GENDE~~R AND JUSTICE~~

Intended for use in courses on law and society, as well as courses in women's and gender studies, women and politics, and women and the law—here is a book that takes up the question of what women judges signify in several different jurisdictions in the United States, the United Kingdom, and the European Union. In so doing, its empirical case studies offer a unique model of how to study gender as a social process rather than merely studying women and treating sex as a variable. A gender analysis yields a fuller understanding of policy diffusion and emotions and social movement mobilization, backlash, policy implementation, agenda-setting, and representation. Lastly, the book makes a nonessentialist case for more women judges—that is, one that does not rest on women's difference.

Sally J. Kenney is the Newcomb College Endowed Chair, Executive Director of the Newcomb College Institute, and Professor of Political Science at Tulane University.

PERSPECTIVES ON GENDER

Edited by Myra Marx Ferree, University of Wisconsin, Madison

GENDER AND JUSTICE

Why Women in the Judiciary *Really* Matter

Sally J. Kenney

Routledge
Taylor & Francis Group

NEW YORK AND LONDON

First published 2013
by Routledge
711 Third Avenue, New York, NY 10017

Simultaneously published in the UK
by Routledge
2 Park Square, Milton Park, Abingdon, Oxon OX14 4RN

Routledge is an imprint of the Taylor & Francis Group, an informa business

Library of Congress Cataloging in Publication Data
Kenney, Sally Jane.
    Gender and justice : why women in the judiciary really matter /
    Sally Kenney.
        p. cm. — (Perspectives on gender)
    Includes bibliographical references and index.
    1. Women judges—United States. 2. Sex discrimination in justice
    administration—United States. I. Title.
    KF8775.K46 2012
    347.73'14082—dc23   2012017964

ISBN: 978-0-415-88143-2 (hbk)
ISBN: 978-0-415-88144-9 (pbk)
ISBN: 978-0-203-12229-7 (ebk)

Typeset in Adobe Caslon
by Keystroke, Station Road, Codsall, Wolverhampton

CONTENTS

FOREWORD

Myra Marx Ferree

The Perspectives on Gender series, to which this volume belongs, has included many distinguished contributions over the years. I have had the privilege of working with authors such as Patricia Hill Collins, whose *Black Feminist Thought* has become a mainstay of feminist theorizing, and Patricia Yancey Martin, whose *Rape Work* represents a deeply insightful integration of decades of her own path-breaking empirical work. I am pleased to now be able to include Sally Kenney in this list. This present volume offers both an important challenge to conventional thinking about gender and an integration of her many comparative empirical research projects on women judges and judging. Rather than a collection of discrete studies, this book pulls together a diversity of cases where gender was and is more or less controversial and offers a new and powerful argument for why and how gender representation matters.

Rather than assuming that there must be some consistent and identifiable difference between women and men in the abstract, Kenney argues that social inclusion of diverse people and perspectives must include gender as a social division with at least potential impact in particular cases. In other words, when the usual argument for the importance of changing the gender composition of the courts is that men are from Mars and women are from Venus, Kenney argues that it is quite enough to suggest that men are from North Dakota and women are from South Dakota—not inherently different as people but at least sufficiently differently positioned that there are cases where their perspectives and interests might diverge. Thus, just as court systems work to include geographic variation, they should work to include gender variation. She traces the variety of instances in which gender difference in the court appointments is seen to matter and the political mobilizations that draw attention and concern to the gender of individual justices as a matter of overall gender justice.

This volume thus stands in a series tradition of paying attention to gender as a matter of political mobilization, a subject position that is made more or less important for both individuals and societies by social movements. Like the earlier books in the series by Verta Taylor, Cheryl Hercus, Patricia Yancey Martin, Angela Miles, and Millie Thayer, this work is a study of the capacity of social movements to construct meanings and make them effective in social relations of power. It also is a model of comparative political research, taking the theoretical problem of gender and representation and tracing it through a variety of levels and systems. Her empirical material ranges from norm-setting policies and practices in the EU and US federal courts to local scrimmages over specific judicial appointments in Minnesota, California, and the UK. The strongly comparative lens brought to questions of gender representation in just judging places Kenney in the good company of other series books such as Bose and Kim's *Global Gender Research* and Luttrell's *School-Smart and Mother-Wise*. By finding both similarities and differences across contexts that vary, whether by nation or by race and locality, these books approach gender as a structural category of analysis rather than a personal attribute.

Sally Kenney also makes an important contribution to the series' focus on intersectionality—that is, the ways that gender, race, class, sexuality, age, nation, and other processes of defining and exercising the power of difference matter in particular contexts. While many see intersectionality primarily in terms of the persons located at the points where exclusions multiply and reinforce disadvantage, a process-based understanding of intersectionality draws attention instead to the historical moments of struggle in which particular subject positions become salient sources of identity and thus able to overcome otherwise divisive differences. Kenney brings such moments forward in her analysis, making the process of women recognizing that gender does matter to them visible in its political particulars.

As a series dedicated to publishing the very best of new feminist scholarship, Perspectives on Gender has made empirical innovation and theoretical power touchstones for inclusion. The attention to intersectional processes, to comparative analyses, and to international contexts that runs through the various books of the series has distinguished it over the years. Sally Kenney's *Gender and Justice* is just the sort of important new work that weaves these concerns together in creative ways and offers insights to all feminist social scientists interested in power, equity, and social change.

PREFACE

Where are the women? Why are there so few? Why have we made so little progress toward equality? Why do we continue to leave women out of our scholarship and fail to consider them fully when making policy and reforming our political institutions? Most scholars who study the judiciary fail to look at gender. Both women and politics scholars and activists seeking to increase the numbers of women in decision-making largely ignore women judges, although many state court judges are elected. Taking a close look at women judges in the United States, the United Kingdom, and the European Union forces us to reconsider core understandings of how policies diffuse and social movements mobilize, how insiders implement policy, how public agendas are set, the nature of representation, and how backlash impedes progress toward equality. When we do turn our attention to women and gender, we too often merely ask whether women judges decide cases differently from men. A query about women expands to asking about gender, but then quickly contracts to a search for essential sex differences. Using sex as a variable in research can provide useful data, but when we understand gender as a social process we go far beyond simple sex differences.

In this book, I demonstrate how to do an analysis of gender as a social process. In each chapter, I situate my inquiry in a different geographical jurisdiction—the State of Minnesota, the US federal system, the United Kingdom, the European Union, the State of California—and take up a different concept—policy diffusion and emotions and social movement mobilization, insider–outsider partnerships and policy implementation, agenda-setting, representation, and backlash. I want scholars and activists to pay attention to women and gender. I want us to move beyond using sex as a variable to understand gender as a social process. This book is also a call to arms to mobilize to reach equality instead of hovering between 25 and 30 percent, or even regressing. To that end, I present an argument as to why it matters that women make up at least 50 percent of the judiciary.

Those who teach American politics, comparative politics, or European politics could use this book not just to cover the third branch of government but to introduce gender as an analytical concept alongside other core political science concepts. Those who teach British politics or the European Union will be particularly interested in Chapters 5 and 6, as almost no academic scholarship on those polities even explores courts, let alone gender and courts. Those who teach women and politics also need to enlarge their field of vision to include the third branch of government. They could benefit, too, from an in-depth analysis of gender as a social process that they can apply throughout the course. And those who teach women's and gender studies could use this book as an exemplar of how to do gender analyses independent of whether they are particularly interested in judges, making it a suitable text for either an introductory course or a graduate course on theory and research methods.

This book is not meant merely for scholars or for the classroom. I hope women judges will read it and use its analysis, quotes, examples, and arguments in the many public speeches they give. I hope that those individuals and groups concerned about increasing women's political power will pay more attention to courts and join the campaign for more women judges. I hope journalists and bloggers, too, will put the arguments to good use. Those interested in women's advancement more generally will see the parallels in other workplaces and benefit from thinking more deeply about the formidable obstacles to progress. And I hope women and their men allies will be inspired enough to mobilize and organize until we reach equality and vow not just to notice but vigorously to contest every reversal.

ACKNOWLEDGMENTS

It is much easier to attach coherence to a trajectory of a project in retrospect. Those interested in scholarly productivity would be advised against directing a Center on Women and Public Policy, launching a project to secure greater gender diversity on the Eighth Circuit Court of Appeals, or uprooting themselves to take up a demanding new administrative position. As a feminist political scientist in the field of comparative public law, I wanted to do something different from the more doctrinal or institutional analyses I had done in the past—something that reflected my growing interest in social movements. The late political scientist Beverly Blair Cook was an anonymous reviewer for my first submission to *Women and Politics* and her helpful comments, and willingness to be identified, began a correspondence that led to a friendship that meant a great deal to me. When she moved into assisted living, she sent me all of her original questionnaires of women judges and urged me to carry the torch. Serendipitously, when she died, Tulane Political Science Professor and my new colleague, Nancy Maveety, collected her papers for the Newcomb Archives. Cook was the first scholar to study women judges systematically, and her research was a catalyst for the formation of the National Association of Women Judges. Most questions I think to ask, Bev already investigated. She did so, however, when university nepotism rules prevented her from being on the same faculty as her husband and with little support for women's studies or women within the discipline. Unlike political science as a whole, I found the subfield of public law to be a relative oasis of nondiscrimination and benefited enormously from the support of senior scholars, such as Martin Shapiro, Joel Grossman, Sam Krislov, and Elliot Slotnick, as well as those with more explicit feminist research orientations, such as Karen O'Connor, Lynn Mather, Kim Scheppele, and Marie Provine.

My first memory of discussing this project was with Martha Chamallas. At the time, I envisaged a comparative study of agenda-setting and was looking forward to perhaps returning to my research in the United Kingdom. She opened the door for me to the National Association of Women Judges, where I made valuable contacts with Judith Resnik and Lynn Hecht Schafran. My friendship with Judge Harriet Lansing and connections with Justice Rosalie Wahl had a huge influence on what I cared about and how I thought about it. Both Harriet and Rosalie had a high regard for the sociologist Norma Wikler, who pioneered the gender taskforce movement. Because Norma had taught them the clear benefits of scholars and social scientists working together for social change, I benefited enormously from the path she had cleared.

My colleague Kenneth Keller actively encouraged me not to give up on my commitment to do comparative research and to hold fast to my belief that one should do comparative work embedded in the community, rather than from afar. I am tremendously grateful to the British Government for their support of this work through the Atlantic Fellowship. At first, I was unsuccessful in winning an Atlantic Fellowship. The selection committee questioned the importance of studying judges and, more importantly, questioned whether it was possible for a scholar to penetrate the secret world of judicial selection. Having already studied the internal workings of the European Court of Justice, I was confident it could be done. When I reapplied, that week's *Sunday Times* had a front-page article alleging the current Lord Chancellor sold judgeships to secure contributions to the Labour Party. How judges were selected in the United Kingdom suddenly seemed a much more important topic to the selection committee than it had the previous year. The scholarly collaboration and friendship I developed with Kate Malleson at the London School of Economics continues to pay dividends in the quality of my work. Several years later, a Fulbright Fellowship to Queen's University, Belfast, allowed me to reconnect with the new Association of Women Judges and I began to update and polish the work I had done.

Two Grant-in-Aid fellowships from the University of Minnesota made parts of this work possible. I was able to spend time at the European Union Institute in Florence and work in its library. I was also able to spend time in the Carter Presidential Library in Atlanta. I am grateful to the University of Minnesota and the Hubert H. Humphrey Institute of Public Affairs for sabbatical support, and to Tulane University, Molly Travis, and especially Michael Bernstein for their support of this project. Tulane paid for my payback year; Molly stayed on as interim director of the Newcomb College Institute so that I might finish a draft of the book; and Michael, a master negotiator and problem-solver, provided the financial support to allow me to complete my sabbatical. Perhaps even more valuable has been Michael's belief in the importance of the project, his commitment to my completion of it, and his frequent encouragement.

I am deeply grateful for the existence and support of the Collaborative Research Network of the Law and Society Association that I co-chair with

Ulrike Schultz. The association is my primary intellectual and political community and I value it immensely. The 140-plus scholars we have found from 17 countries have, through the work of the CRN, developed closer and closer ties, strengthened by LSA annual meetings and conferences in Argentina, organized by Beatriz Kohen, and Oñati, Spain.

At this point, it is customary for men scholars to thank their long-suffering spouses for doing the lion's share of household labor so that they might complete their noble work, unfettered by minutiae. For a woman scholar, arrangements always seem to be different. I am especially grateful to a team of people who support me in all sorts of ways—physical, emotional, logistical— that my husband refers to simply as "my people." They keep this car on the road, so to speak, and I could not do it without them.

I am also grateful to the sustained intellectual support, friendship, and sage academic advice of my dear friend, Kathryn Sikkink, and for the high standard of scholarship and scholarly productivity to which she aspires. She sets the bar high. I am also profoundly grateful to my husband, Norman S.J. Foster, the hardest-working and smartest person I know. Thank you for moving so many times to accommodate my academic career, for your belief in the value of what I do and my ability to do it, for your support in helping me do it "my way," whatever the cost, for your humor, and for your loving support.

I have worked on this project for nearly ten years. Because of my substantial administrative responsibilities, I endeavored to publish pieces of the work as I finished them in case my duties prevented the sustained focus such a book requires. At the eleventh hour, with the encouragement of Myra Marx Ferree, I moved this book to Routledge Press to appeal to a wider audience interested in gender, to benefit from Myra's wisdom as series editor, to be able to reach readers in the United Kingdom and the rest of the European Union, and to work with an editor, Stephen Rutter, with whom I had great confidence and rapport. The manuscript benefited enormously from the scalpel of Susan Mannon as Stephen and I worked toward our goal of making this book accessible to a wider audience, beyond political science and academia. One of my deepest fears is that in an effort to be accessible, readable, and brief, I may have omitted a scholarly citation that helped my thinking as we condensed reviews of the literature. Consequently, I would be happy to share longer drafts of any of the chapters with specialized scholars. For those inadvertently omitted, I apologize.

I have benefited from many readers and research assistants over the years. I presented an earlier version of Chapter 2 to the international meeting of the Law and Society Association in Berlin in 2007, and this paper was subsequently published in the *International Journal of the Legal Profession* 15, nos. 1–2 (2008): 87–110. Thanks to the Taylor & Francis Group for permission to use parts of that earlier publication. I would like to thank Myra Marx Ferree and Patricia Yancey Martin for their helpful comments and Amber Shipley and Lura Barber for research assistance. Thanks, too, for the helpful comments from the Gender and Judging Collaborative Research Network of the Law and Society Association.

Thanks to Ron Aminzade, Susan Bandes, Karlyn Kohrs Campbell, Harriet Lansing, Kathleen Laughlin, Mary Lay Schuster, Patricia Yancey Martin, David Meyer, Mary Jane Mossman, Joe Soss, and Judith Taylor for their helpful comments on the many drafts of Chapter 3 as well as those who critiqued drafts of the public policy teaching case—Kathryn Sikkink, Barbara Frey, Cheryl Thomas, and Justice Rosalie Wahl. Thanks, too, to Lura Barber, Rachel Estroff, Rebecca Moskow, Amber Shipley, and Jaquilyn Waddell Boie for their research assistance. I benefited enormously from the opportunity to present early versions of this paper at Washington University, New York University, the Law and Society Association annual meeting in St. Louis, and the Western Political Science Association annual meeting in Las Vegas. I published an earlier version of this paper in *Mobilization: An International Journal*: "Mobilizing Emotions to Elect Women: The Symbolic Meaning of Minnesota's First Woman Supreme Court Justice," 15, no. 2 (2010): 135–158. Thanks to the journal for permission to use parts of that earlier work.

I received a Grant-in-Aid grant from the University of Minnesota Graduate School to spend a week at the Carter Presidential Library in Atlanta to begin the research for Chapter 4. I presented earlier versions of the chapter at the 2007 Law and Society Conference in Berlin and the 2009 European Conference on Politics and Gender in Belfast, and I benefited from comments made during the panels, especially from Lee Ann Banaszak and Celia Valiente. I also presented it to the Gender and Women's Studies Program at the University of Texas at Austin. Margaret McKenna, Barbara Babcock, Patricia Wald, Virginia Kerr, Phyllis Segal, Nancy Stanley, Rachel Brand, and Eleanor Acheson all provided helpful information, as did Sheldon Goldman, Rorie Solberg, and Elliot Slotnick. Elizabeth Meehan, Mary Lee Clark, Kathleen Laughlin, Susan Hartmann, Cynthia Harrison, Lynn Hecht Schafran, Marian Sawer, Elizabeth Beaumont, and Dara Strolovitch all made helpful comments on drafts. Thanks, too, to Piyali Dalal, Lura Barber, Stephanie Short, and Laura Wolford for research assistance.

I enjoyed the generous support of the British Government in the form of an Atlantic Fellowship in 2002 and a Fulbright Fellowship in 2005 to work on Chapter 5. I also benefited from the comments at presentations before New York University's Law and Society Faculty, University of Minnesota College of Law, the Humphrey Institute of Public Affairs, Queen's University Faculty of Law, the Midwest Law and Society Retreat, and the Atlantic Fellows. I would like to thank Ed Goetz, David Meyer, Kate Malleson, Brice Dickson, Debra Fitzpatrick, K.T. Albiston, and Myra Marx Ferree for their helpful comments on drafts. Thanks also to Natalie Elkan, Sarah Taylor-Nanista, Jaquilyn Waddell Boie, Amber Shipley, Emily Warren, and Renee Klitzke for research assistance, and to Norman Foster for help with data analysis and preparing the figures. Earlier iterations of this work have appeared in the

Journal of Politics 70, no. 3 (2008): 717–735 and *Social Politics* 11, no. 1 (2004): 86–116. Thanks to Cambridge University Press for permission to reprint parts of this earlier publication.

I published an earlier version of Chapter 6, "Breaking the Silence: Gender Mainstreaming and the Composition of the European Court of Justice," in *Feminist Legal Studies* 10, nos. 3–4 (2002): 257–270. Thanks to *Feminist Legal Studies* for permission to reprint parts of this earlier work. Thanks to the Atlantic Fellowship in Public Policy for funding. Thanks to Caroline Naome, Fionnuala Connolly, Judge Ninon Colneric, and Advocate General Christine Stix-Hackl for interviews, and Diana Faber, Carol Harlow, Kate Malleson, and the editors of *Feminist Legal Studies* for comments. Thanks to Andrew Mowbray who read a more recent version and to Noreen Burrows, Rosa Greaves, Susan Millns, Ann Stewart, Antoine Vauchez, and Erik Voeten for sharing work in progress and information. Thanks to Ann Towns for translating the Swedish legal opinions into English. Thanks, too, to the many research assistants who worked on this project over the years, most recently Laura Wolford and Stephanie Short.

Thanks to Michael Bernstein, Linda Greenhouse, Thomas Hilbink, Harriet Lansing, Sarudzayi Matambanadzo, Clare Pastore, Traciel Reid, Judith Resnik, Reva Siegel, Esther Tomljanovich, Margaret Thornton, and Janice Yoder for their helpful comments on Chapter 7. I presented earlier versions of this chapter at the 2010 Law and Society annual meeting in Chicago, at the 2011 Southern Political Science Association's annual meeting in New Orleans, and at a faculty workshop of the Tulane University Law School, where I received helpful comments. Thanks to Lura Barber, Rosalind Cook, Stephanie Short, Libby Sharrow, and Laura Wolford for research assistance.

I presented an earlier version of Chapter 8 to the International Conference on Women in the Legal Professions, Law Faculty, University of Buenos Aires, Argentina; as a Leadership Lecture at Gustavus Adolphus College; at the Indianapolis meeting of the National Association of Women Judges; to the 8th Annual Workshop of the Justice at Stake Campaign; to a Women and the Law class, University of Texas at Austin; to the Center for German and European Studies, Department of Gender and Women's Studies, and the Department of Sociology, University of Wisconsin-Madison; and to the Law and Public Affairs Program at Princeton University. Special thanks to Myra Marx Ferree and Aili Tripp for their comments and to Lura Barber for research assistance.

Lastly, I would like to thank all of my wonderful new colleagues at Tulane University, particularly the staff of the Newcomb College Institute. Without the efforts of Aidan Smith, Katherine Corbett, Rosalind Cook, Laura Wolford, and Katy Smith, this dream would not be a reality. I could not have done it without all of you.

Attending the National Association of Women Judges annual meeting in Newark in October 2011, hearing the keynote address of Justice Ruth Bader Ginsburg, and reflecting on my own emotional reaction to her, I am reminded, once again, why women judges really matter. My hope is that this book serves as a constant reminder to those of us who have intermittently taken up this issue and as a call to arms for a new generation to complete the work and vow never to go backwards.

1

INTRODUCTION: GENDER AS A SOCIAL PROCESS

The first 101 justices of the US Supreme Court were men. It took nearly 200 years for a president to appoint a woman. When Justice Sandra Day O'Connor retired in 2005, Justice Ruth Bader Ginsburg was the only woman serving. President George W. Bush (encouraged by First Lady Laura) wanted to appoint a woman to replace Justice O'Connor but he could purportedly find no woman in the entire country, including his own White House Counsel and close adviser Harriet Miers, who would both pass muster with conservatives and secure Senate confirmation. President Barack Obama made little reference to gender when nominating Sonia Sotomayor.[1] When he nominated Elena Kagan, he briefly noted that women's representation on the US Supreme Court would reach an all-time high of one-third.[2] In the aftermath of these appointments, a *Newsweek* article by Dahlia Lithwick asked the honest, yet provocative, question: "Beyond the fact that the Court will be slightly more representative of the American people . . . what does the difference between having one, two, or three women at the court really signify?"[3] What does having any woman on any court signify?

I read fear and disappointment in this remark. Lithwick's wistful question suggests fear that individual women's presence or even leadership may not bring about the hoped-for empowerment of women when these women integrate mainstream political institutions. Also lurking within this question is the fundamental assumption of core differences between men and women—what feminist theorists call essentialism (fixed characteristics are attached to bodily identities, all women are X, all men are Y). The comment also hints at an ambivalence about that assumption, a fear that those differences may be a mirage or ephemeral at best, vestiges of sex stereotyping. Lastly, Lithwick's question implies that if women do not revolutionize judging or dramatically change outcomes, the achievement of representation and nondiscrimination by their participation does not offer a very compelling reason to mobilize, or even celebrate. This book takes up the question of what women judges signify in several different jurisdictions in the United States, the United Kingdom, and the European Union. In so doing, its empirical case studies offer a model of how to study gender as a social process rather than merely studying women and treating sex as a variable. A gender analysis can help us more fully understand policy diffusion and emotions and social movement mobilization, backlash, policy implementation, agenda-setting, and representation. Lastly, the book makes a nonessentialist case for more women judges—that is, one that does not rest on women's difference.

WHAT'S THE PROBLEM? WHY SO FEW WOMEN?

The US Supreme Court is not alone in having no women for most of its history and even now having very few relative to women's share of the population. Why? Where are the women judges and why are there so few? Why is more than 50 percent of the population so poorly represented in judicial positions? What are the consequences of this underrepresentation? And if we are concerned about these causes and consequences, how may we frame this underrepresentation as a critical political issue in need of a remedy?

Few scholars or activists think about women judges, just as few scholars or activists who study the judiciary think about women or gender. Though I will argue that the appointment of Justices Sotomayor and Kagan were major victories for women's equality, attention to women's representation in the judiciary has been surprisingly scant. Compare the popular interest in Hillary Clinton's bid for the Democratic presidential nomination, Nancy Pelosi's term as the first woman Speaker of the House, or even Sarah Palin's bus tour after her candidacy for Vice-President to the degree of popular interest in Kagan's appointment as the third sitting woman Supreme Court justice. Those who study women and politics have mostly ignored the judicial branch of government.[4] Advocates for more women in politics often neglect or ignore the judicial branch; even organizations of women judges have turned their attention away from campaigning for more women on the bench.

Courts are powerful institutions of government. American courts—state, federal, and municipal—are entangled in every important public matter. It is difficult to think of a gender-relevant public policy issue not judicialized: divorce and custody, battering and rape, discrimination, abortion. As the power of courts grows worldwide, and as judicial selection becomes more contested, we can only expect the composition of courts—who the judges are, who selects them, and using what criteria—to grow in importance. State judicial races now evidence all of the pathologies of campaigns for other offices: they require vast sums of money; candidates face negative television ads that simplify issues and distort records; legislators increasingly draw districts to be homogeneous and safe; and voters, challengers, and the media presume women and minority men to be less competent and treat their candidacies differently from those of white men. In *Republican Party of Minnesota v. White* (536 U.S. 765 [2002]) the Supreme Court held that states may no longer restrict judges from announcing their views on political issues, and in *Caperton v. Massey* (556 U.S. ___ [2009]) it held that judges must recuse themselves when a litigant has made a substantial contribution to their campaigns. Recent elections for the Wisconsin Supreme Court and the confirmation stalemates in the US Senate during the last three administrations reveal a politicization of the state and federal judicial selection process that is unlikely to disappear soon. Worldwide, countries as diverse as France, Russia, Hungary, and Argentina have transferred more power to courts. So also have supranational organizations, such as the European Union (European Court of Justice), the Council of Europe (European Court of Human Rights), the World Trade Organization, the Organization of American States (Inter-American Court of Human Rights), and the United Nations (International Criminal Court and tribunals on the former Yugoslavia and Rwanda).

ONCE WE FIND WOMEN WE FALL INTO LOOKING FOR DIFFERENCE

To return to the question posed by *Newsweek*, why does it matter if women are missing? As I will discuss in Chapter 2, Justice O'Connor's voting record and opinions were disappointing to pioneering judicial scholar Beverly Blair Cook, who had previously blamed the Supreme Court's poor record of deciding equality cases on the fact that only men served. Others worked hard to discover a different voice[5] in Justice O'Connor's opinions—one that did not exist. As soon as enough women ascended to the bench to make quantitative analysis possible, scholars asked whether women decided cases differently from men. They found few striking or consistent differences, with the exception of a greater propensity of women appellate judges to find more often for the plaintiff in sex discrimination cases and to persuade men colleagues on panels to vote with them. The repeated failure to find broad differences did not seem to deter scholars from the quest to uncover them nor to call into question the fundamental assumption of some essential gender difference, whether it came from biology or shared experience.

What was driving this *Groundhog Day*[6] phenomenon of assuming and looking for essential sex differences in the study of women judges? A social scientific methodological habit of asking about gender by running a regression analysis using sex as a variable explains a lot. Adding sex as a variable in quantitative research has been the most frequent way social scientists have operationalized thinking about gender. My late 1970s political science graduate course in American politics covered questions about women and politics by having us read studies showing women to be apolitical, less politically engaged than men, more religious and conservative, voting like their husbands, or for the handsome candidate, and so on. I read a lot of tables but they were all about sex as a category rather than gender as a relationship.

As I argued in an essay about how feminist scholarship entered the subfield of public law,[7] assuming difference was also consistent with a very conservative and a not very feminist understanding of sex differences, the same view of women as private, as outside the public, that had earlier justified their exclusion from the political realm altogether. Now new cohorts of feminist researchers have developed more sophisticated research methods and approaches to gender. As I shall argue throughout this book, we can learn a lot from using sex as a variable, but only if it is coupled with an understanding of gender as a social process that is more complex than binary and essentialist understandings of sex differences allow.

Pointing to the methodological orientation of the discipline or its conservative practitioners cannot, however, fully explain the persistence of asking only whether women judges decide cases differently from men. Feminists, too, have been fascinated by the difference question. As I sat through panel after panel at academic conferences extolling the different voice of women—focused on the web of connection, concerned with relationships, dedicated to the nurturing of others—I was not just puzzled by why this question persisted in the face of scant empirical support for the hypothesis. I also could not help wondering what women these researchers knew. Had none been to a National Women's Studies Association meeting? After thirty years at its core, I have not found feminism to be a warm bosom of sisterhood nurturing its members, or any less lacking in conflict, betrayal, intrigue, and pathology than any other group of people.[8] My naïve assumption that women professors would necessarily be the most supportive of my embryonic feminism was quickly dispelled. Twenty-five years in the academy has disabused me of the belief that women naturally ally themselves with each other; rather, constituting ourselves as a group, when it occurs, is a political accomplishment. Platitudes about women's moral difference, even when reframed as superiority, contradicted my own direct experience and smacked of sexist stereotyping even before the term "essentialism" gained currency.

Moreover, living in Margaret Thatcher's Britain for much of the 1980s disabused me of any notion that women leaders would necessarily use their power to advance women's equality. In the US, I also knew it would be folly to assume that conservative women federal judges, such as Janice Rogers Brown, Priscilla Owen, and Joy Clement, if elevated to the Supreme Court, would advance equal protection doctrine for women as Justice Ginsburg has done. Feminists who argued from a premise of sex difference whipsawed between arguing that women would bring a distinctive perspective to the bench and criticizing those women judges who did not. This book's nonessentialist case for more women judges rejects these two poles as the only alternatives.

WOMEN JUDGES LARGELY REJECT FRAMING
THEMSELVES AS DIFFERENT

If there is any shared feminist methodology, it might be that we listen to women and take seriously the perspectives of the subjects we study.[9] My own experience did not comport with the different voice. Nor, as it happens, did that of many women judges.[10] While not determinative, women judges' hostility to this essential difference frame of reference should give us pause, as should the repeated failure to unearth any essential dichotomous difference across jurisdiction, issue, and time. When I was a Congressional fellow in 1987, nine of us met with Justice O'Connor, just as the *University of Virginia Law Review* published an article arguing O'Connor decided cases with a distinctly feminine voice. Her essential female nature led her, ostensibly, to pay more attention to facts rather than deductively apply legal precedent. One fellow asked Justice O'Connor whether the article accurately captured her unique decision-making process. Annoyed, O'Connor asked rhetorically what judge would not consider the facts before her and dismissed the point. She later wrote, "there is simply no empirical evidence that gender differences lead to discernible differences in rendering judgment."[11]

Justice Ginsburg, who, unlike Justice O'Connor, calls herself a feminist,[12] and who is well versed in feminist legal theory, said this of such studies:

> I am very doubtful about those kinds of [results]. I certainly know that there are women in federal courts with whom I disagree just as strongly as I disagree with any man. I guess I have some resistance to that kind of survey because it's what I was arguing against in the '70s. Like in Mozart's opera "Cosi Fan Tutte": that's the way women are.[13]

Both Justice Ginsburg and Justice O'Connor have quoted Minnesota Supreme Court Justice Jeanne Coyne saying a wise old man and a wise old woman reach the same conclusion. But both at the same time do advocate for more women on the bench and for greater diversity of view and experience to enhance judicial decision-making.

Elaine Martin's survey of women judges in the US in 1987 revealed their similar reticence to embrace different voice arguments. Judges were most in agreement in support of the proposition that we need more women judges because the bench without women does not reflect the total fabric of society (85 percent). The biggest disagreement among women, however, was over whether they agreed that "women judges have an ability in the decision-making process to bring people together in a way that men don't." The largest group (40 percent) disagreed with this statement, 30 percent agreed, and 30 percent were neutral.[14] Martin also surveyed 1989 National Association of Women Judges (NAWJ) conference attendees about the impact of women judges. Ninety-eight percent agreed that women judges were role models for women attorneys. Nearly 90 percent reported making a special effort to encourage other women to run for judicial office. Nearly three-fourths of women agreed that women judges in general work to heighten the sensitivity of other judges to the problem of gender bias, although only one-third reported that they personally had made a difference in how men judges thought about the gender impact of their decisions. Martin's study showed the wide spectrum in how women judges think about the difference gender makes.[15]

Some judges do make difference arguments. Justice Kathryn Werdegar, who served on the California Supreme Court, said of the three women serving, "We three are as different in our decisions as any three randomly chosen justices might be . . . which is not to say that women on the bench do not make a unique and, indeed, vital contribution."[16] Werdegar goes on to reject the different voice argument as unsubstantiated by social science, but does argue that gender and feminist perspectives contribute to better decision-making, that many voices are left out of judicial deliberation, and that individual women who serve as judges can make a real difference. She goes on to argue how important it is that the door to service on the highest court is no longer closed to women, how important it is that women not be seen to be excluded as participants in the judicial system, and how confidence in our institutions requires that they reflect the citizenry.[17] If you parse the more recent remarks of Justices Ginsburg and O'Connor, you will find that they also both reject difference arguments but continue to advocate that courts become more gender diverse. This book follows this same tack.

FEMINIST THEORY'S DETOUR INTO DIFFERENCE

Feminists wanted it to be true that all women would be feminists and feminists would transform judicial decision-making. At the time of the first studies on women judges, feminist theory was often valorizing radical feminist difference arguments, even though many feminists also contested them. In some corners the difference argument became *the* feminist argument, despite the fact that feminists were its most vocal critics. When I became interested in feminist theory in the late 1970s, postmodernism was just emerging and feminist theory drew heavily from Marxism, seeking to develop a theory of patriarchy as Marx had developed a critique of capitalism.[18] The quest was on to find the one true cause of women's oppression: was it sexuality or labor? Which form of oppression—race, sex, or class—was more fundamental, and which came first?

Whether a cause or an effect of this theoretical orientation, at the end of the 1980s and beginning of the 1990s, feminist politics was often deeply ideological and fractured and, as I experienced it in both the United States and the United Kingdom, repressive. Organizers in both countries abandoned national conferences and the elaboration of a shared platform of action in despair as different factions trashed those with whom they disagreed. These practices suppressed intellectual creativity because one feared denunciation, craved to be seen as radical, and sought to display one's feminist bona fides, most easily accomplished through harsh criticism of others. "Liberal" was a term of derision. Law was irretrievably patriarchal; mainstream politics was irrelevant; feminism was narrowed to a politics of sexuality and radical separatism.

As ridiculous as these aspirations sounded for me—a white, middle-class, married woman from Iowa who wanted a life as an engaged scholar—my fear of censure from my feminist colleagues was real. This silencing of intellectual creativity coexisted with a wonderful sense of awakening as I discovered Gayle Rubin, Catharine MacKinnon, Dorothy Dinnerstein, and *Signs* in the basement of the Princeton library and discussed feminist theory with a few trusted friends. One regrettable consequence of this repressive climate was how it constricted the choice of research topic. To study elected officials was to expose oneself as a dreaded liberal accommodationist, unless the study revealed them to be, as one leading feminist political theorist characterized women legislators, "supplicants of the state." Those of us who studied law were galvanized to expose its weaknesses and limitations and to condemn the many compromises its purveyors made along the way. For example, Ruth Bader Ginsburg's decision to challenge discrimination by litigating with men plaintiffs harmed by sex-based classifications was a strategically clever choice, but a demoralizing one as it conceded that men judges could grasp the harm of sex discrimination only when it hurt other men. Yet, in our eagerness to brandish our critique, we had no real alternative vision of social change.

What changed? Living under Reagan and Thatcher may have made our differences a luxury we could no longer afford. Maybe postmodernism exposed the goal of searching for one true and comprehensive theory of women's oppression as misguided. Maybe a new generation of feminists came to political science as scholars rather than through the movement and were less steeped in the old theoretical dogmas or invested in scoring points by trashing other feminists. Maybe radical feminists became more interested in working within institutions as the internationalizing of feminism took hold around the United Nations' 1995 World Conference of Women in Beijing and working together across differences seemed more important. The causes are difficult to untangle. At last, one could study women elected officials without it being assumed that one wholeheartedly endorsed everything about them. One could study women in the military or the Catholic Church,[19] or in foundations, religious groups, and unions, and call them feminists.[20] One could study right-wing women.[21]

These changes do not mean that feminists began to agree with each other more than they ever had before. At the theoretical level, feminists continued to disagree about matters such as international feminism and multiculturalism, but it seems to me that more breathing space and intellectual freedom emerged in the late 1990s. My personal account of the intellectual history of feminist theory provides context for my thinking about women judges because it provides a background for how feminists have thought about women's entry into law and women working inside institutions, a topic I take up specifically in Chapter 4. The polarization has not evaporated, even if more space has opened up for discussion. I still glimpse the old curled lips and rolled eyes of colleagues as I talk about women judges rather than drag queens or migrant workers. And it is important to recognize that although part of the persistence of the different voice approach comes from a narrow disciplinary reduction of gender to sex as a variable, another part lies in some radical feminists' long-standing belief in the irretrievable maleness of legal institutions and their attachment to a difference perspective as being somehow more feminist.

Feminist theory's categories of thought reflect normative commitments that I want to reexamine. Early texts often portrayed the brands of feminist theory in evolutionary terms, with the "winner" (socialist, radical, or black feminist theory, depending on the author) appearing in the final chapter. Feminist theory sought to categorize as the categories proliferated, as categorization itself was going out of intellectual style, and as ever-fewer writers were neatly identifiable as members of a distinctive category. I also find problematic the application of terms to a thinker, or group of thinkers, that she would not use herself. For example, "liberal" was a term of derision socialists, radicals, or postmodernists used to criticize, and therefore not a label anyone applied to themselves. Liberal feminists were either historical figures, such as Mary Wollstonecraft or John Stuart Mill, or those contemporaries one wished to criticize as having a narrow view of women's equality that failed to problematize inequalities based on race, class, sexuality, or global position.

Thus, in part, the tenacity of the difference argument in judging is a legacy of arguments within feminism. Feminist theory went in two different directions. As difference feminism morphed into cultural feminism in the 1980s and became synonymous with feminism itself, anti-difference feminists, often called liberal, were highly critical of difference feminism, along the lines of Justice Ginsburg, and maintained that these stereotypical differences were exactly what feminists were fighting to eradicate. Women had to show they were rational rather than emotional in order to win the vote; that they were persons and independent of husbands in order to practice law;[22] and that they were capable of listening to unsavory details of crimes and of deliberating democratically in order to serve on juries. They thought the methods used to claim a different voice were empirically weak, the arguments for essential differences theoretically misguided, and their implications dangerous.

In the 1990s, postmodern and intersectional theories of feminism questioned the categories "women" and "woman" altogether. If asking about gender leads us to count and study women judges, identify exclusionary practices, and chart how women overcame obstacles, it also leads to productive questions for pivoting the center of focus. Where are the black women? Lesbians? Working-class and poor women? Women from the Midwest or South? Does it make sense to categorize very conservative and very liberal women as sharing a common identity? By now, many feminists find differences between women more interesting than purported commonalities.

Scholars such as Judith Butler (in *Gender Trouble*) carefully traced how thinkers such as Freud, whose entire theory was meant to abandon biological causes, still engaged in a natural fallacy. In other words, she showed how Freud assumed that fixed sex differences exist that are the root of sexuality and gender. Even thinkers dedicated to showing sexuality as socially constructed can fall into naturalizing and essentializing sex differences. Postmodern feminism such as Butler's leads to a fear that if the category of women disappears as relevant, it may not still matter whether women are judges. Feminists began to worry that if the answer to the difference question is "no," the politics of gender inclusion is over. This book is an answer to that fear. I trace what the politics of including women in the judiciary have been and what consequences they have had, and argue that it *does* matter for women—as well as for justice—that women be represented in this portion of our democratic political institutions.

WOMEN JUDGES SIGNIFY BOTH BUSINESS AS USUAL *AND* RADICAL TRANSFORMATION SIMULTANEOUSLY

I part company with many feminists in two ways. First, I argue that we should not make an argument for women on the bench based on difference. Second, I believe we should advocate both for more feminists on the bench and for more women—irrespective of whether they are feminist. By now, the scorn for my supposed "liberalism" in studying elite women may have produced a gasp of outrage from my radical feminist colleagues. Perhaps I am no feminist at all? I argue that the yardstick of radicalness (that Latin American feminists have dubbed a *feministómetro*) is a holdover from feminist entanglements in Marxist and cultural revolutions. Definitions of radicalness that take on board the important insights of postmodern feminism are fundamentally different.

Drawing on theories of performativity and multiplicity of meanings, I argue that, paradoxically, the more women judges look and behave like men, the more radical their presence on the bench can be because it normalizes women's authority and power. This idea is deeply contrary to self-defined "radical" feminist approaches that see all women exercising state power as stooges of patriarchy. I instead suggest that the more women are feminist, progressive, more likely to dissent and use outsider arguments, the more they bolster difference arguments that often lead to women's marginalization and exclusion. To make this argument, I draw extensively on the parallel projects of Ellen Lewin, Joan Scott, and Derrick Bell.

Could feminist incursions be both accommodationist and radical simultaneously? Could women in the legal profession both shore up the disciplinary social control elements of law and challenge the gender order at the same time? Embracing a both/and way of thinking can enhance our thinking about women judges. In *Recognizing Ourselves: Ceremonies of Lesbian and Gay Commitment*, Ellen Lewin[23] proposed that we recast dichotomous thinking on gay marriage that holds that marriage is either a fundamental human right with tangible legal, material, and social consequences that a minority community must win to be equal or an assimilationist betrayal of the queer difference that challenges patriarchal compulsory heterosexuality. The anthropologist Lewin asked what participants intended and experienced in the performance of commitment rituals. She found that the more the ceremonies emulated traditional hetero-sexual weddings, the more their differences and exclusions showed in sharp relief. Same-sex couples confronted department store registries that could enter only bride or groom; family members who lavished gifts on marrying siblings neglected to send gifts to recognize gay unions; family members failed to attend or, if they did, refused to bring their children; parents did not offer to pay for gay weddings. Lesbian couples who dressed as the traditional bride and groom seemed more to be performing drag than conforming to heterosexual norms. The more the ceremony observed orthodox religious practices, the more clergy and congregants had to confront their denomination's refusal to support gay marriage. In short, the more the ceremony conformed to heterosexual rituals, the more it exposed society's rejection of gay unions and challenged the hetero-sexual monopoly.

Conversely, the more camp and queer the ceremony was, reflecting gay cultural practices of parody, the more it affirmed the similarity of gay and heterosexual unions. Lewin offered several examples. The depth of their love and the longevity of their partnership rendered the leather-clad "bear" square dancers' union authentic. Including a prayer for the dead for former partners and community members who had died of AIDS shocked family members only because they came to regard the prayer as part of a traditional Jewish wedding. The intensity of participants' emotional reactions led many to report that the ceremony seemed more real than heterosexual weddings. The partners had freely chosen one another, had risked and endured family banishment and societal disapproval, and their relationships had endured longer than many heterosexual marriages. Strangely enough, the more the ceremonies deviated from conventional weddings, the more spiritual they became and the more authentic the partnerships seemed to the participants. Those who were most deliberately poking fun ended up characterizing their use of symbols as fol-lowing traditions, not engaging in parody. They argued their practices were authentic but not copying heterosexual weddings.[24] Those lighthearted and playful in planning the ceremonies as well as the conservatives determined to avoid spectacle at all cost were both astonished by the depth of emotions they experienced. Proclaiming their commitment before friends, family, and spiritual communities changed the individuals and their relationships. Ceremonies participants structured to be the most transgressive were experienced as most traditional, moving, and affirming while those that were structured to be traditional were experienced as jarring misfits.[25]

By listening carefully to participants and applying anthropological theories of ritual and symbols, Lewin finds the arguments of both poles in the gay marriage debate wanting. She concludes:

> Looking at lesbian and gay weddings further undermines these dichotomous understandings of resistance and accommodation and opens the way for a reconsideration of the entire framework on which these concepts depend. To the extent that resistance facilitates accommodation and conformity depends upon subversion, these complex rituals suggest that a highly dichotomized view of these tendencies does violence to the real subtlety of cultural processes.[26]

Lewin's work on lesbian and gay commitment ceremonies helps reframe gender and judging in at least three important ways. First, her paradoxical finding that the more celebrants conform to nuptial traditions the more their radical challenge to them unfolds in practice bolsters my argument that increasing the number of women judges contributes to social change. This disruption of meaning goes beyond merely seeing women as symbols and role models. Second, her injunction against either/or dichotomies applies in the case of gender and judging as a critique of the assumption that women judges must either be a radical feminist challenge to the patriarchal state or accommodationist supplicants. Fracturing the dichotomy of radicalism and accommodation helps us better articulate why women judges matter, even if they do not on the whole decide cases differently from men. Third, her anthropological approach asks what events mean to participants and takes women's experiences seriously, a key component of thinking like a feminist. This method invites us to think about gender and judging by listening carefully to what women judges, lawyers, and those who work for the appointment or election of women judges say about what having women on the bench means to them, and leads us to expect multiple meanings and contradictory positions, especially in actions sedimented in ritual.

Like weddings, judging has many ritualistic elements, from the "all rise," to the wearing of the robes, to the physical layout and design of the courtroom where judges sit above the parties before them. Judges symbolize many things: the values of the specific community; the power and the disciplinary arm of the state; the neutral, objective, and positionless adjudication, rendered artistically as Justicia—a blindfolded woman holding both a sword and a scale. As I argue in Chapters 3 and 7, women judges symbolize such things simultaneously. In fact, as Lewin argues, rituals achieve their effect precisely "through their ability to evoke multiple meanings sequentially or simultaneously."[27] Lewin's emotional reaction to her own commitment ceremony took her by surprise and signaled that something important was happening, as did the emotional reactions of the people she interviewed. I suggest that the emotions generated by the appointment of Justices Wahl and Sotomayor also signal that something profoundly important has occurred, and this recognition should encourage us to probe more deeply for the meanings of these events.

A second attempt to transcend difference arguments comes from Joan Scott's account of the *parité* movement in France. Embarrassed by France's poor performance in increasing the number of women deputies in its National Assembly (6 percent in 1997) and presidential cabinets, energized by a discourse of women in decision-making in the European Union, and frustrated and humiliated by blatant discrimination against women within political parties, a group of French feminists launched a movement to seek 50 percent representation in the National Assembly. They called for parties to run women as half of their candidates and not to put them at the bottom of the list or in unwinnable seats. That such a demand would arise within France is surprising, since, despite Simone de Beauvoir's declaration in *The Second Sex* that woman is made not born, contemporary French feminism had become synonymous in many corners with the defense of difference. The framers of the parity movement deliberately eschewed difference arguments, drawing instead on core republican values of universal citizenship. They argued parity was different from equality (based on sameness) and neither a form of affirmative action (based on an analysis of discrimination) nor a quota (which the Constitutional Council had declared to be unconstitutional) but "rigorously universalist,"[28] "unsexing the national representation by sexing the individual."[29] Because women, like men, covered the political, economic, and social spectra, they were not a special interest, social group, class, culture, or complement (in the yin–yang sense). As such, they would not represent women but represent the nation—as men did. *Paritaristes* rewrote the national motto as: *liberté, égalité, parité.*

As a practical matter, the *parité* movement benefited from a general sense of malaise about the capacity of political institutions and the crisis of French identity posed by massive immigration and globalization. The French public saw politicians as corrupt—a special interest group of men bureaucrats—who had only weak claims to represent the general will because they were out of touch with everyday citizens. A strong executive branch, an increasingly powerful judiciary exercising judicial review, and an expanding European Union had eroded the power of the National Assembly. The Socialist rout in 1993 led the Socialists to look around for a way to rehabilitate themselves, and becoming the party of *parité* was a method they seized. As in the case for changing the method of selecting judges in Britain that I discuss in Chapter 5, the case for more women in politics was tied to the idea of modernization—women's exclusion became a measure of backwardness.

Parité as a concept was enormously popular with the French Government, if not with the men politicians who would be displaced in any particular application. The *paritaristes* were not arguing from difference but rather from universalism, a paradigm shift in thinking of France as encompassing men and women in every aspect.[30] Their arguments were often misheard and distorted, which once again demonstrates how naturalized difference becomes and how intertwined it is with heterosexuality. What we can draw from this example relevant to making the case for women judges is how the *paritaristes*, before their arguments were hijacked, used French republicanism to make an argument for women's greater representation that did not rest on women's purported difference. They sought to run women as citizens who had a right to be in government and, in so doing, their campaign exposed all of the gender-based assumptions of the polity. I want to make a similar argument for women's judicial representation.

The third example on which I draw is the work that Derrick Bell has done on racial representation. In *Faces at the Bottom of the Well*, Bell captures the both/and way of thinking about race and racial progress.[31] Bell reveals how Martin Luther King Day, Black History Month, and a focus on the success of individual African Americans bring race to the surface at the same time as they announce racism as something overcome, transcended, and in the past. Bell uses fiction as well as essays to communicate this both/and dynamic effectively. *The Onion*'s banner headline after President Obama's election—"Black Man Given Nation's Worst Job"—captures the sense of racial transcendence and the persistence of racism. Obama's election shows both that race no longer matters and that it matters very much, that we are a postracial society and a racist one. It is a landmark of progress and brings to the surface the most shameful backward elements of our society. The campaign sparked a dialogue about the comparisons between racism and sexism, yet commentators do not seem to be looking for the essential race difference in everything the President does or saying he does that "because he is African American." Certainly people have high expectations of him to transform politics. But how much of that should we attribute to expectations of progressives generally and expectations we have of one black man's difference?

THE DANGERS OF DIFFERENCE

Since women began articulating claims for greater equality, they have vacillated between framing their claims in terms of women's sameness to or difference from men. Suffragists, for example, argued that women were equally human and deserved civil and political rights. But they also argued women were naturally virtuous and morally superior to men.[32] Later, progressives (also labeled maternalist or social feminists) more often emphasized women's difference.[33] As I shall describe in Chapter 8, like the suffragists and social feminists before them, women seeking to abolish women's exclusion from juries made both equal rights and difference arguments.[34] During the resurgence of feminism in the late 1960s, feminists, too, diverged over whether to focus on their similarities to men or their differences. Both Catharine MacKinnon[35] and Martha Minow[36] theorized what Minow labeled "the dilemma of difference." If we define equality as sameness, policies may overlook important differences and disadvantage women when they deviate from standards based on male norms. But if we highlight difference, it often leads to women's disadvantage and exclusion.

In *For Whose Protection? Reproductive Hazards and Exclusionary Policies in the United States and Britain*,[37] my analysis of protective legislation led me to conclude that making arguments from women's difference was often empirically inaccurate and politically dangerous for women—difference almost always led to disadvantage. I examined how judges used ideology to construct sex differences rather than exploring them scientifically. Careful textual analysis of legal opinion in two countries convinced me how important judges' views were about gender roles, sex differences, sex discrimination, and women's equality in shaping how they reacted to exclusionary policies. Judges' ideas about gender roles frequently trumped the empirical evidence of a lack of sex differences and a doctrinal mandate for employment equality. I found the differences between men judges more important than the differences between men and women. Not all men failed to grasp the harm of exclusionary policies; nor did all women immediately see why they were problematic.

INDIVIDUALS MATTER; LIFE EXPERIENCES MATTER

Some feminist theorists have attempted to carve out an intermediate path between the simplistic gender essentialism of some radical feminisms and postmodernism's rejection of women as a category altogether. For example, Patricia Yancey Martin and her coauthors rework feminist standpoint theory to develop the case for women judges.[38] Feminist standpoint theory draws from the Marxist idea that social location and experience matter. Experiencing oppression as a member of the proletariat, as a woman, or as a racial or sexual minority provides a material incentive for grasping how the world is structured to favor some groups and disfavor others, all while making the disfavored believe this structure of oppression to be "natural." Experience is necessary, but not sufficient to escape this ideological hegemony. One can have "false consciousness"—that is, fail to see how one is oppressed. Only by struggle can one achieve feminist consciousness. Standpoint theorists part company with radical feminists in thinking something essential about being a woman in and of itself produces a feminist consciousness. But they also diverge from postmodernists because they believe the experience of living life as a woman matters in producing feminist consciousness. Feminist consciousness is still linked to women's bodies, even if it is not automatic. Those who share this view would argue that men cannot be feminists, while recognizing that not all women are.[39] Perhaps this is what Sotomayor meant when she spoke of a "wise" Latina woman.[40] She did not say a Latina woman would come to a better decision than someone without those experiences, but a *wise* Latina woman, presumably one who has reflected on how her gender, race, and class have shaped her experiences. If

Justice Sotomayor had not contextualized (repudiated?) her "wise Latina" comment[41] during her confirmation hearings, we might have had an interesting national debate on how experience affects judging and why a greater representation of social locations on the Court might be conducive to justice.[42] Rather than pursue a case based on feminist standpoint theory, I think the better course is to follow the *paritaristes* and say the case for women does not rest on women's difference.

To say that sex does not produce a difference discernible at the macro level is not at all to say that individuals do not matter. Lady Brenda Hale, the first woman appointed to the House of Lords, Britain's highest appellate court, is a woman, but perhaps more important is that she is an expert in family law and championed no-fault divorce as a law commissioner.[43] She is the author of the first text on women and the law and brings a sophisticated understanding of gender issues to her analysis. Her approach to gender is very different from that of the previous highest-ranked woman judge, Elizabeth Butler-Sloss, who argued that women faced no discrimination in seeking high judicial office.[44] One could make similar observations about the differences between Justices O'Connor and Ginsburg. And one could say that Justice Harry Blackmun, too, made a huge difference on women's issues as an individual, as did Justices William Brennan and Thurgood Marshall, who were often clear voices for feminist decisions. The complicated evidence about women and critical mass in legislative bodies[45] reinforces Elaine Martin's finding that adding more women to a court does not increase that court's propensity to find for women litigants in a simple linear way, any more than adding women to legislatures automatically ensures the passage of more feminist legislation.[46] Women on courts, juries, or in organizations generally can legitimate anti-women decisions or advocate feminist outcomes.

Reading Paula Sharp's novel *Crows over a Wheatfield* inspired me to persevere in completing this book and working to secure women on the bench. The protagonist's estranged husband sexually abuses their child to punish her for leaving him. A male judge repeatedly grants him unsupervised visits. The repeated injuries to her little boy, and her failure to obtain legal redress, lead her to go underground. Living in Iowa City, I watched how the exposure of a woman on the run in violation of a custody order nearly caused the battered women's shelter to close.[47] But I also witnessed a case of alleged paternal child sexual abuse be judged to be a false accusation by a woman judge and woman legislator, both of whom I admired and trusted. One need not teach constitutional law and women and the law, write on sex discrimination doctrine, serve on the board and volunteer for a court-monitoring organization such as Watch, or read feminist novels to notice that it matters enormously who decides cases. We need more feminist judges: judges who understand women's experiences and take seriously harm to women and girls; who ask the gender question, "How might this law, statute, or holding affect men and women differently?"; who interpret equal protection and discrimination law in light of those provisions' broad social change purposes; who value women's lives and women's work; who do not believe women to be liars, whores, or deserving of violence by nature; who question their own stereotypes and predilections and listen to evidence; and who, simply put, believe in equal justice for all. It matters who judges are and what their values are. We are not simply looking for the smartest and most able lawyers for the job. We want the wisest—those who value women and understand gender.

MOVING FROM SEX AS A VARIABLE THAT UNCOVERS DIFFERENCE TO GENDER AS A SOCIAL PROCESS

In this book, I shall argue that gender is not just a synonym for sex or a euphemism for women but a social relationship based on perceived difference and symbolizing power. Gender is not a category, nor the traits or roles ascribed to such a category; it is a social process that actively differentiates by sex and devalues women and the feminine. Gender is institutionalized in many ways; its processes are entangled in diverse other processes of difference and inequality and embedded in the traditions, rituals, practices, and discourses that make up social institutions. Gender is not a thing sitting passively in people to make a difference or not but an institutionalized process of meaning creation that is contested in different ways in each of my chapters' cases, even as each is about women judges. Because gender is a process, it is always contested.

We need to move beyond sex as a variable to theorizing gender as a social process. Gender does not have a fixed meaning attached to bodies. The meaning of gender is continually renegotiated; it is fluid and variable within social groups, across cultures, and across times. Thus, although gender is a tenacious social category, it is continually reinscribed and its content changes. Scientists have shown repeatedly that more variation occurs within rather than between each sex category: that is, many men are more different from each other than they are different from women, and vice versa. Whether the difference is physical strength or scientific reasoning, women differ significantly from each other and much overlap occurs between women and men. Even if the strongest man is stronger than the strongest woman, many women are stronger than many men. Yet whenever a putative sex difference emerges—women are more likely to vote for Democratic presidents than men—we start talking about it as two non-intersecting categories—men vote for Republicans and women vote for Democrats—rather than as a tendency that varies over time. The "men are from Mars, women are from Venus" position has enormous staying power for the public and judicial scholars alike. Sociologist Cynthia Epstein referred to this emphasis on difference as a distorted focus on tails, not centers, of distributional curves.[48]

Women and men do have different life experiences. Some, but not all, women are mothers. Some, but not all, women are in heterosexual marriages where they do most of the caring labor. Most experience the world as a woman, subject to the risks of sexual violence, gender devaluation, and exclusion and discrimination, although in different forms and with different consequences. Yet, using sex as a variable is a risky business. It masks similarities between men and women and it also renders invisible significant differences among women. Other identity characteristics and affinities shape adjudication arguably more than sex, such as one's political party, judicial philosophy, and approach to constitutional interpretation. Other life experiences also shape one's identity, including class, region, ethnicity, and generation.

The recent Wal-Mart case provides a good example (*Wal-Mart Stores v. Dukes*, No. 10-277). Many were quick to point out to me that all three women Supreme Court justices were in dissent in this landmark sex discrimination case.[49] (Justice Ginsburg wrote the dissenting opinion.) That is true. Also in dissent, however, was Justice Breyer, who has not lived life as a woman. All four dissenters were appointed by Democratic presidents; all those in the majority were appointed by Republicans. Which is the more important explanation? Those who discovered in Justice O'Connor a different voice in cases could never explain why men justices joined her opinions. Did Justices Kennedy and Souter have a feminine perspective, too? Or a feminist one?

A WOMAN WHO WILL GET TO DECIDE CASES

I think the important thing about my appointment is not that I will decide cases as a woman, but that I am a woman who will get to decide cases.
(Justice Sandra Day O'Connor)

Feminist scholars have developed a sophisticated way of understanding gender as a social process and have advanced in their thinking of equality and difference, radicalism and essentialism. It is time for the slower-moving mainstream of social science to take note of how constructively this new understanding could alter the questions they ask, too. To be sure, some feminist scholars have also treated male and female as dichotomous, valorized the traits and endeavors society assigns to women, studied only women in their eagerness to rectify centuries of inquiry about only men and boys, and perpetuated the essentialism (men are X, women are Y) that is precisely what most feminists seek to challenge. This book moves beyond merely criticizing this state of affairs and models the study of gender as a social process. I offer a nonessentialist argument for greater equality for women by focusing on the judicial branch of government. Lewin's, Scott's, and Bell's approaches offer bold new conceptualizations of the difference debate that help us think about gender and judging.

Justice Ginsburg dragged herself from her hospital bed to attend the State of the Union Address so that everyone would see that a woman sits on the US Supreme Court. Presumably, she was not thinking only of the effect of the image on young girls and women law students, but of showing that the face of normal judicial power could be female. Strangely, race and gender become relevant only when women or nonwhite people appear, but white men have gender and racial identities, too. Senator Jeff Sessions failed to appreciate the irony in his declaration during the confirmation hearings that he believed Judge Sonia Sotomayor could not rise above her social location. If social location shapes judgment, his location as a white man shaped his judgment. Litigants have asked judges from nondominant groups to recuse themselves without appreciating that if race, gender, or sexual orientation matter for judging, all judges are affected. The furor Judge Sotomayor's nomination caused, a nomination many saw as an easy case, showed just how subversive the mere presence of women, and particularly a wise Latina, is. Robing and adjudicating, sitting on the elevated platform, is both transgressively radical and conservative. Women perform their difference from and their sameness to men simultaneously.

FROM DESCRIBING WOMEN TO GENDERING CONCEPTS: THE PLAN OF THE BOOK

This book provides an example of how to use gender as an analytical framework. I also offer a nonessentialist feminist case for more women judges that I hope will reignite the determination of groups of women judges, those advocating more women in politics, feminists, and the general public to demand women's equal participation as judges. Gender scholarship, well done, makes it impossible to see the general in the same way again, whether it is when the welfare state started,[50] how legislators pass routine legislation,[51] the range of possibilities for thinking about moral questions,[52] when and if a Renaissance happened,[53] who is dependent upon whom,[54] the origins and key players of the civil rights movement,[55] and who participated in second-wave feminism,[56] to name but a few examples. My aspiration is not only to demonstrate how to do gender scholarship and to make the case for women judges, but to persuade my colleagues that gender offers new insight into policy diffusion and emotions and social movement mobilization, backlash and judicial selection, policy implementation, agenda-setting, and representation.

I begin by being interested in women judges. They *are* interesting. Asking about gender and courts offers a lot of analytical traction: how come folks interested in the increasing politicization of state court judicial races fail to look at the first women challenged and removed from the bench? What do social movement scholars miss from understanding critical events by focusing only on rational arguments rather than emotions in social movement mobilizations? How come those who study the Carter Administration often fail to note his transformation of the composition of the judiciary and how judges are selected? How come agenda-setting scholars almost never study women's movements and women and public policy issues? How come members of the European Union are deeply concerned about a democratic deficit and representing nationality on the European Court of Justice but not the majority of the Union's citizens—women? How come those who study and advocate for more women in politics ignore courts? The project begins with looking for women, but quickly moves to appreciating what a gender analysis can add to our understandings.

One of the arguments that I will make in this book is that contemporary analyses of women judges are not really gender analyses at all, even if they use the word "gender." Rather than considering gender, such studies are really about supposed sex differences between men and women. In this book, I explore women's relation to and the gendered nature of the judiciary in various geographic jurisdictions. I begin with women supreme court justices in US states, move to women federal court judges, consider women on the highest bench in the United Kingdom, and end at the European Court of Justice. In each case, I consider how women ascended to positions of judicial power and how gender structures the judicial selection process. I criticize the exclusion of women and gender from judicial scholarship, illustrate how a gender analysis moves beyond a presumption of difference, and advance an argument for why we need more women judges.

As I will discuss in Chapter 2, judicial scholars have hypothesized that women judges are more likely to be concerned with children and to be better at juvenile justice than men; more liberal; pro-choice on questions of abortion and family planning; more likely to employ communitarian reasoning; more inclined to seek mediate solutions; more likely to inflict harsh or lenient sentences; more likely to side with women in divorce or Family and Medical Leave Act cases; more likely to grant asylum; or more likely to prioritize women's issues as chief justices. In most cases, the difference fails to emerge or emerges inconsistently. The most recent and strongest methodological study shows that women federal appellate judges do seem to be more pro-plaintiff in some sex discrimination cases and influence their colleagues when on panels to be more pro-plaintiff.[57]

Chapter 3 examines women's appointments to state supreme courts in the United States. I look at the symbolic importance of women judges by examining the appointment and subsequent election of Rosalie Wahl to the Minnesota Supreme Court in 1977. By promising to appoint a woman, the Minnesota Governor heightened public awareness of the appointment, which helped Wahl retain her seat. The men who challenged her thought the first woman would be easy to defeat. The story of how she succeeded rests on how she "did" gender and how she used emotions to mobilize social movements in support of her candidacy. The meaning of her appointment, victory, and gender all varied because of the context.

Chapter 4 examines women's entry into the US federal courts as they moved from tokens to minority. As with Chapter 3, the focus is on the process by which women made it to the highest bench and the meaning that their presence on the bench has for politicians, feminists, and the public. In this case, I look closely at President Jimmy Carter's women appointments to the federal bench to show how a gender analysis can illuminate our understanding of policy implementation. Carter appointed more women to the federal bench than all previous presidents combined—in total forty women (15.5 percent of all his appointments). Featured in this chapter is the story of Margaret McKenna, a thirty-two-year-old Deputy White House Counsel, who charged the nominating commissions with the task of generating lists that included women and minority men, galvanized the women's movement to lobby for women candidates, and helped Carter connect his policy preferences for merit selection with the policy of appointing women judges. McKenna connected the dots between Carter's commitment to merit selection of judges and women in government and made that policy commitment a reality by a strategic collaboration between well-positioned insiders and outside groups. Lest one think such a pattern constituted a distinctly gendered, feminine, or feminist approach to public policy, it is useful to remember that the same exact winning partnership between outside groups and strategic insiders forced President Bush to withdraw his nomination of Harriet Miers in favor of Samuel Alito.

Chapter 5 looks at the Appellate Committee of the House of Lords in the United Kingdom, now Britain's Supreme Court. Britain appointed the first woman, Lady Justice Brenda Hale, to its highest appellate court in 2002, more than twenty-five years after the United States and Canada had appointed women to their supreme courts. And in a major constitutional upheaval, the Labour Government completely revamped how the country selects judges, changing from vesting power in the Lord Chancellor to creating a Judicial Appointments Commission. The chapter explores how feminists made the case for women's presence on the UK bench by drawing on arguments for modernizing the UK political system. A male-dominated bench, with judges selected in secrecy, had the aura of an outdated political system. A gender-diverse bench, in this case, gave the UK system a sense of both modernity and legitimacy. Unfortunately, because the appointment of women was only an instrumental value, a means of modernizing, feminists have seen no momentum for increasing women's numbers in the higher judiciary, and the failure of the Judicial Appointments Commission to increase the percentages of women judges shows how any judicial selection system can disadvantage women unless diversifying the bench is an explicit priority.

Chapter 6 analyzes the European Court of Justice (ECJ), the supranational court of the European Union. The member states have appointed even fewer women to the ECJ than to their own national courts. This chapter explores how courts as representative institutions differ from legislatures and bureaucracies, but why gender merits representation even so. Because it is a supranational court, where representation is most clearly operative in selection processes, the ECJ provides an excellent case for considering the role that gender should play in making courts representative institutions. Looking at the concept of representation through the lens of gender and law shows legislators to be more like judges in how they represent than previous researchers have recognized.

In Chapter 7, I seek to develop a way of disentangling gender as a process from other causal factors rather than seeing it as an all-or-nothing explanation. Combining an array of phenomena usually seen as separate, or not noticed at all, I argue a backlash against women judges is at work. Theorizing the concept of backlash and applying it to the judicial branch of government reveals some disturbing points about what stalls women's progress in other sectors. I contrast Justice Wahl's success with Chief Justice Rose Bird's failure. The latter's appointment meant very different things to the other justices, to conservatives, and to women than Wahl's in Minnesota, and Bird was gendered very differently by the media, by her colleagues, by the opposition movement, and by herself. Using sex as a variable would be to construct Wahl and Bird as the same—women firsts. But a gender analysis reveals different social processes at work and illustrates the backlash against women judges.

Chapter 8 makes a nonessentialist case for women judges. Examining women's historic exclusion from jury service and the litigation their exclusion spawned exposes the trickiness of difference arguments. Regardless of their position on difference and protective legislation, feminists were united against women's exclusion from jury service, which they regarded as a core component of citizenship and a marker of equal status. They argued women would not have been tried by a jury of their peers if only men judged. All-male juries, just like all-white juries, are illegitimate. The same is true for the judiciary. We can draw on equal opportunity norms and reverse the question to ask why it is acceptable to exclude women from the judiciary. Sex discrimination is wrong, whether perpetrated against feminists or non-feminists. Moreover, if we look closely at international and federal discourses of representation outside of the gender context, it is clear that judges from different nations or states need not speak in a different voice to be deserving of representation. For example, Iowa judges do not have to decide cases differently from Minnesota judges to justify their representation on the Eighth Circuit Court of Appeals. Likewise, women do not have to decide cases differently from men to be deserving of representation on the bench. Instead of resting our arguments on difference, we should draw on broad arguments about citizenship. Whether demanding the vote in the United States, inclusion on juries, equal legislative representation in France, or judicial office, feminists need not rest claims to equality on evidence of difference.

2

GENDER, JUDGING, AND DIFFERENCE[1]

INTRODUCTION

Since women's rights activists first advocated that women serve as judges, to Justice Sandra Day O'Connor's retirement and replacement by a man, to President Obama's nominations of Judge Sonia Sotomayor in 2009 and Dean Elena Kagan in 2010, many feminists and academics have argued that we need more women judges because they will decide cases differently from men—specifically, they will rule more favorably on women's rights cases and bring a gender lens to all adjudication. In this chapter, I shall argue that the evidence shows that view to be largely misguided, reliant on dangerous assumptions about women's essential difference and claims that are empirically untrue.

In the book's conclusion, I call for continued mobilization to ensure the selection of judges capable of a gender analysis and committed to women's equality. I argue that many good arguments also support increasing the number of women judges. In this chapter, I shall argue that the claim that women decide cases differently—and in a more feminist direction than men—is not one of them. Using sex as a variable and conducting quantitative analysis can offer important insights, particularly about continuing discrimination. Scholars should, however, abandon the quest for the essential sex difference, and instead employ the concept of gender as a social process. Assuming that women will automatically decide cases differently from men diverts us from the larger purpose of investigating how women and men judges acquire a feminist consciousness and articulate a judicial agenda for women's rights.

As soon as enough women sat on the bench to make quantitative analysis possible, political scientists began using sex as a variable to examine the difference women made on the bench. More troubling, however, is that new scholars who study gender and judging often fail to build on their predecessors' criticisms of this frame and instead fall into the same trap of essentialism, no matter how many times scholars deconstruct the essentialist assumptions and faulty reasoning underlying this research or produce empirical findings of no difference. It is as if we can think of only one question to ask about women judges: "Are they different?" Even if we find they mostly are not, we keep asking the same question over and over, sure that we will uncover the "true" difference. Is looking for sex differences the only way the conservative discipline of political science can "do" gender, or has the difference approach became instantiated as "the" feminist analytical approach, despite its critics?

As I argued in Chapter 1, the drumbeat of essentialism has a *Groundhog Day* quality. Looking carefully at the tenacity of the assumption of difference in research on women judges proves to be an excellent location for exploring the concept of gender more broadly and a fruitful way to explore both what is helpful and what is problematic about using sex as a variable.

Three political scientists, Beverly Blair Cook, Elaine Martin, and Sue Davis, pioneered the study of women judges and laid a foundation for scholarly investigation. First, they theorized gender as a social process rather than as an essential difference. Second, they investigated sex differences empirically rather than assumed them. Third, they treated women as a varied group and saw feminism as something women (and some men) espoused to different degrees (if at all). Finally, they investigated gender beyond the question of whether women judges decided cases differently from men. At the same time, each of these three scholars occasionally fell into the essentialism trap. What is most intriguing, and troubling, is that none of the three's work followed a simple trajectory of going from more essentialist to less over the course of their careers. Instead, paradoxically, their work sometimes became more essentialist the less empirical support for sex differences they found. The fact that feminist theorists were largely on a trajectory in one direction, criticizing and rejecting essentialism, while political scientists who work on women judges were more inconsistent, and essentialist frames continue to surface, suggests that examining the tenacity of the difference frame has more than historical value as a literature review. This investigation sheds light not only on scholarship on women judges but on the concept of gender more generally. It shows just how tenacious and ubiquitous assumptions of difference are across the board.

HAS GENDER REPLACED SEX? IS IT A NOUN, AN ADJECTIVE, OR A VERB?

As I argued in Chapter 1, "sex"—meaning biological sex differences—has dropped from the popular lexicon, and we now use the word "gender" instead. From the outset of feminist theorizing in the 1970s, feminists employed the word "gender" to challenge the assumption that innate sex differences between men and women existed, were static, dichotomous, and the foundation of men and women's differing social roles. Gender differences thus do not flow inevitably from sex differences; rather, gendering is the process by which we attach meaning to sex differences, most often to devalue whatever society associates with women.[2] Most feminists now recognize gender to be a social process rather than an essential difference. They explore the construction of and asserted content of gender differences empirically rather than assume these differences.[3] And good reasons exist for not assuming such sex differences: for all intents and purposes, they do not exist! Scientists have shown repeatedly that women differ as much from other women as they do from men, whether the attribute is strength, the capacity for mathematical reasoning, or the ability to calm toddlers. Even if some sex differences exist on a bell curve, much overlap exists in the middle. We know from social psychologists' research on cognition, however, that once group identities are created (however arbitrarily— the blue team and the green team, for example), subjects will start to differentiate and attach attributes to each group, regardless of whether such differences have any empirical support.[4]

USING SEX AS A VARIABLE CAN UNCOVER DISCRIMINATION

While feminist scholars have given us good reason to be skeptical about claims of sex differences, using sex as a variable can identify incidences and measure the magnitude of sex discrimination and differential treatment. One useful application is explaining women's underrepresentation in the judiciary and the wide variation in women's representation across the US states and cross-nationally. Rather than argue that women will decide cases differently from men (which has weak empirical support at best, as I shall show, and risks disadvantaging women in unintended ways), using sex as a variable can help us identify and assess discrimination. If sex increases the probability that men will be selected as judges and decreases the probability that women will be selected, we risk excluding the talents and abilities of a majority of the population. Moreover, we have done an injustice to qualified women and unfairly advantaged less qualified men. We have excluded women from a core function of citizenship, participating in one branch of government, symbolically conveying that women are second-class citizens, lacking the ability to participate and contribute. I take up these arguments in Chapter 8.

Many have justified women's absence from high judicial office because women have entered legal education in large numbers only recently. Apologists reassured advocates that women would trickle up to higher judicial office as cohorts with equal numbers of women accrued seniority.[5] Beverly Blair Cook conducted the first pool analysis, asking how many women judges we would expect to see serving on the bench, given the pool of eligibles. She found little change between 1920 and 1970.[6] In 1977, Cook could explain most of the variation in the number of women serving on state courts as a function of the number of women law graduates and the number serving in the state attorney general's office.[7] By 1984, the evidence had changed, and Cook rejected the trickle-up hypothesis.[8] She found a disparity of 50 percent between the actual women judges and the number of women judges we might expect based on the number of women lawyers. If women were 10 percent of the lawyers in a state, about 5 percent of judges would be women.[9] Cook concluded that it was not merely a question of time, since gatekeepers were discriminating against women.[10] Other scholars who followed drew the same conclusion.[11]

A great deal of research suggests that gatekeepers discriminate against women. In Chapter 4, I shall describe how presidents and other selectors failed to consider women fairly. Vital gatekeepers, such as the law professors who suggest law clerks to Supreme Court justices, did not recommend women in proportion to their increasing numbers.[12] Nor have justices chosen them in proportion to the pool.[13] Another important gatekeeper has been the American Bar Association's (ABA) Standing Committee on the Judiciary, which evaluates nominees.[14] Cook showed how this committee's evaluations of potential women nominees thwarted women's progress and echoed the views of many, such as Chief Justice Warren Burger, that no qualified woman existed.[15] When President Ronald Reagan gave the committee O'Connor's name in 1980, it reluctantly accepted the viability of women candidates and had its first woman member, who also became the chair.[16] Nominating commissions, for the federal appeals courts or state courts, also serve as gatekeepers.[17] Cook argued as early as 1984 that the more women on the nominating commissions, the more women on the lists.

Women are herded into the lower-status corners of the legal and judicial professions and then assessed as lacking the prestigious credentials required for high judicial appointment. For example, the ABA's Standing Committee on the Judiciary valued large-firm experience. Yet, when Sandra Day O'Connor sought employment with her third-place ranking from Stanford Law School in 1952, firms openly said they would not hire women. Such exclusion from large firms solidified women's absence from high judicial office. From Northern Ireland[19] to Argentina,[20] women are shunted into family law, then told that it is not sufficiently prestigious for high judicial appointment.[21]

Gatekeepers have used different standards for men and women nominees—for example, holding parenthood against women but not men. Even if selectors use sex-neutral criteria when making judicial selections, such criteria have tended to indirectly discriminate against women, having what we in the United States call a disparate impact. Disparate impact, known as indirect discrimination in the United Kingdom and the European Union, occurs when employers use a sex-neutral characteristic (e.g. height) in hiring and recruitment. In 1982, Elaine Martin explored the disparate impact of using the criterion of being well known by senior judges as the basis for choosing judges.

Her survey found that 43 percent of women felt that they would not have been considered under this system because they lacked political influence and connections.[22] Martin considered a second example of disparate impact, too—how the ABA's criteria of valuing large-firm experience made it nearly impossible for women to pass muster because large firms refused to hire women attorneys.[23] The ABA also tended to favor older, well-to-do, business-oriented corporate attorneys. Women did not need to argue that they deserved a place on the bench because they were different; instead, if we used objective criteria of merit, the women Carter appointed were more deserving than the men.[24] By deemphasizing political connections, Carter's merit commissions let the women candidates' stronger academic credentials emerge.

Do women believe discrimination hinders them in becoming judges? Many women lawyers reported to gender bias taskforce surveys that they thought they were discriminated against. A large gender gap repeatedly existed in what men and women reported about whether the profession discriminates against women (women thought it did more often than men).[25] A gender gap may also exist in political ambition for judicial office as it does for legislative office. Lawless and Fox[26] documented that well-qualified women were less likely than their male counterparts to say they had considered running for office or had been asked to do so. In 1983, Cook reported higher levels of ambition for judicial office among younger cohorts of women, although much of that ambition was focused on state courts.[27] How much of women's lower levels of ambition, if a gender gap does exist, reflect women's expectations of discrimination? Women may have wisely ascertained that applying for judgeships in the past (or running for judicial office) was pointless, despite their ambitions. Williams found that 68 percent of the women attorneys surveyed believed women faced barriers to becoming a judge.[28] Her survey of women lawyers in Texas did not show a large gender gap in political ambition for state judicial office in a state with partisan election.[29] Jensen and Martinek's 2006 survey of trial court judges in New York State actually found women to be more ambitious than men.[30] Examining sex difference in whether lawyers perceive discrimination in the profession and in ambitions for judicial office, as an example, can provide important information explaining women's underrepresentation.

We can also use sex as a variable to explore whether women do better under one method of selection than another.[31] Early analysts proclaimed that the appointive methods of selection granted women and minority men greater access to judicial office than elective measures,[32] but Dubois found that women fared as well under elections as under appointment in California from 1959 to 1977.[33] In 1982, Susan Carbon et al. surveyed women state court judges and found that judges tended to declare whichever system produced them to be their preferred system.[34] By 1988, Cook had concluded that no one judicial selection system produced more women.[35] What mattered was a commitment on the part of gatekeepers to consider women and to discard discriminatory criteria, whether those gatekeepers were executives or commissions. Tokarz's analysis showed how appointive systems could discriminate—what mattered was whether gatekeepers had a commitment to equality.[36] Subsequent analyses confirmed Cook's and Tokarz's findings.[37]

So-called merit selection systems have not produced more women judges, primarily because nominating commissions can discriminate, too, unless they have women members, are trained to avoid discrimination and stereotyping, and make securing a gender-diverse bench a priority. Githens found, for example, that the Maryland nominating commission employed a gender double standard for men and woman applicants. Commissioners saw women as uppity when they sought judicial positions, whereas they saw men as lacking in ambition when they sought judicial positions, since they should have aspired to more lucrative partnerships in large firms.[38] Electoral systems, too, can discriminate against women if gatekeepers keep women from partisan endorsements, if voters discriminate, or if women have difficulty raising money.[39] Torres-Spelliscy et al.'s study of ten state nominating commissions in the US found that some nominating commissioners saw themselves as headhunters who made it their task to recruit a diverse candidate pool while others saw themselves as background checkers who passively waited for candidates to apply.[40] Only the former were successful in selecting a diverse and representative judiciary.

After years of discrimination in the legal profession and by gatekeepers, simple nondiscrimination using current criteria and processes will not be enough to ensure equality. Commissions need to recruit diverse candidates actively, train commissioners on implicit bias, appoint a diversity compliance officer or ombudsperson, and make diversity of commissioners and judges an explicit statutory goal.[41] And we have several examples demonstrating that gender balance is possible. In 1988, the Province of Ontario, Canada, created a committee with a majority of lay members to choose judges, chaired by political scientist Peter H. Russell.[42] It set a goal to increase the number of women judges,[43] advertised widely for candidates, and Russell personally wrote to every eligible woman lawyer, urging them to apply. He received applications from fifty women for the first five openings, and the women he interviewed said they never thought they stood a chance of becoming a judge because they lacked political connections.[44] Half of the first seventy-five appointments were women, adding considerably to the ten sitting women judges, who made up just 4 percent of the provincial judiciary.[45]

Scotland preceded England in creating a Judicial Appointments Board in 2002 and expressly repudiated the process of "secret soundings"—the vetting of judges by informally canvassing senior judges—and the "tap on the shoulder" approach in favor of an application process. The proportion of women in the judiciary increased from 1 to 4 of 32 judges (12 percent), 12 to 23 out of 136 sheriffs (17 percent), and 10 of 58 part-time sheriffs (17 percent). The proportion of women applicants rose from 11 percent to between 20 and 25 percent.[46] But the Scottish Executive never rethought its definition of merit nor explicitly made gender diversity its goal,[47] and its progress stalled. A similar burst occurred in 1996 in South Africa. The Constitution set an explicit goal to have a diverse and representative bench, as did the statute creating federal nominating commissions. Two of the eleven initial justices of the Constitutional Court were women. But in 2004, only 13.3 percent of the judges in the superior courts were women.[48] An explicit goal may be necessary, but the South African case shows that it is not sufficient if the appointees to the Judicial Appointments Commission do not embrace it or take concrete steps to make it a reality. Chapter 7 describes how similar initiatives in the Australian states of Victoria and Queensland created a backlash from sitting male judges and the legal establishment.

USING SEX AS A VARIABLE TO DETERMINE WHETHER WOMEN JUDGE DIFFERENTLY FROM MEN

Once a sufficient number of women were on the bench, research shifted from a focus on the barriers to women securing judicial office to a focus on how decisions of women judges differed from those of men. The first study of the effects of women judges found no differences between men and women in their sentencing behavior, even in rape cases, nor any evidence that the gender of the judge interacted with the gender of the defendant.[49] Later analyses of the same data confirmed that although men and women judges did not differ in their overall sentencing behavior, women judges were twice as likely as men judges to send women to jail.[50] Women judges, more so than men, treated men and women defendants similarly. Gruhl, Spohn, and Welch, however, hypothesized that women would be more lenient on criminals than men. But perhaps the most important finding was buried in a footnote, in which the authors admitted that in their minuscule sample of seven, they found more differences among women judges than between men and women judges.[51]

In 1981, Cook surveyed the 170 women sitting on state courts and a comparative sample of men. She hypothesized that women would be more feminist than men on women's rights cases. Even so, she eschewed an essentialist approach, dismissing what she called the biological model "that women will exhibit a different style of decision-making and emphasize different substantive goals compatible with certain intrinsic characteristics of the sex."[52] Instead, she embraced a socialization model and added a touch of feminist political philosophy: because women experience sexism and discrimination, "male authorities do not feel for or act for women's interests, and women authorities largely do."[53] Patricia Yancey Martin et al. would later call this theory the feminist standpoint.[54]

Cook identified judges by sex, party, and ideology, asked them whether they considered themselves feminist or supportive of the women's movement, and then asked them a couple of hypothetical questions.[55] One question was about temporary alimony for a woman custodial parent so that she could acquire an education. The other concerned a married mother's ability to change her name to her maiden name despite her husband's disapproval. Cook found gender gaps on each of her measures. She found consensus on the hypothetical case involving alimony, but she found that attitude and feminism—not sex and party—predicted judges' stances on the second hypothetical case about name changing.

In 1983, Gottschall compared the voting of Carter appointees on the Court of Appeals over a two-year period to see if they were liberal activists, as critics charged.[56] He found little difference between men and women on rights of accused and prisoners and some differences for race and sex discrimination cases, with the caveat that he analyzed only nineteen votes cast by women. Another study of federal district judges found male judges to be more liberal and women more likely to defer to government.[57] It found no significant differences between men and women US district court judges on issues of women's rights or criminal policy. Women judges, however, were more likely to uphold government regulation and less likely to support personal liberty claims. Allen and Wall's study[58] showed that four out of five women on four state supreme courts were the court's most liberal member.

In Chapter 1, I discussed Elaine Martin's surveys reflecting differences among women judges. Using surveys of judges, Martin modified Cook's protocol and asked respondents whether they were feminists and then compared feminist men and women to non-feminist men and women.[59] Martin's study had many methodological limitations. Her sample was not representative, she did not control for other potentially important variables, and she dealt with self-reported opinions and hypothetical cases rather than actual behavior. Nevertheless, she made several important contributions to the study of gender and judging. First, like Cook, she did not assume sex to be a proxy for feminism but investigated sex and feminism as separate variables. In this sense, she recognized the presence of feminist men, who may differ little from feminist women and even non-feminist women, who, it turned out, differed less than we might have expected from feminist women and more than we might have thought from non-feminist men. Martin showed that feminist ideology may well be more important than sex in predicting different votes in hypothetical cases. Yet, she treated feminism as dichotomous—you either were or were not a feminist, no gradations existed. Moreover, the presentation of the work illustrates recurring problems: feminist ideology morphs into sex differences, and differences in tendencies become essential (dichotomous) sex differences (men think Y, women think X, rather than some women think X and some men think X, too, in varying degrees). Treating overlapping degrees of differences in opinions as dichotomous—men think this, women think that, feminists think this, non-feminists think that—is one of the most troubling ways essentialism works its way into using sex as a variable. It need not be so.

Those who discuss these studies could talk about them in non-essentialist ways, but they rarely do.

Sociologist Patricia Yancey Martin and her colleagues examined Florida judges and found that "compared with men judges and attorneys, women judges and attorneys were more conscious of gender inequality, observed more gender bias in legal settings, and showed a stronger connection between experiences with gender bias and feminist consciousness."[60] Drawing on feminist standpoint theory, Martin et al.[61] argued that feminist consciousness is a political achievement, not an automatic consequence of being a woman or experiencing life as a woman. In this case, women judges observed more gender bias dynamics and were more likely than men to agree with a variety of feminist principles, ranging from property division post-divorce to rejecting rape myths and negative stereotypes about domestic violence. The findings held across race. Therefore, Martin et al. argued that the presence of women judges would make the legal system more objective, more legitimate in the eyes of women claimants, and help all judges raise their consciousness on these issues.

Sue Davis's study of judges on the Ninth Circuit Court of Appeals was grounded in feminist theory.[62] Recognizing that finding a different, female, or feminine voice in one woman jurist hardly proves anything about the category of women, Davis searched for evidence of difference by pairing the women judges on the Ninth Circuit with their most similar men—men appointed by the same president who were similar in education and background, and similarly located on the liberal–conservative spectrum. Davis focused on equal protection and civil rights cases. She found many of the elements of difference in the cases she examined, but little evidence of gender differences between paired men and women. Surprisingly, her findings did not lead her to reject the different voice as a way to frame gender and judging. Instead, she left us with the possibility that the wrong sort of women were serving on the bench (too manly?) and/or that the male system of judging overpowered the feminist voice.

Importantly, Davis found that whether one approached sex discrimination law as a feminist mattered—it determined outcomes in important cases. Davis took a step forward in empirically showing that although women were likely to apply feminist analysis, some, but not all, men did, too. In the end, however, she retreated from an anti-essentialist view of gender and questioned whether women judges could give full expression to either their femininity or feminism, since only "the right sort of women"—women who accepted the yoke of the law—could be appointed in the first place.

A subsequent study by Davis,[63] and an additional study by Songer, Davis, and Haire,[64] expanded the question of whether women judged differently due to some inherent feminine difference by considering the entire Court of Appeals and moving beyond equal treatment cases to cases on criminal procedure and obscenity. Songer et al.[65] found women judges on the Court of Appeals as a whole more likely than their male colleagues to support claimants in sex discrimination cases (63 to 46 percent), and more likely than their colleagues to support the defendants in search and seizure cases (17.7 to 10.9 percent), although they found no significant differences in obscenity cases. The difference narrowed somewhat but persisted when they compared women and men appointed by Democratic presidents in employment discrimination cases, and disappeared altogether between Republican-appointed men and women. Nor did they find differences when they factored the party of the appointing president into their analysis of search and seizure cases.

Davis and colleagues suggested the possibility that theories of difference were quite simply wrong. Alternatively, they opined, evidence of difference simply did not emerge in analyses of decision-making. A third possibility they considered was that the law crushes women's uniqueness and that women, as newcomers to the bench, cannot withstand the law's hostility to an ethic of care. Lastly, women of the generation who were likely to be judges might have had the ethic of care stamped out of them or had been chosen for judicial office because they lacked this supposedly essential gender trait in the first place. Implicit in the authors' conclusion was the assumption that women are essentially different, but we have not yet uncovered that difference empirically—this despite the strong evidence that men judges were using feminist modes of analysis, too.

By 1994, Songer, Davis, and Haire[66] had yet to find evidence of difference in men and women judges. For example, they found gender added nothing to the predictive power in either obscenity cases or in search and seizure cases. They did find that the gender of judges was strongly related to the probability of a liberal vote in job discrimination cases (38 percent probability for men; 75 percent for women). They suggested that women could be more attentive to discrimination generally because of their experiences rather than because they reason differently from men. But they went on to muse whether law school stamps out the different voice in favor of rights and hierarchies, suggesting that it somehow represses women's difference in everything but discrimination cases.

Rather than the law silencing women judges' different voice, what we see is political science (or possibly the difference strand in feminist theory) repressing Davis's more anti-essentialist approach over time. Though she starts with a feminist topic—how gender affects judging—she loses the critical eye and sophistication of feminist theory, adopting instead a tried—and untrue—essentialist argument about women's supposed difference. What is striking is that the farther she moves down the path of statistical analysis, the farther she moves from any real support of the different voice.

After carefully reviewing all the evidence about whether men and women decide cases differently, legal academic Theresa Beiner concluded that "the effects of race and gender of judge are inconclusive."[67] In a recent example, Jennifer Segal studied President Bill Clinton's judicial appointees to the district courts and found that the traditional (i.e. white male) judges were more liberal (pro-plaintiff in sex discrimination cases) than non-traditional (women and minority men) appointees.[68] Even if one conceded that Clinton faced a Republican-dominated Senate and knew that women nominees faced more intense scrutiny than men, one can hardly conclude that his women appointees speak in a distinctive feminine or feminist voice. But there is the possibility that women judges may influence their male colleagues. When political scientist Nancy Crowe explored this proposition in sex discrimination cases in the US Courts of Appeals between 1981 and 1996, she found no evidence of such an effect.[69] Jennifer Peresie, however, examined how the presence of women judges on three-judge federal appellate panels affected collegial outcomes in Title VII cases on sexual harassment or sex discrimination and found that plaintiffs were twice as likely to prevail when a woman judge was on the bench.[70] The presence of a woman judge increased the probability that a man judge would support the plaintiff. Peresie also found that judges appointed by Democratic presidents were the most pro-plaintiff and that Democratic men and Republican women were similarly pro-plaintiff. Interestingly, she found men and women judges more different from each other in sexual harassment cases but the influence of women judges greater in sex discrimination cases, though she lacked an adequate theory to account for these differences.

Elaine Martin and Barry Pyle examined state supreme courts and rulings in divorce cases.[71] They zeroed in on divorce cases as places where we might expect gender rather than feminism to lead to differences in behavior on the part of men and women judges. They focused on the non-unanimous decisions of the Michigan Supreme Court over thirteen years and found Democrats to be more liberal than Republicans, African Americans different from whites only on the issue of discrimination, and men and women to differ from each other but in the opposite direction than might be expected:

> Men cast 52.3% of their votes as liberals in discrimination cases while women cast only 38.3%. The reason for this result may simply be that during most of the time period under study there was only one Democratic woman justice, who, as a former prosecutor and criminal trial court judge, was somewhat less liberal than her fellow male Democrats in two of the three issue areas.[72]

Martin and Pyle's comment reveals the inherent problem in this line of research. Although they were looking at the Michigan Supreme Court over time, they were still only looking at a small number of people and a small number of women and minority men. In addition, they were assuming that gender would or should lead to a distinctive form of judging, rather than looking for that relationship empirically. The gender assumption remains, even though the evidence not only fails to support it but contradicts it.

Martin and Pyle first added Minnesota and Wisconsin to their study, then all state high courts, to examine their hunch that although other studies found few gender differences, divorce cases would provide "the most fertile ground for discovering the impact of judicial gender."[73] This telling phrasing reveals the authors' belief that women's true difference from men would finally become evident in their decision-making. They found that women judges were more likely than men to support a woman litigant in divorce cases. This difference was more pronounced if there were three women on the court but less pronounced if there were two—a non-linear relationship that Martin and Pyle could not explain. Men were more supportive of women litigants when they served with only one other woman and less likely if they were chosen by merit systems. Women who had more trial court experience were more supportive of women litigants.

As Martin and Pyle tried to make theoretical sense of these results, the fundamental flaw in these studies emerged: the researcher looks for and either finds or fails to find sex differences. Then, a story is produced to suggest why essential differences are not found or are found inconsistently. A common story draws on Rosabeth Moss Kanter's theory that posited that women "tokens," isolated on the bench or in their profession, behave just like men.[74] Justice Ginsburg expressly criticized these insulting characterizations in 1986.[75] Presumably, once women reached a critical mass on the bench, their true differences would emerge. But the research does not deploy the evidence to help us decide whether women really do have a different approach to judging. Rather than continuing with this line of research, I argue that it is time for rethinking our theories of gender and judging.

Beverly Blair Cook did not see judges at the highest appellate levels as enmeshed in a legal and political structure that constrained their decision-making and shaped their arguments, but rather as able to pick and choose from precedent and interpretive canons to support their policy preferences. Rather than engaging in a textual exegesis of rules, precedents, and legal arguments, Cook mined legal texts for evidence of judicial attitudes and policy orientations. What mattered to her was who judges were and what they thought and believed about everything, not just law and the judicial role:

> In these cases, what is important is how the Justice feels about women—women on welfare, pregnant teachers, women officers, women jurors—and their demands, in relation to how the Justice feels about the other party—industry, grade school, the military establishment, the courts—and its expectations for the female role.[76]

Cook plotted each of the justices based upon their votes on women's rights cases and the views they expressed in their opinions, other writings, and speeches. She concluded: "The paternalism of the male Supreme Court justices which shines through these cases may only be ended with their closer association with female justices."[77] Yet Cook's later analysis comparing Florence Allen and Sandra Day O'Connor contradicts her assumption that women judges would necessarily support women's rights. Allen, a suffragist, was part of a vast network of women's groups and saw herself as a representative of women. In contrast, O'Connor looked ahead to a time when gender identity would lose its significance.[78]

It has been argued that Justice O'Connor used communitarian, holistic, and contextual reasoning rather than liberal, individualistic, atomistic, and rule-based reasoning—the former being dubbed the "feminine voice."[79] Her opinions do not display a consistently feminist voice, although she did take a feminist position on some issues, particularly relative to her more conservative colleagues. But her gender arguably mattered because she deployed a distinctly "feminine" style of reasoning. This argument was put most fully by legal academic Suzanna Sherry,[80] but several others advanced it as well.[81] When political scientist Sue Davis put these claims to a rigorous empirical test, however, she found little evidence for them, finding merely that Justice O'Connor was less conservative than Justice Rehnquist on some issues and showed greater support for equality claims than other conservatives.[82] Political scientists Jilda Aliotta[83] and Nancy Maveety[84] reached the same conclusion.

An ongoing puzzle is why Davis, as well as Martin and others, continued to use Sherry's theories to frame questions about Justice O'Connor and gender and judging, given that Davis's empirical analysis demolished Sherry's argument. Yet Davis concluded, "O'Connor does not appear to speak 'in a different voice,' but the possibility remains that other women judges do."[85] Justice O'Connor (echoing many of the National Association of Women Judges (NAWJ) members whom Martin surveyed) herself dismissed as absurd the idea that she employed a uniquely or distinctly feminine approach to legal reasoning.[86] To be sure, O'Connor's jurisprudence eschewed bright-line legal rules and she seemed to revel in her power as the swing justice, questioning advocates about facts of particular cases at oral argument. Even if O'Connor did have a different voice, a feminine voice, or a feminist voice, we cannot generalize about all women from this one woman. It is thus astonishing that observers are so determined to find that distinct female essence of judging, when, instead, they could be asking how the experiences of particular judges, shaped by gender, have affected their perspectives.

Unlike the overwhelming majority of women judges that Cook surveyed, Justice O'Connor neither self-identified as a feminist nor supported widespread access to abortion. Cook documented O'Connor's experience of sex discrimination and her work as a legislator in passing some sex equality legislation, though recognized that her commitment to women's equality was weak. She reminded us that upon President Reagan's assumption of the presidency, right-wing Republicans effectively vetoed women judicial candidates as "too feminist"[87] and noted that Reagan's choice of O'Connor "offered more symbol than substance to other women."[88] Cook's analysis of the eighteen sex equality cases O'Connor had considered as of 1978 (Cook excludes abortion cases from this analysis) showed five men justices more favorable to sex equality than O'Connor.

Cook completed a fuller and more comprehensive analysis of O'Connor's role in the Burger Court in 1991. Beginning with an analysis of O'Connor's background and her confirmation hearings, she moved into an analysis of her jurisprudence and found that Justice Brennan, not Justice O'Connor, consistently took the lead in favor of gender equality. O'Connor ranked only sixth.[89] Cook concluded:

> O'Connor performed as the woman justice on the Court only in her extra-judicial activities as a speaker and writer. After her first term, when she raised her voice vigorously for a strong constitutional guarantee of gender equality but for weak remedies for gender discrimination, she retired as a spokesperson on women's rights. She never challenged a Court opinion that denied gender equality. The one attitude that could be associated with her personal experience as a mother in American culture was her sensitivity to children, which appeared in criminal, free expression, and church–state cases ... O'Connor's contributions to the Burger Court's jurisprudence were characterized by her political sensibility, driven by her structural principles, and *unmarked by her gender*.[90]

Cook's choice of words is telling. Here, "gender" means feminine essence or feminist consciousness. I would urge us to see everyone—men and women—as marked by gender, albeit in different ways and with different effects. Even Cook, the most anti-essentialist of the three scholars I examined here, returned to the assumption of difference. O'Connor was a disappointment because she did not speak in a feminist voice—the voice Cook was hoping for when she criticized the all-male Supreme Court's rulings on sex discrimination.

In their 1990 article in *Women & Politics*, O'Connor and Segal[91] examined how the addition of one justice, Sandra Day O'Connor, to the Court may have moved Justice Rehnquist more toward the center on sex discrimination cases. Perhaps, too, Justice Ginsburg's arguments led him to join the majority in the Virginia Military Institute case and perhaps also in *Nevada v. Hibbs*.[92] As intriguing as O'Connor and Segal's findings are for thinking about the difference women make in collegial courts, Barbara Palmer's analysis of Justice Ginsburg's effect on her male colleagues[93] shows the same confounding results that Martin found as the number of women increased on state supreme courts.[94] Palmer found that although O'Connor and Ginsburg wrote more than their share of decisions in sex discrimination cases and were the spokespeople for the Court on women, some male colleagues became more supportive of women's rights claims after Ginsburg's addition; others became less so, making it difficult to argue for a clear gender effect. Justice Ginsburg herself reported being listened to less once Justice O'Connor left the bench.

In a recent chapter acknowledging—but untouched by—anti-essentialist critiques of Gilligan, Carrie Menkel-Meadow reports the findings of her study showing women immigration judges granting asylum at a significantly higher rate than men.[95] Menkel-Meadow wants so-called women's values not just to be included in judicial decision-making but to become the norm. She laments that the issue of gender difference has been operationalized with exclusively quantitative work on decision-making rather than more qualitative work, such as interviews,[96] and concedes the results of studies on gender differences in judging are mixed and inconclusive.[97] She also notes findings that go in the opposite direction from what her Gilligan-esque approach would predict. She does note that women's and men's backgrounds are different: men come to immigration judging from law enforcement; women more from non-profit advocacy work (a pretty straightforward explanation for the difference, in my view), but she appears to control neither for background, nor party, nor ideology. Finally, Menkel-Meadow notes that proclaiming such a sex difference—women are softer on immigrants—might either cause them to compensate, or might cause selectors to disadvantage them.[98] More than thirty years into this debate (longer, if you go back to debates during suffrage or jury service), it seems like nothing has changed: women are different; women are better; a judicial system with different, better women will be different and better. No evidence to the contrary could ever dislodge the position.

Boyd, Epstein, and Martin tackle the issue of the conflicts and method-ological challenges of some of these studies and others in their 2010 article in the *American Journal of Political Science*.[99] They use sex as a variable to see if women decide cases differently from men and if women's presence on a panel makes men more likely to vote for the plaintiff in sex discrimination cases. As sophisticated methodologists, they diagnose the problem of inconsistent and contradictory findings of sex differences as caused by methodological problems with multiple regression analysis. Their method is superior to that of their predecessors, they argue, because women judges are clustered among the more liberal judges, which affects the results, even if one controls for ideology. Instead, they utilize semiparametric matching. When they compare women to their closest men analogues, they find the likelihood of a judge deciding in favor of a party alleging discrimination increases by about 10 percentage points when that judge is a woman, and that men are more likely to rule in favor of the rights of a sex discrimination litigant when a woman serves on the panel. They would not have unearthed these effects had they used the more common regression analysis, which can produce both false positives and false negatives, they argue. They define their most important contribution as methodolog-ical.[100] I am prepared to accept that their methodology is superior to that of their predecessors. And I am persuaded that they found true empirical sex differences in sex discrimination cases. Previous studies (most clearly Peresie,[101] but also Martin and Pyle and Martin et al.[102]) suggested that if differences exist at all, they are to be found in sex discrimination cases (although Martin and Pyle did not find them in Family and Medical Leave Act (FMLA) cases[103]).

But what do their findings prove, beyond the superiority of their method-ological approach, which is significant? Their data come from cases before the

Courts of Appeals from 1995 to 2001. But after eight years of appointments by President Bush, and vigorous campaigns to block any women who might be anything short of ideologically pure on the part of conservatives (such as Harriet Miers), my intuition is that women judges on the Courts of Appeals may now be less clustered among liberals than during the time period they study. (Judge Murphy is one of the most liberal judges on the Eighth Circuit, but, as the only woman, there is no one for her to cluster with, and the Fifth Circuit certainly includes women among its most conservative members.) Moreover, if presidents have employed gender double standards when selecting men and women judges (Clinton's women appointments had more judicial experience than his men; Bush required that women but not men have strong evidence of party loyalty; Carter required women but not men to demonstrate a commitment to equal justice under law, etc.), have they found that women decide cases differently from men and influence their colleagues or that presidents used different critera in choosing men and women? What conclusions do we draw if they did find differences, but they are ephemeral?

They find no effects in the other twelve areas of law they examine. And, while their findings are indisputably significant, they are tendencies. It is not the case that women always side with plaintiffs in sex discrimination cases and men never do—just that being a woman makes you more likely to, and a panel that includes a woman is more likely to rule in one direction. Boyd, Epstein, and Martin wrestle with the difficult question of why they should see these tendencies in some areas of law and not in other so-called women's issues, like abortion. They rightly recognize that while abortion may be indisputably a women's issue, women do not diverge from men in their opinions: many women are anti-abortion; many men are pro-choice. Both Martin et al.[104] and Ifill[105] wrestle with whether public opinion data show fleeting or stable sex differences. Numerous studies, such as those conducted by gender bias taskforces, have shown women perceive there to be discrimination and obstacles more so than men—that a gender gap exists. But not all women see it and some men do; and how do we explain that if it is a sex-based experience? As Ifill shows, gender gaps on issues are more ephemeral and less significant than race gaps. In Chapter 8, I shall show how difficult the assertions of difference were in thinking about juries: are women jurors harder on rape victims than men? Are they more sympathetic to victims of sexual harassment? It is complicated and variable and not readily predictable, stable, or dichotomous.

Although the title of their article is "Untangling the Causal Effects of Sex on Judging," Boyd, Epstein, and Martin[106] use "gender" and "sex" interchangeably and refer to gender effects and the literature on gendered judging. They do not use the term "gender" to mean a social process. They focus on methodology and therefore claim to be examining only the studies that use quantitative analysis, leaving out some of the studies I discuss in this chapter. They say they focus on the empirical, not the normative, but they do not confine themselves to asking what is the best method to unearth sex differences, if they exist, but consider, albeit briefly, where sex differences come from, what effects they have, and what they mean. One of the shortcomings of many of the other quantitative studies that use sex as a variable is that the intellectual energy goes into the methodological analysis rather than into reflecting why you would expect a difference or what the evidence of difference means. That analysis often occurs at the end as an afterthought. I have already criticized the studies that find no difference but continue to assert a difference exists, yet to be unearthed. The converse problem is when studies do find a difference but can only speculate as to its cause because nothing in the evidence would allow you to determine whether the alleged cause produced the reported difference.

Because they look for and find individual effects as well as panel effects, their article, unlike many of the other studies, actually attempts to use their findings to adjudicate between four competing frames of understanding sex differences. They do, however, opt for a weaker claim than causality, saying they are making merely a descriptive inference, limited to one time period and one set of cases: women are slightly more likely to vote pro-plaintiff in employment discrimination cases.[107] Their survey of the quantitative literature leads them to identify four accounts of sex differences in judging. The different voice account (drawing on Gilligan[108]) assumes either biological difference as a causation or gender-based but shared and dichotomous socialization. Because they fail to find difference across different areas of law and find panel effects instead, Boyd et al. say their evidence undermines this account. The account they label "representational" would also lead us to expect no panel effects and individual effects on women's issues. The "informational" category assumes women have had a common experience of discrimination and that experience can be brought to bear on men's decision-making—such as Justice Stevens telling about driving on country roads, or Justice Ginsburg knowing about nudity and adolescent girls, or Justice Marshall being familiar with the shame and physical hardship of exclusion from public accommodation—hotels, restrooms, restaurants—because of race. This account would predict both individual effects and panel effects. Lastly, the "organizational account" assumes that if an essential difference exists, it is overcome by uniformity in professional training which stamps out any sex difference, wherever that difference comes from. If that were the case, we would see no individual effects or panel effects.

Problematic essentialist assumptions underpin all of the explanations. But more importantly, one can see the limitations of thinking about sex as a variable rather than gender as a social process. A more comprehensive engagement with writings on gender and judging (for example Martin et al.'s theorizing about the feminist standpoint) might have surfaced some problems with the informational category the empirical analysis supports. Why do some women fail to support sex discrimination plaintiffs while some men do? Boyd et al. cite Beverly Blair Cook as saying the reason why women organized to campaign for more women judges was because they expected women to decide cases differently.[109] Yet Cook reexamined her assumptions of difference when she confronted Justice

O'Connor's inconsistent record on women's rights cases and examined other empirical studies that showed few differences in outcomes. Boyd et al. also refer to Sherry[110] and Gilligan[111] without stressing how thoroughly their evidence refutes their accounts. They quote Beiner[112] as feeling that something in Gilligan rings true, declaring Beiner to have it "exactly right,"[113] without explaining the end of the quotation: "or at least true based on some stereotyped notion of the way in which women behave." So, is Beiner right that Gilligan led us to expect that women really *are* different in sex discrimination cases, or that we only continue to look for sex differences because of stereotyped thinking?

The final published version of Boyd et al.'s paper no longer claims to have closed the debate about difference once and for all, nor to have proven Justice O'Connor (who claimed empirical studies did not support the existence of sex differences) wrong in favor of those who have argued for difference. Press reports of their study, however, emphasize the difference in the one area of law rather than the sameness in the twelve.[114] As I argue in Chapter 8, I suspect one reason feminists (as opposed to political scientists in general) continue to search for sex differences is because they implicitly fear that if they are unable to show that women decide cases differently, they will not be able to argue why it is important they hold judicial office. It is as if they are saying, "See, it matters, women are different and they decide cases differently from men." They know that feminists on the bench are important, and would like to believe that women are more likely than men to be feminists.

Boyd et al. speculate that the same methodological error that they criticize in the judicial studies may have produced erroneous results in the scholarly quest to unearth the different voice and representational voice among women legislators. By citing Dahlerup,[115] they recognize feminist thinkers are questioning essentialist ideas about women's representation and critical mass. They are well aware that not all women are feminists, some men are, and larger numbers of women do not automatically produce more feminist policy outcomes. Some readers (like the media) may read Boyd et al. and conclude, "Aha, at last we've found the essential sex difference, or at least more evidence of the feminist standpoint." Others may read the article and say the difference is in only one area of law, not that marked, and perhaps ephemeral.

Legal academic Rosalind Dixon took a close look at the cases and opinions that constitute the difference women make and found less evidence of a sharp difference than the numbers alone seem to indicate.[116] She identified the problem of attributing causality to sex or ideology, since the cases in question were all decided by women appointed by Democratic presidents. Her view, like mine (and Beiner's), is that the individual experiences of judges, which include experience of gender-based exclusions, may cause them to interpret facts differently from judges without those experiences. She describes what I call a cohort or generational effect—the gender-based experiences that Justices O'Connor and Ginsburg shared were more alike than those that Justices Kagan and Sotomayor faced.[117]

STUDIES OF OTHER EFFECTS OF WOMEN ON THE BENCH

If significant gender differences exist, they may manifest themselves in ways other than judicial votes cast in cases.[118] Women might conduct their trial courtrooms differently from men by refusing to allow well-documented sexist behavior. They might act differently as administrators—for example, hiring more women law clerks.[119] Men lawyers and judges might moderate their behavior in the presence of women judges, as might women jurors, lawyers, and litigants. In many, but not all cases, a woman justice on a state supreme court was the one to call for the creation of a state gender bias taskforce[120] and women judges have been leaders in establishing race bias taskforces.[121]

A 2003 study of the fifteen women chief justices of state supreme courts examined whether they placed more emphasis than men chief justices on women's issues.[122] The authors deserve praise for looking for the significance of gender beyond dichotomous votes on cases and noting that, as administrators of their state's judicial systems, chief judges can advance reforms concerning juvenile courts, family courts, gender bias studies, and battered women's programs. The study uncovered enormous variation among the chief justices, men and women, even on women's issues. Although the presence of a woman chief judge positively and significantly impacted the likelihood of mentioning a women's issue, the number of mentions does not increase with an increased number of women on the court. Rather, it had the opposite effect. The authors found no statistical significance for the claim that women chief justices are more likely to make women's issues a priority.

CONCLUSION

When writing her judicial biography of Justice Harry Blackmun, *New York Times* legal correspondent Linda Greenhouse had early access to the justice's newly released papers.[123] We learn from Greenhouse that Justice Blackmun, most well known as the author of *Roe v. Wade*, had a daughter who became pregnant out of wedlock, married, lost the baby through miscarriage, and subsequently divorced. Greenhouse's remarkable book showed how Blackmun came to feminism through the issue of reproductive freedom, and thereby came to diverge from the other Republican-appointed justices—most poignantly his lifelong friend, Warren Burger. One could argue that we learn more about gender, women, and feminism from Greenhouse's approach than from Sherry's. First, we learn that men not only have gender but experiences that mark them by gender and lead to positions on women's rights issues. Second, we learn that gender consciousness is acquired; it is not an automatic component of biological identity. As such, it may or may not be acquired by men and women alike. Third, we learn that we must trace gender consciousness and feminist sensibility empirically rather than assume it.

So, how does gender matter? *Does* it matter? The scholarly evidence suggests that researchers have assumed women judges are more likely to be feminist. Accordingly, if we want to promote women's rights, we should promote women judges. Women judges, it is assumed, will be more concerned with children and better at juvenile justice, pro-plaintiff in sex discrimination cases, pro-choice in abortion cases, pro-woman in divorce cases, pro-plaintiff in FMLA cases, inclined to seek mediate solutions, and likely to raise women's issues in speeches. Only occasionally has the evidence supported any of these assumptions. And even when it does support the idea that women judges are somehow or essentially different, the studies tend to be constrained by sample size, limited time periods, or an absence of controls. Other explanatory variables, such as party or ideology (or simply feminism), may predict differences between men and women judges more reliably than sex. Strangely, findings of no difference never seem to challenge the fundamental assumption of difference, or deter the search for it.

Gender shapes men's and women's life experiences in profound ways. Some, but not all, women are mothers. Some, but not all, women are in heterosexual marriages where they do the lion's share of caring labor. Women may be discarded for a younger partner but second or third wives are women, too, and women differ about how they view women's roles and what constitutes appropriate levels of spousal support. All experience the world as women, subject to the risks of sexual violence, gender devaluation, and exclusion and discrimination. Many of these experiences are similar among particular generational cohorts of women. When the women who are now senior judges entered the legal profession, they had profound experiences of exclusion. Many, such as Justice Sandra Day O'Connor, did not enter large law firms but instead worked for the government on mental health issues or—as many women did because it was one of the few places where parents could work part time—for public defenders, as Minnesota Supreme Court Justice Rosalie Wahl did. In the 1970s, Republicans and Republican women supported the Equal Rights Amendment and abortion liberalization, and women judges may have differed less ideologically from each other than they do now. These similarities may well situate women to approach their work similarly and develop a feminist sensibility. But those similarities may have as much to do with generation, ideology, and previous experience as they do with sex. And even in the same sex and generational cohort, we see important variations among women judges. One need only consider the differences between Justices O'Connor and Ginsburg for this point to be clear. As a result, we must move from an assumption of essential sex differences to a discussion of gender as a social process.

A feminist consciousness is not an inevitable result of being female or living life as a woman. Rather, it is a political achievement on the part of both women and men. Bringing a gender lens to judging also results from experience and education but most importantly from the reflection of individuals and organizations. It is not the natural, automatic, or inevitable result of merely adding individual women or a supposed critical mass of women to any court. In fact, the evidence I consider in Chapter 7 suggests that the more women who serve, the less women may feel compelled to inject "a woman's perspective." It is not enough simply to add more women to the mix; we need to create organizations attentive to gender devaluation. As I will show in Chapter 4, one woman, Margaret McKenna, made a huge difference in getting Carter to appoint women to the federal bench. But Peter Russell also succeeded in selecting women to be judges in Ontario.

Quantitative analysis using sex as a variable can reveal discrimination and help us identify patterns of exclusion and the effects of double standards and so-called neutral standards that disproportionately exclude women. We assume that men and women have an equal likelihood of being able to contribute to judging, and a discrimination analysis would investigate how sex makes women less likely to have that opportunity. We should not use sex as a variable as part of a misguided quest to uncover essential sex differences. Differences mostly do not exist, or small differences become mistakenly framed as universal and dichotomous: all men are one thing and all women another. A good example would be the Supreme Court's decision in June 2011 in *Wal-Mart v. Duke*. Immediately, because it was a sex discrimination case, commentators noted that all three women joined the dissent. But all justices appointed by a Republican president were in the majority and all justices appointed by a Democratic president, including one man, Justice Breyer, dissented. (If the case had instead been *Bush v. Gore*, the party of the appointing president might have been highlighted; if the case were on abortion, journalists might have commented on how the Catholics voted.) We can debate which side Justice O'Connor might have joined if she had still been on the Court. Sex is such a powerful identity category that we go to it first, rather than to ideology, religion, region, or area of legal practice. To argue that sex is a poor explainer of outcomes is not the same thing as arguing that individuals do not make a difference. It matters that Justice Ginsburg understands the complex workings of sex discrimination, but it also mattered that Justices Blackmun, Brennan, and Marshall did too, and it matters that Justice Breyer does now. Similarly, it matters that Justice Thomas has a different approach to discrimination litigation.

In the chapters that follow, I look at different jurisdictions to show how a gender analysis could improve upon the quest to uncover essential differences. While I occasionally use sex as a variable to uncover discrimination—showing that women state supreme court justices faced challengers no man had ever faced; or that presidents employed different standards for men and women appointees to the bench; or that the UK press treated men appointed to the Law Lords in a very different way from how they treated women; or that it took a long time to see women serving on the European Court of Justice—I show how a gender analysis helps us understand events more fully. But each chapter is not simply about women judges in different settings; it is about how a gender analysis of women judges in different jurisdictions leads us to rethink core analytical concepts of diffusion of innovation and emotions and social movement mobilization, backlash, the role of insider–outsider networks in policy implementation, agenda-setting, and representation. It may be that scholars continue to look for difference because they anticipate the argument that if women's presence on courts does not change legal outcomes, no harm ensues from excluding them. In each jurisdiction, I show the harms of discrimination. In Chapter 8, I also show how we can make the case for women judges without relying on empirically shaky assertions of essential difference. Statements about essential sex differences—that women will not work hard, that they cannot manage, lead, or control their emotions—sound more like the alleged positions of Wal-Mart managers than a framework to advance equality.

As I argued in Chapter 1, Judith Butler and Joan Scott have demonstrated just how tenacious essentialism can be as a construct. And, as I also argued in that chapter, many feminists made and continue to make the difference argument. Some radical feminists (others call them cultural feminists) genuinely believed that women were morally different from and superior to men because of their larger role in caring labor. Many believed women were less violent by nature. And many believed women were necessarily more feminist. Postmodernism, with its anti-essentialism and rejection of binaries, comports more, in my view, with my own experience and the data. Some studies find sex differences, but many do not. The magnitude and direction can change. Experience matters, to be sure, but no necessary relationship exists between sex and gender consciousness. In the next chapter, I show how one women's movement made the appointment of a woman judge a priority on the governor's agenda and how one woman's way of doing gender mobilized a movement to return her to office when faced with three men challengers.

3

MOBILIZING EMOTIONS: THE CASE OF ROSALIE WAHL AND THE MINNESOTA SUPREME COURT[1]

Using sex as a variable to count women state judges, show large variations, and identify patterns tells us a great deal. But it can lull us into a false sense that the instances are the same, that each case is somehow commensurate with every other, or similar in important ways. We understand much more if we go beyond simply studying women and also explore gender. Thinking about gender as a social process—the process of assigning meaning and significance to sex differences—makes visible how judicial selections are moments where the meaning of gender is constructed by selectors, women judges (and their opponents), advocates, and the media. Understood this way, the differences between cases of women firsts may be more illuminating than the similarities.

In this chapter, I examine a case where gender was highly salient—the dramatic appointment of Rosalie Wahl to the Minnesota Supreme Court in 1977. Wahl's appointment and election became important symbols for women in Minnesota politics. She galvanized the women's movement, and her appointment and election became imbued with gender significance and were profoundly emotional for those engaged. I analyze this case as an example of meaning-making (what sociologists call framing) and social movement mobilization. Scholars have largely downplayed the role of emotions in social movement mobilization and have paid even less attention to how gender and emotions intersect. A gendered analysis of Rosalie Wahl's case that fully analyzes emotions helps us better understand symbolic politics and social movement mobilization more generally.

Those who study women and politics, too, however, have failed fully to understand the emotional connection between women candidates and women voters that is neither natural, automatic, nor inevitable but must be constructed and created anew in each individual case. And they largely ignore women judges, even though more than half of all state judges are elected to office. Walter Mondale's selection of Geraldine Ferraro as his running mate in 1984 sparked an emotional reaction among women, as did Rosalie Wahl's appointment in 1977. But Hillary Clinton's presidential candidacy failed to do so to the same degree, and failed dramatically to connect emotionally with young women, many of whom were more inspired by Barack Obama. As I shall show in Chapter 7, Rose Bird failed to connect emotionally with women and voters in general in California, and lost her seat as the state's first woman chief justice in 1986.

Treating these cases as the same—cases of women judicial firsts—obscures how gender operates vastly differently in different cases. Moreover, thinking of sex as a variable rather than gender as a social process might lull women's advocates into thinking that women will automatically rally behind other women. Understanding gender as a social process, then, lets us see differences in how each individual woman "does" gender, and how her differences are gendered in different ways—for example, the way her race, age, attractiveness, and sexuality affect gender constructions. Women judicial candidates cannot assume that women will necessarily mobilize behind them, identify with them, or see their races as important for women. Seeing gender as a social process— one in which women must construct meaning and emotional connections— will be vital to securing women's progress toward more equal representation on the bench. The politics of judicial races differs from that of legislative races, yet our understanding of women and politics is enhanced by examining how gender works in these races, too.

In Chapter 4, I shall consider the mechanics of how well-positioned insiders collaborated with feminist activists to make President Carter's goal of a diverse bench a reality. We have a great deal to learn from the behind-the-scenes mechanics in each case of a woman first and in increases in the number of women judges, whether they serve on federal or state courts. And we can learn much from the mechanics in Rosalie Wahl's case.[2] It helps us understand gender by showing how the meaning of gender is constructed, if not anew, then with variations in different contexts. In Chapter 5, I will show how advocates in the United Kingdom tied the idea of women's representation to the idea of modernization: a modern court needs to have some women members. The case of Rosalie Wahl, however, is not simply a case about meaning-making or framing but about how meaning-making can trigger emotional responses that motivate people to identify, feel, and act. Both the meaning of gender and the ability to make emotional connections vary dramatically from case to case.

WOMEN AND STATE SUPREME COURTS: POLICY DIFFUSION AND NORMS

In 1977, the Governor of Minnesota expressly set out to implement a policy of appointing the first woman to the state's supreme court. But did Iowa

Governor Branstad do the same when he appointed a woman, Linda Kinney Neuman, nine years later, in 1986? Was Neuman's sex—and the inappropriateness of an all-male bench—part of the calculus? Unlike Rosalie Wahl and Rose Bird, Neuman's selection generated almost no notice. Did Governor Branstad's choice reflect a policy to appoint a woman? Did it reflect the adoption of and consensus around a new norm that an all-male bench was unacceptable and a gender-diverse bench required? The fact that Governor Branstad appointed three new judges in 2011 and returned the Iowa Supreme Court to an all-male bench makes us question the existence of a policy or norm. Although we can learn something by looking at the appointment of the first woman to the highest appellate court in each state as an example of policy diffusion, a gender analysis would lead us to look critically at the meaning and construction of gender in each state when women emerge rather than assume it is the same.

These cases of Minnesota and Iowa (and, in Chapter 7, California) show how different the intentions and motivations of appointers can be, even though both are appointing women firsts. The emergence of the first woman on a state's highest appellate court also means dramatically different things to appointers, campaigners, voters, activists, and the media. Gender may be more or less salient, depending on the case.[3] In some cases, as with Florence Allen and Rosalie Wahl, and, arguably, Sandra Day O'Connor, the election or appointment of a woman represented an achievement of a social movement anxious to demonstrate muscle and clout. In this chapter and Chapter 7, I show how women's representation on the highest state appellate court has been accomplished and how variable its meaning is. Not only is gender more or less salient, but women are gendered in different ways by others, particularly the media. How gender is relevant for an electoral race may differ for a heterosexual mother of five who is a returning housewife (Rosalie Wahl) and a forty-something single woman (Rose Bird). Not only are women different, and gendered differently in different races, but the women themselves "do" gender differently—that is, they actively attach different meanings to the significance of their gender, and some are more effective in their gendered rhetorical strategies than others. The meaning of gender in a race, however, is not controlled or determined simply by the selectors, women themselves, activists, or the media, but rather in a dynamic interplay based on the agency of all. Before I analyze this process in the case of Rosalie Wahl, I shall review women's placement on state supreme courts.

As I argued in the previous chapter, quantitative analysis using sex as a variable is valuable, for example, in demonstrating sex discrimination at work by showing a gap between women's representation in the legal profession and their ascension to the bench. We also need simply to count the number of women to show how slow the progress has been or sound the alarm at reversals. Using sex as a variable helps us identify patterns, things that hold women back or explain their greater success. In 1923, Florence Allen joined the Ohio

Supreme Court to become the first woman in the United States to serve as a judge on a state supreme court. It would be another thirty-six years before Rhoda Lewis joined the Hawaii Supreme Court as the second women to serve on a state supreme court. And it was only in 2002 that the last all-male state supreme court—that of South Dakota—welcomed its first woman. Overall, four women joined their state supreme courts in the 1960s, twelve in the 1970s, eighteen in the 1980s, and twelve in the 1990s.[4] (Three state supreme courts, however, have reverted to all-male courts—Indiana, Idaho, and Iowa.) Scholars study how public policies are adopted across political systems over time and call the process policy diffusion. We could treat having women represented on the state's highest appellate court as a policy and trace its diffusion.

Sometimes, as policies diffuse, they reflect a new norm, "a standard of appropriate behavior for actors with a given identity."[5] Policies that reflect larger social norms are implemented and enforced; failure to implement or enforce policies suggests that particular norms have not taken hold. In Chapter 5, I will consider whether an all-male bench became unacceptable in the United Kingdom and how the issue of women's representation on courts came to be on the public agenda (or not). How do we know a norm is a norm? When women do make it to the bench in particular cases, does their representation reflect the adoption of a new norm that women must be represented? Or does this reflect a policy on the part of their selectors to choose a woman?

While thinking of the first woman appointed to a state's highest appellate court as a singular policy illuminates a gap between women in the legal profession and women on the bench, and allows us to measure progress or identify reversals, the wide variation between states is difficult to explain. Differences in how states select judges do not explain this variation. Some states elect judges in partisan elections; others elect them in non-partisan elections.[6] Others appoint judges and have them stand for retention election with no opponent. Still others use the federal system, with lifetime appointment and no retention election.[7] Scholars have carefully explored whether women do better under one judicial selection system than another and have found that women can do well or poorly under any system—partisan election, non-partisan election, retention, or appointment.[8] Asking this question, however, is another example of a positive use of sex as a variable.

In political science, scholars have studied the innovation, diffusion, and adoption of norms and policies across organizations, states, and countries.[9] Elazar[10] suggests that some states have political cultures that lend themselves to policy innovation. Some states, for example, have professionalized bureaucracies, paid legislators with capable staff, well-educated populations, and economic resources, all of which enhance policy experimentation and adoption. Structural factors, such as easy thresholds for referenda, also facilitate experimentation.[11] Do some states have a political culture that makes them more receptive than others to the idea of women serving as judges?[12] The idea has appeal. We know from research that urban constituencies and Democratic constituencies elect more women to state and federal legislatures.[13] Cook's early studies of women state court judges suggested that women were more likely to represent suburban and urban than rural constituencies,[14] and the pattern continues in Minnesota.[15] Carbon et al. also found that women were much more likely to serve in large metropolitan areas than rural districts.[16]

To explore the effect of state political culture and women judges, Cook divided states into three groups—traditional, individualist, and moralist. She found that "the distribution of the women judges among the states fits the prediction based on political culture."[17] Specifically, the barriers of party organization in the individualistic states and sex-role stereotyping in the traditional states produced similar results: they dampened the numbers and distribution of women judges. Cook then investigated whether states had distinctive gender political cultures. Here, she found that the number of women participating in political party conventions explained some of the variation in women judges. She also found that states with higher women's incomes and lower birthrates tended to have more women judges.[18]

Following Cook, scholars found mixed results for the influence of political culture on the number and distribution of women judges.[19] Bratton and Spill's study showed that relatively liberal states were particularly likely to have gender-diverse courts,[20] but Williams found liberal states to have more women judges only on their trial courts, not their appellate courts.[21] Bratton and Spill's study of women's representation on federal trial courts showed that ideology had little predictive effect.[22] Scholars who study women and politics have argued that the South as a region is less receptive to women in elective office, based on their studies of women in state legislatures. Yet eight of the thirteen chief justices in the South are now women,[23] and many states in other regions have lower percentages of women judges than Southern states. Similarly, on federal courts, the Eighth Circuit is the least gender diverse and the Fifth the most—exactly the reverse of what such regional analysis would lead us to predict. If something about Southern political culture dampens women's representation in state legislatures, why not courts? To conclude, political scientists can explain little about how state political culture determines the likelihood of having women judges.[24]

Lutz[25] and Walker[26] show that states often look to their closest neighbors for solutions to policy problems. If we look at the list of states, however, we see little regional clumping as to which was first or who has the most or the least women state court judges. Ohio and Hawaii are first; South Dakota last. Vermont has the highest percentage; Idaho the smallest. Gray notes, however, that regional effects seem to be diminishing over time, especially as policy professionals use professional associations and the internet, and are able to travel.[27] But states may also want to adopt policies to be in sync with other states and/or in step with international norms. In the case of Britain, for example, as I discuss in Chapter 5, having women on the bench became linked to ideas of what a modern state should be. Likewise, laws on equality for women may be a way of belonging in the world community and being considered a legitimate state.[28] In these cases, adopting a policy does not necessarily mean the state really embraces the norm—it could be just window dressing.

Many scholars who have done event histories or examined policy diffusion argue that the framing of the ideas matters and that some ideas and policies diffuse more easily than others. Ferree et al.'s comparative analysis of German and American abortion rhetoric demonstrates that framing of reproductive rights as women's sexual autonomy is doomed in Germany, just as broad appeals to equal healthcare access get little traction in the United States.[29] Likewise, Judith Hellman and Raka Ray examine how feminists must frame their policies to cohere to state political cultures in Italy and India, respectively.[30] These framing arguments suggest a new way to think about state political cultures—not as feminist friendly or hostile, but as places that are politically and culturally different. Some frames will have more discursive appeal than others, depending on the particular political culture of a state or country.

In *Silent Revolution*, Herb Jacob seeks to explain the trajectory of policy diffusion in divorce reform. He argues that policy stories too often focus on landmark cases rather than routine policy changes that are "under the radar."[31] Activists framed the issue of divorce reform as a technical fix to a narrowly legal problem rather than a sweeping social change, and certainly not as a gender issue. Prior to divorce reform, couples amicably seeking dissolution of their marriages had to claim that a spouse had inflicted cruelty upon them or committed adultery. Lawyers had to counsel such couples to lie in court, and judges pretended to believe them. Arguing such policies created contempt for the legal system and collusion of court officers in a lie, proponents of reform advocated for "no-fault" divorce. They worked behind the scenes to minimize objections of Catholic leaders, to attract little attention, and to work with legal insiders to present the issue as fixing a small problem. In Wisconsin, when the issue became framed as about increasing women's autonomy rather than fixing a corruption of the legal system, passage of reform became more rocky and conflicted. But most states reformed their law with very little conflict or debate. Jacob's case study compares the different state stories and reveals the national networks of policy activists behind the change—what Finnemore and Sikkink call "norm entrepreneurs."[32] The Minnesota case suggests the opposite of what Jacob found—that feminists were more successful when they slipped issues in "under the radar" and framed them as not about women. In Minnesota, it took feminist mobilization to secure a woman's place on the court. While the saliency of gender and the drama of the appointment of the first woman were significantly different in different states, and women may have slipped in without much fanfare in some states, the failure of feminist activists to mobilize in support of women on the bench makes this progress vulnerable to reversal—as in Iowa or, as I shall show, in California and the United Kingdom.

In *Speak No Evil*, Jon Gould seeks to explain the diffusion of campus policies against hate speech.[33] Contrary to the stereotype of liberal professors bent on political correctness to repress freedom, Gould reveals a national network of policy administrators pushing for hate speech policies, despite the policies' constitutional difficulties. Gould explains how, even after it appeared that many codes were legally unenforceable, campus presidents refused to repeal them because they provided an important symbol of their commitment to action against racism. Those who focus on symbolic politics invite us to look beyond the instrumental goals of interest groups for answers to the question of why activists care deeply about certain issues that seem to offer little material redistribution.[34] In *The Symbolic Use of Politics*, Edelman observes that politicians may generate a sense of threat and offer legislation and policies as reassurance that the government has dealt with the threat as a way of generating quiescence.[35] And Klatch argues that symbols are essential to political mobilization as badges of identity and as tools to maintain feelings of community.[36] Treating the appointment of women judges as a case of policy diffusion or looking for differences in state political cultures can only get us so far without digging deeper as to how gender was deployed in different cases and the variable meaning attached to gender. Choosing a woman can signify a little or a great deal about commitment to women's equality or be interpreted, as it was in California (see Chapter 7), as contempt for the judicial branch. Moreover, as I argue in Chapter 7, governors may desire to appoint the first woman or one woman to an all-male court but have little commitment to gender diversity beyond that one appointment. The appointment of a woman does not have one fixed meaning.

THE SYMBOLIC POLITICS OF JUDICIAL APPOINTMENTS

The symbolic meaning of judicial appointments is evident when we consider women's placement on the US Supreme Court. As Richard Nixon considered appointing Mildred Lillie to the US Supreme Court, his concern with appealing to women voters was paramount, coupled with his desire to "stick it to the Senate," who had rejected two of his nominees, and to torment Chief Justice Burger, who had opposed having a woman on the Court.[37] Nixon was determined to appoint what he called strict constructionists to the Court, people who would further his policy goal of reversing the Warren Court's rulings on civil rights and criminal justice.[38] He also had gender-specific policy goals, specifically narrowing the interpretation of the equal protection clause and narrowing the right to privacy. But his discussion of appointing a woman to the Court focused on what such an appointment would signal to voters, and women voters in particular. In short, his deliberations centered on symbolic meanings, not policy objectives. Ronald Reagan, too, sought electoral advantage by promising to appoint a woman to the Supreme Court, something President Jimmy Carter would not do.[39] President George H.W. Bush, the forty-first president, appointed nearly all of his women appointees to the bench after he had nominated Clarence Thomas, seemingly to show women he was not indifferent to their concerns.

Public policy scholars use the term "focusing event" to explain why issues such as homeland security after 9/11, disaster management after Hurricane Katrina, and bridge inspection after the collapse of the Minneapolis Bridge rise to the top of the government's agenda. Likewise, social movement scholars define a "critical event" as one that renders the targets of social movement activity more vulnerable, makes movement resources more available, and encourages individuals and groups to set aside their differences and make coalitions possible.[40] In both cases, emotions are pivotal.[41] Emotions shape the cognitive reassessment of a situation, thereby transforming the possibilities for mobilization. Rosalie Wahl's appointment to the Minnesota Supreme Court in 1977 was a focusing event for Minnesota feminists. Paying close attention to emotions informs our understanding of what this historical event meant and why women in the judiciary matter.

An exception to the scholarly neglect of emotions is Gould's research on ACT UP, which demonstrated how social movements not only harness feelings and legitimize them, but convert feelings from one kind to another: from grief, resignation, and despair to anger, shame, and pride.[42] For Gould, as for others who take emotions seriously, social movements do emotional work.[43] They do not merely harness and mobilize emotions; they frame and transform them. Thus, when we examine what sparks political and social change, we must attend to changes in context and meaning, not simply objective changes in social conditions.[44] Emotions do more than mobilize people to act;[45] they create possibilities for collective action and social movement maintenance during difficult times or doldrums.[46]

The symbolic politics literature also invites us to examine the meaning activists attach to policy goals and why they care so deeply about certain issues.[47] As Gusfield[48] and Edelman[49] argued, certain policy objectives become symbols of the status of particular groups.[50] Laura Flanders's analysis of President George W. Bush's women appointments, *Bushwomen*, employs an even more cynical gender analysis.[51] She argues that Bush strategically appointed pro-choice and moderate women to paralyze liberals and insulate the appointees from media criticism of their more conservative policies on other issues. The Alliance for Justice made the same point with President Bush's decision to renominate two conservative women, Janice Rogers Brown and Priscilla Owen.[52] If appointing a woman was merely tricking the masses, we would expect social movement actors to have been the harshest critics of these symbolic gestures, decrying the appointment of women as mere tokenism. But the evidence suggests that these gestures were symbolically meaningful, however politically motivated. In analyzing the temperance movement, Gusfield[53] demonstrated that advocates of prohibition valued that it would represent a symbolic statement against drinking, even if it would not stop drinking itself. Gusfield's analysis offers important insights into the current debate over gay marriage. Gay activists certainly want domestic partnership benefits, access to loved ones in hospitals, and the ability to bring non-citizen partners into the country. But they also want societal affirmation of their belongingness and the sanctity of their relationships.[54]

Interviews with activists and congratulatory letters to Rosalie Wahl demonstrated that her appointment and election to the Minnesota Supreme Court meant very different things to different people.[55] Unlike Nixon, Reagan, or even Bush, who wanted to hide their lack of commitment to women's issues behind the appointment of a woman, Governor Perpich valued the appointment of women for both symbolic and instrumental reasons. He wanted to appoint Wahl to signal his support both for women's full inclusion in public life and as a way of seeking electoral support. But Perpich alone did not control the symbolic meaning of Wahl's appointment. Instead, Wahl, her supporters, and the women of Minnesota determined its multiple meanings. To understand these multiple meanings, we first must understand the rage and humiliation women's exclusion from political decision-making and the legal profession had engendered. We must also appreciate how the revolution in marriage and divorce laws shattered the lives of "displaced homemakers" and how the feminist movement unleashed a broad range of women's passions. These historical trends converged to create a distinctive emotional climate. Against this backdrop, the nature of Wahl's appointment, the particulars of her biography, and the campaign against her appointment combined to make this a powerfully symbolic and emotionally meaningful woman first.

THE CASE OF ROSALIE WAHL

Little-known Lieutenant Governor Rudolph Perpich became Governor of Minnesota when Governor Wendell Anderson ascended to Vice-President Walter Mondale's vacated Senate seat in 1976.[56] Perpich opposed the Vietnam War and was flamboyant and unpredictable.[57] He also held little fondness for the Minnesota Democratic–Farmer–Labor Party (DFL) machine.[58] (The DFL is one of the state's two major parties, affiliated with the Democratic Party. Hubert Humphrey was one of the leaders of the merger between the Minnesota Democratic Party and the Farmer–Labor Party in 1944.)

At the time, the DFL and other political parties relied on the labor of women who were not employed outside the home to help with organizing and fundraising. Rarely were these women considered for leadership positions or candidacies.[59] The title of Esther Wattenberg's 1971 report for the DFL Feminist Caucus said it all: women were *Present but Powerless*.[60] In the 1970s, however, women in Minnesota began to demand not just a voice, but seats at the table commensurate with their numbers and the work they did for the party. They rejected their permanent relegation to mere volunteers. A button at the time expressed the sentiment: "If we can't make policy, we won't make coffee!"

The DFL Feminist Caucus pressured the party to run more women candidates and to ensure that DFL candidates were pro-choice. Perpich addressed the DFL Feminist Caucus and promised to fill the next vacancy on the state's supreme court with a woman.[61]

Although women were gaining entry into law schools at this time, few made it to the bench. In 1977, no woman had served on the US Supreme Court, only one woman sat on a federal appellate court, and only five women served on state supreme courts.[62] Rahn Westby, a twenty-five-year-old lawyer who later co-chaired the Ramsey County Women's Political Caucus, had been one of four women in her class at William Mitchell College of Law and had endured patronizing remarks by male faculty, an experience shared by many women at the time.[63] She recalled feeling that women lawyers were not getting anywhere professionally and needed to "pole-vault" someone onto the high court to break the gridlock of women in the legal profession.[64] Westby and Carol Connolly, her co-chair in the Ramsey County Women's Political Caucus, made increasing the numbers of women in the judiciary a top priority early on. They wanted a high-profile appointment to break the gender barrier.

Minnesota's system for choosing justices on its supreme court was and remains through non-partisan election.[65] Formally, supreme court justices run for office, but, in practice, sitting justices inform the Governor when they are going to step down, and the Governor nominates a replacement when the retirement is announced, allowing the nominee to run with the ballot designation of "incumbent." If a justice is appointed more than a year before the next election, he or she has to run in that election, and every six years thereafter. As of 1977, only one member of the Minnesota Supreme Court had obtained his seat by election rather than appointment. The last incumbent unseated in an election was in 1900. Serious challenges to sitting justices were rare.[66] Rather than follow the usual practice of naming the new justice with the announcement of the retirement, Perpich announced he would appoint a yet-to-be identified woman. Had he announced his choice of Wahl in the usual way, his appointment would have garnered some publicity on account of Wahl being the first woman. But announcing that he was searching for a woman to appoint heightened public and media interest.[67]

Realistically, there were few women old enough and with sufficient legal experience to consider for such an appointment. Minnesota Women Lawyers (MWL) formed a committee to put forward names of women qualified to serve on the bench. They sent a questionnaire to all women lawyers, asking if they would be willing to be considered for a judgeship. The MWL Endorsement Committee winnowed the list of eighteen names to seven, including Rosalie Wahl's. Wahl was also on the list that the Minnesota Women's Political Caucus and DFL Feminist Caucus submitted to Perpich.[68]

Wahl was part of the feminist movement and had a record of working for women's equality. She also had a rather tragic life. Her mother died when she was three, and four years later she saw her grandfather and younger brother killed by a train. Socially and politically, she lived the Quaker's life of devotion to social justice. In college, she worked to fight racism through the Young Women's Christian Association (YWCA) and lived in a racially integrated communal home at the University of Kansas. After her fiancé was killed in World War II, she married and moved from Kansas to Minnesota, where she lived with friends in a type of collective they called an "intentional community." When this endeavor failed economically, Wahl, at age thirty-seven, armed with an undergraduate degree in sociology and responsible for four children, enrolled in night school at the William Mitchell College of Law.[69] Already a community activist, she gravitated to law because she wanted to be inside the room making decisions rather than hovering outside, as she had in the past.[70] Only one other woman was in her law school class and the law librarian was the only woman on the faculty.

Women lawyers enjoyed few opportunities in the 1960s, a time when law firms would blatantly announce they were not hiring women. The head of the state public defender's office, however, hired Wahl when she graduated from law school in 1967. He was one of the first legal employers willing to appoint women on a part-time basis, an important consideration for mothers of small children. (Wahl divorced in 1972.) The opportunity for women to work in the state public defender's office meant that many prominent women attorneys in Minnesota had experience defending the indigent, an experience that profoundly shaped Wahl's outlook on law and justice. Later, she would help establish the criminal and civil law clinic at William Mitchell College of Law.

Feminists in Minnesota wanted qualified women on the bench, but they also wanted feminists, and they united behind Wahl. Her outsider status as a William Mitchell graduate, a late entry into the profession, and a defender of indigent criminal defendants appealed to Perpich. Although Wahl did not know what was in her file, she was told later that it was thick. Her former students, now lawyers throughout the state, wrote letters praising her. Insiders knew that Perpich would often be persuaded by the person he talked to last. Thus, two women from the DFL Feminist Caucus remained at the Governor's residence late into the evening right before he was to decide, determined to be the last people with whom he spoke.

Although Wahl had been active in her local community, she was not a DFL insider. Nor was she the darling of the Minnesota State Bar Association, which, prior to Perpich's administration, had recommended names to the Governor, who largely rubber-stamped its choice. She was, however, a member of the DFL Feminist Caucus, and she was present at its meeting when Perpich made his promise to appoint a woman to the state's supreme court. She met Perpich for the first time when he interviewed her. Perpich knew that the first woman appointed would have many challengers. If she lost, he would have squandered the power to shape the bench. In addition, it would probably be a long time before any other governor could be persuaded to appoint another woman; nor would any woman be a credible candidate for challenging an incumbent.

Among the candidates, Perpich determined that Wahl would perform best in a state-wide campaign.

Perhaps no aspect of the story of Wahl's appointment more completely reveals the deep emotional meaning of this event than the way Governor Perpich announced his choice. He did so at his son's high school graduation in Hibbing, Minnesota. On the same day, nearly 4,500 women were meeting in St. Cloud to hammer out a platform and choose delegates to the upcoming White House Conference on Women in Houston. When the conference chair, Minnesota Secretary of State Joan Growe, announced that Governor Perpich had stated his choice, the crowd erupted. Wahl came to the microphone and promised that she would "not cease to be an advocate for those whose rights have been denied or infringed." In 1978, the chair of the Minnesota Women Lawyers Endorsement Committee, Judith Oakes, would reflect that "no other government appointment has stirred as much emotion as Wahl."[71]

Even before the Governor decided which woman he would appoint, ambitious men who coveted a seat on the Minnesota Supreme Court had readied themselves. Wahl's opponents did not say directly that a woman should not serve on the bench, but the gendered nature of their attacks lay close to the surface. For the first time in two decades, a seated supreme court justice had a serious opponent—or, in Wahl's case, three opponents. Wahl faced a primary. Ramsey County District Court Judge J. Jerome Plunkett, Rochester District Court Judge Daniel Foley, and former Attorney General Robert W. Mattson filed.

Wahl and Mattson won a hard-fought primary. The general election campaign turned out to be even more negative. Mattson ran a series of negative ads against Wahl, claiming she had a poor record before the state's supreme court, which one might expect since her practice consisted of appeals of poor people who had been convicted of crimes. Another ad charged that "Ms. [sic] Wahl lets rapists loose." This referred to the fact that she was the sole dissenter in *State v. Willis*,[72] a case of a rapist who had held his victim at knifepoint. Wahl had dissented because a trial court had suppressed evidence and the police had unlawfully searched the defendant's house. Another ad charged she let drug dealers loose. At a debate sponsored by the American Association of University Women (AAUW), Mattson made claims that were blatantly untrue, causing the outraged, well-informed women in the audience to gasp in dismay.

Rosalie Wahl won. In 1977, she became the tenth woman to serve on a state supreme court and the first woman to serve on the Minnesota Supreme Court.[73] She retained her seat easily, and without challenge, in 1984. Perpich went on to appoint more women to judicial office than had been appointed by all of the previous governors of Minnesota combined. As Justice Esther Tomljanovich recounted, "He appointed a lot of women without real big track records, and that was a real big risk, but it made a revolution."[74] Until Wahl retired in 1994, the Minnesota Supreme Court was the first state in history to have a majority of women justices (four of seven).[75] Kathleen Blatz, a Republican, became the first woman chief justice in 1998.

Wahl herself had an enormous impact on women's equality, the legal system, and legal education. She wrote 549 opinions over seventeen years. She looked at the judicial system from the bottom up, championing the underdog, the marginalized, and the outcast. Her opinions on race and sex discrimination were especially eloquent. She had what her former clerk, Jane Larson, called "her longest running struggle with other members of the Supreme Court"[76] over how to interpret statutes allowing for the availability of permanent rather than rehabilitative maintenance for long-term homemaker spouses. Wahl would often say that she thought men had trouble understanding the experience of a mid-life woman whose husband is divorcing her.[77]

WAHL AS SYMBOL

Wahl struck a chord with women across the political spectrum and generated a grassroots mobilization and an emotional response. Announcements of appointments to the Minnesota Supreme Court generally garner little attention outside the legal community. Most people cannot name the justices on the court. And many citizens who vote do not vote in judicial elections, or simply follow the cue of the ballot designation of "incumbent."[78] By forecasting his appointment of a woman, Perpich heightened the newsworthiness of the event. The extended speculation over who he would pick captured the attention of a wider community. Moreover, although Wahl was not a DFL insider, she was well known in the wider feminist community. By enlisting the DFL Feminist Caucus and the Minnesota Women's Political Caucus, not just Minnesota Women Lawyers, in the selection process, Perpich ensured that these groups would have a stake in Wahl's election.

In addition to this sense of drama around Wahl's nomination, her own speeches made a connection with women and constructed a sense of history with her nomination. Immersed as she was in women's history and literature, and possessed of great poetic flair, Wahl's oratory broadened the meaning of this event beyond the narrowly legal. Indeed, Wahl always tied her appointment to the wider cause of women, and not just women's success in the legal profession, but their wider aspirations for dignity and recognition. Her gendered appeals were to shared feminist ideals, rather than to her experience as a wife and mother or a trailblazer in the legal profession. In short, Wahl was not just an individual or a woman. She was an important symbol who drew women into the campaign.

As I investigated Wahl's appointment, I conducted interviews with those who worked on the campaign and examined documents in the Minnesota Historical Society collection. In the interviews, I expected activists to identify instrumental goals in their discussion of Wahl's appointment. For example, I expected them to express that policy achievements, such as equal pay and rape shield laws, would be meaningless if men judges applied and interpreted laws indifferent to feminist arguments. But the interviews with activists did not mention these policy implementation goals. Instead, those who devoted the most hours to the campaign talked about their humiliations as women in law school and the legal profession. Wahl, as one of seven justices, was not valued so much for bringing a feminist voice to the table, or for engineering feminist outcomes, but for the visibility of the position. Like blasting Sally Ride into space, Wahl's appointment symbolized that women's political exclusion had dramatically ended; that women were smart and capable of assuming leadership positions; and that the feminist movement had arrived and had clout.

Is the symbolic meaning of Wahl's appointment due solely to the fact that she was first? Being first was certainly important in Wahl's case, but not all firsts have the same symbolic meaning or emotional resonance to wider publics.[79] Being first is a conventional media frame that has mixed blessings.[80] This frame makes women's accomplishments newsworthy at the same time as it marks them as exceptional, coding the domain as appropriately male. Kohrs Campbell suggests that what matters is how the woman who is first sees herself, whether she has a track record that makes her representative of women, and/or whether she is treated by men in such a way that she becomes representative of women in similar circumstances.[81] Wahl was all three.

Many of us recognized an historic breakthrough when Ronald Reagan appointed Sandra Day O'Connor to the Supreme Court. For those of us working in the field of women and the law, it was exciting, even if we had some ambivalence about O'Connor's legal philosophy and policy views.[82] Her appointment, however, did not reach Sewell's threshold of "raising the emotional intensity of life."[83] The interviews with activists on Wahl's campaign reveal an emotional intensity of a much higher magnitude. Twenty-five years later, women can describe the events like they were yesterday. For a few, the Wahl campaign was a highlight of their lives; others can tell you where they were and what they were doing when they heard Perpich had nominated Wahl, suggesting an emotional intensity comparable to the Kennedy assassination. This special emotional resonance is due more to the idiosyncratic personal qualities of Wahl and the historical timing of the feminist movement in 1977, and less to the fact that she was first. Her being first was important, but other firsts in other states or countries did not generate the outpouring of emotions one witnessed in the Wahl case.

No fixed meaning attaches to the mere fact of being first or to being the first woman. The meaning of such events must be constructed. Rosa Parks was the *sixth* person arrested in Montgomery for violating segregation laws, yet she became the symbol of the boycott. Sally Ride became a symbol not because she was the first woman in space but because she was an evangelist for women in science. The Stonewall riots were not the first; activists self-consciously constructed their historical significance.[84] Likewise, the importance of Wahl's nomination was constructed by Perpich, by feminists in Minnesota, and by Wahl herself. In this respect, Wahl's use of emotions was critical. She deployed a keen emotional intelligence in her passion for social justice, her commitment to feminist action, and her rhetorical ability to call women to collective action.

By deliberately acknowledging and triggering emotions, Wahl as a political leader generated the kind of enthusiasm that might stimulate political involvement.[85] In a sense, she acted in the manner of what Aminzade and McAdam would call an effective leader:

> The skills of effective leaders include an ability to assess emotional climates, induce mobilizing emotions that motivate followers by altering definitions of the situation, create/reconfigure emotion vocabularies, and transform emotion beliefs and feeling rules into moral obligations. Such leaders can accurately appraise the mood of bystander publics and authorities, seizing the appropriate time to act.[86]

Wahl did not simply use emotions in her political activism, but in her decisions as a supreme court judge. As Court of Appeals Judge Harriet Lansing has noted:

> Rosalie's opinions, in both her use of language and her analyses, often demonstrate a wider definition of reason that does not artificially omit or ostracize the effect of human emotions on perception and thought. She brings in the emotions to better focus the picture and, when relevant, incorporates them into the decision.[87]

Wahl's papers at the Minnesota Historical Society include hundreds of congratulatory letters, which speak to the emotional intensity of her appointment. Women wrote about how important it was that someone as "human" as Wahl, but also a feminist, was on the court. Most striking, however, are their accounts of the intensity of their emotional reaction, as indicated in this letter:

> I've delayed this letter because I've had difficulty finding words to express the feelings of joy and inspiration I've felt since your appearance at the Women's Meeting. Even now, in recollection, my eyes mist over with tears—then my tears fell for nearly ten minutes. Whenever I'd begin to get hold of myself I'd glance up at Mary Peek, wiping her eyes, and begin anew. But such tears of total happiness are pleasant.[88]

This writer went on to describe the significance of this event not just as a woman and a feminist, but as a practicing lawyer who daily experienced judges who treated women badly and failed to grasp the harm in sex discrimination. She continued:

> The reality of the appointments didn't strike me fully until last week. I was in trial before Judge Johnson in Stillwater and was constantly aware of the positive benefits of having women on the bench—the case, sex-

discrimination, has required a constant educational process for the bench . . . Governor Perpich made a wise and brave choice appointing you, the most likely to speak for those of us who have so long been unheard—not only women, not only defendants—but all of us who fall into categories other than middle and upper class white heterosexual males.[89]

Another writer also spoke of her intense emotional response but defined the meaning of the event differently. She wrote of how Wahl's appointment reduced the social stigma of divorced women:

> I do not have anything unique to add to the many expressions of joy heard over Minnesota Public Radio last evening at Joan's [Growe, in St. Cloud] announcement. But I do want to say that many women in Minnesota are elated for a very special reason, and I think you should know that. We are the divorced, many of us not by choice, and we are coping as best we can in a society which is still confused about our status. (Funny, no one seems confused about the status of divorced men!) You have no doubt been a role model to generations of law students, and to many young feminists. But now you are giving us even one more reason to throw up our banners and rejoice.[90]

Another woman saw the meaning of Wahl's nomination as a reevaluation of older women more generally. As she explained, "Reading about your career in the paper has given me hope for myself in later careers as well."[91] To young women of ambition, Wahl's appointment meant hope for the future. One high school student thanked her for coming to her house to help her write a report and said she made her see that she could do anything. Another had just given the valedictory lecture to her high school class about Wahl, and had then returned home to hear the announcement of her appointment to "much cheering and carrying on in the kitchen!"[92]

Others more subtly expressed their satisfaction that the Governor had appointed not just a woman but a feminist and a person devoted to the advancement of other women:

> Such beautiful news. I cried when I read it in the newspaper. Truthfully, I did not dare hope that any mere male governor would have such supreme good wisdom and judgment. "Congratulations" is not the right word at all. Rather, it is a deeper joy—a selfish one on my part—that I want to express . . . this historical appointment fell on the right woman, with the right philosophy. It's almost too good to be true.[93]

The woman's movement feel you are sharing the honor with them.[94]

Lastly, women wrote about how they felt inspired to press on and refuse to accept gender-based restrictions in their lives. As one explained, "It makes me want to go out and do something with my life."[95]

If Wahl was a symbol, she symbolized different things for different people, which allowed her to mobilize and connect with a broad and diverse group of women. As well as being an historical event, a focusing event, a critical event, or even a transforming event, Wahl's election may have been what Zolberg called "a moment of madness"—a time when new things are possible and politics moves from the instrumental to the expressive,[96] or a liminal moment.[97] Sewell referred to these moments as "collective effervescence."[98] Clearly, the letter writers joined those I interviewed in expressing that level of exhilaration. Rosalie Wahl's appointment meant that it was no longer possible to contemplate an all-male supreme court in Minnesota.[99]

In her study of *Ms. Magazine*, Amy Farrell[100] analyzed how *Ms.* subverted its restrictive dependence on sexist advertising by publishing extensive readers' critiques of its own ads. Like the letters to Wahl, Farrell found that many of the letters were deeply personal, asking not for publication but for what she calls an "understanding reading."[101] Readers writing to *Ms.* and those writing to Wahl shared an intense identification as part of the movement. That shared identity created an expectation that the reader, although a stranger, was simpatico, a kindred spirit, another feminist. Strangers wrote to Wahl *knowing* she would understand. Farrell argued that through their letters, even those letters vehement with anger and betrayal, *Ms.* readers expressed a collective ownership of *Ms.* and an aspiration that it be the voice of the movement, their voice. Likewise, the letters to Wahl were not merely the perfunctory congratulations of other luminaries or the happy outpourings of loved ones. They were from strangers who nonetheless found in Wahl a kindred feminist soul. Wahl, like *Ms.*, actively encouraged such identification by being an active and visible presence in the feminist movement. She framed the significance of her appointment to connect it with the trajectory of women's rights.[102] As such, women could construct meaning in her appointment and in her career—meaning that cemented their identity as feminists and their cause as women's rights.

CONCLUSION

As Jasper has noted, the women's movement was centered on women's emotions, reworking humiliation into rage and rage into action:

> In thousands of consciousness-raising groups women learned to feel less guilty about their resentment toward husbands, fathers, employers, and others . . . As Arlie Hochschild wrote of this process, "Social movements for change make 'bad' feelings okay, and they make them useful. Depending on one's point of view, they make bad feelings 'rational.' They also make them visible." According to Verta Taylor and Nancy Wittier, women's groups regularly try to transform negative feelings that many women have due to their structural positions, including depression, fear, and guilt.[103]

The emotions at play in Wahl's case were slightly different. Women were angry and felt a sense of injustice, to be sure. They felt overworked, undervalued, and excluded within the DFL. Those entering the legal profession felt humiliated, abused, and thwarted in their ambitions. Women in general felt that their talents were not recognized and that they could not attain their dreams.[104] But other emotions were also at work. They shared a sense of hope and opening. Aminzade and McAdam argued that "it is only when anger gets joined with hope that the forms of action we normally associate with social movements and revolutions are apt to take place."[105] In this case, the fact of being first is relevant, if not decisive, for creating that sense of hope and opening. In the electoral context, hope makes people more attentive to information and more likely to follow a race.[106]

We can see a few examples of how emotions can change the tenor of political events in the electoral campaigns of Hillary Clinton. In a debate during her first run for the US Senate in 2000, her opponent, Representative Rick Lazio, pressed himself into her space, demanding that she sign a pledge. Lazio's boorishness drew support for her from many women who could identify with the threat of male intimidation. The night before the New Hampshire primary in 2008, when Senator Clinton's voice quavered in response to a question about where she finds the strength to carry on, "[h]er display of emotion brought her gender front and center. That led more women to identify with Clinton."[107] As political pollster John Zogby said, "When she showed emotion, they said, 'Her struggle is mine.' They related to her."[108]

Kornblut argues that the conventional understanding of this moment as humanizing Clinton has been overstated, and the fact that Clinton had women lawmakers in the state sewn up as her supporters, who then made a last-minute push, was more significant.[109] But she does argue that the comments about whether Clinton was "likeable enough," the media focus on her hair, and her Iowa defeat made voters see her as the first viable female presidential candidate who was about to lose.[110] Like Wahl, the Clinton case provides an excellent example of how paying attention to the emotional aspects of identification of voters with candidates and mobilizing social movements shows us the fluidity and variety of "doing" gender. Clinton's campaign strategy was not to run as a woman,[111] since voters' previous hesitancy to make a woman commander-in-chief had proved an insurmountable obstacle.[112] The strategy was to focus on experience, preparedness, and hawkishness. But the campaign strategy, focused too soon on winning the general election, not a primary against Barack Obama, failed to predict how emotions would affect Obama's ability to attract supporters. Young women were inspired by Obama as the first African American president, and Clinton's support for the war proved a liability, as did voters' ambivalence about Bill Clinton. Women did not universally support Clinton rather than Obama. Some thought Clinton failed to capitalize on the growing sense of injustice women felt, as Wahl did;[113] some older feminists were ambivalent about Clinton; and many young women did not feel that sense of gender injustice strongly enough to identify with Clinton. Meanwhile, although many women empathized with Sarah Palin's struggles as a new mother, recognized a clear double standard between questions about her parenting and President Obama's, and worried that the media's close scrutiny of her family might deter women from seeking public office, they did not see her as part of the women's movement or feel she understood and could speak for them. She energized the Republican base, but failed to attract women moderates and Democrats.

Women candidates have often benefited from public perceptions that they are more moral, less corrupt, and bring to office different modes of doing politics than men. People who met Rosalie Wahl felt deeply that she was sincere, not just another politician telling them what she thought they wanted to hear. One letter writer declaimed, "she's just so *human*."[114] In contrast, many women feared that neither Palin nor Clinton would really change things for women, and politics as usual would continue. Instead, Obama became the likeable, inspirational candidate of change for many.

The emotional and symbolic importance of politics is also evident in the gay rights movement. Armstrong and Crage describe the politically powerful emotions of the first march commemorating Stonewall:

> Activists discovered that bringing homosexuals together in public had a magical emotional impact—the ritual created collective effervescence by visually and experientially counteracting the view that homosexuality is private and shameful . . . A parade proved to be ideal for the affirmation of gay collective identity and for the production of feelings of pride central to the emotional culture of the movement.[115]

Wahl's appointment and election inspired an emotional response in much the same way. The important point here is that this emotional response solidified a collective feminist idea and galvanized a larger feminist movement. It was not simply an outcome of women's advancement; it was the engine of women's advancement.

Perpich's choice of Wahl sanctioned the importance of the women's movement and women in public life. When thousands of Minnesota women gathered to advance their claims for greater status in preparation for the Houston conference, what better indicator of their rising status than an appointment of the first woman to the Minnesota Supreme Court? Wahl's was not a routine appointment, given to notice only within the legal community. It was a signal of a significant change in status, not just for women lawyers or women switching courses in mid-life, but for all women in Minnesota. This unique sequence of events would not have been true of just any first, or even of a first at a different historical moment, although the breakthrough quality of the first is clearly relevant.

The symbolic meaning of a woman appointed to high judicial office is highly variable, depending on the individual involved, the timing, and many other factors. As I discuss in Chapter 6, even those knowledgeable about European Community law could probably not name the first women judges of the European Court of Justice. And as I shall discuss in Chapter 5, only a handful of feminists in the legal community celebrated the hard-fought appointment of Brenda Hale to the House of Lords. In Chapter 7, I shall show how Rose Bird, the first woman to serve on the California Supreme Court, did not connect emotionally with voters or run as a woman, nor was the campaign to unseat her framed as a threat to women and their movement's progress. If we want to replicate and diffuse the success (i.e. make the exclusion of women from high judicial office unacceptable and create a norm of a gender-diverse bench), scholars and activists would be well advised to go beyond studying the judicial selection process, and even the women's movement, to analyze the activation of the symbolic meaning of the appointment. In some circumstances, this symbolic meaning creates such a powerful emotional response that it galvanizes a grassroots movement.

This case of Rosalie Wahl shows how paying attention to emotions in social movement mobilization demonstrates the plasticity of gender.[116] If we conceptualize sex as merely a variable rather than gender as a social process, we search for generalizable patterns of women running for office. And they do exist. In Wahl's case, opponents used her gender in predictable ways (women are soft on crime, inexperienced, distracted by family caretaking responsibilities, poor leaders and managers, and lack prestige credentials). These frames may resonate with voters based on recurring gender stereotypes and gender devaluation (assuming women are deficient and "affirmative action" candidates rather than possess superior qualifications). Despite these patterns, gender is different in different cases. It is not a constant, but a construction. Many agents participate in constructing the gender of women candidates, including the candidate herself, who makes decisions about how much she wants to run as a woman, as Rosalie Wahl did. As Sapiro shows,[117] gender shaped how Margaret Thatcher was constructed as a leader by cabinet colleagues, voters, and the media, but this is not the same as how Nancy Pelosi's or Benazir Bhutto's leadership has been gendered. Fidelma Macken, the first woman judge on the European Court of Justice, did not want to be framed as the first and only woman judge, even though, as I shall show in Chapter 6, she claimed the Irish government's determination to appoint a woman was decisive in her selection.

Not only do not all women candidates "run as a woman," but not all women candidates are the women's candidate. Rosalie Wahl was a divorced mother of five who went to law school later in life. She had been active in traditional women's political issues and in newly emergent radical feminist groups. No one doubted her commitment to feminism or women's collective fate. This case not only provides a window into how gender emerged in a judicial race; it shows how one woman constructed her gendered identity not just to appeal to women voters but to mobilize women as active supporters. She did so not by promising substantive representation, but by shaping the meaning of the event to be about hope for women's future. We need to look for patterns among women judges and women firsts, to be sure, but we must also look at the unique way gender emerges in each new context.

4

STRATEGIC PARTNERSHIPS AND WOMEN ON THE FEDERAL BENCH[1]

If we included gender issues in our public policy analyses and brought those who study women and public policy into conversation with each other, along with those who study policy implementation, we would vastly improve our understanding of the policy process. In this chapter, I show that we can explain how President Jimmy Carter's policy to appoint more women to the judiciary became a reality only if we understand the partnerships between feminists inside the administration and interest groups and social movements outside of government. Exploring this transformative moment, this turning point, reveals the three indispensable ingredients for successfully implementing the policy of getting women appointed to the judiciary: a discourse that explicitly makes gender equality a goal; the commitment and determination of individuals in positions to make that goal a reality; and the mobilized support of interest groups and social movements to bring the policy into being, to exert pressure and generate public support at key moments, and to hold policy-makers accountable for results. Feminists can enjoy some policy successes, to be sure, with only one or two of these ingredients (as I demonstrate in other chapters), but those changes can stall or be reversed if any one component is missing.

Recognizing the importance of all three factors helps us understand the large variation in presidential appointments of women to the federal judiciary. Focusing on the gender of political appointments, and how the gender of judges became an issue in judicial appointments, thus illuminates important elements of the judicial appointment process that are mostly overlooked. If we understand gender, we understand more about the judicial appointment process. Since President Franklin Delano Roosevelt appointed the first woman to the federal bench in 1934, the number of women judges presidents have appointed has varied considerably. This reality is contrary to the perception that now that women make up half of all law school graduates, we will see slow and steady progress of women onto the bench. Women's progression is not steady, natural, or inevitable. The appointment of women does not follow a slow, upward trajectory; rather, it increases or decreases dramatically, not incrementally, and even reverses, depending on who is in office. To explain this variation, scholars have identified relevant demographic determinants, highlighted the role of judicial appointments in presidential electoral politics,[2] and documented the importance of political ideology,[3] all of which is important as an explanation but comprises only part of the story of policy change.[4] Individuals in key positions, often working in concert with others in social movements, bring about change. When new policy-makers take up their positions, policy advances can be quickly reversed. No necessary relationship exists between women's progress in the legal profession and their representation in the judiciary. The former does not ensure the latter. Nor is policy change irreversible.

Looking at this important gender case, then, reveals important dimensions of the policy process that are too often overlooked. Public policy analyses tend to shortchange policy implementation, focusing instead on how policy-makers came to adopt a policy position or how "Mr. Bill becomes Mr. Law," focusing most often on dramatic, landmark policy changes—such as passage of the Social Security Act, the Civil Rights Act, or healthcare reform. Getting policy-makers to adopt a policy, however—even high-profile and important policy-makers, such as the President—and passing legislation or adopting an agency rule are necessary but not sufficient conditions to make policy change a reality. As fictional Captain Jack Aubrey commands, someone has to "make it so."[5] Most public policy studies, however, fail to include women and public policy issues as one of their examples.[6] And scholars who study women and public policy are dispersed in other fields, often not in conversation with each other.

President Carter appointed more women to the bench than all previous administrations combined and put the issue of the race and gender of judges on the public agenda. Thus, his administration is particularly instructive with regard to feminist policy success. Drawing on archival sources, interviews, and secondary sources, I argue that the insider–outsider collaboration during the Carter Administration explains this administration's success in getting women on the bench. In this case, insiders provided critical resources to outsiders, such as notification of an impending decision, information on which lever to pull and when, and suggestions of strategies. Using influential feminists in the Carter Administration as a case study of these resources at work, I show that, without insiders' strategic knowledge, feminist groups and other social movements cannot be as effective in exerting political pressure for women appointments. At the same time, in the absence of outsiders' political pressure, insiders cannot obtain the leverage and support they need to implement bold changes and usher women onto the bench.

In the sections that follow, I outline scholarly thinking on how feminists engage the state and I review the history of Carter's appointments as an illustrative case of such engagement. I show how Carter's relationship with feminists evolved, resulting in an unprecedented record on appointing women judges. I then comment on the state of that partnership in subsequent administrations and offer some conclusions.

FEMINISTS ENGAGE THE STATE

During the 1960s and 1970s, radical feminists developed theories of the state as irretrievably patriarchal. Distinguishing themselves from liberal feminists, radical feminists valorized autonomous feminist organizing and characterized working with the state or within government as cooptation.[7] Although she had used the phrase to criticize racism within the feminist movement, Audre Lorde's famous quotation, "the master's tools will never dismantle the master's house,"[8] served as a mantra for the radical feminist argument of not engaging in conventional politics.[9] After 1980, however, many radicals joined socialist and liberal feminists in engaging the state.[10] They were compelled to do this as feminist policy gains evaporated under President Ronald Reagan and Prime Minister Margaret Thatcher.[11] Later, such feminists seized opportunities for policy change presented by President Bill Clinton's election,[12] the election of Labour governments in Australia and the United Kingdom, and the election of progressive governors,[13] and opportunities within international and supranational organizations such as the United Nations and the European Union.

In Australia, those feminists who entered governmental administration called themselves femocrats.[14] Those who studied the phenomenon applied the term more loosely, encompassing advocates within women's policy machinery such as the US Women's Bureau, the Equal Employment Opportunity Commission (EEOC), and Ministries for Women.[15] The term also came to include feminist political appointees and civil servants, though typically not elected officials. Within the European Union and in the field of international economic development more generally, feminists developed the policy tool of gender mainstreaming, using a gender lens to evaluate all policy proposals, from trade to economic development, much as environmentalists advocated environmental impact assessment for building projects.[16] Gender mainstreaming was intended to extend feminists' reach outside of the traditional women's policy machinery.

As feminists began to engage the state, scholars began to theorize the state as an arena (albeit not a gender-neutral one) rather than a unitary, monolithic tool of patriarchy.[17] The path-breaking work in this regard was *Feminist Organizations: Harvest of the New Women's Movement*.[18] In this book, the question was not whether feminists in the US should engage the state, but when, under what conditions, and to what effect. As Lovenduski put it, "effective feminist intervention in state institutions is necessary, possible, and difficult."[19] To be effective, feminists needed to pursue two strategies simultaneously: maintaining autonomous organizations and infiltrating the state.[20] This work and others accepted that feminists could (and should) join the state and remain explicitly feminist. Following Tilly,[21] Banaszak criticized scholars who have located social movements as independent actors outside of the state.[22] She also criticized femocrat scholars for conceptualizing feminists inside of government as professionals or allies rather than social movement participants.[23] Finally, she rejected the idea that social movements mobilize and then enter government to secure their policy objectives. Instead, she showed that feminists in government predated second-wave feminism[24] and that government insiders played a role in creating feminist organizations, such as the National Organization for Women.[25] Working within government is not necessarily demobilizing and, in fact, may be mobilizing.[26]

As I have suggested, insiders provide the movement with several critical assets. First and foremost, they provide information. Insiders alert outside groups about upcoming proposed changes in regulations and legislation. For example, they sounded the alarm about the EEOC's poor record of enforcing the sex discrimination provisions of Title VII that led to the formation of the National Organization for Women. Telling outsiders what is going on and identifying pressure points are two of the most valuable resources insiders offer. But insiders do more than share information: they also propose and shape the strategies of outside movements, suggesting protest actions or organizational formations; they bring the movement's concerns to the attention of those higher up; and they help frame how their superiors and colleagues think about issues.

The importance of feminist insiders comes to the fore when we consider judicial appointments by US presidents. The appointment of women judges has ebbed and flowed, depending on the presidential administration. Only eight women had served on Article III federal courts when President Carter took office in 1976.[27] He then appointed more women than all previous presidents combined—forty, or 15.5 percent of all his appointments. Reacting to evidence of a widening gender gap in support for his presidency, Ronald Reagan out-flanked Carter during the 1980 campaign by promising to appoint a woman to the US Supreme Court, which he did.[28] The fanfare over the appointment of Sandra Day O'Connor deflected attention from the fact that only 7.6 percent of Reagan's judicial appointments were women. President George H. W. Bush (the 41st president) appointed few women in the first two years of his presidency, but following his appointment of Clarence Thomas to the Supreme Court and the backlash surrounding Anita Hill's testimony, he appointed thirty-six—nearly half in the year he ran for re-election. Though 19.5 percent of his appointments were women, most were Reagan appointees he elevated from the district to the circuit appellate courts, which did little to change the overall gender composition of the federal bench.[29] Despite facing a Republican-controlled Senate after 1994, 28 percent of President Bill Clinton's appoint-ments to the federal bench were women, compared to 22 percent for President George W. Bush (the 43rd president).[30]

What conclusions can we draw from these data? I suggest that we can understand at least some of this variation by looking at the role of feminist insiders. In short, we need to look at feminists inside the government who helped exercise leverage on the policy process. Kingdon or Bardach would call such strategic insiders "process players" or "policy entrepreneurs."[31] During the second wave of feminism, beginning in the late 1960s, the National Women's Political Caucus and the National Organization for Women's Legal Defense and Education Fund championed the cause of integrating more women into public service.[32] That campaign has included a demand for more women judges, a demand that the newly formed National Association of Women Judges also championed. But understanding the pressure of these outside groups does not fully explain when and how women judges are appointed. To comprehend how outside pressure for women's representation on the bench becomes a reality, we must also examine how these outside forces partnered with feminist insiders to enable policy successes.[33] Other studies have recognized the importance of partnerships between insiders and outsiders in explaining the success of women's policy agencies.[34] Verloo calls such interactions in Europe "velvet triangles,"[35] while Vargas and Wieringa describe the phenomenon as "the triangle of empowerment."[36] The insiders I examine, however, are not within a women's policy agency but the White House itself. They are not civil servants, but political appointees.[37]

Appointments to the federal bench have always been party patronage positions, even though senators or presidents occasionally recommend judges from another party. As a formal matter, the President recommends candidates to the US Senate, which must confirm them by a simple majority vote. Traditionally, the President deferred to senators of his own party from the home state for district court judges, relied upon them heavily for circuit court appointments, and consulted key senators as a whole on appointments to the Supreme Court. Senators from the state of the vacancy of either party, however, may in effect veto an appointment or subject committee hearings to delay by not returning their "blue slip" on the nominee.[38] In addition, the chair of the Senate Judiciary Committee may delay or refuse to hold hearings and the Senate majority leader may refuse to schedule a floor vote. More recently, senators have threatened the filibuster to prevent confirmation. Thus, senators have many ways of delaying or opposing judicial nominees.[39]

From 1953 to 2000, when President George W. Bush suspended the practice, presidents called upon the American Bar Association's (ABA) Standing Committee on the Federal Judiciary to rate nominees before their public nomination as a regular part of the process.[40] The ABA champions the ideal of merit rather than political loyalty,[41] though feminists have criticized the gender composition of this committee and its standards.[42] Brooksley Elizabeth Born was the committee's first woman member in its twenty-five-year history, serving from 1977 to 1983 and as its chair from 1980 to 1983.[43] As for standards, the committee favored judicial experience and large-firm practice over academic work, government lawyering, or public defenders and legal aid. It also demanded trial experience (particularly membership in the American College of Trial Lawyers).[44] And, in Carter's time, it automatically gave judges older than sixty-four an unqualified rating.[45] Feminists argued that these standards indirectly discriminated against women, who are more likely to work in academia or for the government and who are more likely to work as public defenders.

Outside of this broad framework, each president has had his own system for choosing nominees, sharing responsibilities between the attorney general (overseeing the Department of Justice with the staff to investigate large numbers of candidates) and the White House counsel's office. President Nixon was the first to make ideology rather than party loyalty or personal connections the most important criterion for selecting federal court judges.[46] Keeping his campaign promise to appoint strict constructionists, or judges who were supportive of the police and not interested in expanding the rights of the accused, Nixon charged his attorney general, John Mitchell, to vet judicial candidates to ensure that their policy views aligned with his.[47]

CARTER PUTS GENDER ON THE AGENDA

The voters elected Jimmy Carter President in 1976, when feminist activism was at its zenith[48] and antifeminist forces were only in the early stages of organizing. Congress passed Title IX, outlawing sex discrimination in education, in 1972, and the EEOC started enforcing the prohibitions against sex discrimination in Title VII. The Supreme Court had declared the right to an abortion as part of a constitutionally protected right to privacy in *Roe v. Wade*. And Ruth Bader Ginsburg at the American Civil Liberties Union's Women's Rights Project had successfully challenged governmental sex-based classifications by urging the Supreme Court to expand its interpretation of the equal protection clause. Feminists across the ideological spectrum marched and organized. The far right was only just beginning to organize the counter movement that would defeat the Equal Rights Amendment, scale back abortion rights, and sweep Ronald Reagan into the White House.

To review, President Roosevelt appointed the first woman to the federal bench in 1934. Sixteen years later, President Truman appointed a second. President Eisenhower appointed no women to the federal bench. Presidents Kennedy, Nixon, and Ford each appointed one; President Johnson three. President Carter's appointment of forty women to the federal bench was thus a very dramatic policy change. He declared a gender- and racially-integrated bench to be a priority, charged his staff with implementing that policy, and altered the way he chose federal judges. As Meyer and Minkoff have demonstrated, the election of a Democratic president creates opportunities for progressive social movements,[49] and feminists seized the opportunities Carter's election provided.

When Carter took office, six women sat on the federal bench—five out of nearly 400 federal district court judges, and one out of 97 on the federal courts of appeal. Only eight women had *ever* served.[50] So women made up less than 1 percent of the federal judiciary, even though they were 15 percent of recent law school graduates and 9.2 percent of all lawyers.[51] To be eligible for appointment, lawyers had to possess twenty-five years of practice, which put the percentage of women closer to 3.5 percent of those eligible. Carter's record is impressive, considering how gatekeepers defined the eligible pool at the time.

How and why did Carter come to make such a radical leap in the number of women judges? His early record of appointing women judges was poor, leading many feminists to criticize his campaign promise of appointing more women as empty. The story of how they convinced him to fulfill his campaign promise is the subject of the remainder of this chapter.

Carter's "peanut brigade," the term reserved for his group of campaign volunteers, ran a grassroots campaign that challenged the party machine. Hailing from Georgia, in the Deep South, Carter spoke passionately about how class and race worked to deny equal justice to many, and he was skeptical of the Democratic Party machine and its resulting judicial appointments.[52] He was a firm believer in merit selection and believed strongly that party loyalty should not be the most important criterion in choosing judges. After the Watergate debacle, the ethos of the times turned against partisanship, so Carter's call for merit selection resonated with an electorate increasingly realigned as independent. As we shall see, because of his reliance on the Federation of Women Lawyers' Judicial Screening Panel, his women nominees all had a deep commitment to equal justice under law.

Goldman[53] and others have provided a detailed analysis of President Carter's judicial appointments.[54] I want to explain these appointments by spotlighting the acts of one well-placed feminist who made diversifying the judiciary one of her top priorities. Margaret McKenna was the first woman to hold the position of deputy White House counsel. She was only thirty-two years old. Having been editor of the *Law Review* at Southern Methodist University Law School, she tried race discrimination cases as a trial attorney in the Civil Rights Division of the Justice Department,[55] and later coordinated the Rhode Island Carter–Mondale campaign.[56] She served on the transition team for the Justice Department and worked closely with Carter's designate for attorney general, Judge Griffin Bell. Deputy White House Counsel Douglas Huron and McKenna's boss, White House Counsel Robert Lipshutz, shared her commitment to a racially and gender-diverse federal bench, but it was McKenna who made it happen. As she explains:

> Unless you stay on top of it and it's a high, high priority, you just stop pursuing it. You have to be so dogged about it or it slips by. It has to be really important to you. All of us [Lipshutz and Huron] had the same

values. This [affirmative action in judicial appointments] was a significant part of my job. And I never let go of it.[57]

Assistant Attorney General Barbara Babcock, who attributes her own appointment to Carter's platform,[58] agrees that McKenna made it happen: "You are right to focus on folks like Margaret McKenna—she had a huge hidden role . . . A young feminist without a high-level appointment who knew how to manipulate all those who did, and who really got things done."[59] Babcock also insists:

> It was wonderful, the way she really threw her weight around. She was [Lipshutz's] deputy and not the President's, but she would say, "This is what the White House wants." It was great assurance. She had a lot to do with getting the names through . . . It was very much a collective effort among women.[60]

McKenna, Lipshutz, and Huron had to overcome a number of significant obstacles to meet their goal of getting women on the bench. First, McKenna had to connect Carter's commitment to merit selection in judicial appointments to his commitment to bringing women into governmental positions more generally. Second, she had to persuade the newly created circuit nominating commissions, and later senators advocating for federal district court appointments, to include women on their lists of recommendations. Third, she had to wrest control over the decision on judicial nominations from the Justice Department, and particularly from Attorney General Bell and Associate Attorney General Michael Egan. Fourth, she had to help the administration overcome the American Bar Association's tendency to rate all the women and minority men candidates "not qualified," which inevitably destroyed their chances at confirmation. McKenna succeeded because she made these tasks a priority and because she worked strategically with a network of women's groups on the outside. Her connections with women's groups outside the administration were critical to her success. According to McKenna herself, women's groups were "enormously helpful." Neither would have been able to prevail without the other. It was the partnership, the working in tandem, that was the key to policy success.[61] As Clark concludes:

> Contemporaneous with Carter's commitment to appointing more women judges was women's rapidly increasing entry into the legal profession, as well as rising activism by women's legal and political advocacy groups around the issue of women's judicial appointments. New organizations specifically focused on promoting women's appointments to the federal judiciary formed at this time, and existing organizations undertook new initiatives to lobby for women's appointments. These organizations were better organized, better connected, and more sophisticated at using the

media than had been their predecessors. The pressure brought to bear by women's legal and political advocacy groups was critical in altering the political landscape in which women's judicial candidacies were considered—complementing and indeed spurring Carter's efforts to reform the judicial appointments process to name more women judges.[62]

Indeed, once candidate Jimmy Carter promised to increase the representation of women in the federal government, women's groups and the media held him to his promise and kept an exact count of the number of women Carter appointed. But what, exactly, did they do?

FEMINIST POLICY ACHIEVEMENTS

To get the issue of women judges on the agenda, to ensure that they were nominated to the bench, and to help secure their confirmation by Congress, feminists working inside and outside the state had to accomplish many tasks. First, they had to interrogate the assumption that judges are men. When Justices Harlan and Black retired in 1971 and Nixon promised to eschew litmus tests and "appoint the best man for the job," Liz Carpenter, Lady Bird Johnson's press secretary, who was well connected with women in the Washington Press Corps and on the National Women's Political Caucus (NWPC), phoned Virginia Kerr, an NWPC staff member, and urged the NWPC to issue a press release in protest. Under Carpenter's direction, Kerr wrote a release and delivered it later that day, pointing out that the "best man for the job" might be a woman. As Kerr recalls, "the NWPC's public relations campaign was an unqualified success in placing women in the rhetorical field of consideration for future Supreme Court vacancies . . . the NWPC turned the taken-for-granted male monopoly into a gaffe."[63]

Feminists also had to generate names of women for potential nomination. In the case of the Carter Administration, NWPC Chair Mildred Jeffrey oversaw and Susan Ness led the NWPC's Legal Support Caucus, formed immediately after Carter's election to encourage women to apply and to conduct training sessions about how to apply.[64] By forming broad coalitions, they ensured a wide audience for their efforts, troops to deploy across a broad spectrum of the women's community, and clout on their letterhead when they wrote to the White House as the "Judicial Selection Project." Moreover, by forming coalitions with progressive and civil rights groups, they broadened their influence beyond the feminist community. Kerr even corralled the Daughters of the American Revolution to join forces: "I was actually the one who thought of contacting the DAR," she remembers. "I have always felt that Sandra O'Connor owed a big debt to the NWPC for making appointment of women to the court a bipartisan feminist cause."[65] These groups helped funnel names of potential nominees to McKenna and Barbara Babcock in the Justice Department.[66]

Women's groups had to lobby on many fronts in this struggle. They met with the administration to suggest names of panelists for the new circuit nominating commissions, pressured senators to appoint women to their nominating commissions, criticized recommendations of only white men, and pressed for the women who appeared on the list. They testified before the Senate Judiciary Committee about the slow pace of women's judicial appointments.[67] They publicized and protested obvious omissions from lists, such as the Ninth Circuit Panel's failure to suggest Herma Hill Kay or the Second Circuit Panel's failure to suggest Ruth Bader Ginsburg.[68] They advocated for stronger language in the executive order implementing the Omnibus Judgeship Act and challenged the criterion of twelve–fifteen years of legal experience. They called for one-third of the new seats from the Omnibus Judgeship Act (which created thirty-five new judgeships) to go to women.[69] And they wrote questions for nominating commissions—both procedural ones about what they had done to ensure a wide group of potential nominees was considered, and substantive ones, proposing a specific battery of questions for probing candidates' commitment to equal justice under law.[70]

One of the effective strategies that feminists used in the Carter Administration was to set up their own screening panel. Feminists were dissatisfied with both the ABA's and the Justice Department's definition of merit and their lack of attention to a candidate's commitment to "equal justice under law."[71] President Carter sent Attorney General Bell to hold a meeting with women's organizations to develop ideas about how to increase the number of women's names submitted by screening panels. Mildred Jeffrey asked Bell whether women's groups could set up their own screening panel, and he agreed to submit all names of prospective nominees to what became the Federation of Women Lawyers' Judicial Screening Panel. Phyllis Segal, the first director of the National Organization for Women's Legal Defense and Education Fund, organized the effort and recruited Lynn Hecht Schafran to be its national director. They limited their evaluations to questions about the candidates' demonstrated commitment to equal justice under law.[72] At least one candidate was forced to withdraw because of what this screening panel unearthed. Finally, in 1979, feminists formed an organization of women judges—the National Association of Women Judges—which advocated women's appointments at the federal, state, and local levels, as well as training women for election and selection.[73] One of its first resolutions was to call for the appointment of a woman to the US Supreme Court, and the organization lobbied both presidential candidates to commit to this. Ironically, Reagan took the pledge while Carter refused, even though the NAWJ had just honored him for his efforts to appoint women judges.

In the end, Clark credits both the multi-pronged approach of the groups and their working together in coalition for their success in getting women on the bench. I argue that the insider–outsider connection was particularly determinative. As I shall demonstrate later in this chapter, Carter had a weak policy commitment to appointing women to the bench. Without feminist groups putting pressure on the White House and the Senate and arguing the case in the media, McKenna would likely not have had the leverage she needed to press the issue. Equally, without McKenna's insider knowledge, feminist groups would have been less effective at exerting pressure at precisely the right points and precisely the right times. Feminists inside the Carter Administration formed a Washington Women's Network that grew to more than 1,200 women who networked with each other and liaised with outside groups.[74]

The key to successful policy implementation, then, is the combination of tenacious insiders linked to well-organized outsiders. As Babcock concludes: "I think that all the women judges would never have been appointed . . . without the strong presence of women bosses in the Carter administration. It was very, very striking."[75]

THE ISSUE OF JUDICIAL SELECTION

President Carter wanted Attorney General Bell, a highly regarded appellate judge, to choose judges by merit, not by party or ideology. To that end, Bell hired Michael Egan, a lifelong Republican,[76] as his assistant attorney general in charge of judicial appointments. Moreover, Carter rejected Nixon's politicizing of the Justice Department and its criminal investigations. We should thus recognize that wresting exclusive control of judicial appointments from the Justice Department was a major accomplishment for McKenna, given the firewall[77] Carter wanted between the White House and the Justice Department on other matters[78] and Carter's profound commitment to merit selection.[79]

The clash over control of judicial appointments was not the first conflict between the Justice Department and the White House counsel's office. When the Supreme Court decided to hear *Regents of the University of California v. Bakke*, a white man's challenge to a medical school's affirmative action policy, the Justice Department prepared a brief in favor of Bakke. Lipshutz joined the President's Special Assistant for Domestic Affairs Stuart Eizenstat and Secretary of Health, Education, and Welfare Joseph Califano in pressuring the Justice Department to rewrite the brief to support affirmative action. Lipshutz's comments lend further support to the contention that, but for someone like McKenna, Bell would not have forwarded the names of women and minority men for President Carter to appoint to the bench:[80] "[We] all knew what the president's position was, but we found early on that unless someone really got heavily involved . . . to do something about affirmative action, it was too easy . . . [to] end up with all white males again.[81]

If Carter was going to institute merit selection, let alone affirmative action, he first had to wrest control from individual senators who had the power to confirm and jealously guarded their prerogatives. His commitment to reforming judicial selection was part of his campaign,[82] and even before taking office, he and Bell met with Senate Judiciary Committee chair James Eastland. Senator Eastland opposed taking district court appointments away from senators, but agreed to set up nominating commissions for circuit court judgeships. Carter issued Executive Order 11972 four weeks after he took office, which created panels to "include members of both sexes, members of minority groups, and approximately equal numbers of lawyers and non-lawyers." The order charged panels to recommend five well-qualified persons for each circuit court vacancy, leaving the President to select one to nominate. The panels succeeded in being diverse—45 percent women and 24 percent minority[83]—but their recommendations were not. The six panels recommended no women and only one minority man. Carter subsequently revised the executive order (with Executive Order 12059 in May 1978) to implore panels "to make special efforts to seek out and identify well qualified women and minority groups as potential nominees." Lipshutz, Huron, and McKenna were still unhappy with the results, though. At the end of the first two years, Carter had nominated no women to the circuit courts and only three African Americans, two of whom were Johnson appointees on the federal district courts.[84] McKenna traveled to a conference of the nominating commissions in Chicago in July 1977, personally to deliver the message that the panels needed to do better.[85]

In 1978, the nominating commissions for the Fifth and Sixth Circuits each included a woman on their lists, including Phyllis Kravitch as a second choice for the Fifth.[86] Lipshutz wrote a memo stressing the dissatisfaction of women's groups that none of the twelve circuit judge nominees so far had been women and recommended that Kravitch was the stronger of the two candidates.[87] Also, the First Lady wrote a handwritten note urging the President to choose Kravitch.[88] Although Carter approved Kravitch, Bell successfully delayed her nomination for three months as he sought to reverse the decision. He was very angry over having to share decision-making on judicial appointments with White House staff. Indeed, Bell considered resigning over the issue, and was particularly antagonistic toward McKenna, about whom he wrote:

> *Bob* Lipshutz [emphasis added], as I have noted, is not a combative, overly assertive individual. But he had working on his staff *Ms.* [emphasis added] Margaret McKenna, a lawyer dedicated to protecting and expanding women's rights . . . I thought the need for affirmative action in picking federal judges had run its course. Enter Ms. McKenna. Some women's organizations took issue with our rate of progress, despite our statistics . . . The women's groups turned to Margaret McKenna . . . The new judgeships thus upped the stakes in what Ms. McKenna and the women's groups were seeking. Mr. Lipshutz and Ms. McKenna departed from the historical precedent by attempting to assert White House staff control over the judicial nominations. Their claim was that they were not trying to take over the process but simply were trying to assure that I did not overlook minorities and women in my recommendations. They set themselves up

as the keepers of the morality in the area of discrimination, as if I and others at the Justice Department lacked their degree of concern.[89]

Lipshutz believes Bell tried to get McKenna fired.[90] Regardless, Bell eventually left office and despaired that he lost control over judicial nominations to the White House. We can only speculate as to whether it was a simple conflict over who controlled the process or whether McKenna's gender or the gender of the judges she championed played a part. Clearly, Huron and Lipshutz agreed with McKenna on the importance of diversifying judicial nominations. Without the pressure of all three, Carter may have deferred to Bell. McKenna reported relations easing somewhat after Benjamin Civiletti replaced Bell as Attorney General midway through Carter's term.[91]

An opportunity for more women judicial appointments arose when Congress passed the new Omnibus Judgeship Act of 1978, creating thirty-five new circuit court judgeships. With the expanded judicial pie, Carter could now more easily please both senators who expected patronage and interest groups that wanted a more diverse judiciary. Lipshutz urged the President to seize that opportunity. Carter's Executive Order 12059 explicitly charged the circuit nominating commissions to seek out qualified women and minority groups. Lipshutz criticized Bell's ad hoc method of selecting judges one-by-one and called for concentrating on multiple vacancies at both the circuit and district levels. He grasped what those studying women in organizations and particularly multi-member electoral systems have long known: selectors are more likely to chose a diverse group if they can select more than one at a time. The Omnibus Judgeship Act gave the administration a unique opportunity to introduce such a selection system, thereby dramatically enhancing the chances of nominating women and minority men.

Thus, after several years working with the circuit nominating commissions, the White House team and McKenna had developed a system and practice for generating the names of women and garnering support for them. But obstacles remained. Only 24 percent of district court screening panel members were women, and one-third of these panels included no women lawyers—those most likely to know qualified women.[92] Moreover, men chaired all the panels.[93] Thus, although they focused on merit, the selection panels merely institutionalized the old-boys' network upon which senators had once relied to make recommendations.[94] Among the questions that panels asked potential women nominees were whether their husbands would be jealous if they were appointed, whether they would be able to sentence criminals to jail, whether they could handle the workload, and who would take care of their children.[95]

The ABA Standing Committee on the Federal Judiciary also proved to be a problem in diversifying the list of potential nominees. For example, Joan Krauskopf, a law professor, received unanimous support from the Eighth Circuit nominating panel, and the support of Senator Eagleton and the judges of the Eighth Circuit. Yet, the committee rated her unqualified because of her lack of trial experience.[96] It rejected two other women nominees for the same reason. In Krauskopf's case, Bell met with the committee and asked the members to change their rating, but they refused and Carter chose not to overrule them. Krauskopf commented ruefully, "The effects of past sex discrimination in the legal profession, which prevented me from having more extensive trial experience . . . prevented me from serving on the Eighth Circuit Court of Appeals."[97] Likewise, the ABA rated a female law professor in Puerto Rico under consideration for the First Circuit "not qualified," and Carter dropped her nomination even though she would have been the first woman and the first Hispanic to serve on that circuit.[98]

While the so-called gender-neutral standards disadvantaged women, having what we would call a "disparate impact," disparate treatment discrimination was also at work in the ABA's process. Bell succeeded in getting the ABA to reconsider its "not qualified" rating for Diana Murphy for the district court in Minnesota.[99] (President Clinton later nominated Judge Murphy to the Eighth Circuit Court of Appeals, where she has served with distinction since 1994.) The Tenth Circuit panel recommended Stephanie Seymour, the first female partner in a major Oklahoma firm,[100] who had prepared numerous documents and appeared in court but never tried a case herself. Nancy Stanley,[101] one of the lawyers who had vetted Seymour for the Justice Department, was surprised to learn that the ABA Committee was about to rate her "not qualified." Seymour had a reputation as a "lawyer's lawyer" for the oil and gas industry, but some powerful men wanted the nomination for themselves. The Justice Department demanded a new investigation with a different circuit representative and Carter nominated Seymour.[102]

Seymour's case was not the only time Bell intervened in the ABA process, and he apparently told the ABA that they must either reconsider their ratings or the President would stop giving them privileged status in assessing prospective nominees—a threat President George W. Bush eventually carried out. Some accounts emphasize Bell's interventions with the committee; others also credit Lipshutz.[103] On five occasions, the administration proceeded to nominate candidates the ABA had rated "not qualified." The Senate confirmed two of the white men so rated—David O'Brien and William Matthew Kidd. It also confirmed one African American so rated—U.W. Clemson. Once Carter had chosen a woman nominee, McKenna could rally women's groups to apply pressure at key points, but securing ABA approval and Senate confirmation remained in the hands of the Justice Department.

Feminists involved in the process came to believe that the ABA rating system was deeply flawed, both in the criteria it used and in its process more generally. According to Lynn Hecht Schafran, they used to say that if the nominee was male, white, and had not tried a case in twenty years, the ABA would consider him a star.[104] Political scientists carefully examined the ratings of all of Carter's nominees based on the questionnaires they filled out under oath for the Senate Judiciary Committee and found that the non-traditional nominees (women and minority men) were not less qualified as a group than the white male nominees. They were simply different—younger, less wealthy, less likely to be Republicans, more likely to have been born outside of the jurisdiction for which they were nominated, more likely to have done criminal work, less likely to have been involved in political campaigns, less likely to have more than twenty years of legal experience, and more likely to have experience as public defenders or to have worked as legal aid lawyers. Most importantly, however, they were less likely to have received one of the top two ABA ratings—"exceptionally well qualified" or "qualified."[105]

Once McKenna and her colleagues had persuaded the senators and nominating commissions to recommend women, they still had to fight the Justice Department to get the President to select the women on the list. Once Carter chose a woman, they had to fight to ensure that an unwarranted ABA rating of "not qualified" did not sink the nomination. Moreover, the Senate delayed and obstructed some nominees. Right-wing groups, unhappy about Carter's ability to shape the federal bench with the 150 new positions created by the Omnibus Judgeship Act of 1978, challenged liberals and nominees they considered to be "activists." Did it so tar women and minority men with that label? Or were those nominees more likely to have been politically active in liberal causes, particularly advancing the causes of women and minorities? One of the two women assistant attorney generals in the Justice Department and that department's liaison to Congress, Patricia Wald, faced fierce opposition over her appointment to be the first woman on the D.C. Circuit Court of Appeals. Canned editorials branded her "anti-family" because of her work on children's rights, though she had been a stay-at-home mother of five for ten years, and Senator Gordon Humphrey called her a "wild and wooly woman."[106] Wald's case presages the politicization and gridlock over women and minority men nominees perceived to be left of center and tied to social change causes in later administrations.

CARTER AND FEMINISTS

Just as feminists were ambivalent about participating in mainstream electoral politics,[107] they were ambivalent and divided about Carter himself.[108] Women worked hard to elect him, although many progressive feminists, disappointed with Carter's record as president, supported Senator Ted Kennedy's challenge to Carter's renomination in 1980. As a born-again Christian, Carter personally opposed abortion.[109] He supported the Equal Rights Amendment,[110] but many feminists claimed that he did not use enough of his political capital to ensure its ratification.[111] Although the experiences of his wife and mother sensitized him to women's economic vulnerabilities, his determination to bring women and minority men into government may have stemmed in part from his hostility to the party machine and his commitment to merit over partisan considerations.

The United Nations had declared 1976 "International Women's Year" and would later extend that year into a decade. In celebration, President Ford and Congress supported Congresswoman Bella Abzug's bill to fund a national conference on women made up of delegates from each state.[112] The conference produced a National Plan of Action and Carter appointed Abzug to chair his National Advisory Committee on Women. That committee publicly criticized the administration's slow progress on women's issues. At its final meeting with Abzug as chair, Carter implored women to help him persuade liberal senators, saying, "I would love to have half women [judicial appointments], but you must help me with the local Senators."[113] He would eventually fire Abzug for her public criticism of the administration, precipitating a crisis within women's groups. Gloria Steinem and Abzug pressured members of the National Advisory Committee on Women to resign, but half of the forty-member group stayed on.[114] As this scenario illustrates, Carter's relationship with feminist insiders was complex. Though he sympathized with their cause, he did not agree with them on all issues, or make them top priorities.

Sarah Weddington, the lawyer who argued *Roe v. Wade* before the US Supreme Court, became Carter's special adviser on women's issues. She worked to get more women appointed to public office, campaigned with the President for reelection, and helped craft his message on women's issues. Even Weddington—who, after Abzug, presented the more mild-mannered face of feminism[115]—was not fooled into thinking she was a top adviser. Criticizing the release of candid photographs of Carter working in the Oval Office, Weddington wrote in a memo: "Mainly through our efforts the outside world would think there are women in the inner circle. For the sake of the President, it would be good to perpetuate that myth."[116] She and the First Lady supported McKenna's efforts to create a diverse and representative bench. It may well be, too, that McKenna and Weddington were effective insiders because they were seen as more palatable, less radical, and simply easier to deal with than other feminists.

Once Congress passed the Omnibus Judgeship Act, McKenna succeeded in charging the circuit court nominating commissions with putting women on their lists and pressured senators to consider women for district court nominations. Along with her colleagues in the White House counsel's office, she intervened with Carter to override Bell's recommendations of white men and succeeded in persuading the President to nominate women and minority men once their names began to appear on the lists. She worked indirectly with others to pressure the ABA Committee not to rate all of the women nominees "not qualified." Her efforts and the effects of those efforts are evidenced by the testimony of insiders, the statements of successful nominees, the paper trail of memos in the presidential papers, and her own statements. So far, then, the story is one of tenacious policy implementation. McKenna succeeded in getting herself assigned to the task of securing women appointments and, having done so, pursued that task relentlessly, overcoming barriers within and outside the administration. In short, she and her colleagues helped President Carter develop and solidify his commitment to appoint women and minority men to the bench.

During his presidential campaign, Carter had declared he would consider women for all governmental positions.[117] This promise included appointing women to the federal judiciary (explicitly in both the Democratic and Republican party platforms in 1976).[118] Carter charged Abzug and then Weddington with working with women's groups to gather names of potential women nominees and appointees. They were the bean counters within the administration whose task it was to ensure that women were appointed across the board. Reading the presidential papers, however, one has the sense that, in the early years, the administration pursued two separate policy tracks: merit selection of judges; and appointment of women to governmental office. McKenna and her colleagues in the White House counsel's office deftly persuaded the President to connect the dots and link those two issues.

Indeed, from the beginning of his presidency, Carter was committed to integrating women into the federal government in general, rather than the judiciary in particular. In his speech before the US National Women's Agenda Conference, for example, he pledged his support for their agenda in its entirety.[119] He spoke of how his mother worked as a teenager for the Post Office and then as a nurse until the age of seventy, and how his wife Rosalynn had to work in a beauty parlor to help her mother after her father died when she was thirteen. He talked about discrimination and women's underrepresentation in the federal government and called on members of the audience to help identify qualified women. He mentioned virtually every feminist issue (aside, of course, from abortion and lesbian rights), but not the importance of women serving in the judiciary.

As I have shown, Attorney General Bell and Associate Attorney General Egan were slow to challenge the conventional standards or procedures of judicial selection, which directly or indirectly excluded women and minority men. They were, however, willing to make slightly more token appointments than their predecessors, if they could find candidates who met their narrow standards of merit. Carter was committed to merit selection and abhorred the idea of political interference with the workings of the Justice Department. In July 1977, White House Chief of Staff Hamilton Jordan sent the President a memo about whom Carter should select for the First Circuit Court of Appeals. Jordan recommended that the seat should go to someone from New Hampshire and Carter replied, "Why are we deciding which state gets a judge? This is not merit selection."[120]

McKenna recalls that the issue of women's representation on the bench "wasn't that high on Carter's list." In her recollection, Carter thought they would "take the politics out of it" and that the "ABA's role would be good."[121] Although Carter instituted the nominating commissions for the circuit courts, he appointed only one woman during the first two years of his administration.

It is interesting to speculate what might have happened had McKenna not been so strategic and effective a feminist insider. Weddington's files show tangential involvement with judicial selection. Outsiders clearly identified her as the conduit on women's issues, but it was McKenna who handled judicial appointments. As McKenna recalls, "they [Abzug and Weddington] were aware of judicial appointments and we involved them but it was not their thing."[122] Clearly, it was McKenna who pursued the issue on judicial appointments in particular.

Carter's recognition of the need for a more racially diverse judiciary may well have been his path to embracing a more gender-diverse judiciary. He said to a black reporter that his goal was "to have black judges in Georgia, Florida, the Carolinas, Mississippi, Alabama, Louisiana, indeed, throughout the country."[123] In 1977, he called upon the National Bar Association (a group of black lawyers) to review the qualifications of judicial candidates,[124] and he met early on with a committee whose purpose was to appoint African Americans to the Fifth Circuit Court of Appeals. In his speech to the Los Angeles Bar Association on May 4, 1978, he said:

> I grew up in a community in Georgia that often did not provide simple justice for a majority of our citizens because of the divisions of privilege between those who owned land and property, and those who did not, the divisions of power between those who controlled the political system and those who were controlled by it, the wall of discrimination that separated blacks and whites . . .
>
> The passage of the Omnibus Judgeship Act, now pending in a House–Senate Conference committee, will provide a test for the concept of merit selection . . . The passage of this act . . . offers a unique opportunity to make our judiciary more fully representative of our population. We have an abominable record to date.[125]

This speech reflects the evolution of the President's priorities for a diverse bench: first through a focus on merit; second through the appointment of African Americans; and finally through the selection of women. It also marks the moment when a diverse and representative bench was put firmly on the agenda.[126]

In his signing speech for the Omnibus Judgeship Act, Carter declared:

> This Act provides a unique opportunity to begin to redress another disturbing feature of the Federal judiciary: the almost complete absence of women, or members of minority groups . . . I am committed to these appointments, and pleased that this Act recognizes that we need more than token representation on the Federal bench.

He went on to say that he intended to write to the chairman of every circuit court nominating commission to remind them of this obligation and that he hoped that the Senate would work with him to "achieve a more representative judiciary."[127]

By the time of his reelection campaign, Carter was firmly committed to the principle of a gender-diverse bench. Although he refused to commit to appointing a woman to the US Supreme Court should a vacancy occur (in contrast to the promise made by his challenger, Ronald Reagan), Carter's debate preparation reveals a deep policy commitment to the issue.[128] Women's issues became critical to Carter's campaign as he tried to keep feminists in the fold after Kennedy's challenge and to capitalize on the fact that women were less likely than men to support Reagan. Ultimately, though, he lost the 1980 election, taking much of the wind out of the sails of accomplishing a gender-diverse bench. He was no perfect feminist, to be sure, and it took a feminist insider, partnered with outsiders, to help him unify his concerns about judicial selection and women in government jobs. But during the Carter Administration all three elements of success were present: explicit policy commitment to gender equality; strategically located, motivated, and tenacious insiders; and outsiders applying pressure. They overcame the obstacle of the ABA some of the time and wrestled with individual senators rather than the Senate as a whole—as Clinton and Obama have had to do. As we will see in the next chapter, all three elements are either absent or exist to a lesser degree in the UK, where activists face additional structural barriers.

AFTER CARTER

After President Reagan took office, he made good on his promise to appoint the first woman justice to the US Supreme Court. Her name was Sandra Day O'Connor and her appointment was a major woman first in the history of the judicial branch. Even so, Reagan's overall women appointments amounted to half of Carter's. Women were entering law school in even greater numbers by the 1980s, filling the pipeline even fuller with qualified women. Reagan, however, had none of Carter's commitment to merit selection, affirmative action, or a diverse judiciary. Nor did he consider women's groups to be a key constituency meriting direct White House access. And he appointed no Margaret McKenna, no Sarah Weddington, and no Barbara Babcock to press the case. Without a policy commitment to gender equality, and with no insiders, Carter's progress was quickly reversed, even as women's numbers in the profession continued to rise. And the outside groups, having neither an insider to leverage nor the support of the President, turned their attention to defending other policies under threat.

After twelve years of Republican control, the Democrats retook the White House in 1992, and President Bill Clinton faced a vastly different legal and political environment than had existed under Carter. Clinton and First Lady Hillary were both lawyers.[129] In addition, the trickle of women into law schools in the late 1960s had become a torrent: women now made up nearly half of all law school graduates and the women who had earned law degrees during an earlier era had made partner, received tenure, accumulated years of trial experience, organized state women's bar associations, and secured positions on state and federal benches. Indeed, Clinton had a much larger pool of women candidates to choose from than Carter had enjoyed, including many who met the conventional criteria. Furthermore, although there had been a backlash against affirmative action, the demand for proportionate representation of women at all levels of government had strengthened. But the judicial appointment process had become more contested and politicized than it had been under Carter. Conservatives were furious that successive appointments to the Supreme Court had not yet resulted in a clear overruling of *Roe v. Wade.*

Owing in part to his strong support among women, Clinton had not promised merely to integrate women at all levels of government, but to have a federal judiciary "that looked like America." Like Carter, however, Clinton bristled over feminist groups' scrutiny of the number of his women appointments. The first ever woman attorney general, Janet Reno, appointed Eleanor D. Acheson to be her assistant and to run judicial appointments.[130] Acheson had been Hillary Clinton's college roommate at Wellesley and she later served as the National Gay and Lesbian Taskforce's general counsel.[131] One of her greatest challenges was to get the administration to focus on and prioritize judicial appointments when so much else was going on in the White House. But securing confirmation of the administration's nominees was also a major obstacle, particularly after the Republicans became the majority party in Congress in 1994. During the 105th Congress, it took 161 days to confirm federal judge appointments, compared to just 59 days for the 103rd,[132] which incurred a rebuke from Chief Justice Rehnquist and local bar associations, who warned of the dire consequences of a high vacancy rate on the federal courts.[133]

Women nominees had particular difficulty securing Senate confirmation. It took women and minority men six weeks longer than white men to clear the confirmation hurdle, despite their higher ABA ratings.[134] Many of the so-called "non-traditional" nominees were the ones the Senate voted down or never acted on.[135] Women signaled "liberal activism" in the minds of Republican senators.[136] The ABA Standing Committee rated 63 percent of Clinton's nominees well qualified, 10 percentage points higher than the Reagan and Bush (41) Administrations',[137] and the highest rankings since the ABA began formally evaluating nominees in 1953.[138] During Clinton's first term, 31 percent of those nominees were women, a rate that was twice that of Carter and significantly higher than that of Reagan or Bush (41).[139] Clinton also appointed the second woman to the US Supreme Court, Ruth Bader Ginsburg. Regardless, in this case, a president determined to appoint a woman, a White House counsel doggedly pushing for women appointments, and interest groups aggressively pressing could not consistently overcome the obstacle of a hostile Senate.

After nominating John Roberts to fill Justice O'Connor's vacancy, President George W. Bush was determined to appoint a woman. First Lady Laura Bush also pressed the case for a woman. The President got his opportunity when Chief Justice William Rehnquist died,[140] but his nomination of White House Counsel Harriet Miers infuriated conservatives, who were determined not to have another David Souter (a conservative Republican who proved to be a moderate on the court and failed to cast his vote to overturn *Roe v. Wade*).[141] Moreover, Miers did not do well when meeting with senators or learning constitutional law in preparation for her confirmation hearings. Ultimately, Bush withdrew the nomination in favor of Samuel Alito. The President could neither overcome the objections of his own core constituency nor allay broader concerns about competence. In the case of Miers, two of the three elements for success were present: the President wanted a woman and strategically placed insiders identified a candidate. Lukewarm support for Miers among Democratic senators and feminist groups—who did not see her as either a feminist or a progressive—only bolstered conservatives' belief that, if Democrats and feminists did not immediately oppose her, she was not reliably conservative enough for them. The opposition of outside groups nixed her appointment, and the President abandoned his commitment to appointing a woman—his own close adviser.

Bush's commitment to appoint a woman did not survive conservative opposition. Nor did it extend to lower-court appointments. When asked whether the President took gender into account in judicial appointments and valued a gender-diverse bench, Assistant Attorney General Rachel Brand said she believed Bush's numbers to be commensurate with those of his predecessors. But they were not. More than 28 percent of Clinton's appointments were women, compared to only 22 percent of Bush's.[142] All three ingredients were absent. The Bush case is a significant counter-example should one extrapolate from Margaret McKenna to posit that the effective partnership between insiders and outsiders is a uniquely feminine or feminist way of policy implementation. Conservatives learned the lesson of McKenna, or, more likely, the defeat of Robert Bork's nomination by progressive interest groups. The Senate would have likely confirmed Miers, but the President demurred to conservative groups and withdrew the appointment. Conservative social movements linked strategically to White House insiders (ironically, in this case Miers herself) caused Miers to withdraw and the President to select Alito. Their success shows the generalizability of the McKenna case: the constraints of Senate confirmation notwithstanding, social movements linked to insiders can implement policy. In Bush's case, however, the policy success was the appointment of conservative judges rather than women and minority men.

Like Carter and Clinton, Obama has placed advocates for greater judicial gender diversity in key positions in his administration.[143] Indeed, his nominations of Judge Sonia Sotomayor and Dean Elena Kagan demonstrate his administration's commitment to a diverse and representative bench. Of the nominations Obama has made for the federal courts, nearly 46 percent have been women,[144] but the vitriol conservatives unleashed in response to Sotomayor's nomination[145] suggests that the President's future appointments will meet considerable resistance.

Obama needs no Margaret McKenna to persuade him to nominate women and minority men. And, unlike Carter, he does not have to search hard for candidates with Ivy League educations, litigation experience, large firm practices, and judicial experience. But seemingly gender-neutral standards may well continue to disadvantage women, and they still face double standards, as Sotomayor's confirmation demonstrated. Unless feminists organize and mobilize, we can expect to see women and minority men take longer to win Senate confirmation and be more likely to fail.

Contrary to the perception that women are making slow and steady progress onto the federal bench, then, the evidence suggests the emergence of new—and the strengthening of old—obstacles. Only by understanding the networks of insiders and outsiders can we explain the enormous variation in presidential records on judicial diversity during the last thirty years. The irony is that conservatives, not feminists and progressives, have taken the lessons of the Carter Administration to heart. The withdrawal of Miers's nomination reflects the recognition that policy success requires a network of insiders and outsiders with considerable media savvy.[146] Unless feminists and progressives develop strategies for overcoming the new policy obstacle of Senate confirmation, they will fail at policy implementation. The lesson feminists and progressives should take from the Carter Administration, and from the subsequent conservative legal movement, is that they must reproduce and strengthen the outside organizations that mobilized with insiders. Feminists, of course, have been ambivalent about engaging the state and have not shown the ability to sustain that engagement through Republican administrations. But unless organizations from women's bar associations to the National Association of Women Judges recommit to the actions they took in the 1970s, we will continue to see a disproportionate gap between the number of women a president nominates and the number who are confirmed. The policy of securing a diverse and representative bench will not be implemented.

Most studies of policy implementation fail to consider gender issues, such as the appointment of women judges. Moreover, many fail to consider the role of law and courts as policy-makers and the importance of the third branch of government. Those who do study women and public policy often do not engage each other's arguments, nor interact with those developing more comprehensive theories of policy implementation. This chapter shows how bringing a gender lens to policy implementation can expand, enlarge, and challenge ideas of policy implementation. Feminists enjoyed policy success only when they succeeded in securing explicit policy support from the President, had the support of a tenacious, effective, and well-positioned policy insider, and mobilized as a network of outside groups working closely with insiders.

5

GENDER ON THE AGENDA: LESSONS FROM THE UNITED KINGDOM[1]

INTRODUCTION

In Chapter 4, I showed how understanding the connections between policy insiders and outsiders helps explain how President Carter's promise of a more gender-diverse bench emerged and became a reality, even though feminists had advocated for it previously. Looking at a gender policy case reveals important dimensions of policy implementation that have been overlooked. In this chapter, I examine the concept of agenda-setting—the process of transforming a condition into a problem that the government must solve. Theories of agenda-setting generally postulate elements of magnitude and sequence: that is, sufficient consensus must first be reached to produce a tipping point or identifiable moment when the issue is indisputably on the agenda. Conventional accounts hold that this process involves convincing sufficient numbers of people that a problem exists by creating a groundswell or consensus around the issue. My evidence will show that policy changes that increased women's representation on the bench in Britain occurred *without* such a groundswell or consensus. The story of how the absence of women from higher judicial office in the United Kingdom[2] came to be seen as a problem that the government had to address is very different from Chapter 4's account of the United States. The machinations that lead to the appointment of women judges vary from state to state, country to country, and even between international organizations. Extending our scope of inquiry to gender (and also the third branch of government, the judiciary) improves our understanding of agenda-setting. As with the concepts in the previous chapters, looking at agenda-setting through a gender lens alters and deepens our understanding.

In this chapter, I shall argue that rather than producing a groundswell around the absence of women judges, feminists in Britain succeeded by linking this issue to the Labour Party's discourse on modernization. By so doing, they persuaded well-placed government officials, policy-makers, and opinion leaders that Britain needed more women judges, not so much for gender equality in itself, but because gender equality signaled a modern judiciary. In this case, feminists were able to capitalize on several trends that had little to do with gender: changes in the Labour Party's philosophy toward courts and law; a decline in public confidence in the courts; an increasing recognition that the role of the Lord Chancellor in judicial appointments was problematic; and the momentum of several decades' worth of efforts to reform the judiciary.

This case invites us to consider how feminists deploy arguments about legitimacy, equality, and representativeness in their arguments for women judges. As I shall show, agenda-setting theories posit policy windows—short opportunities for change that are time limited. British feminists successfully took advantage of an open policy window in 2003. But while they succeeded in changing the judicial selection process and securing the appointment of the first woman law lord, the absence of a larger mobilization and commitment to greater gender diversity on the bench has limited future policy success.

Why was it so much harder to place the issue of the gender of judges on the agenda in the United Kingdom than it was in the United States? Why did Britain appoint its first woman to its highest appellate court only in 2003, more than twenty years after the United States and Canada had made such an appointment? At least initially, we might expect convergence between the United States, the United Kingdom, and Canada. They share common intellectual and political heritages; they have similar numbers of women in the legal profession; women have held high political office in varying degrees in all three countries; and organized feminism has pressed its case in all three. Ideas about policy and governance have moved between the three countries since the colonies were founded, whether they relate to anti-slavery, suffrage, or welfare policy.[3]

Two factors made it harder to frame the absence of women judges as a problem in Britain and to break through the barrier and secure the appointment of the first woman to the highest appellate court. First, judging is much more of a specialized domain in Britain. Senior judges there are not public figures to the same extent as Supreme Court judges in Canada and the United States. Feminists have therefore not targeted judges as a way to showcase women's increasing power. More importantly, until recently, judges in Britain were chosen from a very narrow and select pool of candidates by gatekeepers who did not prioritize a gender-diverse bench. In fact, one gatekeeper, the Lord Chancellor, successfully resisted pressure for change throughout the 1990s and was indifferent to international comparisons that made Britain appear behind the times in terms of women's representation in the judiciary.

THE CONCEPT OF AGENDA-SETTING

Scholars have long asked how an issue moves from being a non-issue to a public issue and then to an agenda item in public policy circles.[4] In the literature, the spread of ideas is understood as a kind of epidemic with a dramatic tipping point. Malcolm Gladwell, for example, uses a contagion model to understand the spread of ideas. For him, ideas, like viruses, are contagious: they spread from person to person. They take off dramatically, not incrementally, and little changes can have huge effects. Likewise, Rochon uses the metaphor of an earthquake to describe the role of social movements in agenda-setting.[5] The case discussed in this chapter seems to be an exception to the idea that agenda-setting and policy change result from a dramatic tipping point. To return to Rochon's metaphor of an earthquake, the size of the fault that causes an earthquake may be less important than we think. To understand how the absence of women judges came onto the UK agenda, we need to understand how advocates framed arguments to piggy-back onto other arguments rather than created a groundswell of support.

Katzenstein[6] and Mansbridge[7] call discursive politics "the politics of reflection and reformulation . . . involving words and images."[8] Scholars have emphasized the importance of discursive politics in understanding how political change occurs. Kingdon, for example, recognizes that ideas can spill over from one sphere to another.[9] Likewise, Baumgartner and Jones recognize the circulation of ideas and the importance of tone.[10] Finally, Ferree et al. have analyzed what Gladwell calls the "stickiness" of ideas by evaluating the discursive field in which abortion activists make arguments in Germany and the United States.[11] In Germany, justifying access to abortion by arguing it enhances women's autonomy is a framing that fails to resonate. In the United States, pro-choice activists get traction with arguments about the dangers of intrusive government, but not by pointing out the hardships of lack of access for poor women. Those who want to understand agenda-setting and political change must consider these discursive politics, even if they may be difficult to measure.[12]

The case explored in this chapter features an issue—the underrepresentation of women on the bench—that simmers rather than boils to the surface. In this case, no groundswell of activism rose up to make this an issue that the government had to address. Instead, it "snuck up" on policy-makers and the public, slipping in through the back door as the public debated other, related issues. Here, the government did not respond to a social movement at all. In fact, one could argue that it sparked a social movement through its political reform. This point is important, since many feminists presume that an issue must become an agenda item before a policy change can occur.[13] In emphasizing the role that government action plays in building a grassroots movement, I join policy scholars who emphasize that policy may be an input and not merely an output.[14] As I suggest, not all policy change conforms to the contagion model outlined by Gladwell and others. It can occur without much groundswell and in fact may be a key component in creating a groundswell.

WAS THE ABSENCE OF WOMEN A PROBLEM?

Was women's underrepresentation in the judiciary a problem? Was it on the public agenda? Kingdon's study of agenda-setting revealed that the policy community was largely in agreement about whether an issue was or was not on the agenda.[15] I interviewed policy-makers and activists and read every national newspaper article in a twenty-year period that discussed judges, judicial appointments, judicial selection, or the composition of the judiciary. In addition to simply counting the number of articles per year (and noting their infrequency), I counted how many times an article about judges noted the absence of women.[16] My interviewees were not convinced that this issue was on the agenda in 2002. As for the results of my newspaper analysis, Figure 5.1 indicates the emergence and evolution of this issue over time. What is striking about Figure 5.1 is how little coverage judicial selection and the appointment of a new Law Lord received in the United Kingdom.[17] It is hard to imagine a

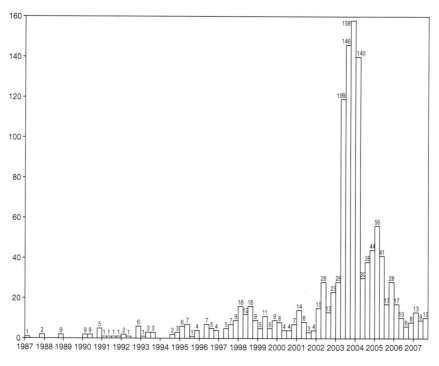

FIGURE 5.1 Number of stories about the judiciary in major UK newspapers, 1987–2007 (by quarter)

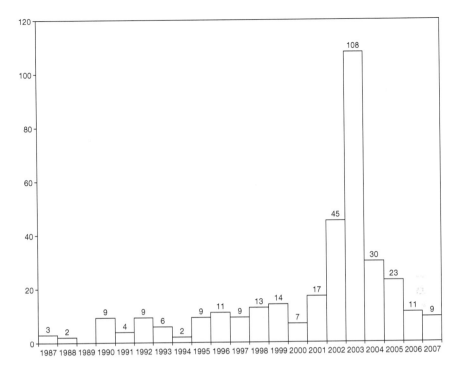

FIGURE 5.2 Number of stories noting the gender composition of the judiciary in major UK newspapers, 1987–2007 (by year)

US Supreme Court appointment garnering only three or four news stories. I coded stories as to whether they discussed the gender composition of the bench. Figure 5.2 confirms what my interviewees suggested: that the issue was not on the public agenda as late as 2002. In 2003, however, coverage of the issue skyrocketed. Why? Simply because advocates attached gender to the issue of constitutional reform, which *was* on the agenda. The surge in coverage that we see is due to the larger debates around constitutional reform in 2003, not the issue of gender per se.

Putting aside momentarily this question of how feminists attached this issue to constitutional reform, we may ask why the issue of women judges emerged only recently and quite late, by international standards, in the UK. To understand why it took so long for the gender composition of the judiciary to make its way onto the public agenda in the UK and why the first woman was appointed to the highest appellate court only in 2003, we need to know the basics of several parallel stories that have little or nothing to do with gender or the women's movement.

In contrast to the United States, judges in the United Kingdom are not recognizably powerful public figures. Historically, the Lord Chancellor chose judges from a narrow pool of distinguished barristers, with virtually no parliamentary scrutiny and little political influence.[18] One becomes a senior judge in England by first becoming a barrister.[19] Until recently, one also had to be a Queen's Counsel (QC), which the Lord Chancellor chose utilizing the same system of consultation as for judges.[20] Consultation is more often referred to as "secret soundings." The Lord Chancellor would poll members of the senior judiciary about prospective candidates. People could be eliminated from consideration either because they were not known or because someone had a negative opinion of them. A candidate would not even necessarily know she was being considered, nor for what reason she was disqualified; nor would she have the opportunity to address alleged faults. Successfully vetted candidates would receive the tap on the shoulder, asking them to serve. Before the constitutional reforms of 2003, the Lord Chancellor appointed barristers to the High Court bench after twenty-five years of distinguished advocacy. A select few rose to the Court of Appeal and the Law Lords. The Lord Chancellor generally chose judges for the House of Lords from among judges on the Court of Appeal and judges on the Court of Appeal from High Court judges. High Court judges are chosen mainly from QCs with years of experience in oral advocacy. Thus, although a judicial progression exists, it is only from the High Court; judges from lower courts generally do not move up the rungs of the judicial ladder in the way that a state court judge in the US might aspire to the federal bench.[21] Few members of this elite group are women, although, if one goes farther down the hierarchy, more women serve.[22] Indeed, in 2004, only 8 percent of QCs were women, inching up to 10 percent in 2010, which limits the number of women holding high judicial office in the UK.[23] Thus, when Brenda Hale took her seat, the UK had a comparatively low proportion of women holding high judicial office (12 percent). That continues to be the case today.[24]

Though the system of judicial selection in Britain clearly has discriminatory effects, it has never been a primary focus of feminist politics. Because Parliament does not confirm judicial appointments and because what judges do is framed as carrying out rather than making policy, most legal practitioners and scholars would be hard pressed to identify by name the members of the highest appellate court—as of 2009, the Supreme Court.[25] For these reasons, British feminists seeking visible symbols did not tend to target judicial appointments and were unlikely to see integrating the courts as a political objective. Given this state of affairs, the puzzle is not why the gender of judges came to be a political issue so late, but why it ever emerged as an issue at all. I suggest that many of the changes in Britain that rendered the time ripe for increasing the number of women on the bench had little to do with gender. Instead, other trends produced what Kingdon would call "spillover effects." These developments made it easier for feminists to attach the issue of women judges to non-gender policy issues.

CHANGES THAT CREATED A MORE RECEPTIVE CLIMATE

One of the most significant developments that brought the issue of judicial selection to the fore was the Labour Party's position on the Constitution. Historically, Labour had been very suspicious of courts because judges traditionally interpreted the common law as restricting strikes and trade union organizing. Thus, in debating a Bill of Rights in the 1980s, many on the left were skeptical of giving more power to judges, who were seen as upper class, from privileged educational backgrounds, and politically conservative.[26] Two factors, however, eroded Labour's historic opposition to the courts. First, eighteen years of sweeping Conservative policy changes had convinced many left-wing constitutional thinkers that Britain, too, needed to strengthen its courts as a check on government. Second, courts and judicial power have been on the rise throughout the world. Much of this has been supranational judicial power, such as the European Court of Human Rights and the International Criminal Court.

It was not just Labour's changed constitutional policy that was relevant with respect to the gender composition of the judiciary. The party's victory in 1997 doubled the number of women members of Parliament—from 60 to 120.[27] Women also took up leadership roles in the government, including many longstanding feminists, such as Harriet Harman.[28] Labour's endorsement of a policy of women-only shortlists in some open seats, and its subsequent legislation to amend sex discrimination law to permit such positive action, legitimated larger arguments about gender and representation. Labour created the Women's Equality Unit, a cabinet-level office to advocate for equal opportunities policies. Moreover, the Prime Minister's wife, Cherie Booth, a QC and part-time judge herself, became an outspoken advocate of women's greater political participation, including participation on the bench.

Outside of these developments in Labour Party policy, a number of incidents in the 1990s diminished public confidence in the judiciary. The courts overturned several high-profile convictions of alleged Irish Republican Army (IRA) murderers. When the IRA's campaign of violence moved outside of Northern Ireland to the mainland and struck at pubs and even the Conservative Party's conference hotel, the criminal justice system faced enormous pressure to bring the perpetrators to justice. Although, in many cases, the fault lay with the police—who faked evidence or forced false confessions—many criticized the judiciary for not subjecting policing practices to sufficient scrutiny and for taking too long to rectify the situation when the evidence mounted that innocent people were in jail. The judiciary's failure to function as an independent check on governmental power made it complicit in human rights abuses. Moreover, the public perceived judges to be out of step with ordinary life: they were elderly, from a narrow social stratum, and disconnected from popular culture. In short, they were no longer seen as adequately representing the British people.[29]

Perhaps the most important turning point was the Pinochet case.[30] In this case, a Spanish magistrate had granted a motion to seek to extradite eighty-two-year-old General Augusto Pinochet of Chile to stand trial in Spain for his alleged crimes against humanity. Pinochet, having left Argentina to obtain medical treatment in London, appealed against the extradition. On November 25, 1998, the House of Lords ruled (three–two) that Pinochet did not enjoy immunity for his alleged crimes while in office.[31] After the ruling, however, it emerged that one of the five judges, Lord Hoffman, was a chairperson and unpaid director of Amnesty International, and his wife worked for the organization. Pinochet asked the House of Lords to set aside its decision because of a conflict of interest, which it did. The next panel found the same result (six–one), although on different legal grounds. Ultimately, Home Secretary Jack Straw refused to extradite Pinochet on health grounds. From its inception through the miners' strike of the 1980s, the Labour movement had argued that conservative judges were partisan and ideological, not neutral appliers of principle. The Pinochet case, however, demonstrated outside of the class-conflict frame that outcomes hinged on who heard the case. Judges were not merely legal technocrats deciding cases according to arcane legal rules, but people with political positions. The case raised the specter that judicial outcomes turned on the luck of the draw and which judges the Lord Chancellor assigned to the case.

In the same year as the Pinochet case, the role of judges became an even greater matter for public consideration. That year, Parliament at last passed the Human Rights Act, requiring courts to interpret domestic law so as to be compatible with the European Convention on Human Rights. This act gave higher courts the power to declare a legislative or administrative act incompatible with human rights, returning the issue to the government for remedy. Nearly every news article discussing the Human Rights Act mentioned the resulting increase in judicial power.[32]

THE LORD CHANCELLOR AND LEGAL PROFESSION ARE GATEKEEPERS THAT KEEP OUT WOMEN

Interviews with legal and political insiders suggested that the two most important reasons why so few women were in high judicial office were the narrow pool from which judges are chosen and the concentration of power to choose them in the hands of one person—the Lord Chancellor. Both the process of judicial selection and the power of the Lord Chancellor became major issues for the Labour Party. The 1992 Labour Manifesto, for example, called for a reduction in the power of the Lord Chancellor and the creation of a judicial appointments commission. Feminists were then able to piggy-back on Labour's unrelated concerns about judicial power and the position of the Lord Chancellor. By 1997, however, as Labour was about to come to power, the proposal for reducing the power of the Lord Chancellor mysteriously vanished. Indeed, Lord Chancellor Irvine effectively blocked such reform for six years. Given that he had the power to appoint all members of the higher judiciary without parliamentary approval, Lord Irvine could have diversified the bench, just as reforming appointers in the United States, such as President Jimmy Carter and Governors Jerry Brown (California) and Rudy Perpich (Minnesota), had done. Instead, he drew even more heavily from a narrow elite than had his Conservative Party predecessor.[33] When challenged to explain the absence of women from higher judicial office, Lord Irvine repeated the notion, shared by many judges, that such consideration would pose a serious threat to merit selection.[34]

If Prime Minister Tony Blair thought Lord Irvine was no longer moving forward on Labour's constitutional reform agenda, why did he not force him to resign? Lord Irvine was not only one of the architects of Labour's election victory (disarming the far-left wing of the party) but the barrister who hired both Cherie Booth and Tony Blair fresh out of university and one of the most politically powerful Lord Chancellors of modern times. He spearheaded major constitutional reforms,[35] but he effectively vetoed changes in the judicial selection process. Eventually, though, on June 13, 2003, Blair fired Irvine and appointed an interim, Lord Falconer, while the government explored the idea of abolishing the office of the Lord Chancellor altogether.[36] The position of Lord Chancellor had been under attack as an unacceptable concentration of power.[37] He exercised legislative functions as the leader and a sitting member of the House of Lords, and as a member of the cabinet and an adviser to the Prime Minister. He exercised judicial functions as the person who appointed and disciplined all sitting judges. He exercised executive functions as the head of a 12,000-person civil service department that administered the judiciary. The parliamentary debates after Blair announced he was abolishing the position stressed the theme of modernization and eliminating such concentrated power. Feminists and others were thus able to frame and defend both the separation of powers and a gender-diverse bench as elements in the modernization of the nation's political structure.

REFORM OF THE JUDICIAL SELECTION PROCESS

The issue of gender and the judiciary was clearly on the horizon in the UK, although it was not on the agenda in the sense of likely governmental action. Margaret Thatcher's Lord Chancellor, Lord Mackay, set in motion incremental reforms paving the way for Labour's proposals. In 1990, he removed the ban on solicitors holding judicial office. He began publicly advertising judicial positions and interviewing candidates. He actively encouraged women to apply for Queen's Counsel and junior judicial posts. Thatcher saw the issue as one of free market competition thwarted by a monopolistic

Bar, rather than modernization and gender diversity (she was the only post-war prime minister not to have a woman cabinet minister). Lord Irvine also initiated many procedural reforms that affected women and the judiciary, including developing equal opportunities policies, arranging for lay members to serve on the committees that made the initial short lists of judicial candidates, and allowing lawyers to spend a day shadowing members of the judiciary, but he did not significantly increase the percentage of women judges. And nearly all the reforms were confined to lower judicial office. After the Peach Commission recommended an independent audit of appointment procedures in December 1999, the Lord Chancellor appointed Sir Colin Campbell to be the first Commissioner for Judicial Appointments.[38] His three annual reports, special investigations, and responses to consultation bolstered criticisms of the existing system.[39]

The next Lord Chancellor, Charles Falconer, dramatically changed the discourse about gender and judicial appointments, marking a turning point, if not a tipping point. In sharp contrast to his predecessor, Falconer no longer framed diversity as the antithesis of merit:[40] he recognized that diversity on the bench could be achieved without compromising merit. As part of the Constitutional Reform Act of 2005, Parliament created a Judicial Appointments Commission to recommend candidates for high judicial office. The government opted to retain the system of Queen's Counsels under a reformed system.[41] The Judicial Appointments Commission continues to select mostly barristers and QCs as high court judges. In December 2009, only 10 percent of QCs were women.[42]

Parliament also created a new Supreme Court, which convened in 2009.[43] Members of this court no longer also serve as legislators in the House of Lords as the Law Lords had. The Constitutional Reform Act transferred the judicial functions of the Lord Chancellor to the President of the Court of England and Wales. The President is the head of the judiciary and represents its interests to the government. The Lord Chancellor no longer sits as a judge or represents the judiciary, and no longer must be a lawyer or a peer. The Constitutional Reform Act enshrines a duty of governmental ministers to respect judicial independence. In a dramatic move signaling his determination to diversify the bench, Lord Falconer named a woman of Indian descent, Baroness Usha Prashar, the first chair of the Judicial Appointments Commission in October 2005.[44]

Despite these seeds, it was not until the discussion of constitutional reform that the issue of women and the judiciary was substantively raised. How did feminists ride this wave of judicial reform and attach the issue of a gender-integrated bench to it? Clearly, women were woefully underrepresented in the judiciary. Although Parliament outlawed the exclusion of women from the legal profession in 1919, the Lord Chancellor did not appoint the first woman English High Court judge, Elizabeth Lane, until 1965. The next twenty years saw only five more women added to the High Court bench. The number of women in the legal profession, however, was rapidly increasing. In 1973, only 13 percent of newly admitted solicitors were women and 10 percent of those called to the Bar.[45] Since then, women have flocked to legal studies and are now more than half of all law students. The percentage of female solicitors has grown tenfold since 1984: Law Society annual statistics reveal that in 2008/9 women made up 46 percent of solicitors on the Roll and 60 percent of admissions to the Roll, while the Bar Council reports that 34.4 percent of barristers in 2009 and 52 percent of those called to the Bar in 2008/9 were women.[46] Despite these increasing numbers, though, women still face many obstacles to full participation in the legal system. Not only are they paid much less than men,[47] but they leave the profession in much higher numbers.[48] One in three reports sexual harassment.[49] Studies report barriers to women's success at each point in their career, from obtaining a pupilage to getting clerks to assign them work.[50]

Lord Irvine argued that the problem was simply the pipeline. Once women became more than half of all law students, it would only be a matter of time before they trickled up to QCs and judges. But despite a torrent in the pipeline, no trickle occurred. And though the size of the judiciary in England and Wales increased tenfold—from 300 in 1970 to 3,000 in 2000—the percentage of women appointed to the bench remained unchanged.[51] The case of Britain shows clearly that the composition of the judiciary does not change seamlessly as a matter of course as the pool of candidates widens to include women. Instead, feminists have to make a case for women judges. But in Britain this demand did not come about due to grassroots mobilization or any surge in public awareness of gender inequality. Instead, it arose as a result of what Rochon has called "critical communities"— groups of thinkers who put forth new ideas about an issue.[52] They do not necessarily mobilize to change the political structure. Rather, they offer a way to think about a social problem and possible remedies for it. Though members of a critical community may cross over into a social movement that seeks to put these ideas into action, the existence of a critical community in itself will not bring about large-scale change. This absence of mobilization is exactly what we see when we consider the case of women and the judiciary in Britain.

LITIGATION HELPS CHANGE THE DISCOURSE AND REFRAME THE ISSUE

Just as agenda-setting scholars tend to overlook gender and women's issues, they overwhelmingly focus on the legislative process. In Chapter 4, I focused on how important the executive branch is to setting the agenda and policy implementation. And especially in the United Kingdom, the land of parliamentary sovereignty, political scientists have ceded the study of the judicial branch of government to legal academics and ignored the role of litigation in politics and the policy process.[53] As I will discuss in Chapter 7, social movement scholars have also tended to be skeptical about whether courts and litigation can bring about social change. So far, the story of the UK has been one of a narrow pool of eligibles and a recalcitrant gatekeeper. Feminists had to tie their demands to the issue of modernization. But an equally important, and easily overlooked, decisive factor in this story is the role of lawyers and litigation in helping to change the discourse and reframe the issue. Lawyers were an important part of the critical community and they helped change the discourse about gender diversity in the UK judiciary. Legal groups, feminist organizations, and advocates for women's issues used the political openings afforded by Labour to broaden the focus on an out-of-touch judiciary to reframe the issue as about equal employment opportunities, legitimacy, and representation.

First, the critical community applied equal employment opportunities norms to judicial selection. Britain's Sex Discrimination Act of 1975 prohibits employers from treating either sex less favorably than the other (direct discrimination). But it also prohibits indirect discrimination—for example, using a height requirement or paying part-time workers (who are predominantly women) less than full-time workers. Discrimination law has mandated a set of practices as well as created a normative discourse about fairness. Though critics charge that the law has failed to deliver equal employment opportunities and is more advantageous to male plaintiffs than to women, it is clear that personnel practices now make it more difficult for men simply to hire their friends without drawing up a job description, advertising the job, and assessing each applicant on written criteria.

Although these norms have never been extended to the process of judicial selection,[54] two court cases attempted to extend them to the hiring of governmental legal advisers. By extension, this could then be applied to the process of selecting judges. The first case was brought by Josephine Hayes, a barrister, against Attorney General John Morris over his appointment of Philip Sales as First Treasury Junior. Hayes headed the Association of Women Barristers and blasted the Lord Chancellor in the fall of 1997 for abandoning Labour's pre-election pledge to create a judicial appointments commission.[55] She claimed that using the system of secret soundings to appoint Sales was discriminatory and disfavored women. The case was settled when Morris contributed an undisclosed amount to charity so as to avoid an embarrassing public hearing.[56]

Jane Coker and Martha Osamor brought the second case against the Lord Chancellor when, in 1997, Lord Irvine appointed Garry Hart as his special adviser without advertising the post or considering other candidates. Coker was a solicitor with twenty years' experience and had been short-listed for the job of assistant recorder. Osamor was Nigerian and an adviser in a law center, though not a lawyer. Both challenged Hart's appointment under the Sex Discrimination Act and EU Equal Treatment Directive, with Osamor also bringing suit under the Race Relations Act.

The employment tribunal gave the direct discrimination claim short shrift. But in a bold and surprising move, it upheld Coker's claim of indirect discrimination. The law of indirect discrimination has four components: the employer must have imposed a neutral requirement or condition; fewer women than men must be able to meet it; it cannot be justifiable; and it must be to the detriment of the complainant. In this case, the tribunal found that the neutral requirement was that all acceptable candidates must be personally well known to the Lord Chancellor. It determined that fewer women than men could comply with this requirement, and that the Lord Chancellor failed to justify the requirement. It was to Coker's (but not Osamor's) detriment. The tribunal found that the 1,500 pages of documents the Lord Chancellor submitted, which included equal opportunities policies for his department, merely "put into sharp relief the inadequacies of the Lord Chancellor's personal way of proceeding in respect of the appointment under scrutiny."[57] Nor was it persuaded that the longstanding practice of appointing special advisers justified the outcome. The tribunal also "accepted as obvious . . . that 'word-of-mouth' recruitment tends to perpetuate discrimination situations."[58] It concluded: "We do not say that all such posts should be subject to civil service recruitment standards, only that the particular minister should ensure that his selection is free from discrimination."[59]

Both the Lord Chancellor and Osamor appealed. The Equal Opportunities Commission (EOC) decided to support Coker as one of the three cases it brought to promote women's greater participation in public life.[60] Julie Mellor, chair of the EOC, said:

> The arguments against his method of appointing his special adviser are exactly the same as those against the traditional way of appointing judges. Having transparent selection procedures and recruiting from a wide pool of people not only helps employers ensure they are not discriminating against certain groups of people, it also enables them to appoint the best people for the job.[61]

Ultimately, however, the employment appeal tribunal panel held that although the Lord Chancellor did impose a requirement that the candidate be well known to him, doing so did not have a disparate impact on women because the pool consisted of only one person—Garry Hart.[62] Moreover, because Coker did not know about the job until the announcement of Hart's appointment, she had suffered no detriment. The minority view of the tribunal was that Coker *did* suffer a detriment—namely, the opportunity to be considered for a post.[63]

The *Equal Opportunities Review* argued against the tribunal's reasoning:

> Garry Hart was an excellent appointment, but that was not the point. The vacancy was filled by word-of-mouth recruitment, a process notoriously prone to discrimination . . . This decision raises the spectre that employers

can circumvent the constraints of discrimination law . . . by selecting their candidate in advance . . . So the result of *Coker*, if it stands, would be to create a category of exceptions to the legislation that would operate in respect of appointments of specially privileged people by specially privileged people. The idea that you cannot show indirect discrimination in respect of the filling of a job vacancy if you did not know the vacancy was being filled is a novel gloss on the statute, and one with little merit to it.[64]

Neither of the plaintiffs won the legal battle, but they did win the discursive battle. In this case, they helped make a connection between equal employment opportunities norms and the process of judicial selection. And the conceptual leap of seeing the selection of judges as an employment process governed by equal employment laws was a critical step forward. As a result of these cases, the Lord Chancellor's system of secret soundings was brought to light and depicted as exclusionary, anachronistic, and out of step with modern hiring norms. Moreover, the legitimacy of the Lord Chancellor's office and the conduct within that office were called into question. The practice of secret soundings and the clubbiness of the insider circuit of senior barristers and male-dominated committees are examples of what sociologists call "homosocial reproduction"—a selection process by which employers select individuals who are socially similar to themselves[65]—which has long been recognized as disadvantageous to women in other contexts.

These two cases were not about judicial selection, and the Commission for Judicial Appointments was not involved. It did, however, share the plaintiffs' position that the judicial selection process—the "tap on the shoulder" system of secret soundings—looked more like a discriminatory process of homosocial reproduction (continuing the all-male clubbiness of the inner circle of the legal profession) than the meritocratic system Lord Irvine touted. The commissioners, widely experienced with post-1975 employment requirements of nondiscrimination in their fields of education and business, brought equal employment opportunities norms to bear, finding "a picture of wider systemic bias . . . [and] evidence of narrow and inappropriate views about who is suited" for judicial positions.[66] It rejected the claim that women would naturally trickle up.

British feminists and feminist groups framed the issue as a question of representativeness and diversity. Certainly, British feminists were slow to wage an organized campaign to change the composition of the judiciary. But leading public intellectuals did connect the narrow stratum from which judges (nearly all male) were chosen and the adverse policy outcomes and the poor treatment of women in court. In the 1980s, for example, Judge Bertrand Richards fined a man £2,000 for raping a seventeen-year-old girl. He said the girl had been "guilty of contributory negligence" because she had hitched a ride home after missing the last bus. Women organized a mass demonstration in London and called for the judge to be removed from the bench. The legal establishment rallied around Richards and stressed the importance of judicial independence. Some feminist legal theorists used such incidents to argue that the law was irretrievably male. Although they did not help form a movement to advocate for more women on the bench, activists later drew on these discursive resources.[67] In its 2010 report, the Advisory Panel on Judicial Diversity stressed the need for the judiciary to reflect the population, and also framed its argument in terms of equal opportunities and legitimacy.[68]

Feminist activists have also been propelled by wider policy discussions in the European Union. At the 1993 Vienna Conference, they demanded an International Criminal Court to hear cases about crimes against humanity, including gender-based claims, such as rape in war. Preparation for the 1995 Beijing Conference linked British feminists more deeply to an EU network that used the language of gender mainstreaming and called for gender balance in decision-making. During the campaign to appoint women to the newly established International Criminal Court, British feminists joined an international coalition, mobilized for action, and deployed representational discourse to the composition of courts. Groups such as the Women's Equality Unit, the Fawcett Society, and the National Alliance of Women's Organizations have begun to extend the EU-led discourse about women in decision-making to the judiciary. (In Chapter 6, I take up the issue of the gender diversity of a supranational court—the European Court of Justice.)

By 1996, advocates for more women on the bench in Britain used the composition of domestic courts (all-male) to criticize outcomes in cases. In a letter to *The Times*, Josephine Hayes and Daphne Loebl, both barristers, expressed their outrage that some High Court judges were forcing women to undergo Caesarean sections without their consent. They asked:

> Is it a coincidence that the judges of our High Court, and the appeals courts to whom they must answer, are nearly all men, while all those on the receiving end of these orders are women? We think not. What collective experience of giving birth have the higher judiciary? What collective understanding have they of the violation involved in cutting open a healthy adult's womb against her will? Half the population is virtually unrepresented on the bench.[69]

Both the European Court of Justice and the UK's higher judiciary are concerned about improving their legitimacy, and the appointment of women to the bench may be a convenient means to that end.

Beginning in 1995, the Association of Women Barristers and the Association of Women Solicitors organized conferences in which Lord Irvine was called to account for the low numbers of women judges and QCs. The media covered these events, which kept the issue in the public eye. On the occasions when groups such as the International Bar Association or the World Women Lawyers Congress met in London, well-known public figures such as

Cherie Booth and Helena Kennedy used the platform and the ensuing media attention to call for more progress.

Events in 2002 are illustrative. At the one-day Women Lawyers' Forum, Booth issued her most hard-hitting criticisms of the system yet, saying that "an old boys' network" was to blame for women's underrepresentation at all levels of the legal profession.[70] The small number of women judges, she argued, undermined public confidence in the judiciary. The Lord Chancellor's Department responded that Lord Irvine had done much to promote equal opportunities.[71] As we can see from Figure 5.2, however, such publicity was relatively low level and never reached any kind of crescendo until the constitutional reform crisis. Thus, although women lawyers may not have created a social movement to press for the advancement of women judges, they did create the first vehicle for holding the Lord Chancellor publicly accountable, something neither the Labour Government nor Parliament appeared able or willing to do.

In October 1997, the Labour Social Security Secretary and Minister for Women, Harriet Harman, issued a press release stating that as part of the government's determination to tackle domestic violence, Lord Irvine had taken important steps to increase the number of women judges. In what the *Daily Mail* reported as "a withering slap-down,"[72] the Lord Chancellor's Department immediately responded that "we cannot have positive discrimination and all appointments must continue to be made on merit."[73] Moreover, the statement said: "The Lord Chancellor has the fullest confidence that all judges, regardless of gender, already deal with cases of domestic violence with impartiality and consideration for the victims of domestic violence."[74] Described as "the most spectacular and embarrassing public telling-off yet administered to a senior member of the Blair Government,"[75] the statement left no doubt as to whom the Lord Chancellor believed had exclusive right to speak about the composition of the judiciary. Harman was not to be deterred, though. On June 5, 2002, the *Guardian* reported that she was promoting a special scheme of law scholarships to bring more women (and lawyers from ethnic minorities and working-class backgrounds) into the judiciary and championing the right of crown prosecutors to become judges, noting that Black women, in particular, had made few inroads into the judiciary in the UK.[76]

Unlike the previous highest-ranking woman in the judiciary, Baroness Elizabeth Butler-Sloss, both Lady Hale[77] and Lady Justice Mary Arden, one of only four women on the Court of Appeal, often speak out on the need for more women judges. For instance, at the 2008 annual meeting of the Association of Women Barristers, Arden issued a "blistering" attack on the continuing lack of women appointed to the bench, highlighted by the legal editor of *The Times*, Frances Gibb.[78] Arden noted that in the last three years, twenty-nine men and only one woman had been chosen. Moreover, the sole woman merely replaced another who had died, meaning no progress toward gender equality had been made. Gibb noted that the new Judicial

Appointments Commission was under scrutiny for its poor performance on diversity in the higher judiciary, although women had made some progress on the circuit and district benches.

These episodes notwithstanding, it was an important court case in 2001 that made the biggest discursive leap in extending the question of political representation to the judiciary. In *R v A*, the Fawcett Society expanded the discourse of representation to include courts and took its case to the Law Lords.[79] In this case, a male defendant charged with rape argued that the Youth Justice and Criminal Evidence Act of 1999, which precluded him from adducing evidence of his prior sexual relationship with the alleged victim, violated his right to a fair trial under Article 6 of the European Convention for the Protection of Human Rights and Fundamental Freedoms incorporated into British law by the Human Rights Act of 1998. The Fawcett Society filed an application for permission to intervene in the case.

The application to intervene argued that, without women on the panel— at least two of the five—the court would not comprise an "impartial tribunal" as required by human rights treaties. It argued that an impartial tribunal is essential for the public to have confidence in the courts in a democratic society. All twenty-seven people eligible to hear an appeal—twelve Lords of Appeal in Ordinary (Law Lords), fourteen other Lords of Appeal (former Lords of Appeal in Ordinary), plus the Lord Chancellor—were men. The Fawcett Society argued that, in the Youth Justice and Criminal Evidence Act, Parliament sought to balance two competing rights—the right of the defendant to a fair trial and the right of the woman not to be examined on her past sexual conduct—and that if an all-male court set aside the balance struck, such a decision would have grave democratic consequences.[80] When deciding this very question in a different case, three women justices sat on the Canadian Supreme Court.[81] The Fawcett Society argued that for a fair-minded person to conclude that justice is done, at least two women must participate in the decision.

The Fawcett Society's brief had little legal impact—the Law Lords denied the petition to intervene and did not refer to the petition or the issue in its opinion. Thus, in its decision concluding that the defendant did have a right to question the alleged victim on a prior sexual relationship, the Law Lords made no mention of the Fawcett Society's argument. Yet a connection was made between international treaty obligations on women's political participation and the composition of the English bench. Such a connection paved the way for future cases and debates highlighting the UK as a laggard in diversifying its judiciary by international standards and as a country not in compliance with its international treaty obligations. The brief moved beyond mere criticism of sexist judges to a demand for a representative judiciary. The intervention questioned not just the representativeness of the judiciary but the legitimacy of an all-male panel. Judges and leading politicians may not have been concerned about equality for women, but they were concerned about the public perception that the judiciary was out of touch.[82] The brief's significance, then, lay in providing an important discursive shift. Erika Rackley has argued that Lady Brenda Hale brings such a different perspective to her decisions in the Law Lords.[83] In the end, feminists in the UK have made progress in framing the argument, despite limited mobilization behind the issue. They have linked their cause to other efforts for judicial reform.

By comparison, women judges in England have been slow to organize.[84] At the 2002 meeting of the International Association of Women Judges in Dublin, only five English judges attended, and several were clearly prodded to do so from above at the last minute.[85] The UK delegation was smaller than those of Canada and the United States. It was also smaller than the delegations representing Uganda, Taiwan, and Nigeria. But the UK Association of Women Judges was founded in 2003, under Lady Hale's leadership, and, after modest beginnings, it has now doubled in size to boast more than 200 members. It hosted the biennial meeting of the International Association of Women Judges in 2012. Hale wrote the first textbook on women and the law, calls herself a feminist, and has written about why it is essential to have more women on the bench.[86] Women judges in the UK now have a leader—an articulate spokesperson who has a scholarly career studying the significance of gender. The group responded to the Lord Chancellor's consultation papers on increasing judicial diversity and constitutional reform, organizes regional and national meetings, and advocates for a gender-diverse judiciary.[87]

In 2009, a group of legal academics formed the Equal Justices Initiative to promote the equal participation of men and women in the judiciary in England and Wales by 2015. They track and disseminate data on appointments, circulate policy material, speeches, and commentaries, and respond to consultation documents and events. They have succeeded in expanding and organizing the critical community advocating for a gender-diverse bench beyond the sphere of legal correspondents and individual academics but have not yet succeeded in a broader mobilization.[88]

Rochon recognizes the role of the media in legitimizing critical communities.[89] Newspaper coverage of the gender of judges over the last twenty years is indicative in this regard. Because the papers in the UK have clear political lines, journalists are free to take clear positions, such as arguing for the appointment of more women judges. And they have. For instance, Clare Dyer and Marcel Berlins, in the *Guardian*, and Frances Gibb, in *The Times*, have often placed the issue front and center. These writers regularly observe the low numbers of women on the bench and the absence of women from the Law Lords. Leading barristers such as Cherie Booth, Vera Baird, and Helena Kennedy receive serious attention rather than ridicule from these journalists when they criticize the composition of the judiciary. The journalists also quote the heads of the Association of Women Solicitors and the Association of Women Barristers. Figure 5.2 demonstrates how a feminist critical community raised the issue of women in the judiciary in the media. This coverage did little to sustain movement for policy change, but it did contribute to the wider public perception that judges were out of touch.

CONCLUSION: REFORMING THE PROCESS, DISAPPOINTING RESULTS

On June 12, 2003, when Prime Minister Blair announced that he would abolish the office of Lord Chancellor and reform the Constitution, the new Secretary of State for Constitutional Affairs, Lord Falconer, emphasized that no woman had ever served on the Appellate Committee of the House of Lords, known as the Law Lords.[90] In doing so, he framed gender diversity as a priority. Feminists helped achieve this end by attaching their demand for a more gender-diverse bench to the call for modernization of the judiciary, rather than creating a wave of social change themselves. Most importantly, they helped remove the major obstacle of the Lord Chancellor himself. In a 2002 interview, Cherie Booth had despaired that women would never make any progress on the bench under Lord Irvine. As Kingdon has noted, changes in personnel, most often resulting from elections, can dramatically alter governmental agendas.[91] Had the Lord Chancellor decided himself that he wanted more women on the bench, he could have appointed them easily, without being forced to do so by parliamentary committees, journalists, or feminists. Instead, he blocked the issue, and his monopoly of power allowed him to continue to do so until Prime Minister Blair removed him.

In this case, feminists seized the opportunities provided by powerful emerging discourses on equal employment opportunities and representation. These were modern discourses that dealt as much with updating the judiciary as with gender equality. The UK feminists successfully connected these modernization discourses to a gender agenda, or rather highlighted the inherent gender issues embedded in these discourses. In terms of equal employment opportunities, though employment laws may not apply to judicial appointments, the norms of fairness that this discourse upholds and promotes are being applied to questions of judicial selection. If the pool of eligible women differs vastly from the numbers of women on the bench, increasingly commentators will draw the inference that discrimination has occurred. As I will show in the next chapter, the European Union has issued statements on the importance of women participating in decision-making and, at last, this discourse has spilled over to the bench. Gender is now viewed as an appropriate basis for representation at various political levels, including the judiciary. Moreover, many policies, such as rape laws, are now widely recognized as having a gender dimension. Formulating these sensitive policies without any women's consultation or participation is increasingly regarded as illegitimate.

Focusing on the discursive aspects of politics and the uncoordinated actions of individuals who litigated and constituted a critical community highlights the importance of this case to our understanding of agenda-setting and policy change. Prior to the formation of the UK Association of Women Judges and the Equal Justices Initiative, Cherie Booth, Helena Kennedy, Josephine Hayes, Harriet Harman, Colin Campbell, Kate Malleson, Brenda Hale, the EOC, Fawcett, and others were not necessarily acting in concert to create a social movement around feminist policy initiatives.[92] Their actions were more serendipitous, random, and chaotic than conventional accounts of policy change. These players did create a discourse around equality and representation that might extend to the absence of women judges. They embedded these discussions in the larger question of modernizing the UK judiciary. Close inspection of Figures 5.1 and 5.2 reveals that while gender stories in the news increased dramatically in 2003, they were part of the larger story of constitutional reform. A mere 26 percent of the stories on constitutional reform mention gender. Figure 5.2 reveals that there has been a faint but steady drumbeat of stories on gender issues, but not a great groundswell of consensus. Policy change, in this case, was more incremental than dramatic. Indeed, even the major constitutional reform that occurred in 2003 was less the result of consensus than it was the result of incremental demands to modernize the UK's political system.

Many scholars of agenda-setting and social movements ignore the role of courts as arenas of discursive contest and law as a discourse.[93] Ignoring courts as political actors and as arenas for setting agendas and framing debates is especially strong in the United Kingdom, where there is little tradition of public interest litigation, where no written constitution empowers courts to review legislation, and where courts are not regarded as coequal political branches of government. A focus on courts should lead us to think more deeply about the influence of discourse in shaping the direction of policy change.[94] Litigation provided British feminists with the opportunity to frame the debate as one of representation, equal employment opportunities, and legitimacy. Feminists are not, by any means, setting the agenda by framing the issues on their own terms. They have, however, benefited from the government's framing of the issue as one of modernization.

In the end, feminists linked their cause instrumentally to the goal of modernization; they did not succeed in persuading policy-makers or the public that women judges were necessary. Lord Falconer's rhetoric and policy changes may have done more to create a consensus for women on the bench than necessarily have been a function of it, suggesting a reversal of our understanding of the policy process. A lesson for activists from this case might be to take heart because small, uncoordinated efforts of a critical community may yield significant results. For success, groups need not achieve consensus, but only persuade decision-makers, such as Falconer. Moreover, they may not even need to persuade such targets of the desirability of their cause (in this case integrating the judiciary), but rather that advancing their cause serves the target's other interests (in this case modernization).[95]

Developments since 2003, however, suggest caution and expose the limitations of such an approach. Just as those studying public interest litigation and particularly women's human rights, women's reproductive rights, and GLBT rights know, relying on courts too heavily as a public policy strategy may achieve some policy successes, but, ultimately, social movements need to garner a strong foundation of public support. Furthermore, advocates need to mobilize beyond their critical communities to ensure more success beyond a token first. Justice Brenda Hale continues to be the only woman member of the Supreme Court, even though two vacancies have occurred since her appointment. The Judicial Appointments Commission has enjoyed some success in encouraging women and minority men to apply for lower judicial office and has selected numbers consistent with their representation in the applicant pool, but it has made little progress in appointing women to higher judicial office.[96] An Advisory Panel on Judicial Diversity issued a report in 2010, calling for changes in the selection procedures to achieve a more diverse judiciary,[97] and the House of Lords Select Committee on the Constitution called for evidence for an inquiry on May 13, 2011.[98] Perhaps most discouraging is that recent discourse has returned to the "diversity as the enemy (rather than the servant) of merit" argument in both the call for evidence and recent parliamentary hearings. It is troubling that the Justice Secretary, Kenneth Clarke, had no idea how many women sit on the Supreme Court.[99] In other places, too—Ontario (Canada), Victoria and Queensland (Australia), and South Africa[100]—we have seen spikes in the number of women judges that have not been sustained because no organized group continued to press the case. Once the constitutional moment passed, or the key decision-maker who valued diversity left, the momentum faltered. Piggy-backing discursively to another item on the agenda, in this case modernization, is a clever strategy of the weak, but it has its limitations and cannot be a substitute for a broader mobilization.

This case does, however, show the value of exploring agenda-setting through a gender lens by looking at how the absence of women in the higher judiciary became a problem. More thoroughgoing policy change may require broader consensus in the policy community as well as a sustained mobilization of outsiders who will hold policy-makers accountable. As Kingdon points out, policy windows can close quickly.[101] While advocates for gender equality have succeeded in finally getting a woman appointed to the highest appellate court, creating a Judicial Appointments Commission, and having women appointments to lower courts better reflect their representation in the qualified labor pool, they have not succeeded in changing the overall composition of the higher judiciary. Attaching the issue of gender equality to modernization may have been enough to break the barrier of a woman first and eliminate the largest obstacles for women in the judicial appointment process, but it has been insufficient to generate a deeper commitment to gender equality, which is necessary to move women from token to parity.

6

A CASE FOR REPRESENTATION: THE EUROPEAN COURT OF JUSTICE[1]

A GENDER THEORY OF A REPRESENTATIVE JUDICIARY

Political scientists and feminists alike often fail to recognize courts as political institutions and judgeships as decision-making positions that require gender balance. So it comes as no surprise that theorizing about the concept of representation has almost exclusively focused on non-judicial elective offices. Nor is it a surprise that few political scientists have conducted a gendered analysis of the concept of representation or questioned whether women must be represented in all political institutions, including the judiciary. This chapter attempts to fill both lacunae by offering a non-essentialist gender analysis of the concept of representation as it extends theories of representation to the judicial branch. Because it is a supranational court—a hybrid of an international, federal, and constitutional court—where national representation is clearly operative in selection processes, the European Court of Justice (ECJ),[2] the highest appellate court of the European Union, provides an excellent location for bringing a gender lens to an analysis of courts as representative institutions. Analyzing discourse around the membership of this court is particularly helpful in generating arguments to help make a non-essentialist case for women judges in Chapter 8.

A gender analysis of courts as representative institutions, however, does more than shine a spotlight on two heretofore neglected aspects of important political concepts. Dissecting how courts are representative institutions allows us to question the true relevance of principal agent and acting-for models of legislative and executive representation. In short, other forms of representation, upon closer reflection, may be more like judicial representation than we had previously assumed. Similarly, focusing on the absence of women and the rejection of gender as a legitimate representative factor exposes how often judicial selectors fail to employ narrow standards or legal merit as the decisive criterion and how often other factors, such as representation, politics, and even cronyism, shape judicial selections. This chapter's analysis, therefore, is directly relevant to those interested in representation, even if they are indifferent to equality for women, uninterested in gender, and not particularly interested in courts and law.

Because the very notion of judicial independence requires that judges apply the law rather than take instructions from their political appointers or any other constituency, follow polls, appeal to majorities or what is popular, or even follow their own policy preferences, many have concluded too readily that courts, unlike legislatures, are therefore not representative institutions. In this chapter, I shall boldly argue against conventional wisdom and assert that courts, particularly supranational and federal courts, *are* representative institutions, even if their representative functions differ from those of legislatures. Representation of geography, nationality, legal system, and area of legal expertise has routinely factored into judicial selection processes, as have other non-merit factors—most importantly, having a close relationship with the appointer. Yet, strangely, when women or minority men demand representation on courts commensurate with their proportion of the population or the legal profession, opponents assert that courts are not representative institutions, decry the terrible precedent-breaking deviation from a pure merit standard, and predict a precipitous drop in judicial quality.[3] It is impossible to advance a gender argument about courts as representative institutions without also speaking to the fundamental issue of what judging is. But before I develop a gender theory of judicial representation, I must first describe the court, the appointment process, the women members, and the history of advocacy for more women members.

The ECJ has been a key engine in increasing the effectiveness of EU policy instruments that promote equal treatment,[4] so much so that Susan Millns has labeled the ECJ's championing of gender equality "judicial gender mainstreaming."[5] A higher percentage of women serve in the European Parliament than in most member state national assemblies. Yet, the ECJ has lagged behind many member state highest appellate courts, if not international courts,[6] in the number of women serving as members.[7] The Court of Justice had had only one woman member until Ireland appointed Fidelma Macken in 1999. With the Netherlands' appointment of Alexandra (Sacha) Prechal in June 2010, a total of seven women have now served as judges, and five as advocates general. As of August 2010, five of twenty-seven judges are women and three of eight advocates general (nearly 23 percent). Like so many other courts and law schools, the ECJ's robing room is lined with portraits of retired members. The passage serves as a daily reminder to the eight women of their exceptionalism.

Women in the United States and Canada actively campaigned to increase the number of women judges in the 1970s.[8] Justice Sandra Day O'Connor joined the US Supreme Court in 1981; Bertha Wilson joined the Supreme Court of Canada in 1982, seventeen years before a member state appointed a woman judge to the ECJ. European feminists were much slower to extend the demand for women in decision-making to courts, first voicing that demand in preparation for the 1995 U.N. meeting in Beijing, strengthening that demand with the addition of Sweden, Finland, and Austria to the European Union, but not really developing the case until 1999, when the European Commission published a report: *Women and Decision-Making in the Judiciary in the European Union*. Given feminist organization around the European Union more generally, feminists have mobilized surprisingly little around the issue of women members of the ECJ. Before I examine their efforts and arguments in greater detail, I must first describe the appointment process to the ECJ.

HISTORY OF JUDICIAL APPOINTMENTS TO THE EUROPEAN COURT OF JUSTICE

It is not surprising that feminists have been slow to tackle the issue, because the process of selection is secretive and idiosyncratic to member states, and the court issues a single collegiate judgment and is studied more for its doctrines than its politics.[9] The European Union's founders considered different methods of selecting judges,[10] including a role for Parliament similar to the Assembly of the Council of Europe's role in choosing judges for the European Court of Human Rights.[11] The Court of Justice of the Coal and Steel Community had no requirement that judges have any legal training, only that they be independent and competent.[12] The Treaty of Rome, which created the European Community, required judges to be able to fulfill the conditions required for holding the highest judicial office in a member state. Article 223 of the Treaty of Amsterdam stated that the judges and advocates general shall be appointed by common accord of the governments of the member states for a renewable term of six years. The Committee of Permanent Representatives (COREPER) circulated the names of the national nominees to member states.[13] In reality, each member state government had "unfettered discretion"[14] to follow its own internal selection procedure and simply informed the Council of its nominee. One scholar of the ECJ has observed, "In practice, no Member State openly questions the candidate put forward by any other Member State— common accord is generally always achieved."[15] After the 2007 enlargement, twenty-seven judges now sit on the ECJ, one from each member state. Also sitting are eight advocates general, chosen by the same selection processes as judges. Members are former judges, civil servants, politicians, practicing lawyers, or professors.

As Voeten noted, "International judicial appointments rarely incite much public scrutiny. This leaves government officials free to browse their preferred networks for suitable candidates."[16] One explanation is that Europeans accept and consider a higher degree of secrecy normal; consequently, judicial appointments are among many matters left to elites. In Britain, for example, Parliament neither scrutinizes nor approves judicial appointments,[17] and only in 2002 did the British Parliament create a Judicial Appointments Commission. The Austrian Government's decision in 2000 to submit the name of Christine Stix-Hackl to the National Parliament after open hearings is the exception. Britain advertised and sought applications for the first time when replacing Advocate General Francis Jacobs in 2006,[18] after following a similar procedure for its appointment to the European Court of Human Rights in 2002. Even the appointees themselves claim to know little of the processes that led to their own appointment.[19] Member states choose members of the ECJ within "the muffled atmosphere of ministerial cabinets and diplomatic meetings."[20] Judge Mancini observed that "few supreme courts in the western world are so lacking in links with democratic government."[21]

One reason why judicial appointments receive so little attention is that Europeans view the relationship between law and politics differently from Americans and Canadians; they see law as separate from politics. As Shapiro and Stone Sweet have noted: "Unlike the United States, where political science has always counted 'public law' as one of its sub-fields, European social science has noticed law and courts, if at all, as discrete parts of larger projects: for example, the sociology of lawyers as part of the sociology of the professions."[22] Scholars and judges alike resist classifying and studying the ECJ as a political institution, despite its evolving constitutional status. This denial of the political role of courts persists, notwithstanding the increasing role of national courts in shaping public policy in France,[23] Germany,[24] and the United Kingdom,[25] as well as the growing impact of supranational courts[26] and the ECJ's recognized role as the engine of European integration.[27] Members of the ECJ are deeply suspicious of any political participation in choosing judges, even from member state governments, let alone from legislatures or, horror of horrors—as in some American states—the electorate.

Each country faces the task of representing its own set of interests and cleavages: party, language, region, legal system, governmental department. Just as the Council takes great care to balance and distribute the leadership of EU institutions among the member states, a different balancing process occurs within the member states themselves. They may distribute court appointments —advocate general, judge, judge at the General Court, or across international courts, such as the European Court of Human Rights, International Court of Justice, or International Criminal Court[28]—among parties or languages. Appointments to the ECJ sometimes display many of the same features of diplomatic appointments: exile for a party luminary who is in trouble; a retirement prize for exemplary public service; the removal of a competitor within a party; or a consolation prize for a failed judicial appointment at home.

Appointment to the ECJ has always been political in the sense that personal connections to the appointing executive, family connections, and party credentials are paramount, even if the appointments are not necessarily motivated by specific policy goals.[29] Voeten speculated that what he found for the European Court of Human Rights is most likely also true for the ECJ: member states more favorably disposed toward European integration choose their judges accordingly, concluding "politics plays a role in international judicial appointments, as it does nationally."[30] Burrows's interviewees' declaration that "political affiliation is indispensable for nomination to the ECJ in Germany" has been echoed in interviews of scholars examining other countries.[31] Member states do not make appointments exclusively on merit. The Belgian Government's appointment of Melchior Wathelet in 1995 drew the wrath of Members of the European Parliament who were concerned about his judicial abilities and events during his tenure at the Belgian Ministry of Justice.[32] Ireland, too, has appointed politically connected top jurists who may know little EU law. Cearbhall Ó Dálaigh, former Attorney General and Chief Justice of Ireland, served fewer than two years and left complaining of difficulty with both the French language and EU law. Appointments may be delayed in anticipation of a change of national government, and member states have occasionally chosen not to renew a judge's or advocate general's mandate because of political ideology and policy differences.[33] But perhaps most importantly, the principle of one judge per member state trumps any merit determination. At best, the judge is the most meritorious Luxembourgeois or Cypriot judge, *not* the best candidate throughout the European Union.

The Council created an entirely new system for selecting members of the European Civil Service Tribunal, established in 2004. It abandoned the principle of unfettered state discretion (the secret "tap on the shoulder" system) and the principle of one position for each member state. Candidates now apply through an open competition and a committee comprising former members of the ECJ, the General Court (formerly the Court of First Instance), and lawyers of recognized competency gives an opinion on candidates' suitability, recommending twice as many candidates as vacancies. Rather than having a judge from each member state, the Tribunal has just seven members and the Council must balance geography and national system, but not gender. Following the recommendation of former President Ole Due, the Convention on the Future of Europe had proposed that member states select judges and advocates general from a list developed by an advisory panel.[34] Hazel Cameron, the UK member of COREPER at the time, reported a majority of member states agreeing to an application procedure, but the other changes were controversial and took three presidencies to resolve.[35] The compromise of the committee recommending twice as many nominees as vacancies meant the Council, rather than the committee, remained the decision-maker. Despite the Council's statement that the process for the Tribunal, a specialized body, should not be considered a precedent for other judicial appointments,[36] the precedent of applications, expert examination of credentials, and abolishing one position for each member state dramatically changed judicial selection.[37]

The Lisbon Treaty, which came into force on December 1, 2009, amended Article 255 of the Treaty on the Functioning of the European Union and changed the appointment process for members of the ECJ. A panel of seven persons chosen from among former members of the ECJ and the General Court, members of national supreme courts, and lawyers of recognized competence, one of whom is proposed by the European Parliament, acting on the initiative of the President of the Court of Justice, now gives an opinion on candidates' suitability to perform the duties before the Council acts on a member state's appointment. The Council appointed two women and five men to the panel.[38] One of the women, Ana Palacio Vallelersundi, is a lawyer and a former member of the European Parliament. Only one judge, Sacha Prechal, has been appointed under the new process and received a favorable recommendation by the panel. Three appointments to the General Court may have been rated unsuitable by the panel: Greece withdrew its appointment of Christos Vassilopoulos; Romania withdrew its nomination of Judge Valeriu Ciucă; and Hungary resubmitted its appointment of Judge Otto Czúcz. Unlike its announcement of Judge Prechal, the Council issued no statement saying the panel had approved Judge Czúcz.[39] Blogger Pescatorius pointed out that the panel is no more transparent than member states, nor its criteria, nor even, it seems, its decisions.[40]

THE FIRST WOMEN MEMBERS

Prior to 1999, only France had appointed a woman, Simone Rozès, to the ECJ as advocate general, in 1981. Rozès had served as a judge on the Tribunal de la Seine before being appointed President of the Tribunal de Grande Instance. She oversaw the École Nationale de la Magistrature for the Ministry of Justice and subsequently left the ECJ to serve as the first president of the Cour de Cassation. ECJ President Josse Mertens de Wilmars remarked on the significance of her appointment—"a reflection of the finest spirit of modern times"—and on the ECJ's commitment to equal treatment for men and women in its rulings. He declared that France chose her neither because of nor in spite of her gender, but because she was the best person for the job.[41] The appointment of Rozès was not the result of feminist agitation or a deliberate intention on the part of France to advance the cause of women. France has enjoyed a high number of women judges overall, although women are disproportionately clustered at the lowest ranks.[42] It is not surprising, then, that the first woman member of the ECJ came from that country. Although, in 1994, one of the French members confided to me in an interview that his chief judge had advised him not to take the appointment "too seriously," which I interpreted as meaning that French judges at the time saw appointments to the ECJ as something of a sabbatical from the real work of the judiciary, which was done by French courts.

One of the important functions members play is hosting delegations of lawyers or law students visiting the ECJ from the member states. And it does not escape the notice of women law students, who routinely make up half or more of these groups, that few women have served. When I attended oral arguments in 1994, delegations would ask the information officer why there were currently no women on the ECJ. I, too, asked why the ECJ had only ever had one woman member. Staff were clearly defensive about this issue. The well-rehearsed answer was that the fault, if any, lay with the member states, and the new Scandinavian members could be counted on to appoint women members (as if only the Scandinavian countries had women, or women lawyers). As it turned out, it was Ireland in 1999 and then, among the new members, Austria and Slovenia, not the Scandinavian countries, that appointed women to the ECJ (although Finland and Sweden appointed women to the Court of First Instance in 1997). Not until 1994 did the absence of women generate any press notice,[43] and then it was merely a passing comment.

In 1999, Ireland appointed the first woman judge, former High Court judge Fidelma O'Kelly Macken, a barrister specializing in commercial law who also taught at Trinity College, Dublin. Characteristic of the low level of press attention any ECJ matter receives, most accounts confined themselves merely to noting that she was the first woman judge. Macken refused my request for an interview. According to her staff person, Mona Hickey, "She feels that she would not be in a position to contribute anything constructive to your research and therefore an interview would not be fruitful."[44] Apparently, Judge Macken actively discouraged framing her appointment in terms of gender. The tone of the *Financial Times*, however, was different. Entitled "Her Turn," the article stated:

> Not that the Luxembourg-based body is itself entirely free from the spectre of sexism. It seems that Macken is, amazingly, the first woman judge to sit on the court in its 47-year history. (People at the court blame the member states for only putting forward middle-aged males up to now.) It is almost worth taking action over.[45]

Judge Macken did grant an interview with New York University professor Joseph Weiler on September 4, 2003.[46] She described both her parents as feminists, especially her mother, who was poised to compete for Ireland in the Olympics at the time of partition. She declared, "Every judge who has been appointed to the Court of Justice has had some political connection,"[47] and said her predecessor at the ECJ had wanted to come back to the Irish Supreme Court as soon as there was a vacancy, which happened to be right after the Irish Government appointed Macken to the Irish District Court. But the most important factor, she argued, was gender:

> They wanted to appoint a woman. We have a very strong background in this area; we have our second woman President at the moment and the

very first woman permanent representative, who has the status of ambassador to the Community, was an Irish woman also. The second woman appointed to the Court of Auditors in Luxembourg is an Irish woman. So they really wanted to appoint a woman and they asked me if I would go.[48]

Weiler asked Macken how relevant it was to her function as a judge that she was Irish and a woman. She declared that it mattered "not at all" in terms of being Irish, since one removes one's national hat entirely and dons a European judge's hat.[49] As to being a woman, she found "nothing to distinguish me in any way whatsoever"; and, despite being, like all Irish women she alleged, "feisty," she thought her colleagues treated her no differently from any other judge. Nor did she think it mattered to have a woman judge on the panel in cases of gender discrimination.[50] After Ireland renewed her for a second term, she returned to the High Court in 2004 and then the Irish Government appointed her to the Irish Supreme Court in 2005.

For feminists, Germany's appointment of Ninon Colneric to the ECJ in 2000 was a watershed; yet it, too, generated little publicity. Colneric has a Ph.D. from the University of Munich and has been a part of the European Union's Equality Network. As President of the Labour Appeals Court of Schleswig-Holstein, she worked to dismantle the barriers to women serving as lay members of industrial tribunals simply by grouping openings so that several positions could be filled simultaneously. She left the ECJ in 2006.

Advocate General Christine Stix-Hackl also arrived at the ECJ in 2000, to become the third woman serving at that time. She had a background in legal diplomacy after completing her legal studies at Vienna University and the College of Europe, Bruges. Not only had she been on the team negotiating Austria's accession to the European Union and the European Economic Area, but she had argued cases before the ECJ, having worked in the European Commission's Legal Service and served as head of the European Union's Legal Service in the Federal Ministry of Foreign Affairs. Austria's selection process differs from those of most member states: the government submits the candidate's name to the legislature and both houses and the President must agree. Hearings are open and the qualifications are presented and defended. When I interviewed her, Stix-Hackl reported that gender played little role in the discourse surrounding, or the justification for, her appointment, although *Zeit Online* reported her "flashing a smile" when she reported that she was "only the second woman" to hold the post of advocate general.[51] At an address to the Congress of the European Women Lawyers Association in Budapest in 2006, Stix-Hackl noted that the Court of First Instance was more balanced, with nine out of twenty-five judges being women, compared to two (plus three advocates general) out of thirty-three at the ECJ.[52] She added: "Given that a wide array of backgrounds should be ensured among the members of courts at a European or international level, member states could also contribute to ensuring a certain representation of the plurality of our 'European' society by being more open to appoint women to the ECJ."[53]

After noting the ECJ had declared nondiscrimination on grounds of sex to be a right and had championed women's equality, and that the European Union had instituted gender mainstreaming and positive action, Stix-Hackl did not argue that women judges generated different outcomes: "Community law is increasingly shaped and applied by women and has, to a significant extent, incorporated the specificity of women's situation. Whether there is an interaction remains, however, difficult to evaluate."[54] She left the ECJ in 2006.

Spain appointed Rosario Silva de Lapuerta in 2003 and renewed her mandate in 2009. She served as state legal counsel in Malaga and at the Ministry of Transport, and then at the legal services of the Ministry of Foreign Affairs, where she headed the unit dealing with the ECJ and later handled EU matters for the Ministry of Justice. She served as a member of the Commission's "reflection group" on the future of the Community's judicial system and headed the Spanish delegation on reform of the Community's judicial system in the Treaty of Nice. She also served as a member of the Committee on the Future of the European Legal System (which issued the Due Report that recommended retaining one judge per member state but making the term a single, non-renewable one of twelve years),[55] and as president of the Fifth Chamber and the Seventh Chamber.

Also in 2003, Germany appointed Juliane Kokott as advocate general. Kokott received her Ph.D. from the University of Heidelberg, studying the Inter-American system for the protection of human rights. She received her LL.M. from American University, Washington, D.C., as a Fulbright Scholar, and also studied at the Academy of International Law in Tunis, the Max Planck Institute, the University of California, Berkeley, and Harvard University. She held a chair in International Law, International Economic Law, and European Law at the University of St. Gallen, Switzerland.

Slovenia appointed Verica Trstenjak as a judge of the ECJ in 2006. Trstenjak had previously served for two years as Slovenia's judge on the Court of First Instance after the Slovenian Parliament voted overwhelmingly to support her nomination.[56] A professor since completing her doctorate of laws, she studied in Germany, Switzerland, and the Netherlands, served in several governmental capacities, including as head of the Legal Services, participated in numerous lawyers' associations (president of the Association for European Law, 2003 Lawyer of the Year for Slovene Lawyers), and published widely on private law.

Pernilla Lindh had served for eleven years on the Court of First Instance when Sweden appointed her as a judge on the ECJ in 2006, replacing Stig von Bahr. In a rare press commentary on the gender composition of the ECJ, the *Herald Sun* (Melbourne) erroneously announced Lindh as one of the "First Women Judges for the Court of Justice" (even though Finland was appointing Virpi Tiili to the Court of First Instance, and the article later noted that

Advocate General Rozès had been the first woman to serve on the ECJ).[57] The *Guardian*, under the mildly diminutive heading "Women's Day," noted the first two women members of the Court of First Instance but announced they were the first in the ECJ's forty-three-year history, without noting Rozès, Macken, or Trstenjak.[58] The Australian *Age*, under a list of international events involving women, had previously noted Tiili's and Lindh's appointments to the Court of First Instance.[59] Lindh had served as a judge on the Stockholm District Court and on the Stockholm Court of Appeal. She had been the legal adviser in the office of the Chancellor of Justice, legal adviser and director general of the Legal Service of the Trade Department of the Ministry of Foreign Affairs, vice-president at the Swedish Market Court, responsible for legal and institutional issues at the time of the European Economic Area negotiations, and deputy chairperson of the European Free Trade Association group at the time of Sweden's accession to the European Union.

The United Kingdom appointed Eleanor Sharpston advocate general in 2006 (and reappointed her in 2008), making her the first woman appointed to the ECJ by Britain and the first member appointed by that country to be selected in an open competition. Sharpston grew up in Brazil and studied economics and modern languages at King's College, Cambridge, where she also did graduate studies in law. She was called to the Bar, and then held various academic posts teaching European law. Her scholarly publications focused on the EC single market, principles of EC law, EU enlargement, and European citizenship. For five years, she practiced law in Brussels and then served as Judge Gordon Slynn's *référendaire* (law clerk) for three years. She appeared in over fifty cases before the ECJ on behalf of and against the UK Government, as well as in cases before the European Court of Human Rights. She "took silk" (became a Queen's Counsel) in 1999. Sharpston received a "Blue" for rowing at Cambridge, sails square-riggers, plays the violin and classical guitar, and the photo in the *Times* announcing her appointment pictured her in full motorbike gear—in leathers, holding a helmet.

Romania appointed Camelia Toader to the ECJ as a judge in 2007. Her career, like those of many of the others, spanned work in academia, serving on the bench, and working on legal and European matters for her national government. After earning her doctorate in law, she became a professor of civil law and European contract law. She held visiting appointments at the Max Planck Institute and in economics at the University of Vienna. She served on the Court of First Instance in Buftea and later Bucharest, and then as a judge on the High Court of Cassation and Justice between 1999 and 2006, participating in reform of the Romanian legal system. She served as head of the government's European Integration Unit and taught at the National Institute for Magistrates. Romania renewed her mandate in 2009 and her colleagues elected her president of the Eighth Chamber where she, like many of the other members, is no doubt well served by her fluency in European languages: German, French, and English.[60]

Austria appointed Maria Berger as its first judge to the ECJ (making its first two appointments to the court women) in 2009. Berger had studied law and economics, received a doctorate in law, worked as a university lecturer and briefly as a university administrator when she began working for the Federal Ministry of Science and Research, and then served as head of European integration at the Federal Chancellor's Office. She was elected a Member of the European Parliament in 1995, headed the Social Democratic delegation, and served on the Legal Affairs Committee and as a substitute on the Constitution and Women's Rights committees. She became Minister of Justice in 2007 and championed a domestic partnership law for same-sex couples.[61]

The appointment in 2010 of Alexandra (Sacha) Prechal was an even more important milestone for gender equality than the appointment of Ninon Colneric. Prechal is a leading authority on EU gender equality law, a recognized leader of the European Union's Gender Equality Network (its coordinator for sixteen years[62]), and committed to the realization of equality for women as a human right. Although she has not served as a national judge, her credentials are impeccable: Ph.D. thesis on the doctrine of direct effect, former *référendaire* at the ECJ, professor of European law, member of the Dutch Academy of Arts and Sciences, member of the editorial board of numerous EU law journals, and principal investigator on EU law research projects, such as on the coherence of EU law. She is a member of what Cohen would call the family of EU law insiders.[63] She is multilingual, knowledgeable about EU law and the workings of the ECJ, and poised to contribute significantly to doctrinal development on the integration of human rights jurisprudence, one of the most important challenges facing the ECJ and an area of her special expertise. It is hard to think of a more qualified Dutch citizen, and it is very unlikely that her gender or feminism gained her a higher place in the queue. Nor does any evidence suggest that feminists campaigned for her appointment or that the Dutch were especially motivated to appoint a woman. Nonetheless, it is also hard to think of a judge better situated to contribute to the advancement of equality jurisprudence because of the depth and breadth of her legal knowledge and her insider's understanding of the workings of the ECJ, and EU law generally. More so than Sir Gordon Slynn, the British advocate general and then judge who served on the Employment Appeal Tribunal and was knowledgeable about equality law, Prechal is a sophisticated analyst of equality doctrine and feminist legal theory,[64] networked to her counterparts throughout the European Union, and an architect of proposals for improving equality law.

THE EUROPEAN PARLIAMENT CHAMPIONS THE APPOINTMENT OF WOMEN

A few voices have demanded increased public participation in judicial selection. For instance, joined by the occasional editorial writer[65] and Thomas Goppel, the Bavarian Minister for European Affairs,[66] *The Economist*[67] has called for either the European Parliament or national parliaments to play some role in judicial selection. The ECJ, with a few exceptions, however, has been adamantly against such involvement as a threat to judicial independence. From its call for a committee to screen candidates, it is clear that it largely wants to restrict the role of political decision-makers (including the executives of member states) rather than expand the discussion of who should serve and what makes them qualified. Nor has the ECJ as a collectivity been a voice for championing greater diversity in the selection of its members.

Members of the European Parliament first raised the question of judicial selection and the gender composition of the European judiciary to little effect. The European Parliament's power lies more in its ability to question and scrutinize the Council than in proposing and controlling legislation, although its powers are growing concomitant with the widening scope of EU activities and worries over the so-called "democracy deficit."[68] The most important decisions are made secretly by non-elected bodies (the Commission, the Council, and the ECJ).

Parliament has made repeated requests for a greater role in judicial selection. As early as 1980, MEPs Hellmut Sieglerschmidt and Ernest Glinne submitted written questions to the Council asking why Parliament had no role in selecting judges and why the process differed from that of the Council of Europe.[69] In 1982, as part of a proposed reform of the treaties, Parliament once more called for greater participation. In 1989, with the creation of the Court of First Instance, 261 MEPs signed a written declaration calling for member states to appoint women to that court. In 1993, the European Parliament passed a resolution calling for it, in conjunction with the Council, to appoint judges to the ECJ by majority vote for non-renewable terms of nine years. This proposal was then incorporated into the Parliament's proposed constitution. Furthermore, also in 1993, MEPs Siegbert Alber and Manuel Medina Ortega argued that the ECJ's transformation into a constitutional court rendered the intergovernmental method of selection outdated. MEP Ortega claimed it lacked "transparency and democratic accountability" and called on the Council to consult the Committee on Legal Affairs and Citizens' Rights. Members of the Legal Affairs and Women's committees do not seem to have pressed the issue since, although feminists objected to the small number of women appointed to the convention to draft a new constitution.[70]

Why did member states not appoint the first woman judge until 1999? The pipeline or pool argument does not provide a satisfactory explanation. Although women in Europe have joined the legal profession in numbers comparable to the United States, they have only recently been able to penetrate the inner circles from which member states make prestigious judicial appointments. In the United Kingdom, for example, women may be barristers, professors, or even Queen's Counsels (top 10 percent of the Bar), but they have not served as Treasury Counsel. Ireland, likewise, had always sent one of its top three judicial officers to the ECJ. Fidelma Macken was a barrister and professor but "only" a High Court judge. Qualified women abound, but if member states set as the criterion cabinet member and best friend of the prime minister, rather than competent jurist, fewer women than men will meet the standard. In the last five years, however, we have started to see women candidates present the specialized credentials that are valued in appointments to the ECJ: service as *référendaires*, professorships in European law, judicial experience, and experience in legal ministries managing accession or EU matters. If the Council, or even member states, made judicial appointments in groups rather than singularly, they would be more likely to look for balance and representativeness.

DEVELOPMENTS POST-1995

The year 1995 was a turning point for advocating for women members on the ECJ. The European Union actively participated in the Fourth World Conference on Women in Beijing,[71] which resulted in calls for the balanced participation of women and men in decision-making that the Fourth Action Programme for Equal Opportunities codified (1996–2000) and the Council supported by a recommendation to member states.[72] The Beijing Declaration and Platform for Action called on governments and international institutions to "aim for gender balance when nominating or promoting candidates for judicial and other positions in all relevant international bodies."[73] Appointees from three new member states (Austria, Finland, and Sweden) also actively promoted greater gender equality.

The demand for equal participation in decision-making took some time to trickle into the legal arena. Anasagasti and Wuiame's 1999 report, *Women and Decision-Making in the Judiciary in the European Union*, was the first occasion when the Council, the Commission, the Directorate-General for Employment, and the Equal Treatment Unit addressed the paucity of women on the European bench. Director of Social Dialogue, Social Rights, and Questions of Equality Odile Quintin opened the report by recognizing the balanced participation of women in decision-making in all sectors as one of the objectives of the Fourth Action Programme for Equal Opportunities between women and men.[74] The report declared: "The balanced participation of women and men in decision-making is considered crucial to the legitimacy of representative and advisory bodies, and therefore also our European democracies . . . The judiciary influences society at all levels and it is therefore crucial that women form a significant presence within it."[75] The report also pointed to the increasing law-making power of judges and mirrored the gender bias taskforce investigations in the United States. The investigators conducted a survey of men and women on the bench and collected data, and, while they recognized that the number of women judges is increasing, they documented both vertical segregation (the glass ceiling) and horizontal segregation (ghettoizing women into a few specialties). The recommendations of the report are familiar: to identify the discretionary criteria (being known to top male decision-makers) that enables some judges (men) to rise to higher levels of appointment; to make the procedures more open and transparent; to generate policy support at top levels; and to monitor the percentage of women. Lastly, the report challenged member states and the European Union to examine working patterns that favor male norms, make family life difficult, and create hostile working environments and conditions.

The survey revealed that the overwhelming majority of respondents believe that a judge's gender makes no difference. A significant minority of judges (more women than men), however, believes that gender makes a difference in certain kinds of cases, such as violence against women. The report discusses the structure of the judiciary and path to higher office in member states and notes that only Austria and Sweden have a positive action policy in favor of women in the judiciary. Interviewees criticized the years-of-service criterion for promotion as well as the objectivity of so-called merit criteria. The variation among the number of women judges in member states is intriguing, and the gap between the number of women lawyers, women in member state courts, and women in European courts is unexplained. Public prosecutors were the most vocal about barriers to achievement, and the survey revealed that women judges were more likely than men judges to report barriers to women's advancement.

In the 1990s, the European Union shifted its policy from equal employment opportunities to "gender mainstreaming," a term not used in the United States. Gender mainstreaming moves beyond the arenas of equality law or even women's issues to analyze all policies for their potential effect on equality between men and women.[76] Just as preparing an environmental impact statement would require developers to assess how their proposed projects affect the ecosystem, a gender mainstreaming analysis goes beyond disparate impact or indirect discrimination analysis in employment discrimination. So-called neutral standards—such as being close personal friends of the appointers, having many years of service, or having uninterrupted employment—can disproportionately exclude women more than men. Gender mainstreaming brings a gender lens to the evaluation of all policies, rather than having the women's or equal opportunity office over in the corner working on narrowly defined women's issues. In the United States in the 1970s[77] and Britain in the 1990s,[78] feminists, as well as calling for more gender-balanced results, demanded changes in the process of selection, removing it from the exclusive purview of the elite of the legal profession and calling for the inclusion of lay members on merit advisory panels. As I described in Chapter 4, they demanded that the pool of candidates be widened and that the list of qualifications be rethought.

In 1997, the Amsterdam Treaty made equality between men and women (as opposed to just equal treatment in employment) a central goal of the European Union and explicitly affirmed positive action.[79] The German *Länder*, or states, had each actively debated their equal opportunities policies and had come up with different results.[80] Yet, according to Judge Colneric, when the ECJ struck down an affirmative action policy in *Kalanke v. Land Bremen*,[81] German feminists for the first time openly criticized the all-male composition of the court. As I described in Chapter 5, British feminists made similar arguments about the illegitimacy of the all-male Appellate Committee of the House of Lords (known as the Law Lords) deciding whether a rape shield law violated a defendant's human right to a fair trial. In 1997, member states amended the Treaty of Rome to add Article 13, which prohibited discrimination in relation to race, ethnic origin, sexual orientation, religion or belief, age, or disability, giving equality constitutional status.

Although those who pressed for more women in decision-making positions in the European Union did not generally mention judges or courts, the logic of their arguments could easily extend to them. Equality law may not apply to judicial appointments, but its discourse, underlying rationale, and decades of evolution of employers' sense of what constituted best practice reasoning started to make judicial selection processes seem anachronistic and difficult to defend.[82] The critique of an all-male bench resonated, not only because principles of equality and gender mainstreaming were becoming more accepted in the European Union, but because the European Union felt itself vulnerable on the question of democratic legitimacy and public approval. In the 1990s, defensive ECJ staff predicted that the new Scandinavian members of the European Union would help to break the court's all-male monopoly, and they were not too far wrong. Despite its aspirations to be the gender-equal state,[83] Sweden did not appoint a woman to the ECJ immediately, but a Swedish woman judge was the first to invoke EU equality law to challenge her country's selection of a man for its first judicial appointment to the court.

LITIGATION FRAMES WOMEN'S ABSENCE AS DISCRIMINATION

In 1995, Sweden appointed Hans Olof Ragnemalm—a former professor of public law, Dean of the Law Faculty at the University of Stockholm, Parliamentary Ombudsman, and judge on the Supreme Administrative Court of Sweden—to the ECJ. Brita Sundberg-Weitman, a district court judge, wrote to the Equal Opportunities Ombudsman, protesting the dearth of women from the 150 top judicial posts in Sweden and arguing the selection system had discriminatory effects in violation of the EU's Equal Treatment Directive.[84] In reply to the Ombudsman's letter asking which criteria had been applied in Ragnemalm's selection, the Ministry of Justice wrote that it had no obligation to supply him with this information and the Ombudsman closed the case. Sundberg-Weitman brought her case to the Stockholm District Court, which held it need not refer the case to the ECJ, that Ragnemalm was clearly the superior candidate, that the Equal Treatment Directive did not apply, and that Sundberg-Weitman was not eligible for damages. Sundberg-Weitman claimed her Ph.D., published books and articles on EC law, greater practical experience in Swedish law as a long-serving judge, and fluency in French made her the stronger candidate. While conceding that her French was probably better, the district court said she was not on the same internationally recognized prestige level as Ragnemalm, who was more like other member states' nominees. She argued Sweden's practice of looking for the person with the highest prestige was indirectly discriminatory against women.

On appeal to the Labor Court over the district court's determination that she pay costs (approximately $10,000), Sundberg-Weitman argued the district court never answered the question as to what the relevant criteria should be—it merely declared its evaluation of her as inferior. She noted that only three of sixty-five deans, six of forty-seven professors of law, and six of forty-one members of the Supreme Court were women, making it difficult for women to obtain the relevant high-prestige qualifications. Moreover, she noted that, at the time, not one woman was serving on the ECJ and, given these numbers, the burden of proof should be on the state to be transparent about what non-discriminatory criteria it was using. Lastly, she argued that awarding costs against her was a deterrent to those seeking to vindicate fundamental rights. The Labor Court ruled that Ragnemalm was the most meritorious candidate and that Sweden's appointment of Pernilla Lindh to the Court of First Instance demonstrated that women could succeed under current standards. It concluded that it should refer the matter to the ECJ only if it concluded Sundberg-Weitman had been discriminated against, but said it was not its place to develop selection criteria for appointments to the ECJ. Because Ragnemalm was most like the other ECJ judges in qualifications, appointing him could not hurt women.

Sundberg-Weitman lodged a complaint with the European Commission's Legal Service, and Linda Steneberg, Swedish Representative to the Commission, inquired about the complaint. In a letter dated September 16, 1998, Odile Quintin, head of Directorate General V (which deals with equality matters) and author of the stirring introduction to *Women and Decision-Making in the Judiciary in the European Union*, wrote that Article 167 of the Treaty of Rome

> clearly leaves every Member State, within the criteria it defines, a complete margin of appreciation as regards the choice of the person it intends to submit for appointment. The same provision further stipulates that the appointment is made by the Member States and not by the Council. It is therefore not up to the Commission to comment.[85]

Moreover, she declared, the Equal Treatment Directive was not applicable to judicial appointments. What is now Article 253 of the Treaty on the

Functioning of the European Union (TFEU) specifies that judges are appointed with "the Common Accord of Member States." Nothing in the treaty requires one judge from each member state or that the other member states defer totally to each member state's selection. That is a matter of practice, not a requirement of the treaty. Sundberg-Weitman then brought her case to the European Court of Human Rights.

Although none of the British plaintiffs nor Sunberg-Weitman was successful in using equality law to challenge the exclusion of women from high judicial office, these cases show that plaintiffs and others are starting to apply the discourse of equal employment opportunities to judicial appointments, and it will be increasingly difficult for member states to continue their closed system of selection if they continue to appoint only men, or disproportionately few women, to the ECJ.

MAKING GENDER REPRESENTATION AN EXPLICIT REQUIREMENT

The International Criminal Court was the first court to specify not only a fixed quota of women judges but that some judges have legal expertise on gender-based violence, particularly rape in war.[86] (I discuss the ICC further in Chapter 8.) Two other international courts, the African Court on Human and Peoples' Rights and the International Criminal Tribunal for the former Yugoslavia (ICTY), have gender requirements for the nomination and election process.[87] Next to these three, the Council of Europe, of which the European Court of Human Rights (ECHR) is a part, has gone furthest toward requiring gender diversity in its judicial selection process. Shortly after 2000, the Assembly of the Council required member states to submit a shortlist of three names, rather than simply announce its appointments (as member states do for the ECJ).[88]

When I interviewed him in 2002, Sir Nicolas Bratza, the first UK appointment to be chosen in an open competition in the UK and the first UK nominee to submit to this process, clearly regarded the Assembly as incapable of meaningful participation in the selection process. Since then, the Assembly has required member states to submit a list of three that contains no more than two members of the same sex. Malta repeatedly submitted a list of three men's names and the Assembly repeatedly rejected its nominations. Malta asked the ECHR to issue an advisory opinion as to whether such a requirement constituted sex discrimination in violation of European human rights laws. The court said that such a requirement did violate equality law if the Assembly did not allow for exceptions.[89] Malta finally submitted a list with one woman on it, and the Assembly chose Malta's preferred candidate—a man. But the Assembly also chose a candidate from Norway's list of three that was not that country's first choice. Clearly, the Assembly exercises far more selection power than the European Parliament, the Judicial Merit Body, or even the Council.

And it has chosen to press the issue of a more gender-representative bench. Just as the U.N. Security Council jettisoned its requirement of gender balance while vigorously upholding adequate representation of the principal legal systems of the world and an equitable geographical distribution when selecting judges for the ICTY,[90] the ECHR, in its advisory opinion, said that gender representation was not sufficiently important that it should trump nationality.[91] In short, Malta's 400,000 citizens must have a representative on the European Court of Human Rights, but the millions of women in the countries of the European Union need not.

ORGANIZING AND MOBILIZING FOR WOMEN

Women lawyers have occasionally raised the issue of a more gender-representative bench in Europe. As I described in Chapter 5, in the 1990s, the Association of Women Solicitors and Association of Women Barristers in the UK joined the Equal Opportunities Commission in demanding that the Lord Chancellor appoint more women to the bench and reform the judicial appointment system,[92] and more recently they formed the Equal Justices Initiative.[93] The European Women Lawyers Association held its founding conference in 2000.[94] In its statement on "The Obligation to Name Women for Top Positions" in 2009, however, it makes no reference to members of the ECJ.[95] The International Association of Women Judges has not chosen to focus on increasing the number of women judges. Anasagasti and Wuiame's 1999 report, *Women and Decision-Making in the Judiciary in the European Union*, followed a similar format to the gender bias taskforce reports in the United States that I described in Chapter 4, but it failed to inspire women to take up the issue of gender bias in the courts or to campaign for more women on the bench. European women have not organized or mobilized in any systematic way around the issue of women in the judiciary.

Perhaps because the ECJ does not hear cases on divorce and custody, domestic violence, or sexual assault, it fails to attract the attention of feminists whose EU lobbying is concentrated in their national capitals or in Brussels. Most ECJ personnel decamp to their nations' capitals on weekends, and not even journalists with an EU beat base their operations in Luxembourg. Litigation comes from member state courts that pose preliminary ruling questions of interpretation, rather than parties and litigants who seek redress and attend hearings in Luxembourg. All of these factors contribute to few feminists—even those with an EU focus—complaining about the composition of the judiciary, the way judges treat them, or the substance of the ECJ's rulings. Some question the framing of the problem more than the outcomes per se,[96] and merely appointing women members, as I argue in Chapter 1, is no guarantee of a feminist sensibility or a gender lens. Nonetheless, sitting in a Luxembourg courtroom as an all-male bench discusses the fate of Europe's women is troubling. To explain why, I now turn to thinking about courts as representative institutions.

REPRESENTATION AND THE JUDICIARY

Are courts representative institutions? What identities deserve representation? Should representativeness be a more important factor of consideration in the appointment of judges to supranational or international courts than to national or state courts? The answers to these questions depend both on what judging is—how courts are different from other political branches—and on what representation is. Pitkin distinguished between representation as "standing for" and representation as "acting for."[97] Legislators are clearly engaged in the latter—whether one sees their function as merely conveying fully formed, pre-existing interests and preferences, or as deliberating, constructing the policy agenda, and actively deciding what is best for the public, or at least constituents. Perry argues that any kind of "acting for" representation conflicts with judicial independence.[98] She distinguishes between appointments based on merit and those based on representativeness, as if the two factors were mutually exclusive. Clearly, if judges are representatives, the nature of that representation is different from that practiced by legislators. Rather than taking instructions from constituents, or at least acting in their interests and making bargains so as to ensure reelection, the judicial role requires judges to be independent rather than delegates. In a democratic system, judges are to decide cases according to law, not popular opinion, governmental instruction, or even their own policy preferences.

Perry's conceptual dividing line, however, obscures the fact that representativeness and other non-merit factors (meaning things other than legal acumen) have *always* played a role in judicial appointments,[99] particularly in judicial appointments to federal, constitutional, international, and supranational courts, and, more importantly, are defensible and legitimate considerations. The question is merely what identities need representing? Geography and political entity (region, state, nation, and legal system) have always been paramount. It is mere convention and not a requirement of the Treaty of Rome (and now of the TFEU) that has dictated that there be one judge from each member state on the ECJ.

Pitkin thought "standing for" representation irrelevant and that anyone could act for others, whether she shared an identity or not. Yet, I argue that representation in Pitkin's "standing for" sense is essential for legitimacy. As Solanke writes, "Diversity and independence are not ends in themselves, but means to an end: legitimacy."[100] The political consequences of not having a judge from each member state and the consequent problem of legitimacy become apparent when one ponders whether Ireland would accept a decision by the ECJ that it had to allow the advertisement of abortion services available in London if no Irish judge had sat on the case? Or whether Denmark would accept that it had illegally restricted contractors on a bridge to Danish companies if a Danish judge had not been president of the court that had issued the ruling? Or whether the United Kingdom would accept that the Equal Treatment Directive did indeed mean that employers could not fire pregnant workers if a former chairman of its own national Employment Appeal Tribunal had not sat on the case? Ensuring the compliance of national courts and governments has been difficult even when a member from the member state who can explain and defend the ECJ's rulings *has* participated in the case.[101] The Irish, Danish, and British judges neither "speak in a different voice" nor "act for" their countries in Pitkin's sense of principals and agents. Nevertheless, their absence would render the decision less legitimate for the same reason that all-white and all-male jury pools increasingly came to be regarded as illegitimate (as I discuss in Chapter 8). Justice must not only be done; it must be seen to be done. Without member state judges, it would be easier for critics of the ECJ to urge noncompliance with its rulings and characterize them as decisions of a remote or occupying power.

As the European Coal and Steel Community of six became the European Union of twenty-seven, the ECJ adapted by dividing itself into chambers and reducing the quorum for its plenary formation rather than hearing cases with the full court.[102] Some worried about how representative these smaller formations were, and whether small states would be able to decide cases affecting large states. Addressing this concern, former ECJ President Alexander Mackenzie Stuart recognized how participation from each member state's judges legitimated the ECJ's decisions:

> I dislike the word "representative" although it is one much used by commentators, particularly in the responsible government departments of Member States, since we do not "represent" anyone, but none the less, it is a word of some significance, if understood in the proper way. That is to say, *in order to carry conviction*, both to the litigant and the Member States, a decision of this Court should be pronounced by a body which represents a sufficiently broad spectrum of legal thinking. In the eyes of many, a Court of three is too restricted.[103]

Nation, then, becomes a proxy for legal thinking, even though several countries have more than one legal system (England and Scotland in the UK, for example).

In addition to member state and legal system, a third factor long recognized as important in the representativeness of courts has been political party.[104] In the European Union, each member state makes its own decisions as to how to balance party. In Germany, for example, judicial appointments alternate between the parties; in Austria, party affiliation is an indispensable qualification. Other exceptions to merit are the obvious ones of friendship, political connections, and political ideology. Rewarding friends, getting rid of competitors, and, allegedly, avoiding obligations to appoint particular women to seemingly more important domestic courts are all concerns that have shaped the composition of the ECJ. Representativeness is therefore not some horrible deviation from the ideal or practice of strict merit appointments. The Council does not choose the most qualified person in the entire European Union when a vacancy arises; it chooses one per member state, often alternating among parties, and selecting those who move in the circles of the appointers.

Perry's construction of a dichotomy between representation and merit is emblematic of a larger phenomenon that appears to be idiosyncratic to gender (and race), whereby calls for representativeness are denounced as particularly antithetical to merit selection.[105] This rhetorical linkage deserves further scrutiny. When treaty drafters proposed that members of the ECJ should be chosen by the common accord of member states, and that translated into a convention that one judge from each member state sit on the ECJ, I assume that nobody sneered, "Do you want just *any* Luxembourgeois judge?" or inquired whether the Council was supporting him *just because* he was from Luxembourg. When we require judges to have a certain number of years of practice, or to be balanced between areas of practice, no one questions, "Do you want just *any* old or experienced lawyer, or just *any* commercial lawyer?" Yet, to advocate for a gender-diverse bench inevitably triggers such questions. Any selection criterion that attempts to balance the ECJ, so that it represents the diversity of the European Union and legal practice, necessarily restricts the choice. Why is it not seen as a deviation from merit to exclude the possibility that the ECJ could consist of twenty-seven German judges but a terrible deviation from merit to prohibit it from being all male? Choosing the best woman judge is no more antithetical to applying merit standards than choosing the best Cypriot judge. The difference is that requiring diversity of nationality or geography has been accepted as a representative restriction, whereas gender diversity has not.[106]

Another frequent rejoinder merits scrutiny. Many have repeated "some version of Pennock's trenchant comment, 'No one would argue that morons should be represented by morons.'"[107] Once again, representativeness is framed as the enemy of merit with undertones of misogyny: "OK, you can have your women, but quality will suffer!" A parallel argument attacks with the reverse formulation: "We'll know we've achieved equality when we have as many mediocre women (judges, legislators, presidents) as men." The argument has the virtue of recognizing that merit selection has more often been honored in the breach. Defenders of President Nixon's lackluster appointments of Haynesworth and Carswell to the US Supreme Court, or Clark in California (see Chapter 7), have weakly declared something along the lines of "the mediocre need representation, too." Neither is a compelling argument for a particular nominee.

Merit is not an empty concept. I favor choosing well-qualified judges. They should be well versed in EU law (although not all have been) and fluent in French (although not all have been), possess astute legal minds, and have strong research and writing skills.[108] During its recent selection process for an advocate general, the British Foreign Office developed a list of criteria that included: good understanding of EU law; the ability to produce high-quality opinions; an awareness of how judicial decisions impact the legal systems of the member states; experience of legal practice; good interpersonal skills; good organizational skills; and knowledge of French.[109] But once past this threshold, in the top echelons of the legal profession, we should not pretend that we can easily rank candidates' merit rather than weigh a balance of factors, such as the value of having an intellectual property lawyer and a French speaker versus a more senior member of the judiciary or one with closer ties to governmental decision-making. But Perry's dichotomy between merit and representativeness also conceals similarities between legislators and judges, particularly judges of the highest appellate, constitutional, or international courts, such as the ECJ. The many advocates general Solanke interviewed in the course of her research emphasized the importance of knowing the law as well as their staff did, and of possessing the ability to write in a way that could be comprehended by the larger public and would not be subject to misinterpretation by the media.[110] They argued for the value of political as opposed to narrowly legal merit; or, to put it another way, that, at this level, solid legal decision-making required political judgment, not merely doctrinal exegesis.

Just as political theorists of representation would argue that in order to understand representation we need to know how we conceptualize democracy and legislative activity, similarly, in order to think about how judges should be representative, we need a theory of what judging is. Some decision-making is discovering the right legal answer in the sense that some decisions are more consistent with precedent or treaty provisions than others. But other forms of decisions mean having a conception about what the European Union is, for example, and what place the ECJ should have in bringing about that vision, rather than simply applying technical legal rules. So what does merit mean in such cases? The person who can recite the most case law? Or the one who crafts the best decision that ensures member state compliance? The one who has argued the most cases before the ECJ? Or the person most committed to the European ideal rather than defense of national sovereignty? Once judging is conceived as making choices about public policy, less justification exists for allowing only a narrow segment of the legal profession to serve. Nor can we easily operationalize what merit means and objectively declare which candidates are the most meritorious.

One sees this aspiration for a European policy visionary rather than a legal technician in current debates about reforming the European Union's judicial selection process.[111] First and foremost, the legal community is concerned about the threat to judicial independence posed by judges who serve only six-year renewal terms. Member states can decline to renew a competent judge or advocate general because they do not approve of his or her decisions (Germany did not renew Manfred Zuleeg in 1994, for example).[112] Similarly, reappointment (or renewal of mandate) provides an opportunity to have partisanship and political ideology play an even greater role in selection than it does in the initial appointment. Second, EU scholars also recognize the policy role of the judge, even though most commentators, like the legal community world-wide, would prefer that only an inner circle of lawyers choose judges, rather than opening up the decision to policy-makers, legislators, or citizens more generally.[113] But advocates general have stressed the importance of having an international outlook which goes beyond the national legal system, having a vision of EU law, being sensitive to trends within and outside of the ECJ, being able to modernize EU law, possessing a political position on European integration, and even being sensitive to the mood of the ECJ. These are not narrow questions of legal expertise.[114]

Openly recognizing the non-merit factors that have always been part of the selection process (geography, nationality, party, friendship, and political ideology) and recognizing the policy role judges play provide the foundation for reexamining representation in the judicial context. Judicial independence requires that member states, interest groups, and citizens do not directly lobby judges. Yet, all three have a very structured opportunity to do just that in the legal proceedings—the citizen by bringing a case; the member state by being the opposing party or intervening; and third-party interveners, such as the Commission, by submitting written observations. In labeling courts "the least dangerous branch," Alexander Bickel saw them as the "arena of principle," where citizens (or their legal advocates) "lobby" their judges through arguments, rather than by contributing money, ensuring their reelection, or taking them out to dinner to tell them how to vote.[115] In theory, principle, not power, governs; instead of counting preferences and consulting polls, judges weigh arguments. In the EU context, then, by design, judges are not accountable to citizens in the same way as legislators are. What Mansbridge calls "promissory representation" (making and keeping campaign promises) or even "anticipatory representation" (behaving in a way that you think will please voters) would be unethical.[116] Judges are not agents and voters principals.

Thinking about judges as representatives provides an opportunity to develop a more sophisticated view of judging, rejecting legal formalism, but also to develop a more sophisticated view of legislative representation, at least in the modern context of Western democracies. Especially in the American context, with separation of executive and legislative functions, safe seats, almost limitless campaign spending, and extremely low voter turnout, does it make sense to think about constituents and legislators as principals and agents? Mansbridge argues that once we think of representation as something other than a poor substitute for direct democracy,[117] only a deeper theory of democracy can help us figure out what our normative expectations of legislators should be. Her concept of gyroscopic representation, which comports more with the Burkean idea of the trustee, has a judicial parallel. "The representatives act like gyroscopes," she describes, "rotating on their own axes, maintaining a certain direction, pursuing certain built-in (although not fully immutable) goals."[118] The judge, unlike the legislator, is not supposed to act on his or her particular policy preferences (in a predictable, transparent, and principled way), but we expect her to act consistently on what she considers to be the best interpretation of the law rather than to cynically deploy principles to suit her naked policy preferences. As Howard Gillman demonstrates in his careful analysis of judicial decision-making in *Bush v. Gore*, we can see this principled consistency in practice when judges vote against policy preferences and the short-term interests of the political party that appointed them.[119] Judges, particularly the judges of each jurisdiction's highest appellate court, may not be democratically accountable to constituents in elections, nor take instructions from them, but they are acutely aware of how the public might respond to rulings and are anxious to have their decisions implemented and seen as principled, legitimate, in accord with the law, and good public policy.

In developing her theories of representation, Pitkin, like nearly all theorists, contemplates the legislator, not the judge. She dismisses descriptive representation because she sees legislators as "acting for" not "standing for" constituents. For Pitkin, no necessary relationship exists between one's characteristics and one's ability to represent one's constituency by carrying out their wishes or making sure their interests and perspectives are considered in deliberation. She anticipates the anti-essentialist turn of postmodern feminists and the findings of Elaine Martin I discussed in Chapter 2. Feminist men judges can advance the equality agenda just as antifeminist women judges can impede it. If women judges neither promote a singular women's point of view or different voice and style of reasoning, nor represent women in the sense of taking instructions from them, why must they be represented? One answer lies in returning to the arguments for representation of legal system and nationality. To say that a German must be on the ECJ does not necessitate showing that she decides cases differently from an Austrian. It is important to have a German judge on cases not for the narrow purpose of advocating German interests, but for bringing to bear on deliberations German ways of legally approaching an issue in light of Germany's precedent and history. For this to be intelligible, we have to infer neither a singular German interest nor a German point of view. The presence of a German judge is not merely for legitimacy in a limited and cynical sense to "sell" the decision back home, but is to legitimate the ECJ through that judge's agreement with the outcome and participation in the decision. If a German judge concludes that EU law dictates that the German Government has lost its case, one has more confidence that the "right" answer has been reached, just as when a feminist judge concludes that the current rape shield laws have gone too far and are now depriving defendants of their human rights. Justice must not only be done, it must be seen to be done, which is why the exclusion of women and minority men from juries became so troubling.

If one need not "stand for" in order to "act for" in Pitkin's definition—that is, if men can represent women and Italians can decide cases for Germans—

why are member states so determined to have their own representatives on the ECJ? And why are women, and minority men, troubled by the absence of their groups in legislatures and courts? Both Phillips and Mansbridge offer answers not steeped in a notion of essentialist difference, such as the argument that only those of a given identity can act for that group or that members of the group necessarily do. Phillips argues Pitkin is too quick to dismiss the idea of descriptive representation and perhaps should consider a weaker form of "acting for."[120] In arguing for positive action to increase the number of women legislators, she points out that even though we reject essentialism, feminists think the idea that men should speak and act for women is patronizing. Husbands and wives may often vote the same, but our notion of citizenship does not mean that we can exclude women from voting if their votes would not change electoral outcomes. Democracy requires that those affected by public policy should, if capable, participate in its development. To exclude them suggests that they lack the capacity for self-government. Including women on the bench indicates the belief that women are capable of judging and considering their experiences and perspectives is important to democratic deliberation. Moreover, it signals that judging, like politics in general, is not an exclusively male preserve.[121]

Mansbridge develops these arguments. She recognizes the limitations of the empirical evidence that claims women represent women's interests (or even think that they do).[122] Nor does a singular women's interest exist. Mansbridge makes the point that to say that men cannot represent women would be to offer up the corollary—that women cannot represent men, something feminists would be loath to concede. Unlike Pitkin, however, Mansbridge invites us to consider what features of the electoral (or, by extension, judicial selection) process have resulted in lower proportions of women, whether the members of the group consider themselves able to represent themselves adequately, and whether any evidence exists that dominant groups in society have ever intentionally made it difficult or illegal for members of that group to represent themselves.[123] The answers to these questions help refute the slippery-slope argument that, if we require gender representativeness, how will we be able to refuse the demand to represent the left-handed (or some other identity that is meant to be ridiculous). Mansbridge makes the additional important point that in the contexts of communicative mistrust and uncrystallized interests, vicarious representation by those who do not share the experience is unsatisfactory to the unrepresented.[124]

As we advocate for the experiences women bring to the bench, we must take care not to essentialize men's and women's differences. It is more significant that Ninon Colneric and Sacha Prechal have been part of the Gender Equality Network than that they, like Simone Rozès, are women. Sharing an identity does not directly translate into fixed judicial ideology. As Phillips argues, the more ill-defined the interests and weak the methods for holding representatives accountable, the more important is the question of who the representatives are.[125] Mansbridge puts it another way: "When interests are uncrystallized, the best way to have one's most important substantive interests represented is often to choose a representative whose descriptive characteristics match one's own on the issues one expects to emerge."[126] Surely, then, that is most true of the highest appellate courts that are setting doctrine and interpreting complex law. Both Mansbridge and Phillips argue that descriptive representation may alter how interests are framed,[127] and whether they are pursued with vigor. As judges assume ever more policy-making power and the European Union becomes ever larger, they run the risk of being further distanced from the experiences of the millions of people whose lives are shaped by their decisions. Given this awesome power, it is important that judges are drawn not just from the best legal minds of the European Union, but from the diversity of experiences within it. It is not a big leap from the unquestioned position that someone from the UK must be on the ECJ to the position that there must be women on the ECJ.

CONCLUSION

Examining how strongly member states cling to the importance of national representation on the ECJ demonstrates clearly that courts are representative institutions. Feminists are not deviating from established norms of judicial appointments in calling for women's representation; they are merely extending the argument to include gender along with nation, region, and legal system as one factor deserving consideration. Moreover, looking closely at how member states select judges shows that representativeness as well as other non-merit criteria have always been paramount in choosing members of the ECJ, as they have been for other international and constitutional courts.

Looking closely at why women deserve representation and how courts are representative institutions does, however, challenge legal formalist ideas about what judges—particularly judges on the highest appellate courts, constitutional courts, and international courts—do. It becomes harder to characterize legal decision-making as apolitical—not in the sense of taking instructions from political leaders or constituents, but in the sense of crafting the future legal and political order for Europe. When political theorists such as Jane Mansbridge and Anne Phillips bring a gender lens to thinking about legislative representation, the differences between what judges and legislators do shrinks, although it does not disappear. Just as they articulate a non-essentialist case for why women and minority men deserve legislative representation, this chapter makes the case for judicial representation of women and urges those interested in women's equality and gender balance in political decision-making not to overlook courts and judges.

Litigation in Sweden and the United Kingdom and developments over appointments to the European Court of Human Rights show that judicial selection systems that never generate women as the best person for the job will be increasingly subject to challenge under equal opportunities norms. Just as member states require national representation to give the ECJ's decisions legitimacy, all-male judicial panels ruling on positive discrimination, caring labor, abortion, and other sensitive gender issues will increasingly be seen as illegitimate. An ECJ that includes women members enhances the legitimacy of its decisions and shrinks the democratic deficit of the European Union, thereby enhancing compliance; it implements the European Union's policy of including women in decision-making; it acts in a consistent manner with its own promulgated norms of equal employment opportunities; and it institutes genuine merit selection. In making the case for women's representation on the ECJ, this chapter shows how a gender lens illuminates the concept of representation and how that concept is further developed by considering courts as representative institutions.

7

BACKLASH AGAINST WOMEN JUDGES[1]

Justice Sonia Sotomayor observed that she was subjected to a higher standard of scrutiny than men nominees to the US Supreme Court. For example, she was interrogated on personal matters, such as her divorce. She was even asked to name everyone she had dated.[2] Opponents attacked her as racist for musing that a wise Latina woman might dispense better justice on some issues, and they characterized her as mean and overbearing in oral argument.[3] Justice Elena Kagan, too, had her personal life scrutinized. The press openly speculated about her sexuality, not to mention her practice of sitting with her legs uncrossed.[4] Both women were trashed as "too fat."[5] What role does gender play in explaining this (mis)treatment? In this chapter, I consider the gendered treatment of women judges by analyzing forms of hostility and retaliation against them. I argue that these forms of hostility and retaliation constitute a backlash against women judges. And I use the case of Rose Bird, the first woman judge appointed to the California Supreme Court (in 1977) and the first California appellate judge to be voted out of office (in 1986), to illustrate the nature of this backlash.

Unlike theoretical concepts I considered in other chapters (e.g., emotions and social movements), scholars have already utilized the concept of backlash to think about gender. The term is most associated with Susan Faludi's book *Backlash*,[6] which argued that the 1980s saw an organized backlash against feminists. The concept of backlash can provide insight into the gendered underpinnings of judicial selection.[7] To make the gender aspects of judicial selection visible, I identify five separate examples and argue that they constitute a backlash against women judges. Women judges have faced tougher confirmation battles than their men counterparts; they have had their competence and objectivity more frequently and brazenly called into question; and they have been removed from office in states where judges are routinely retained. These are just a few examples of the ways in which women judges experience gender bias in the judicial system. When considered with others, they constitute a pattern that I label "backlash."

Antifeminists offer competing explanations for individual women's failures, women's slow progress toward equality,[8] and women's lower status.[9] Indeed, the evidentiary question of proving gender is at work is a difficult task for feminist legal scholarship and feminism more generally. To prove employment discrimination, for example, plaintiffs need to show more than that sexism occurred in the decision-making process or the workplace environment. They need to demonstrate a causal relationship—that an employer did not promote a woman because of gender bias[10] or that sexism rose to such a level that it created a hostile environment that impaired a woman's ability to do the job.[11] Moreover, they must aggregate a series of events to show an underlying pattern, rather than highlight individual isolated incidents. Feminists seek to show that men and women are subjected to different standards, but doing so requires a male comparator (i.e., "this would never have happened if she were a man"). This evidence is difficult to come by in the case of women judges, who are often women firsts. Thus, in this chapter, I restrict my analysis to reviewing the phenomena that may constitute a backlash against women judges and to illustrating the case of California's first woman chief justice, Rose Bird, in which all of these phenomena play some role.

THE CONCEPT OF BACKLASH

The term "backlash" emerged in the aftermath of the passage of the 1964 Civil Rights Act.[12] It denoted "a sudden violent movement backwards, as the recoil of waves or the rebound of a falling tree."[13] Mansbridge and Shames define backlash as a politically conservative reaction to social or political change.[14] Those in power resist attempts to change the status quo, reacting to their declining power. Backlash can vary widely, from ridicule and ostracism[15] to lynching and assassination.[16] Social movement scholars often use the term "counter-mobilization" rather than "backlash."[17] Opponents counter-mobilize because they see the tide of opinion and policy turning. If successful, they manage to preserve the status quo, as anti-abortion activists were doing at the state level when the US Supreme Court decided *Roe v. Wade*.[18]

The concept of backlash implicitly assumes that the reaction against women's progress is qualitatively different from plain old sexism: that is, women's progress unleashes a new force that is distinct from the forces that impeded their progress in the first place. Backlash has an important emotional dimension: women's progress unleashes rage. Mansbridge and Shames assert that the loss of capacity is experienced more intensely than the absence of capacity,[19] since position holders come to view their status as the natural order.[20]

They assert, too, that moving too far, too fast in the direction of social change can trigger backlash. In support of this claim, they reference *Brown v. Board*, which declared racially segregated schools unconstitutional, and *Roe v. Wade*, which held that the constitutional right to privacy encompassed a woman's right to an abortion.[21]

Sanbonmatsu entertains the "too far, too fast" claim in examining whether 1992, the Year of the Woman, triggered the Year of the Angry White Male.[22] She suggests that it may not be that women are progressing too quickly, but that some women in the vanguard violate gender norms. In this sense, backlash may be a form of social control against those who step out, rather than a reaction to women's progress per se. Women politicians and women judges are especially vulnerable to the charge that they violate gender norms. Hillary Clinton is too confident and ambitious; Sonia Sotomayor too mean.[23] Elena Kagan and Rose Bird were too single. Women who pursue a feminist agenda or fail to marry and parent may be particularly vulnerable, whereas women who do not may be more tolerated. The question of whether it is women's progress or individual women's gender nonconformity that triggers a backlash is difficult to answer.

Sanbonmatsu shows that as the number of women legislators increases, the opposition to them and their agenda increases, too.[24] Yoder, drawing on Blalock and Reskin, labeled this phenomenon "an intrusiveness effect."[25] The number of women in nontraditional fields surges, threatening the majority. The majority responds with hostility[26] to what they fear is "feminization."[27] Epstein described backlash as follows: "Like white cells surround offending matter, . . . [t]he new entrants may be sabotaged as the majority group, protecting its community, . . . musters its forces to control its culture and its boundaries."[28] Such hostility is well documented for women in nontraditional fields, from firefighting to soldiering.[29]

In light of the research on backlash, many scholars, Sanbonmatsu among them,[30] have called into question the idea that as women break down barriers, women's changing roles become normalized. Kanter, for example, initially hypothesized that as more women entered the workplace, they would suffer less from heightened attention and visibility, and probably would not be so encapsulated in gender-stereotyped roles.[31] In the afterword to the 1993 edition of her book, however, she acknowledges resistance could increase rather than decrease as women's numbers rise in the workplace.[32] Women tokens do not threaten the male ethos of an occupation and therefore the masculinity of its occupants.[33] They simply become honorary men.

In research on why the progress for women academics has been so slow, Backhouse uses the concept of "the chilly climate" rather than backlash.[34] But the chilly climate shares many of the features of backlash. Sarkees and McGlen,[35] for example, enumerate key features of the chilly climate in academia: derisive comments, hostility of colleagues, denunciation of feminist research, and a pronouncement that women can "write their own tickets" while men have no chance.[36] When the Massachusetts Institute of Technology identified measurable inequalities between men and women scientists—from salaries and square footage of lab space to the paltry number of women tenured professors and the absence of women from academic leadership—and began to equalize them, rumblings that MIT expended "too much effort to recruit women" emerged from faculty and students. Approaching equality in this case and others looks and feels like special treatment.[37] This phenomenon is not limited to academia. When more than 46 percent of Attorney General Rob Hulls's appointments to the bench in Victoria, Australia, were women, one senior barrister opined that it was an advantage *not* to have testicles.[38] Thornton concludes, "As the percentage of women appointed creeps toward 50 percent and approximates the proportion of women law graduates, complaints about the sacrifice of merit and the evil of affirmative action . . . become more vociferous."[39]

It is difficult to investigate empirically whether a slower rate of change is less likely to trigger a backlash. Keck, for example, examines the argument that state supreme court decisions on the right for gays and lesbians to marry are counterproductive because they fuel a counter-mobilization, secure policy reversals on gay and lesbian issues across the board, and set back a movement that has been proceeding steadily and incrementally.[40] He operationalizes backlash as a response to policy change in advance of public opinion that mobilizes opponents, undercuts moderates, and sets back the cause,[41] and debunks the argument that the supreme court cases went "too far, too fast." Other empirical investigations have demonstrated that states would not have moved incrementally toward abortion liberalization but for the Supreme Court's decision to legalize abortion. Post and Siegel[42] and Greenhouse and Siegel,[43] for example, carefully documented how the Catholic Church mobilized against abortion liberalization before *Roe*, how Republican strategists changed positions on the abortion issue to win Catholic voters, and how evangelicals did not join the cause until long after *Roe*. Thus, the anti-abortion movement had emerged and counter-mobilized *before Roe*, in response to shifts in public opinion and state efforts at liberalization.[44] Indeed, rather than being too far, too fast, Justice Harry Blackmun's opinion in *Roe* was consistent with majority public opinion, including Republicans, who supported abortion at higher levels than Democrats (68 versus 59 percent).[45]

The main text advancing a theory of backlash—Susan Faludi's blockbuster *Backlash*—did not explore the "too far, too fast" argument. On first read, the book reads like a catalogue of sexist episodes, rather than a carefully analyzed pattern. For Faludi, the agents of backlash in the 1980s were the media who created a narrative, a frame, to convince women that they had achieved equality but were miserable as a result. Faludi demonstrated that women were not miserable and that inequality, not equality, caused their suffering. Importantly, she denied that women had achieved full equality and argued that "the antifeminist backlash has been set off not by women's achievement of full equality but by the increased possibility that they might win it. It is a preemptive strike that stops women long before they reach the finish line."[46]

Derrick Bell is especially eloquent at deconstructing the parallel "racism is over" narrative and demonstrating how this narrative undercuts efforts to challenge ongoing racial oppression. Although he does not use the term "backlash," Bell articulates the mechanism of divide and conquer that allows racism to persist—picking out some winners to advance the argument that the game is fair but also keeping the have-nots from seeing their plight as shared.[47] Thomas joins this argument by articulating how the backlash narrative works to divide women.[48] Combining these two insights, we can see how the backlash narrative works by blaming individuals for their failure to advance rather than recognizing that racism (and sexism) still holds back groups of people. Hillary Clinton's electoral difficulties were caused by her individual failings, not because she was a woman; women are not CEOs because they have "chosen" motherhood (rather than that they have "chosen" motherhood out of frustration with a glass ceiling in the workplace). Whether the phenomenon at present is a group-based pattern or an individual situation is disputed.[49]

THE FIVE KINDS OF BACKLASH AGAINST WOMEN JUDGES

I define and operationalize backlash somewhat differently from Faludi. In my view, backlash is not simply a narrative or frame in response to women's progress, but more a repertoire of conservative responses that includes narratives and actions. The force of backlash brings powerful narratives to the fore. In the judicial system, those narratives include the idea that representativeness and diversity are the enemies of merit, women would ascend to the bench if they were qualified, and the appointment of women signals the abandonment of merit and the primacy of special interest politics. But there are also concrete acts to consider as part of our understanding of backlash. As the legislative literature has found, backlash may involve policy setbacks.

With respect to the judicial system, I identify five phenomena that constitute backlash. First is the discrimination faced by women judges in the judicial selection process. Women are more likely never to receive a hearing or a vote, take longer to confirm, and are disproportionately likely to lose confirmation votes. Second is direct hostility to women's ascendancy to the bench— the denial of the professional courtesy that judges routinely and heretofore universally extend to all other judges, independent of party, ideology, and ability. It is the failure to let women into the fraternity. Hunter calls this "holding women in contempt for being women,"[50] and it includes openly attacking women judges in ways that would be unthinkable for men judges. Third are actions by lawyers and litigants that challenge women's positional authority on the bench. This might include patronizing remarks, forms of address that deny women's professional status, and formal challenges to women's objectivity and ability to serve, known as motions for recusal.[51] Fourth are more serious actions against women judges, such as charges of misconduct, campaigns to vote "no" on retention, and electoral challenges. Fifth and finally, one might consider reversals in women's numbers on the bench a form of backlash. When benches revert back to being men-dominated or even men-only, we may take this as a sign that progress toward gender parity on the bench is not moving smoothly forward.

A Gendered Judicial Selection Process

Justices Sotomayor and Kagan both received scrutiny from the media and the Senate Judiciary Committee that their men predecessors had not. As women trailblazers appointed in the 1970s have retired, they have increasingly revealed the gender bias they experienced, including in the nomination and confirmation phases of the judicial selection process. Women, but not men, were asked who would care for their children. The Nixon tapes captured how the President, White House staff, and the Attorney General talked about women judges' sexuality and marriages. President Nixon and his advisers were relieved that prospective US Supreme Court nominee Mildred Lillie was not one of those "frigid bitches" or "hags" and joked about how uncomfortable having a woman on the Court would make Chief Justice Burger and how women should not be allowed to work for government and especially not serve in the cabinet. A woman court of appeals clerk, later a federal district judge, reported that before giving her a clerkship, the judge made her promise that she would not have children.[52] Such subterranean evidence about gender double standards is only beginning to become public as retiring women speak out.

After the Senate failed to confirm Robert Bork for the US Supreme Court and judicial nominations became more contentious, women were more likely never to receive a hearing or a vote and to take longer to confirm, and they were disproportionately likely to lose confirmation votes. When the presidency and the Senate are held by different parties, being a woman and/or non-white becomes a proxy for being an extreme activist, such that centrist women judges face the demonization and demagoguery normally reserved for the most ideologically extreme nominees. Once President Clinton faced a Republican-majority Senate in 1994, for example, the women he nominated to the federal judiciary took longer than men to confirm.[53] The Senate failed to act on Clinton's nominations of Elena Kagan for the D.C. Circuit Court of Appeals and Bonnie Campbell for the Eighth Circuit, for example.

In times of divided government, the gender and race of nominees become more salient, and conservative women and minority men have also faced difficulty securing confirmation. Senate Democrats also took longer to confirm Bush's women nominees.[54] It was conservative groups, however, not Democrats, who forced President George W. Bush to withdraw his nomination of Harriet

Miers for the US Supreme Court, even though the Senate would probably have confirmed her. Bell found that women took longer to confirm than men during periods of divided government.[55] As one party seeks to delay the other's judicial appointments as a presidential election nears, women and minority men may receive special scrutiny. Senator Chuck Grassley, for example, recently questioned the credentials of four of President Obama's women nominees.[56] One can see the questioning of women's credentials that I trace in other sections during the confirmation process.

Initial reports suggested that Obama's women nominees for judicial and non-judicial appointments were taking twice as long to obtain Senate confirmation. When Senate Republicans delayed the vote on Elena Kagan by one week, Senator Patrick Leahy compared the twenty days between the conclusion of the Senate hearings on Kagan and the twelve days for Samuel Alito and the seven days for John Roberts.[57] Later in the Administration, women and minority men were not taking longer to confirm to appointments at the Court of Appeals.[58] Looking at discrimination in the judicial selection process, we need to look at the aggregate numbers, using sex as a variable, but must also scrutinize gender at work in how interest groups, who signal to Senate Judiciary Committee members which nominations merit their attention, decide whom to challenge.

Brazen Hostility toward Women Judges

Another indication of backlash is the hostility men judges show to women colleagues who have been appointed or elected to the bench.[59] Put simply, men judges do not always welcome their women colleagues. Florence Allen won election to the Common Pleas Court of Ohio in 1920, becoming the first woman to serve on a general jurisdiction court in the United States.[60] In 1922, she won election to the Ohio Supreme Court, the first woman on any state supreme court. And in 1934, President Roosevelt appointed her to the US Court of Appeals for the Sixth Circuit, where she served until 1959. With respect to her final appointment, Allen's male colleagues did not welcome her and had in fact opposed her appointment. Three judges failed to write a customary letter of congratulation. One took to his bed for several days.[61] The men judges regularly lunched together at an all-male club when they sat in Cincinnati, while Allen lunched alone.[62]

The instances of hostility are not limited to the Allen case or the US judicial system. Canadian Supreme Court Justice Antonio Lamer refused to rise from his chair with the rest of his colleagues when Justice Bertha Wilson, the first woman appointed to the Ontario Court of Appeal in 1976 and the Supreme Court of Canada in 1982, entered the conference room for her first judicial conference.[63] Claire L'Heureux-Dubé, the first woman appointed to the Quebec Court of Appeal in 1979 and the second woman judge on the Supreme Court of Canada, reported that one of the justices refused to speak to her for three months until he determined that she had passed her probation.[64] On the day she was appointed, a neighbor girl whose father was a trial court judge ran up to her on the street bursting with enthusiasm that "they have appointed a woman as a judge and my father says she's a nobody."[65] And when California Governor Jerry Brown appointed a woman, Chief Justice Rose Bird, and an African American man, Justice Wiley Manuel, to the state's supreme court, both appointees were startled to learn that only Manuel had been invited to a welcoming luncheon.[66]

Hunter quotes a woman Australian judge in dissecting this hostility as including "a presumption of 'incompetency, inadequacy and unsuitability' in respect of women as judges."[67] Judge Allen's colleagues, for example, told background investigators for the FBI that she was "naturally unqualified" because of her sex.[68] Those colleagues labeled the possibility of her appointment "lamentable, laughable, disastrous," adding that it "would make the Circuit Court appear ridiculous and would lower the high traditions of that bench."[69] Setting aside the presumption of incompetency, it is noteworthy that senior officials were willing to voice their negative opinions to the press and that the press were willing to take seriously the question of women's competence. California Chief Justice Rose Bird joined a court with a member who had been known to all insiders as senile and another who was widely regarded as an incompetent Reagan crony. Nevertheless, the press openly challenged her credentials, not theirs. Hunter's Australian examples[70] were so striking that the State of Victoria's attorney general confronted the issue directly in a speech:

> Women who accept appointment continue to be measured against some sort of paternalistic yardstick, required to jump higher and faster than any male candidate lest they be labeled an undeserving token. It is at this point, Your Honour, that I cannot hide my disappointment in some quarters of the profession who persist in undermining women in senior office, referring to them in patronizing terms or ranking them in some sort of unspoken contest in which, I suspect, they themselves would not fare well.[71]

In the case of Brenda Hale, the first woman Law Lord, the press reaction was so hostile that it would have made "Rush Limbaugh blush."[72]

In her concurring opinion in a case overturning an acquittal of a thirty-four-year-old man's sexual assault of a seventeen-year-old girl, Justice L'Heureux-Dubé argued that a woman did not consent to sex with a man by living with him, having a child out of wedlock, wearing shorts, or acquiescing to her prospective employer's demand that he interview her in his trailer. Though she joined the majority of the Canadian Supreme Court in her ruling, it was L'Heureux-Dubé's opinion that sent the author of the Court of Appeal's decision, Judge John McClung, into a fury. He published an open letter in the *National Post* (Toronto) attacking her for feminist bias, which, he argued, rendered her unfit for judicial office. In rape cases, the media routinely judges the behavior of the victim rather than scrutinizing the actions of the perpetrator. Similarly, the media frenzy of reporting focused on L'Heureux-Dubé's alleged "feminist terrorism" rather than the accused's abhorrent conduct or McClung's unprecedented intemperate response. The Canadian Judicial Council reprimanded him for his letter, but lawyers wrote that L'Heureux-Dubé had disgraced the Supreme Court.[73] The message was clear: "Feminists were unqualified to render judicial decisions. Women judges who took positions that could be depicted as 'feminist' would attract swift and vitriolic public attack. Feminists who sat on the judiciary did so at their peril."[74]

The hostility toward women judges is not simply a remnant from a sexist era long past. Surveys, hearings, focus groups, and state and federal taskforces on gender bias conducted in the 1980s and 1990s routinely found that women judges received less respect from lawyers and other judges.[75] Sociologist Bryna Bogoch's study of courtroom discourse in Israel found that women judges were treated with less respect than men. She found lawyers were more likely to address men judges as "his honor" and more likely to address women judges simply as "madam," a pattern that was most striking when men and women judges served together on a panel.[76] Some lawyers denied the presence of the women judges altogether by referring to all judges as "his honor."[77] Bogoch also found that judges, witnesses, and lawyers were more likely to interrupt, take over the questioning of witnesses (Israel has a more inquisitorial system of justice than the United States, with judges routinely taking an active role in soliciting relevant information from parties), and show disrespect for women lawyers. This study was particularly worrisome given the high percentage of women judges and women lawyers in Israel.

Challenges to Objectivity

Backlash may also include actions by lawyers and litigants that challenge women judges' positional authority. Perhaps the most striking challenge to women judges' authority, and the greatest failure to grant them positional authority, is through motions to recuse: that is, asking judges to remove themselves from the case for bias or the perception of bias and allowing another judge to serve in their stead. Unfortunately, neither federal nor state courts keep track of such motions, so we have no systematic way to gather data on whether women or minority men receive more of them. We do, however, have anecdotal evidence that suggests it is commonplace in cases that raise diversity issues, gender, race, or, most recently, sexual orientation.[78] In the US, such motions are generally left to the discretion of the judge herself to decide.[79] A 1993 Canadian Bar Association report found that women were often accused of bias because of their gender.[80]

Returning to the United States, Federal District Judge Constance Baker Motley describes one such incident. In 1968, Diane Blank brought a discrimination-in-promotion case against the law firm Sullivan and Cromwell. Motley was only the fourth woman ever appointed to the federal bench and the first African American woman.[81] Sullivan and Cromwell filed a motion that she disqualify herself from the case since she herself had suffered race and gender discrimination. She denied the motion and the Second Circuit affirmed. Similarly, Judge A. Leon Higginbotham, an African American man, denied a request that he recuse himself from a race case in 1974,[82] a frequent occurrence, according to Derrick Bell.[83]

In the United States, for example, the Grand Dragon of the Ku Klux Klan filed a motion to recuse against Judge Gabrielle Kirk McDonald, the third African American woman appointed to the federal bench. He argued that he would not receive a fair trial from a "Negress." McDonald, first in her class from Howard Law School and an accomplished civil rights lawyer, received threats and even a one-way ticket "back" to Africa.[84] She recalled, "I said that if race was an issue, then being white was an issue too. I may be a Negress, but I'm a Negress with a black robe and the gavel and the law."[85]

To become judges, women first have to show that they have the intellectual acumen and legal training to perform such public service. But the association of men with reason and women with emotion makes this demonstration difficult. Women have the dual challenge of showing not only that they are rational but that they are not excessively emotional. They have to show that they can be objective and dissociate their social location from their judgment. The social location of white, upper-middle-class, and largely Protestant men, of course, is never called into question or associated with potential bias. Only those marked as "other" are viewed as imbued with a social location that renders them unable to be objective or open-minded. Non-dominant groups must be excluded, in part, because their entry into the field brings up the question of all judges' social locations in ways that threaten the narrative of impartial judgment.

Studies have repeatedly shown women judges complaining that their colleagues refused to let them sit on sexual assault cases on the grounds that they were not capable of objectivity.[86] If they were not assigned cases in the first place, they could not even get to the point of a motion to recuse, because their colleagues had already determined them to be unfit. In commenting on the recent motion asking Judge Vaughn Walker to recuse himself from the gay marriage debate in California, Clare Pastore remarked that this is "precisely where we were 30 years ago with African American and women judges, when those [recusal] motions went down in flames."[87]

Punishing Women on the Bench

A fourth example of backlash involves more serious actions against women judges. These actions may include charges of misconduct, campaigns to vote "no" on retention, and electoral challenges. We need to consider whether women face harsher discipline for things that are tolerated when done by men; whether women face campaigns to vote them out in retention elections when men are routinely retained; and/or whether women face electoral challenges when men in comparable positions run unopposed. The point is not to suggest that gender bias is at work every time a woman is sanctioned in some way, but merely to explore whether a double standard is operating in challenges to women judges.

Judge Bonnie Reed—who had developed a reputation for being tough on batterers in her ten years on the San Antonio, Texas, bench—was jailed for contempt in 1995 for refusing to let a lawyer postpone a hearing about his client's alleged domestic violence.[88] In this case, the lawyer, John Longoria, also served in the legislature and the law entitled lawyer–legislators to such postponements, known as continuances. Judge Reed did schedule the hearing for a day the legislature was not in session, but refused the continuance, believing the victim to be in danger if she postponed the trial.[89] The Fourth Court of Appeals had Judge Reed taken away to jail in handcuffs, and she served thirteen days—the first time in more than twenty years that a sitting judge had been jailed for criminal contempt in the United States, and the first time ever in Texas.[90] Longoria later filed a complaint to the Texas Commission on Judicial Conduct against Reed, and Reed resigned.[91]

In 1997, a woman provincial court trial judge in Nova Scotia, Canada, was hearing a case of a fifteen-year-old who allegedly interfered with the arrest of another youth. She dismissed the charge, arguing that police officers have been known to overreact when dealing with non-white groups.[92] Two Nova Scotia appeals courts overturned her decision on the grounds that her comments gave rise to a reasonable apprehension of bias, though the Supreme Court of Canada upheld her decision in a joint judgment written by two women justices— L'Heureux-Dubé and Beverley McLachlin. Rather than characterizing the judge as laudably upholding the Canadian Charter of Fundamental Rights, which prohibits discrimination, commentators vilified her as a racist.

Likewise, if women judges comment about gender discrimination, they are savaged. When Madam Justice Bertha Wilson of the Supreme Court of Canada conducted a survey of women federal and provincial judges in Canada, she found that 44 percent had experienced discrimination on the bench. Men judges were outraged and demanded that Justice Wilson disclose the names of the judges who had reported discrimination, characterizing Wilson herself as a "man-eating monster."[93] Wilson found the fallout from the survey enormously painful and "an unequivocal and deeply personal experience of gender discrimination."[94] Hunter argues further that the "overt terrorization and more subtle disciplining of and resistance to women" deter them from acting to make institutional change and from aspiring to judicial office.[95]

We have some evidence that women are more likely to face electoral challenges in states that elect judges; that women's incumbency gives them less of an advantage in comparison to men; and that their fundraising dollars produce fewer votes than those of men. Admittedly, however, the research on gender and judicial elections is mixed. Jennifer Lucas examined partisan and nonpartisan state supreme court elections from 1990 to 2006 and found that women won more often than men in both partisan and nonpartisan elections, and Republican women won most of all. Controlling for both incumbency and partisanship, Lucas found women candidates to have won 3 percent more of the vote in their judicial races than their men counterparts. She found women to have done better in nonpartisan election states than in partisan election states, but women did better than men in both.[96]

In contrast to Lucas, Traciel Reid found that women in races for North Carolina District Court between 1994 and 1998 raised more money than men, but "men received significantly more electoral bang for their campaign buck than women."[97] Women incumbents facing men challengers vastly outspent them, but did less well than men incumbents who outspent their challengers. Moreover, women running for open seats against men had to spend a lot more to win by narrow margins. In the aggregate, women raised more money than men and did better than men as a group, but it appears that both women incumbents and challengers were more likely to be exceptions to the rule that the candidate who spends the most prevails: women who outspend men do not always win.[98] Reid's work suggests that the relatively good news for women candidates in judicial elections may mask situations where gender disadvantage may be at work.

When women are targeted for defeat, they do not always lose, but much depends on how aggressively they fight back and whether they are willing to raise money and actively campaign. The attacks against Rose Bird and Rosalie Wahl in 1978 were only the beginning of a series of campaigns against women state supreme court justices.[99] In 1986, the year when voters removed Chief Justice Bird of California, voters also ousted Chief Justice Rhoda Billings of North Carolina. Republican Governor James Martin had named Billings Chief, breaking a tradition of giving the position to the most senior jurist on the court.[100] Democrats rallied behind the court's senior member, James Exum, who easily defeated Billings. Voters ousted Penny White from the Tennessee Supreme Court in 1996. As with Bird and Wahl, White's opponents zeroed in on a criminal law case. White joined three justices who called for resentencing in a rape and murder case because the rape failed to meet the statutory definition of an aggravating circumstance—namely, that it involve torture or serious physical abuse. Victims' rights advocate Rebecca Easley joined conservatives in criticizing White, saying, "The fact that a woman would agree that rape is not torturous or heinous is worse than a man saying it."[101] White later described herself as "naïve" for not fighting back against these charges. She also argued that women are easier to get rid of because of their higher visibility and because it is easier to tar women as liberal and therefore soft on crime. She felt that she was targeted because she would have assumed the role of Tennessee's first woman chief justice if reelected.[102]

In 2000, the Chamber of Commerce spent millions (some of it illegally) to attempt to defeat Ohio Supreme Court Justice Alice Robie Resnick in a dirty campaign where it claimed justice was for sale. It was not successful. In 2006, opponents of Georgia Supreme Court Justice Carol Hunstein accused her of voting to free a savage rapist and throwing out evidence against convicted cocaine traffickers, describing her as a one-legged Jewish female. (Hunstein is not Jewish, but she did lose a leg to cancer in her youth.) Hunstein retained her seat, but her campaign manager described it as the Georgia version of Swiftboating.[103] Alabama's Sue Bell Cobb, the state's first woman chief justice, defeated an incumbent in 2006 in the most expensive state judicial race yet, spending $2.5 million to her opponent's $4 million.[104] Wisconsin Chief Justice Shirley Abrahamson has been similarly aggressive in her campaigning. From the evidence, it appears that women who fight back do as well as men, though they may face vicious gendered attacks.

Reversals: Women Judges Replaced by Men

Despite the assumption that women are making steady progress in the judiciary, their progress is not steady and it is reversible.[105] As I described in Chapter 4, Presidents Carter and Clinton increased the number and percentage of women appointed, but Presidents Reagan and Bush (41) went backward. At the state level, I have identified forty-eight reversals—defined as a woman judge replaced by a man (see Table 7.1). Three states that once had a woman on their state supreme court now have none—Idaho, Indiana, and Iowa. (Eighteen states have gone from one woman justice to none at one time.) Fourteen states have had a majority of women on their supreme courts at one time but six of them

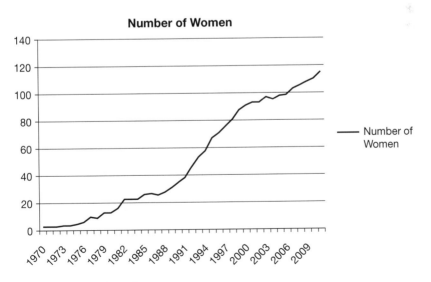

FIGURE 7.1 Number of women on state supreme courts

TABLE 7.1 Reversals: women on state supreme courts replaced by men

State	Year	Number
Arizona	1975–76	1 to 0
Arizona	2009–10	2 to 1
Arkansas	1977–78	1 to 0
Arkansas	2007–08	2 to 1
California	1987–88	1 to 0
Connecticut	2010–11	3 to 2
Florida	1994–95	1 to 0
Georgia	2009–10	2 to 1
Hawaii	1967–68	1 to 0
Idaho	2000–01	2 to 1
Idaho	2008–09	1 to 0
Indiana	1999–2000	1 to 0
Iowa	2003–04	2 to 1
Iowa	2010–11	1 to 0
Kansas	2009–10	3 to 2
Kentucky	2004–05	1 to 0
Maryland	1984–85	1 to 0
Massachusetts	2000–01	4 to 3
Michigan	1982–83	2 to 1
Michigan	1997–98	4 to 3
Minnesota	1993–94	4 to 3
Minnesota	1997–98	3 to 2
Mississippi	2001–02	2 to 1
Montana	2008–09	2 to 1
Nevada	2003–04	3 to 1
New Mexico	1988–89	1 to 0
New Mexico	2007–08	2 to 1
New York	2007–08	4 to 3
North Carolina	1979–80	1 to 0
Ohio	1934–35	1 to 0
Ohio	1964–65	1 to 0
Ohio	1983–84	1 to 0
Ohio	2006–07	4 to 3
Oklahoma	1999–2000	2 to 1
Oregon	1986–87	1 to 0
Pennsylvania	1974–75	1 to 0
Pennsylvania	2008–09	2 to 1
Rhode Island	2003–04	2 to 1
Texas (civil)	1983–84	1 to 0
Texas (civil)	2002–03	3 to 2
Texas (civil)	2004–05	2 to 1
Virginia	2007–08	3 to 2
Virginia	2010–11	2 to 1
Washington	1995–96	3 to 2

State	Year	Number
Washington	2006–07	4 to 3
West Virginia	1999–2000	2 to 1
Wisconsin	1999–2000	3 to 2
Wisconsin	2005–06	4 to 3

have reverted to a minority. Thus, although there has been progress, much of it has concealed reversals, as courts revert back to being male-dominated. Table 7.1 shows how the steady progress in Figure 7.1 conceals these reversals.

As early as 1978, Cook observed that as women moved up the judicial hierarchy, they would not necessarily be replaced by other women.[106] For example, although he initially nominated Harriet Miers to replace Justice O'Connor, President George W. Bush ultimately replaced O'Connor with a man. Bratton and Spill's research showed that President Clinton was likely to replace African American judges with other African Americans, but he replaced only one of the five women who left the bench with another woman.[107] Likewise, Bratton and Spill found that governors were more likely to choose a woman for their state supreme court if that court had no women members.[108] Their research suggests that selectors wanted at least token representation and the credit and attention for appointing a first. But once that first woman had been appointed, no pressure forced further progress or even to replace her with another woman if she left. We see reversals even in Queensland, Australia, and Ontario, Canada, where enormous efforts were made to increase the number of women on the bench.[109]

THE CASE OF ROSE BIRD

It is puzzling that those who study judicial elections have paid so little attention to the California electorate's decision not to retain Chief Justice Rose Bird in 1986. The campaign not to retain Bird was just the first round of conservative campaigns against so-called liberal justices. One of the so-called "Bird-hunters," State Senator John Doolittle, remarked, "This is an attack on the state courts, and tomorrow we will attack the federal courts . . . The juggernaut is moving fast, and it's only a matter of time before we take over."[110] Before the campaign against Bird, nearly all state judicial races were uncontested and incumbents virtually never lost. But in Bird's reelection bid, opponents spent more to oust her than had ever been spent in a judicial campaign.[111] Ultimately, they were successful, and "[t]o this day, Ms. Bird's name remains a kind of reflexive shorthand in California for 'soft-on-crime liberal.'"[112]

Looking at the successful campaign to unseat Rose Bird allows us to think through the implications of backlash theory, as virtually all of the elements this chapter analyzes are present in her case. It was no mere coincidence that judicial races became hotly contested just as women and minority men ascended to the bench. Neither journalists nor scholars have carefully analyzed how gender contributed to these events. John H. Culver and John T. Wold's otherwise exemplary analysis of the retention election of 1986 reveals the shortcomings of how scholars think (or fail to think) about gender as an explanatory factor. To be sure, Culver and Wold raise the possibility that Bird's gender was a political liability, but they argue that it was difficult to document such a claim, stating, "Available data indicate that on balance, her gender neither helped nor damaged her in the 1978 contest."[113] To support this claim, they cite Stolz, who had concluded: "Bird's sex apparently was not influential with the voters, although without a male opponent it is impossible to assess this factor definitively."[114]

In one of their articles on the case, Culver and Wold include just one paragraph about gender, but dismiss it as an explanation because *only* 31 percent of voters believed the attacks on her stemmed from the fact that she was the first woman on the court.[115] They do concede, however, that her gender made her more visible and therefore an easier target.[116] Patrick Brown draws a similar conclusion: voters did not care that Rose Bird was a woman but did care that she opposed the death penalty.[117] But in her essay in *Ms. Magazine*, Deirdre English echoes Sanbonmatsu's suspicion that the public was not ready for certain kinds of women leaders:

> The Rose Bird story is about more than the ways in which a justice tagged as "one of the last of the red-hot liberals" can become the target of a sophisticated political campaign to unseat her. It is also a story that suggests that women in positions of power are extraordinarily vulnerable, particularly if they are considered "too far ahead of society."[118]

English also emphasizes Bird's age and her nontraditional status as a single woman. Bird herself equated her appointment to making a nun the pope. So we have at least some reason to think that gender might be at work in this case. We should abandon an all-or-nothing approach to gender as an explanatory factor—it explains either everything or nothing—and instead examine how it intersects with other factors.[119]

THE RISE OF CHIEF JUSTICE ROSE BIRD

Before I demonstrate how gender might help explain California voters' failure to retain Rose Bird, I need to describe the events in question. Rose Bird was born on a chicken farm outside of Tucson, Arizona. Her father, who was sixty-six when she was born, died when she was just five.[120] When Rose was twelve, her mother moved the family back to her home state of New York, where she worked in a plastics factory, instilling in Rose a lifelong concern with workers' health and safety, as her mother suffered many adverse health effects because of her job.[121] An honors student, Bird received a scholarship to attend Long Island University, where she excelled in English, history, and economics. She chose political science as her major because she wanted to be a foreign correspondent.[122] She received a Ford Foundation grant to serve as a legislative intern at the California State Assembly while doing graduate work in political science at UC Berkeley. This experience apparently led her to switch from graduate study in political science to law at Boalt Hall, where she graduated with honors. Early on, her professors tried to discourage her from pursuing work as a trial lawyer because it was nearly impossible for women to get such work.[123] She served as a law clerk for the chief justice of the Nevada Supreme Court, who praised her intelligence, energy, diligence, and "magnificent personality."[124]

Like other pioneering women of her time (e.g., Minnesota's first woman justice Rosalie Wahl and US Supreme Court Justice Sandra Day O'Connor), Bird found opportunity in public service at a time when most large firms openly refused to hire women. Initially, the public defender told her he would not hire a woman and polled the attorneys who, for the most part, voted against hiring her. But the African American and Hispanic attorneys voted for her, and, despite the majority's opposition to her, the public defender decided to hire her as the first woman deputy public defender for Santa Clara County.[125] Bird went on to head the newly created Appellate Unit, acquiring the trial work she sought and arguing many landmark cases before the California Supreme Court.[126] She also worked with clinical law students at Stanford, who voted her best professor, and collaborated with death penalty opponent Anthony Amsterdam and the group Death Penalty Focus. Her public defender work earned her the admiration of her colleagues, who described her as an excellent appellate lawyer,[127] but this work would also cost her the support of police groups later, when she was seeking nomination.[128]

Bird first met Edmund G. (Jerry) Brown when they were both living in the International House at UC Berkeley.[129] She drove him in her Dodge during his campaigns for Secretary of State and then Governor. And she organized San Mateo County for him, which he unexpectedly won.[130] In 1975, Governor Brown appointed Bird as California's first woman cabinet officer, Secretary of Agriculture and Services, a position that had always previously gone to a grower.[131] She would go on to incur the wrath of agri-business for her work in drafting and securing passage of the Labor Relations Act, which guaranteed farm workers the right to a secret ballot if they wanted to unionize. She also helped outlaw the short hoe, which crippled workers.

Bird broke many barriers and logged many firsts: first woman Nevada Supreme Court law clerk, first woman public defender in Santa Clara County, first woman Stanford law professor, first woman cabinet officer in California, first woman secretary of agriculture in California, first woman California Supreme Court justice, first woman chief justice in California, and first justice the electorate voted not to retain on the California Supreme Court. As I discussed in the case of Rosalie Wahl, "first woman" is a media frame that garners much positive publicity for such women, but it also positions them under a public microscope, with their every move (and mistake) noted. As Bird herself reflected:

> I've always said when you're the first of your sex or race in a position, three things apply to you. One—you're always placed under a microscope. Two—you're allowed no margin for error. And three—the assumption is always made that you achieved your position on something other than merit.[132]

THE REACTION TO BIRD'S APPOINTMENT

Governor Brown's maverick persona, his liberal ideology, and his open disdain for the judiciary influenced how judges and legal insiders interpreted his appointment of Bird in 1977.[133] Her gender and outsider legal status (she had no previous judicial experience and no elite commercial legal practice), combined with Brown's reputation, made her a symbol of Brown's contempt for the judiciary. One commentator described her appointment as "the worst joke yet" that Brown had pulled on the judiciary.[134] Brown insisted that he himself should swear in Bird, breaking with tradition further still.[135] Though he was perhaps hostile to the judiciary in general, Brown, like President Carter during the same time period, also favored a more diverse bench. He appointed more women and minority men to the judiciary than any previous governor. When he left office, women comprised 17 percent of the judiciary, while minorities comprised 27 percent.[136]

Bird, too, helped secure judicial appointments for women and assigned large numbers of women and minority men leadership positions.[137] In 1977, the California Supreme Court led the nation in progressive jurisprudence, striking down miscegenation statutes, ruling the death penalty unconstitutional, and striking down abortion restrictions.[138] Thus, Bird was not California's first liberal justice, nor even in the minority.[139] She was, however, chief, and that may have been the most important factor contributing to her being singled out by conservatives. In short, Bird became the "lightning rod for people's unhappiness with the criminal justice system."[140] Unlike Rosalie Wahl, who joined the Minnesota Supreme Court as its most junior justice in 1977, Bird may also have failed to win the affection of other liberal justices because she was the chief. Indeed, her appointment thwarted many of the other justices' ambitions and expectations of promotion. In part, Bird's case supports the argument that hostility toward women judges is incurred by moving too far, too fast. But this was not because she was the first woman on a state supreme court (California was the eleventh state to appoint a woman to its state supreme court and the second to appoint a woman chief justice). Rather, it was because Governor Brown appointed her chief justice, a position that required her to administer a court on which she had never served as a judge. These issues were particularly offensive to Justice Stanley Mosk, who had expected to be the new chief. Thus, Bird's natural ideological allies on the court became enemies, and they pounded the Governor's desk in furious objection.[141] This anger was aggravated by the fact that the person who had overtaken them was a woman.

Some argue that Governor Brown did Bird no favors by appointing her chief; others went further in suggesting that Bird's appointment cost Brown reelection in 1978. To be sure, Brown could have made a safer appointment— such as Secretary of Education Shirley Hufstedler, whom President Carter was grooming for an appointment to the US Supreme Court. Indeed, when women's groups learned Brown was considering Bird, they lobbied instead for Hufstedler or UC law professor Herma Hill Kay.[142] But the women Brown passed over enthusiastically supported Bird's appointment before the California Judicial Appointments Commission, and this support "made a critical difference in winning confirmation."[143] Women like Dorothy Nelson, then dean of the University of Southern California Law School, wrote letters of support.[144] Bird's appointment also met with an unprecedented public outcry to the Commission on Judicial Appointments. Fervent letters poured in echoing Oliver Wendell Holmes's age-old objection to women judges: they were too emotional and therefore too weak to sentence criminal defendants. Lower court judges openly declared Bird's appointment a source of shame and urged the Commission to vote against confirmation.[145] The Commission ultimately voted two–one to confirm, but only after noting that Bird was minimally qualified and not necessarily the best person for the job.

In order to appreciate the gender-based challenges to competency and gender-based stereotypes of being "soft on crime," we must compare the treatment of Bird to the treatment of men judges in similar positions. Like Bird, US Supreme Court Chief Justice Earl Warren served when the political tide was turning and hence became a symbol of the court. His case counters the argument that gender was the factor in Bird's case. Bird may also be compared with the two sitting justices that the California electorate voted not to retain in the same election as Bird. Since voters threw two other liberal, anti-death-penalty justices out of office at the same time as Bird, we might conclude that factors other than gender were at work. If, however, gender were not a factor, and voters were motivated by the issue of the death penalty, why did Bird receive only 34 percent of the vote while the other two justices—the first Latino on the court, Justice Cruz Reynoso, and Justice Joseph Grodin— received 40 and 43 percent, respectively?[146] Was it because Bird was chief, and took more of the blame? Because she was the most visible target of the opposition movement? Because she was a woman? Or a combination of all three? If the death penalty were the only issue, we would have expected Bird, Reynoso, and Grodin to receive the same percentage of votes.

Two other comparisons, however, do suggest that gender was a factor in the Bird case. The first involves Justice Marshall McComb, who served on the

California Supreme Court. For years, justices, the legal establishment, and the media hid the fact that McComb was senile. As Medsger explains, "He did not do his own work, instructed his staff to plagiarize opinions, fell asleep during public hearings, and during this entire time was unable to discuss any case before the court."[147] Yet no one ever proposed or launched a retention campaign against him. Nor did the media, other justices, court staff, or lawyers expose his foibles.

A second, perhaps more interesting, comparison could be made with Justice William P. Clark. Governor Reagan appointed Clark in 1973 after he had abolished merit selection. Clark had flunked out of college and law school, and his practice gave him only minimal trial experience.[148] Yet Reagan appointed him to the state superior court and then the court of appeals. Later, he was appointed to the California Supreme Court, where "Clark was apparently so incapable of understanding the law that he could not discuss cases even in the justices' private conferences."[149] Medsger alleged that he regularly called the Governor's office with updates on the court's pending cases and consulted outsiders on legal opinions. Most importantly, she alleged that Clark leaked a story to the press that Justice Mathew Tobriner was holding back the announcement of a judicial decision until after Bird's first retention election in 1978. That judicial decision concerned the case of *People v. Tanner*, which overturned mandatory prison sentences when criminals used guns. Clark was suggesting, of course, that the court was nefariously delaying decisions in order to conceal damaging information from the public until after the election. The *Los Angeles Times* ran this story on election day, when voters narrowly voted to retain Bird with a vote of 51.7 percent. Bird called for an investigation of the charges, and the open hearings exposed the tensions of the supposedly collegial court.[150]

Although Justice Clark was arguably incompetent, unethical, and an ideologue, his tenure did not spark the mobilization of a campaign to remove him from the bench. Nor did he earn the scorn of the media, his colleagues on the bench, or court staff and lawyers.[151] In fact, until voters voted not to retain Chief Justice Rose Bird, no justice on either the California Supreme Court or the state's courts of appeal had been rejected by the voters.[152] Nationally, only thirty-three state court judges were not retained between 1934 and 1980.[153] When incompetent and unethical men are spared from scrutiny, while competent and ethical women are not, we have strong evidence that gender is at work.

UNDERSTANDING BIRD'S DOWNFALL

What motivated State Senator H.L. Richardson to undertake a campaign to ask voters not to retain Bird? What motivated those who funded this campaign? And what motivated the electorate to vote against Bird? We may never truly know. We do know that Bird received hate mail and death threats throughout her tenure,[154] and that these threats became so severe during the 1986 campaign that she moved her elderly mother out of her home.[155] We also know that Bird and the other two justices rejected by voters in 1986 were outspent four to one.[156] Opponents spent an unprecedented $8 million to defeat Bird alone, with the largest contributions from oil and gas, agri-business, auto dealers, and real estate interests. The coalition of conservatives that funded and directed the campaign to unseat Bird used direct mail and negative radio and television ads. One mailing attempted to link Bird with Tom Hayden and Jane Fonda, though neither had any tie to Bird.[157] San Diego Sheriff John Duffy required his 200 deputies to distribute postcards to the public urging Bird to resign from the court.[158]

For many, what best explains Bird's demise is that she was progressive and pro-labor and, thus, she was targeted and defeated by business interests. The campaign against her, however, emphasized her death-penalty decisions. Bird voted in favor of criminal defendants in 75 percent of the cases. She also voted to overturn the sentence and/or conviction in every capital case before the court during her tenure.[159] But surveys suggested that 75 percent of California residents supported the death penalty—a sign, perhaps, that the political tide had turned in the state.[160]

Three other explanations for Bird's demise merit consideration here. One argument is that she made administrative mistakes. Because she had not served on the court previously and wanted to "hit the ground running," she brought in her own team of lawyers who interviewed the various staff members about court administration. Their presence was unwelcome and longtime staff treated her as "an intruder in the village."[161] Particularly affronted was the director of the Administrative Office of the Courts, Ralph Kleps, who expected the Chief Justice to delegate all administrative power to him—as Bird's predecessors had. Bird may have lacked judicial experience, but, as an experienced public defender and appellate advocate, she had ideas about how the courts should work, and she did not appreciate Kleps's condescension toward her. After he left the court, he routinely blasted her in his column for the *Los Angeles Daily Journal.*[162] Bird believed justices should do more of their own opinion writing and, if necessary, rely on temporary rather than permanent clerks. She enlarged the pool of judges who could sit *pro tem* to include trial judges.

A court of appeals judge with matters pending before the court turned the key in her office door one night, surprising Bird and her staff, who were working late. Bird subsequently changed the locks to protect the confidentiality of the documents in her office.[163] She moved the conference table and replaced drapes with blinds to let in more light, scheduled judicial council meetings in state buildings rather than resorts, and sold the court's Cadillac. She forbade staff from conducting the practice of law in the court, grading bar exams, or operating blackjack counseling services on court time.[164] Her style was to move swiftly once she had identified a problem, but, in retrospect, she reflected that it might have been better to implement the changes over five years, rather than one.[165] She clearly failed to recognize the importance staff attached to court traditions.

Gender contributed to Bird being constructed as a bad manager. Here, it is useful to compare her case with that of Chief Justice John Roberts. Roberts—like Bird in the 1970s—is young and is leading a group of justices older than himself who may have had designs on his job. He is seen as vigorous (despite some serious health scares), modern, brilliant, and capable—all characteristics that a gender-neutral assessment might have applied to Bird. Bird was not a bad administrator but a decisive one, and it is hard to argue with the substance of her decisions. The media's frame of her as administratively incompetent was arguably unfair, sexist, and driven by leaks from men bearing grudges: the court administrator whose wings were clipped; associate justices who thought they should have been chief; and ideological opponents who sought to discredit her. The media accepted such a narrative because of the sources, because the media itself was sexist, and because the intrigue made for good copy. And the public readily accepted that an "inexperienced woman" could neither lead nor manage.

A second explanation for Bird's demise was that she was simply unlikeable. In her obituary, for example, the *New York Times* referred to her "brittleness."[166] The charge of being unlikeable is a common one for strong women leaders. In the Democratic presidential primary of 2008, for example, debates swirled around whether Hillary Clinton was likeable, with Barack Obama only grudgingly admitting that he found her "likeable enough" in a debate. Certainly, Bird was faced with the same double bind: to be a strong leader, she had to be tough, but to be a "good" woman, she had to be soft. Even so, the memorials to Bird after her death recounted many examples of warmth, kindness, and generosity: from kind notes to newcomers to the court, to the effort she made to find special gifts for each staff member, to giving her winter coat to a homeless person, to housing a Native American woman charged with prostitution and paying her way home.[167] Bird was not unlikeable; she was not liked because she was a woman leader.[168]

A third explanation for Bird's downfall is that she ran a bad campaign or failed to run much of a campaign at all. She never enjoyed the comfortable, easy relations with the press as had her predecessor; nor did the media shield and protect her as they had justices of an earlier era, all of whom were men. She fired the first firm she had hired to run her 1986 campaign because she disagreed with its counsel, which was to raise a lot of money and run negative campaign ads. She believed judges should be above the political fray and wanted to frame the election as being about the importance of an independent judiciary. But television ads pleading for judges to be free of political influence were no match for the mothers of murdered children whose killer was spared the death penalty.[169] Thus, her advisers pushed her to strike back hard on environmental issues and against corporate interests. In the end, she let her opponents define her as a liberal incompetent. Perhaps her biggest mistake was blocking the formation of an independent campaign committee that would have defended all six of the justices up for retention.[170] As we learned from Rosalie Wahl's case in Minnesota, judges working together are more effective in defeating challengers than one justice campaigning alone.

THE ROLE THAT GENDER PLAYED

How much blame should we attribute to Bird herself and how much should we attribute to gender? Bird's appointment to the court shares many similarities with the case of Justice Rosalie Wahl, the first woman appointed to the Minnesota Supreme Court in the same year, 1977. They were both appointed without previous judicial service; they both came from the public defender's office; they were both appointed by maverick governors who were somewhat hostile to the legal establishment; and they both faced immediate external challenges—Bird, a campaign to not retain her; Wahl, three electoral challengers. But the cases have important differences. Wahl had been married (although she was divorced), she was the mother of five, and she looked like "everybody's favorite kindergarten teacher."[171] Bird was younger, unmarried,[172] and was appointed chief justice rather than the court's junior justice. Wahl's colleagues, many of whom were ideologically simpatico, embraced her. Bird's colleagues, many of whom were also ideologically simpatico, did not embrace her, in part because several of them felt entitled to the position of chief justice themselves.

Despite similarities, the two cases differed significantly. The Minnesota legal establishment was wary of the trend of judicial campaigns (e.g., negative ads, big money) and did not favor democratizing or politicizing judicial selection. Wahl enjoyed a mobilized, organized, and most importantly bipartisan campaign from the moment the Governor appointed her. Although opponents targeted her as soft on crime, Minnesota had no death penalty and Wahl, a mere associate justice, did not shoulder the "blame" for the court's jurisprudence. She may have enraged men who felt they had been "beaten by a girl" to a seat on the Supreme Court, but she did not face the hostility of the other justices, since she was their junior. Most importantly, as I argued in Chapter 3, Wahl was a vigorous and effective campaigner, connecting with women, progressives, and the legal establishment across the state. She was also the beneficiary of having an opponent many disliked, whereas Bird did not.

Though Bird arguably ran a poor campaign, gender is not irrelevant. Gender can work in tandem with other issues. For example, it might be easier to frame a woman as "soft on crime," anti-business, or a bad manager. Indeed, if we consider the five elements of backlash, all are present in Bird's case. Her qualifications were immediately suspect, which was not the case for her predecessors or for other men appointed by Governor Brown. As such, she had vocal opposition from nineteen district attorneys and a vote against her confirmation. Her colleagues did not extend the conventional courtesy they showed to all other colleagues, thereby delegitimizing her position of authority. For example, Justices Mosk and Clark did not even attend her swearing-in, and staff failed to grant her the positional authority of chief.

The media routinely reports on women candidates with "husbands, hemlines, and hair," focusing on their gendered attributes of femininity rather than policy positions and campaign successes.[173] And professional women face a double bind in that they must either present themselves as attractive and feminine, making them appear likeable but less competent, or downplay their femininity, making them appear competent but less likeable. Prior to the 1986 campaign, Rose Bird had such a dramatic makeover that students participating in an experiment looking at before and after photos failed to identify her as the same person.[174] Sigelman et al. describe her transformation as going from dowdy, late middle-aged woman to stunningly beautiful woman. In the experiment they conducted, men and women students were shown different photos and descriptions of Bird, as well as photos and descriptions of male candidates (used as controls). The candidates' sex and support for the death penalty directly affected whether students reported they would vote for the candidate.[175] The more attractive Bird was, and the more she was described in feminine terms, the more likeable but less dynamic she was perceived to be. Though attractiveness did not influence voting patterns, the attractiveness interacted with other factors to make her seem more feminine and therefore more likeable.

As this experiment shows, gender and attractiveness affect people's willingness to credit women with leadership ability and grant them positional power. In short, gender is a lens through which other information about judges and candidates is filtered and weighed.[176] Because Bird was a woman, it was easier for opponents to undermine the public's sense of her legal and managerial competency, while the capabilities of other justices went unexamined. It was also easier to frame her as "soft on crime" and harder to frame her as the people's justice, especially since she did not participate actively in her own defense. In fairness, women judges had little guidance in how to campaign in 1977. Later, Ohio Supreme Court Justice Alice Robie Resnick and Wisconsin Supreme Court Justice Shirley Abrahamson could draw on the lessons of Bird's failure and Wahl's success. Bird did not have the benefit of this experience.

Perhaps if the media, or others, had been more effective in naming the gender bias in the backlash against Rose Bird—as Jessie Jackson had identified the racism in the Willie Horton ads and Katie Couric had called out sexism against Hillary Clinton—Bird might have been a more difficult target.[177] But at least in retrospect we can acknowledge the role that gender played in her defeat. After she left office, Bird made the following remarks:

> If we judges and lawyers are not to be popular, let it be because we are standing on the forefront of protecting people's rights during a time of

transition. Let it be because we have the courage to represent unsympathetic individuals and make difficult rulings in order to give life and breath to our constitutional guarantees. Let it be because we have the integrity to do justice, even though such actions may be met with criticism and disapproval. Let it be because we see our role from the perspective of its noble traditions, not from the pressured viewpoint of the moment.[178]

Chief Justice Bird's statement suggests she, too, placed more weight on the death penalty for generating the campaign against her, yet she often identified gender as a factor in her speeches and writings. Upon her exit from office, the male monopoly on the court was restored. California Governor George Deukmejian appointed Malcolm Lucas, his former law partner, to replace Bird.[179] And until 1989, the California Supreme Court had no women serving. Now, of course, four of the six justices on the California Supreme Court are women (one position is vacant). I am reminded here of Mary Catherine Bateson's (Margaret Mead's daughter) famous quote that institutions celebrate their transition from all-male to gender-integrated by sacrificing their first women members.

CONCLUSION

Backlash can be useful. The viciousness of the attacks on Hillary Clinton and Sonia Sotomayor revealed the depths of hostility to women leaders and the continued struggle for gender equality. If, as social psychologists argue, social movement activists respond more to threats than to opportunities, such backlash may galvanize women to action. Yet, if social movement theorists are correct in identifying hope as the crucial ingredient in getting activists to incur risks, the evidence of hostility, open attacks on women, and reversals of women's progress may sober women into silence and deter them from seeking judicial office. As Backhouse concludes:

> Women judges are surely some of the most privileged and powerful individuals in Canada. Unlike most females working today, they have "no more ceilings through which to push." They "hold and deploy the power of the state." However, a closer inspection "inside the robes" shows that gender "trumps" even judging.[180] If women this powerful cannot escape the effects of misogyny and discrimination, then no woman can. The very message is simply shocking.[181]

Did Hillary Clinton lose the Democratic nomination because the media were biased against women candidates and voters? Did women voters, especially younger women, recoil because she was ambitious, voted for the war, was too centrist, and ran a bad campaign?[182] Were the media biased against

Sarah Palin because she was a woman, or because she was conservative and uninformed about public policy? Did independent women fail to support her because they hold women to higher standards than men or because party trumped gender and voters do not vote on the basis of vice-presidential candidates? While feminists from Katie Couric to the Women's Media Center and the candidates themselves raised the gender question in the 2008 presidential campaign, it is rarer to ask about gender in the case of judging and judicial elections, as Justice Sotomayor did. Using sex as a variable to explore whether women as a group are more or less likely to win judicial elections can provide important evidence about discrimination.[183] We need to add to that a gender analysis.

A gender analysis reveals the scaffolding that judges, lawyers, voters, and so many others use to evaluate and make judgments on elected and appointed leaders. Just as feminists in the 1970s identified a set of behaviors that they argued constituted a pattern of sexual harassment,[184] scholars should explore whether the five phenomena I have identified constitute a backlash against women judges. This backlash may have parallels in other arenas, such as presidential politics or academia, which may help us make sense of women's stalled progress toward equality. One step toward acknowledging gender's explanatory power would be to understand how it interacts with other factors and investigate why some women succeed while others fail.

If we want women to progress, we need to understand the complex role of gender in shaping outcomes. Doing so means we must recognize that women "do" gender in different ways and are vulnerable to gender-based attacks in different degrees, based on their individual characteristics as well as the political context. The case of Chief Justice Rose Bird shows an intersectional approach to gender—not in the conventional way that term is used to look at multiple identity characteristics, but in the sense that gender can be a contributing factor. Moreover, gender interacts with questions of legal competency, managerial ability, and campaign strategy. Women's progress is neither inevitable nor a guaranteed response to women's increasing representation in the legal profession; rather, it unleashes formidable forces of opposition we have only begun to name and understand.

8

CONCLUSION: DRAWING ON THE HISTORY OF WOMEN'S EXCLUSION FROM JURIES TO MAKE THE CASE FOR A GENDER-DIVERSE JUDICIARY[1]

After President Franklin D. Roosevelt appointed Florence Allen to the Sixth Circuit Court of Appeals in 1934, it took feminists in the United States nearly fifty years of campaigning to persuade a president to appoint the first woman to the Supreme Court—Sandra Day O'Connor, in 1981. In 2009, after President Obama appointed Justice Sonia Sotomayor, the US returned to its high-water mark of two women out of nine justices on the US Supreme Court, and exceeded that in 2010 with the appointment of Justice Elena Kagan.[2] Still, just over a quarter of all state and federal judges in the United States are women—a far cry from half. The record since the Carter Administration demonstrates that without organized pressure, women lose ground; their progress can be reversed. Despite evidence of judicial reversals, new groups seeking to increase the number of women in politics ignore the judiciary, and groups who once championed this cause have moved on to other issues. If we want to progress and to move from minority to parity, feminists need to mobilize again, organize, and make our strongest argument.

The best case for a gender-diverse bench does not rest on difference. The most persuasive arguments appeal to democracy and legitimacy, recognize the symbolic role of judges, call for simple nondiscrimination, and draw analogies between gender and geographic representation. An historical examination of women's exclusion from juries provides a good example of the pitfalls of arguing from difference and why it is unnecessary to do so. Asking where women are and why they are missing is an important first step. Using sex as a variable can yield some important insights. But if analysis stays at the level of such sex differences research, the likelihood of an essentialist understanding of gender is unacceptably high. Essentialism and its prescriptions are what feminism emerged to challenge, even if feminism has too often been itself trapped by the naturalization of differences. Arguments based on an understanding of gender as a social process are better than those based on sex differences.[3] As in all the previous chapters, thinking about women judges can help us advance a theory of gender. Equally, thinking about gender can illuminate the relationship between judging and other forms of governing power, the nature of impartiality and objectivity, why representation is essential for legitimacy, and why it is discriminatory to exclude women.

The argument from difference resonates because it is so familiar. I revert to it, too. Why can't my husband find things in the refrigerator? Although women's difference arguments resonate with some feminists, such arguments more often resonate with antifeminists, both positively and negatively, as the Sotomayor case demonstrates. This book has shown that very little, if any, evidence exists for an essential women's difference in judging. I reject the difference approach first and foremost because I believe it to be empirically untrue, and because it does not comport with my feminist theory. I also believe that sameness arguments, as advocates for women on juries discovered, resonate better with the liberal values that are dominant within the US[4]—these arguments work. Different political systems have developed distinctive approaches to gender equality reflective of their political cultures. Feminists in the United States capitalized on legal advances that attempted to eradicate racial discrimination; in Europe, feminism evolved out of a welfare state that recognized women's different social roles in performing caring labor.[5] Each paradigm has its strengths and its limitations. In the United States, for example, feminists have failed to get basic provisions of paid parental leave. In Germany, women were largely shut out of business and academe, in part because employment discrimination prohibitions were neither enforced nor incurred significant penalties. While recognizing different paths, non-essentialist arguments are best for making the case for women judges in general. Because they are based on sound empirical scholarship, because they comport with the best feminist theory, because they work, and because difference arguments are intrinsically risky, we should use equality arguments even in contexts outside of the US that might be more amenable to maternalist arguments.

Scholars I deeply admire make arguments from difference. The three I admire most do so in full knowledge of the theoretical problems of essentialism, the possibility that claiming difference will lead to disadvantage, and the significant limitations of the empirical evidence. Sociologist Patricia Yancey Martin and her co-authors reworked feminist standpoint theory to try to make sense of the surveys of lawyers that showed women were significantly more likely than men to perceive discrimination in the legal profession.[6] In making the case for African Americans on the bench, legal academic Sherrilyn Ifill[7] does not argue that black judges necessarily decide cases differently from white judges but rather that because African Americans *as a group* hold different opinions from whites and have shared experiences that are different, they must be represented on the bench.[8] She extends this difference argument to women, although her case for differences in public opinion between men and women is weaker than between African Americans and whites.[9] Legal academic Theresa Beiner wrestles with her intuition and experience that women, as a group, bring something significantly different to the enterprise of judging.[10] All of these scholars are strategic thinkers about feminist politics. All of us agree that a jury or judiciary drawn from the full range of citizen identities and experiences is more conducive to the production of justice, will yield better deliberations, and will command more support than a judiciary drawn from a narrow cross-section of the public. As I argued in Chapter 1, wisdom and experience matter.

I am forever grateful to Sherrilyn Ifill for prompting me to think about juries very late into this project. Yet I part company with Ifill, Martin, and Beiner, and those who share their views. An historical analysis of the jury cases can show that feminists need not agree about difference to advocate for more women on juries, or, by extension, more women judges. Like the *paritaristes* arguing for gender quotas in the French National Assembly, we can argue for women's representation without arguing they are different or expecting them to behave differently. Simply, they are citizens, and citizenship in a democracy requires their inclusion. In their opinions, judges deciding jury cases have also reversed the question, as I shall argue feminists should do. The first kind of reversal asks us to consider if we would tolerate exclusion from jury service if states excluded men from jury service. Would we still regard a jury's decision as fair and legitimate if only women served? The second kind of reversal shifts the burden of proof, asking those who seek to exclude to justify their position rather than placing the burden on those who want to include. The opinions in the jury cases reflect the recognition that perceptions matter. It may not be the case that black jurors would vote differently from whites or women from men, but justice must not just be done. It must be seen to be done. When women or minority men are excluded from jury service, many might question whether justice has been done. Representation is necessary for legitimacy. Lastly, the jury cases wrestle not just with whether women are different from men, but whether exclusion carries an unacceptable stigma that calls into question the legitimacy of our legal system, implying that women and minority men cannot perform the functions of citizenship. Judges are different from jurors because they are employed in a paid job; they are not merely performing a public service along with other citizens. As such, employment discrimination norms apply to the judiciary as a workplace. But this point, too, is amenable to reversing the question. Just because equal employment opportunity statutes do not apply to jurors (nor, as I showed in Chapter 5, to judges in the UK), we could shift the burden of proof to inquire why it is morally defensible (if not unlawful) to engage in discrimination against prospective jurors or judges. Because the jury cases illuminate so much about making arguments for women judges, I analyze them at length before making the case for a gender-representative judiciary.

WOMEN'S EXCLUSION FROM JURIES: A WOMAN'S FLAVOR?

In thinking about how to make the case for women judges, we can learn from the extensive campaign waged by women for the right to serve on juries. The opinions in the litigation over women's exclusion from juries show judges wrestling with parallel arguments about sameness and difference and what harm results from women's exclusion. Because the courts have said that juries drawn from pools that exclude women are not drawn from a fair cross-section of the community and that lawyers may not strike jurors because of sex, the decisions support the case for more women judges. After suffrage, women's rights activists, the League of Women Voters, Business and Professional Women's Clubs, the National Woman's Party, and the Federation of Women's Clubs fought a state-by-state campaign to end women's exclusion from juries.[11] The few women serving in state legislatures often championed the cause, as did many women lawyers.[12] As with suffrage, women framed their demands using both difference and sameness arguments: women were citizens who had an equal right and duty to serve; women brought a distinctive perspective to juries such that, if excluded, women defendants would not have been judged by a jury of their peers.

State legislation either barred women from serving altogether, or, more commonly, achieved the same result by requiring women to register for jury service, dismissing them for the slightest reason, simply administratively excluding them from the pool, or a combination of all three.[13] Comparing campaigns in fifteen different states—from Washington, which allowed women to serve as early as 1911, to South Carolina, which did not remove its exemption until 1967—McCammon et al. found that advocates framed their arguments emphasizing the rights and duties of women jurors rather than focusing on a woman's right to be tried by a jury of her peers, and they were more successful when they did so.[14] Activists in Texas, for example, believed so strongly that the rights argument was more effective than the difference argument that the kit they put together to train volunteers implored advocates to make rights and duty arguments.

The cases against gender and racial exclusions were intertwined, and they were joined most eloquently by an African American woman lawyer, Pauli Murray.[15] Unsurprisingly, given the history of the Equal Protection Clause, the Supreme Court struck down racial exclusions first. It grasped the harm of African Americans convicted by all-white juries, whether such juries came into existence because state laws prohibited African Americans from jury service or, later, because lawyers used their peremptory challenges to remove all African Americans from a particular jury. Over time, however, as Babcock documented,[16] the arguments shifted from an appreciation of the harm to African American criminal defendants convicted by all-white juries to how potential African American jurors may be harmed by excluding them because of race-based stereotypes of how they might decide cases. African American jurors were viewed as being more suspicious of the police and sympathetic to the criminally accused; women were viewed as being softer on crime, particularly if a defendant or his lawyer was handsome. The harm of excluding jurors on the basis of race or gender shifted from disadvantaging a defendant from an oppressed group to the harm of stereotyping jurors. At the same time, the legal basis shifted from the Sixth Amendment right to trial by an impartial jury to a Fourteenth Amendment claim of equal protection, paralleling the shift in doctrine on affirmative action. The focus shifted from a harm to an oppressed group—racial minorities, women—to a wrong of using race or sex as a category, where the harm could be to the dominant group. The Supreme Court's new way of thinking about sex- and race-based classifications sees them as harmful to whites and men, not just to non-whites and women. Whites and men can now be the victims of race- or sex-based classifications, either because they were stereotyped by sex or race as prospective jurors or as defendants who suffered because non-whites or women were not on the jury.

Feminists making the case for women jurors pursued a two-pronged strategy: trying to persuade state legislators to remove impediments to women's full jury service; and trying to persuade courts to strike down statutes and administrative practices that resulted in all-male juries. The 1946 Supreme Court opinions in *Ballard v. United States* displayed the contradictory arguments judges have made on these questions. The US Department of Justice had approved women jurors on all federal courts in 1935.[17] Congress required federal courts to select jurors using whatever rules the host state had for jury service. If a state banned women from jury service, the federal court would do so, too; if the state permitted women to serve, they could serve on the federal jury convened in that state. The federal government charged Edna Ballard and her son with mail fraud for soliciting contributions for the "I Am" religious movement as divine messengers. An all-male jury drawn from a pool of men convicted them, although California had permitted, but not obliged, women to serve on juries since 1911, before suffrage.[18] A dissenting judge on the Ninth Circuit argued, however, that women were more religious than men and might have been more sympathetic to the Ballards. Ironically, the government sent Beatrice Rosenberg to argue before the US Supreme Court that excluding women from juries raised no constitutional problems. Writing the majority opinion for the US Supreme Court, Justice William O. Douglas referenced the requirement that juries represent a "cross-section of the community" and be "truly representative of it."[19] Moreover, Douglas noted, "Jury competence is an individual, rather than a group or class, matter."[20] Overturning the appellate court's upholding of the conviction, he wrote:

> It is said, however, that an all-male panel drawn from the various groups within a community will be as truly representative as if women were included. The thought is that the factors which tend to influence the action of women are the same as those which influence the action of men—

personality, background, economic status—and not sex. Yet it is not enough to say that women when sitting as jurors neither act nor tend to act as a class. Men likewise do not act as a class. *But, if the shoe were on the other foot, who would claim that a jury was truly representative of the community if all men were intentionally and systematically excluded from the panel?* The truth is that *the two sexes are not fungible; a community made up exclusively of one is different from a community composed of both*; the subtle interplay of influence one on the other is among the imponderables. To insulate the courtroom from either may not in a given case make an iota of difference. Yet *a flavor, a distinct quality is lost if either sex is excluded.* The exclusion of one may indeed make the jury less representative of the community than would be true if an economic or racial group were excluded.[21]

Justice Douglas found that excluding women from juries harmed not just the defendant, but the jury system itself, the law as an institution, and the very idea of democracy.[22] He proposed a standard for judging fairness that still resonates: the unfairness in women's exclusion would be readily apparent if men were excluded. He also interjected difference arguments by finding that women and men were not fungible, or interchangeable, without articulating the precise nature of that difference, beyond a "flavor."[23]

In 1957, when Gwendolyn Hoyt came to trial for first degree murder for killing her husband with a baseball bat while he lay on the couch, only 218 women's names were on the jury roll in Tampa, although 46,000 women were registered to vote.[24] The statute permitted women to serve if they registered, but court staff enjoyed wide discretion to select names, and officials excluded those who registered just after the law changed on the grounds that these women were too political and therefore not trustworthy.[25] The box from which court administrators drew names for Hoyt's jury included 3,000 men's names and 35 women's names (1.2 percent), and all 60 names they drew were men's. It took the six-man jury twenty-five minutes to convict Hoyt, and the judge sentenced her to imprisonment with hard labor for thirty years. On appeal, Hoyt's lawyers persuaded Judge T. Frank Hobson that she had not been tried by a jury of her peers and that women's entry into public life made their continued exclusion from jury service discriminatory. Using Justice Douglas's test for discerning fairness, Hobson wrote that if the court found the Florida law constitutional, "then we must hold that the legislature could validly require all women to serve but limit male service to volunteers and thus, in effect, create an all-female jury system."[26]

Dorothy Kenyon, a New York feminist, lawyer, judge, and American Civil Liberties Union (ACLU) board member, wrote an *amicus curiae* brief for the ACLU supporting Hoyt—its first in support of a sex discrimination case.[27] After noting women might be more sympathetic to Hoyt's plea of temporary insanity, given her husband's suspected infidelity and his rejection of her efforts at reconciliation, Justice John Harlan rejected the claim that Hoyt had a right to a jury "tailored to the circumstances of the particular case," saying she had a right only to a jury indiscriminately drawn from the eligible pool.[28] Although women may have been "emancipated" from the "restrictions and protections of bygone years," and were active participants in community life, Harlan wrote, "Woman is still regarded as the center of home and family life."[29] Harlan saw nothing sinister in the way administrators winnowed down the pool from those who had actually registered and declared that "this case in no way resembles those involving race or color"[30] where the Court found similar practices to be discriminatory. Despite Hoyt's lawyers' best efforts to keep the case focused on the state's failure to try Hoyt by a jury of her peers, the court continued to frame the case as women enjoying the privilege of exemption from jury service based on their differing social roles. Notwithstanding Justice Douglas's opinion in *Ballard*, the court would not take this question up again until ten years later.

Kerber credits Pauli Murray, more than anyone else, with successfully linking race and gender in the jury cases.[31] Murray, an African American feminist, had graduated from Howard Law School and written an influential paper entitled "Jane Crow" that analyzed race and gender discrimination together. She recognized jury service as a strategic locus for thinking through the issues of the dilemma of difference.[32] Her research documenting sex-based classifications, including women's exclusion from jury service, became part of the report of the President's Commission on the Status of Women in 1962. Kenyon brought her onto the ACLU board, and together they urged the ACLU to tackle race and sex discrimination as twin and related evils. Their first victory came in *White v. Crook*, when the Federal District Court for the Middle District of Alabama held unconstitutional the state's practice of restricting jury service to a small group of white men.[33] Murray and Kenyon's successor at the ACLU, Ruth Bader Ginsburg, also recognized the strategic importance of women's exclusion from jury service.[34]

The breakthrough came in a civil case of a woman whose hair had fallen out because of a defective home permanent. She argued that women—who in Louisiana, as in Florida, came to be on the jury rolls only if they registered for jury service—would be more understanding than men of the trauma of hair loss for women, and brought a class action on behalf of women civil suit litigants similarly disadvantaged by not having women on their juries. In 1973, a unanimous Federal District Court for the Eastern District of Louisiana in *Healy v. Edwards* declared itself to be explicitly overturning *Hoyt* based on subsequent Supreme Court rulings on equal protection.[35] Justice Alvin Rubin argued that women added not a "flavor" of difference, but "qualities of human nature and varieties of human experience." The absence of women "is significant not because all women react alike, but because they contribute *a distinctive medley of views* influenced by differences in biology, cultural impact and life experience, indispensable if the jury is to comprise a cross-section of the community."[36]

Despite *Ballard*, the Supreme Court did not strike down women's exclusion from jury service until 1974, in the case of a white man sentenced to death by an all-male Louisiana jury (*Taylor v. Louisiana*), chosen under a selection system where few women registered for jury service. Quoting *Glasser*, which struck down the exclusion of blacks from juries, Justice Byron White wrote for the US Supreme Court: "our notions of what a proper jury is have developed in harmony with our basic concepts of a democratic society and a representative government" and the court now understood that the jury must be "a body truly representative of the community . . . , and not the organ of any special class."[37] White quoted Congress in passing the Federal Jury Selection and Services Act of 1968:

> It must be remembered that the jury is designed not only to understand the case, but also to reflect the community's sense of justice in deciding it. As long as there are significant departures from the cross-sectional goal, biased juries are the result—biased in the sense that they reflect a slanted view of the community they are supposed to represent.[38]

White argued that "community participation in the administration of the criminal law, moreover, is not only consistent with our democratic heritage, but is also critical to public confidence in the fairness of the criminal justice system."[39] Referring back to *Ballard*, but not *Hoyt*, White made a strong difference argument: "This conclusion necessarily entails the judgment that women are sufficiently numerous and distinct from men, and that, if they are systematically eliminated from jury panels, the Sixth Amendment's fair cross-section requirement cannot be satisfied."[40] In a footnote,[41] White quoted extensively from Justice Thurgood Marshall's opinion in *Peters v. Kiff*. Justice Marshall had written:

> Moreover, we are unwilling to make the assumption that the exclusion of Negroes has relevance only for issues involving race. When any large and identifiable segment of the community is excluded from jury service, the effect is to remove from the jury room qualities of human nature and varieties of human experience, the range of which is unknown and perhaps unknowable. It is not necessary to assume that the excluded group will consistently vote as a class in order to conclude, as we do, that its exclusion deprives the jury of a perspective on human events that may have unsuspected importance in any case that may be presented.[42]

Justice White then went on to cite studies which showed that "women bring to juries their own perspectives and values that influence both jury deliberation and result."[43]

Justice William Rehnquist's dissenting opinion objected to the Court overturning a verdict without showing that the jury in question had been unfair or prejudiced. He noted that Hoyt, as a woman facing an all-male jury in a case of intimate partner violence, had a much stronger case to claim bias than a white man facing a white jury, but the Court had rejected her claim a mere thirteen years previously. Rehnquist mocked *Ballard*'s reference to a "flavor" as "mysticism" rather than law.[44] He believed the ready exemptions granted to doctors, lawyers, or other groups were more likely to skew results than the exemption Louisiana granted to women. Ruth Bader Ginsburg reported the following astonishing exchange at oral argument for *Taylor*. Justice Rehnquist inquired:

> Mr. King, when we used to try cases where I practiced [in Arizona], we used to follow a maxim, which is perhaps an old wives' tale, that "woman is man's best friend but her own worst enemy," and the idea was, if you had a male client, you wanted a bunch of women on the jury, and if you had a woman client, you wanted a bunch of men on the jury. I take it, in your area, Mr. King, they don't follow any such handy maxim.

Ginsburg continued her account:

> Mr. King was perplexed. His was a male client, but the jury selection system he assailed offered no opportunity to follow the handy maxim. In Louisiana, at that time, it was a bunch of men or no jury. On this occasion, the reaction of the courtroom observers was unmistakable. Women from several law schools attended the argument. Their groan was audible throughout the chamber . . . Yes, women and men are individuals of equal dignity, they should be counted equally by their Government and before the law. But they are not the same, they have distinctive qualities most of us value highly. Few would disagree with the French in applauding the difference. Still, petitioner's attorney did not relish the no doubt well-meant humor in the concluding comment Justice Rehnquist made when the attorney finished her argument and was about to sit down: "You won't settle for putting Susan B. Anthony on the new dollar then?" The attorney held her tongue, although she was sorely tempted to say, "No, your Honor, tokens will not do."[45]

The last significant case on women and juries, *J.E.B. v. Alabama*,[46] displays many of the same features as the earlier cases. It draws the analogy with race, shifts the harm from defendant or group to individual juror, and equivocates about the relevance of gender differences. The State of Alabama brought a paternity action for child support against J.E.B. The state used nine of its ten peremptory challenges to remove male jurors, while the petitioner used all but one of his strikes to remove female jurors. The all-female jury found J.E.B. to be the father. Writing for a six-justice majority in 1994, Justice Harry Blackmun drew parallels with race cases. The Court had struck down race-based peremptory challenges almost twenty years earlier. Blackmun compared *J.E.B.*'s arguments with those who defended the exclusion of women from state juries altogether and noted, "Respondent offers virtually no support for the conclusion that gender alone is an accurate predictor of juror's attitudes."[47]

Quoting *Powers v. Ohio*, Blackmun noted that active gender discrimination against jurors

"invites cynicism respecting the jury's neutrality and its obligation to adhere to the law" . . . It denigrates the dignity of the excluded juror, and, for a woman, reinvokes a history of exclusion from political participation. The message it sends to all those in the courtroom, and all those who may later learn of the discriminatory act, is that certain individuals, for no reason other than gender, are presumed unqualified by state actors to decide important questions upon which reasonable persons could disagree.[48]

Blackmun concluded: "*Equal opportunity to participate in the fair administration of justice is fundamental to our democratic system.*"[49] Only in his footnotes does one find a discussion of the evidence on gender differences in juries. He cited a 1983 study which concluded that the majority of studies showed no difference, although some evidence supported the proposition that female jurors were more conviction-prone than male jurors in rape cases.[50] Another footnote catalogued the abundant gender stereotypes in handbooks on jury selection and reiterated that the Equal Protection Clause forbids stereotyping, even if it contains a measure of truth, because stereotypes stigmatize and perpetuate discrimination. And in a third footnote, Blackmun noted Barbara Babcock's observation that lawyers for both sides were particularly likely to strike women of color.[51]

Justice O'Connor, writing a concurring opinion, disagreed with Justice Blackmun's dismissal of gender differences in jurors as mere stereotyping. She wrote, "We know that, like race, gender matters," and cited a "plethora" of studies about rape and the absence of similar studies where she expected gender differences, such as sexual harassment, child custody, spousal or child abuse. "One need not be a sexist to share the intuition that, in certain cases, a person's gender and resulting life experience will be relevant to his or her view of the case," she suggested.[52] O'Connor would limit the Constitution's prohibition to the government's use of gender-based challenges. She worried that a battered woman who killed her husband would be barred from striking the men from her jury. Chief Justice Rehnquist, in dissent, distinguished between race and gender discrimination. Not only were women a majority, but "the two sexes differ both biologically and, to a diminishing extent, in experience. It is not merely 'stereotyping' to say that these differences may produce a difference in outlook which is brought to the jury room."[53]

This series of jury cases is helpful for thinking about how best to make arguments for more women judges. Until a few commentators criticized *J.E.B.*, feminists had agreed that excluding women from jury service was not a special benefit women enjoy by virtue of their different social roles but a discriminatory exclusion because women lacked the rationality and independence to deliberate. Women's roles have changed, and, while no one would argue men and women now share caring labor equally, we cannot assume that the duty to care for children or put dinner on the table (something the court seemed overly concerned about in *Hoyt*) precluded all women from jury service.[54] Such an assumption is overbroad at best. At worst, it constitutes harmful stereotyping to suggest that women, whatever their social roles, cannot or should not contribute to this essential duty of citizens in a democracy, and reminds us how recently in human history women have been regarded as full citizens. Whether the state bars them outright, requires them to register voluntarily, or strikes them on the basis of sex using peremptory challenges, women are harmed by the assumption that they cannot contribute, and the justice system as a whole is brought into disrepute. As a matter of constitutional doctrine, complicated issues crop up about whether race is a more disfavored category of discrimination than sex, whether women and men suffer equal harm if they are struck from jury service based on assumed sex differences, and what standard of review each cause of action entails. The larger point remains: assuming all women lack the ability to serve on juries is no longer acceptable in our constitutional democracy.

The jury cases reveal conflict, if not muddled thinking, about other aspects of the harm of women's exclusion. The harm to the individual juror is comparable to the harm done to women suffering employment discrimination that excludes them from judicial office. For both, not just individuals are harmed; rather, a judicial selection system riddled with discriminatory exclusions, like a jury system based on sex stereotypes, brings the system as a whole into disrepute, undermines its credibility, destroys citizen confidence in it, and therefore undermines its legitimacy. Timothy reported how members of the courtroom hissed when counsel struck the one black woman who would have been impaneled to hear black radical activist Angela Davis's case in 1972.[55] When black women are struck in open court based on their group identities, it is hard to miss the badge of second-class citizenship.[56]

Similar evidence of "trafficking in stereotypes" comes in the *voir dire* process, where counsel interviews prospective jurors about their objectivity.[57] Since women are supposed to think like their husbands (but not vice versa), women jurors may be asked about their husbands' occupations. When a California attorney named Carolyn Bobb reported for jury duty in 1982, she objected that only prospective women jurors were asked about their spouses' occupations and so refused to answer. The judge held her in contempt and she spent a day in jail. The judgment of contempt was overturned on appeal.[58] The treatment of prospective women jurors in *voir dire* is very similar to interviews of prospective judges in which only women candidates are asked who will care for their children. In Iowa in 2011, for example, the commission asked the woman candidate for the state supreme court more extensively about parenting and work/life balance than the men.[59]

Litigants sought to keep their cases focused on the Sixth Amendment right to a fair trial, which, as a matter of legal doctrine, might subject the exclusion of women or minority men to a higher standard than equal protection analysis. Hoyt claimed having an all-male jury hurt her because women, her peers, might have decided the case differently. For justice to be done, and to be seen to be done, we need not agree that women decide cases differently from men as either jurors or judges. We might argue instead that litigants facing deciders who are unlike them in key identities implicated in oppression—sex, race, nationality—may come to believe justice has not been done. Legitimacy requires that justice be seen to be done, which means that large categories of people—in this case the majority of the population—cannot be excluded if the public is to regard the system as fair.

The fair trial argument, more so than the equal protection argument, however, does suggest (if not insist) that real differences, not just mere stereotypes, separate the sexes. Hoyt argued women might be more sympathetic to her plight of being abandoned. Healy argued that women better appreciated how other women would be harmed by chemically induced hair loss. J.E.B. believed women were more sympathetic to the paternity case against him than men would have been. As Justice Rehnquist's reference to the "handy maxim" in oral argument in *Taylor* suggested, and as Justice Blackmun's review in *J.E.B.* noted, juror selection advice has been riddled with assertions of sex differences and has contained many untested assumptions based on stereotypes or outright sexism.[60] The justices' opinions in *J.E.B.* reveal disagreement over what the social science studies showed. Justice Blackmun's opinion gave the studies short shrift. Justice O'Connor's concurrence said gender matters and claimed it is true that women are more sympathetic to gender-based violence against other women. The social science, however, is murkier. As I documented in Chapter 2, proponents of difference mostly ignore evidence to the contrary.[61] Studying jurors may be more difficult than studying judges, and much of the data relies on experiments with mock trials drawing on college students. The evidence is mixed: some studies find differences; others do not. What should we make of this conflict? Do we pick one side or the other and declare it to be the better evidence, as Justices Blackmun and O'Connor did? Do we pick the side that comports with what we think we know: that men and women are more alike than different, and that differences tend to be manufactured and magnified rather than real; or that everybody knows that women are different from men in predictable and constant ways?

Babcock argued that there is some basis for assuming race and sex do lead to different decisions,[62] yet she counseled against the harm of "trafficking in the core of the truth in most stereotypes."[63] Like women's rights activists from 1920 to 1975, regardless of one's position on difference and other sex-based classifications, women lawyers were united in advocating for eliminating sex discrimination in jury selection.[64] Rhonda Copelon, who, like Babcock and Ginsburg, challenged sex discrimination in jury selection,[65] went on to campaign for the appointment of more women judges—in particular, on the International Criminal Court. Only after *J.E.B.* did some commentators defend the sex-based peremptory challenge. Grossman heralded *J.E.B.* as "treating jury service as a right of citizenship rather than a privilege of difference" and argued that the foray into difference (a jury of one's peers) came about only because women so decisively and repeatedly lost the equality argument: in arguing they were citizens and therefore could vote and serve on juries before suffrage; in arguing they could serve on juries as citizens once they had the vote; and in showing that excluding jurors on the basis of sex, like race, denied jurors equal protection.[66]

Another conclusion that we might draw is that if we think of sex as a variable and sex differences as causing predictable different outcomes, we might find that it does in some times and places but does not in others. Most feminist litigators find themselves more likely to agree with Justice Rehnquist's handy maxim in *Taylor* than they would like. Women do not always support women candidates, are not always sympathetic to rape victims, find ways to blame and distance themselves from battered women, and can be hostile to women going through divorce if the women divorcing made different choices than they did about work and parenting, for example. Men can sometimes be chivalrous and sometimes even feminist. If we stop using sex as a variable, however, and think of gender as a social construct that becomes more or less salient and operates in different ways in different cases (as I did in Chapter 7 when discussing Rose Bird), we might conclude that men and women will sometimes diverge sharply from one another, and other times will not. Justice O'Connor is right that gender matters, but sex does not reliably predict juror or judge behavior in a consistent, dichotomous, and patterned way. The best social science suggests it is exceedingly difficult to predict how an individual will behave, even based on an ostensibly true sex difference.[67] What matters most of all is the strength of the case. Overland observed:[68]

> Most of the academic research on juror decision-making has reached the rather surprising conclusion that jurors' personal characteristics, including their race, gender, socioeconomic status and so on, have relatively little, if anything, to do with their verdicts in most trials . . . [A]mong all these factors, the most powerful determinant of a juror's verdict in both civil and criminal cases is the relative strength of the competing evidence.[69]

Currie and Pillick concluded that "sex-based generalizations have a stubborn vitality among lawyers," even when they have no basis in social science.[70] (As I argued in Chapters 1 and 2, sex-based generalizations have a stubborn vitality in some corners of social science as well.) If the jury cases do not offer a clear gender analysis of sex differences and how they operate in society, they do offer a blueprint for making arguments about women judges. Both those who believed in essential sex differences and those who did not could conclude that excluding women from juries was wrong, because excluding them utilized a sex-based classification in violation of equal protection; or because it stigmatized excluded jurors as inferior and brought the jury system in disrepute; or simply because, for justice to be done and to be seen to be done, women must be included, even if their exclusion does not change the outcomes or process.

Just as the justices were divided about the difference women made on juries in *J.E.B.*, after suffrage, women's rights campaigners fractured over sex-based differences and the law.[71] Social feminists who wanted labor protections for women opposed an equal rights amendment to the Constitution because they feared it would prohibit protecting women in the workplace. Women's rights campaigners, however, were united in seeking to overturn women's exclusion from jury service.[72] (That is not to say that all women agreed. Just as some women did not favor suffrage, others, particularly rural women, were happy to have the choice of whether to vote but were not keen to have the duty to serve on a jury.[73]) The first women to serve in state legislatures pushed hard to change the laws on jury service. Women's rights activists recognized the connections between the right to vote, the right to serve on juries, the right to practice the professions (especially law), and the right to hold public office. They believed women deserved all of these rights, should have had them as a matter of course as citizens, deserved them once Congress passed the Fourteenth Amendment, but surely possessed them once the states ratified the Nineteenth Amendment.[74] Whatever their views on the matter of sex difference, all understood "the powerful truth of women's most persuasive argument for jury service: that unless women took up the full burdens of citizenship they would always be treated as second-class citizens."[75]

Social movement theorist Joshua Gamson has called for creating forms of action that do not require oppressed groups to construct stable identities as different in order to engage in political action.[76] Historian Joan Scott documented a similar convergence in arguments for *parité* in women's legislative representation in France.[77] Advocates framed the issue as transcending the difference argument: one could support *parité* without appealing to difference.

As in the case for juries, feminists need not resolve their differences over difference in order to campaign for a gender-representative judiciary. It is time for women and their allies to come together across their positions on difference and press for parity. The case of the United Kingdom demonstrates that having a gender-representative bench as a mere byproduct of reforming to create a modern judiciary will not produce continuous progress toward parity. A comparison of judicial selection systems reveals some to be better than others, but without an explicit goal of reaching parity, and without active behavior to attain that goal, we will not secure it as a natural or inevitable byproduct of the growth of women in the legal profession.

THE CASE FOR A GENDER-DIVERSE BENCH[78]

Do Not Argue from Difference

For the most part, women judges as a group do not decide cases differently from men. So why does it matter whether women serve as judges? Perhaps an unconscious reason why we continue to search for the essential sex difference and fall into the essentialist trap in our arguments is because we fear that if we cannot demonstrate difference, we cannot persuasively argue that we need women on the bench. If women do not decide cases differently from men, what is the harm of excluding them? Not in failing to produce different case outcomes, certainly. The jury cases can be of great help here, even though, as I have argued, the reasoning in the opinions is muddled. Most notably, the case for women jurors does not rest on a conviction that women judge differently from men (although those arguments are present, for example, in Justice O'Connor's concurrence in *J.E.B.*). In cases about the exclusion of women and minorities from juries, and in discussing the recusal of judges, courts repeatedly say that it is important not only that justice is done but that justice is seen to be done. If a black man faces an all-white jury, a woman faces an all-male jury, or a Greek national faces an international court made up only of Germans, justice may not be seen to be done. We cannot exclude women from juries or judging because, if we do, justice will not be seen to be done. The process and the result will both lack legitimacy. This legitimacy argument does not rest on a difference argument.

Reversing the Burden of Proof

The later jury cases also provide a second argument for women on the bench that rests on what citizenship is in a democracy. We should reframe the question from "What is distinctive, unique, or different about women that renders their presence necessary on the bench?" to "What justifies their exclusion?" Why not reverse the burden of proof? Why should women be excluded? Political theorist Anne Phillips makes this argument for legislative representation.[79] In a modern democracy, surely the burden of proof should be on those who want to exclude citizens from representation and participation in core tasks of citizenship, such as serving on juries or as judges, as the jury cases argued. Women did not vote dramatically differently from men after they won the vote.[80] Husbands often vote the same way as their wives. But no one would now argue that it is therefore justifiable to exclude married women from voting as they are "covered" by their husbands. Because voting is now understood to be a core function of citizenship, it is no longer defensible to exclude women from the franchise or juries, and we do not need to have evidence that they vote differently from men to make that argument—as we once did. It is not a big step from a representative jury[81] to a representative judiciary. Justice Abrahamson compares the two roles explicitly after serving on a jury.[82]

As I showed in Chapter 4, feminist advocates asked the President through the media whether the best man for the job of Supreme Court justice might just be a woman. Similarly, feminists have been working within the European Union to reframe debates about the democracy deficit to advocate for representation in decision-making. The European Council has pressed member states to explain why they have not included any women's names on their shortlists for consideration for appointment to the European Court of Human Rights. Feminists need to continue to reframe the question of what is the harm of excluding women to what justifies their exclusion.

Exclusion Stigmatizes

The jury cases, particularly the cases about peremptory challenges, also identify a concern about the message sent when jurors are struck solely because of their sex or race: that these citizens, unlike white men, are incapable of impartiality or objectivity.[83] Such actions not only harm those struck, but bring the entire justice system into disrepute. The same arguments apply to recusal motions against women and minority men judges. Whether it is schoolchildren visiting the US Supreme Court, law students visiting the European Court of Justice, or people looking at pictures of the Iowa Supreme Court, when they gaze at a court and see only men, they receive a powerful message of exclusion. Justice Ginsburg made a similar point about three women on the US Supreme Court: "When the schoolchildren file in and out of the court and they look up and they see three women, then that will seem natural and proper—just how it is."[84] Was there not one woman in the whole of England qualified to serve as a Law Lord prior to 2002? Not one woman in all of the European Union capable of serving on the European Court of Justice prior to 1999? Not one woman in all of Idaho, Indiana, or Iowa capable of serving on those states' supreme courts in 2012? Only one woman in all of the seven states of the Eighth Circuit who has ever been qualified to serve? Not one woman in Malta capable of serving on the European Court of Human Rights?

The argument about diversity on the court is often dismissed or denigrated as mere symbolism. If women do not decide cases differently from men—producing different outcomes—then, arguably, the only reason we might want them on the court is for window dressing or political correctness. The presence of women disrupts the normal assumption that heterosexual white men are the only citizens capable of performing the core ritual of rendering objective judgment, that only privileged men are naturally suited to assume authority on behalf of the state and to exercise their patriarchal care on behalf of all of society. In Chapter 1, I drew on Ellen Lewin's work to demonstrate how women's presence disrupts these powerful narratives. Sonia Sotomayor clearly triggered anxiety about expanding the deciders to include women of color. Privilege and authority are joined in ways that seem natural and proper, and appointments such as Sotomayor's disrupt these naturalized links and enable us to see exclusion. Chapter 3, which examined the case of Rosalie Wahl, argued that we should not underestimate the important symbolic role of women in such a public office—not just for the girls or women law students who visit the court, but for the effect it has on everyone, from colleagues on the bench to litigants to the general public. Chapter 4 revealed that presidents have understood this symbolism when appointing federal judges. It is profoundly important that women sit in judgment, whether they do so on television or in real life. It is no accident that the exclusion of women from mandatory jury service was one of the last statutory sex-based classifications to be struck down as violative of the US Constitution's Equal Protection Clause. Women exercising judgment breaks a powerful taboo in our society. Since at least the 1850s, women have argued that, under conditions of inequality, men could not be considered women's peers and so it was unfair to have only men judge them. But they also recognized that "making women jurors changed their status to make them the peers of men."[85] They wanted to be peers and to be full citizens. As Ritter observed, "If women were to remain a separate grade, then they deserved their own justice. Likewise, if women were men's equals then they could not be excluded from the jury box."[86] Serving on a jury was a path to justice and a marker of status.

Applying the Norm of Nondiscrimination

Furthermore, we can draw on the conceptual frameworks of employment discrimination to infer discrimination from a vast disjuncture between the qualified labor pool and women in the job—in this case, judges.[87] The harm of excluding women may not be that they would have produced different outcomes, but that discrimination is wrong. If we conceptualize the harm of women's exclusion as an instance of discrimination, rather than argue that women's difference would produce different results, then we might argue for a broad ideological representation of women on the bench, not just feminists. For cases of disparate impact (in Europe, indirect discrimination), when a selection system results in far fewer individuals with a characteristic from the pool, the burden of proof shifts to the employer to defend the criteria and process. If women receive more than 50 percent of law degrees but do not hold high judicial office, the assumption is something about the selection process or path toward promotion operates to winnow them out unfairly.

Feminists used employment discrimination standards of disparate impact to show how the American Bar Association's standards of, for example, ten years of large-firm experience disproportionately weeded out women, especially those who, as Justice O'Connor did, came of age at a time when large firms openly discriminated against women. Similarly, the UK's "tap on the shoulder" system, which requires candidates to be known to judges, discriminates against capable women who may not have invested their time schmoozing with judges as members of the male-dominated Inns of Court. Just as we might ask whether there is not one woman member of the Iowa Bar who is capable of serving on the state's supreme court, we might have asked, as President George W. Bush was appointing one conservative man after another to the Eighth Circuit Court of Appeals, was there not one conservative woman in all of the seven states? Was Harriet Miers the only conservative woman suitable for nomination to the US Supreme Court? (And even she proved not conservative enough.) Why do conservative women fail to run the gauntlet of conservative groups and the Senate Judiciary Committee while conservative men, such as Chief Justice Roberts and Justice Alito, fly through? Is sex discrimination acceptable if non-feminist women are its victims? Many feminists ask, "Do you want just *any* woman on the bench?" Another popular formulation is: "Do you support her *just because* she is a woman?" Once again, I advocate for reversing the question. Why should women *not* be considered? Why is it acceptable for conservative women to be discriminated against on the basis of sex?

Women on the bench matter, not because they necessarily render feminist judgments, but because they disrupt narratives of male power and deserve equal treatment. In Chapter 5, I described how British women challenged the discriminatory nature of governmental appointments. Judicial appointments may be exempt from certain employment discrimination statutes, but they are not exempt from equal protection norms.

Gender Merits Representation

The final argument is the strongest: representation. As I discussed in Chapter 6, courts are representative institutions. In developing arguments about why judges must be broadly representative and why women need to be included that do not rest on showing that women comprise an essentially different group, drawing analogies using representational discourse in other areas besides gender—most obviously geography—is helpful. Prior to the Civil War, the US Supreme Court was precariously balanced between Southerners and Northerners.[88] More recently, presidents such as Ronald Reagan argued that we needed more justices from the West, resulting in the appointments of Justices Rehnquist, O'Connor, and Anthony Kennedy. My research in President Carter's papers showed that the same senators who decried the deviation from a pure merit system when Carter sought a more racially and gender-diverse bench strenuously objected if their state was in danger of losing a seat on the relevant circuit court of appeals.[89]

Lady Hale made this same point about the United Kingdom. Historically, the Law Lords have included two from Scotland and one from Northern Ireland, but no woman had ever served before Hale was appointed. At the international level, it would be unthinkable for the European Court of Justice not to have a German judge, even though the Treaty on the Functioning of the European Union does not require a judge from each member state. To justify this state of affairs, no one argues that geographic representation endangers the court as a meritocratic institution. Nor does anyone believe that an Arizonan judge or a German judge is a different species of judge or will vote differently from, say, a Californian judge or a Belgian judge. No one has to talk about different voices, or suggests that Germans or Arizonans are a "flavor."[90] Simply put, our notions of fairness demand representation in these cases. Why? The geographic representation "requirement" recognizes that judgments command more legitimacy if people from different states/countries/regions participate in the deliberation. In short, a more representative bench commands more legitimacy and is seen to be fairer. A parallel argument exists for representation in legislatures. We do not need to show that senators from one state vote differently from senators in another to demand that both should be in the Senate.

Women Are Not Deficient but Meritorious Candidates: Taking a Hard Look at Where Our Standards of Merit Come from and How Consistently We Apply Them

A danger is that by focusing on the case for gender diversity on the bench, women candidates become the "affirmative action hires" rather than the most meritorious candidates for the job. A good example is the case of Lady Brenda Hale. Her superior qualifications—clearly she was the best person for the job— were eclipsed by the controversy surrounding her feminism and the framing of the discussion in terms of whether it was "time for a woman." President Carter's appointments, however, offered a powerful lesson. Once merit rather than cronyism and patronage become the standard, women did better. In fact, using objective standards of merit, Carter's women appointments were better qualified than the men. If genuine merit replaces cronyism as the criterion for appointment, more women become eligible. They are appointed because of merit, not in spite of merit. Being known to the appointer—cronyism—never seems to detract from men's appointments, unless they are grossly unqualified. (And sometimes it does not even detract in those cases, as we saw with Justice Clark in Chapter 7.) But being appointed "because" she is a woman undermines that woman's credibility. Funny how the best person for the job for the Eighth Circuit Court of Appeals is the Congressman's college roommate, or the Senator's law partner, but when Chief Justice Rose Bird is appointed to the California Supreme Court, for example, the fact that gender was a consideration undermines her legitimacy.

Representation, Merit, and Nondiscrimination

When Florence Allen was appointed to the Sixth Circuit Court of Appeals, the Attorney General was asked whether he was pressing for her appointment because she was a woman. He replied that he was merely trying to make sure she was not barred from office because of her sex. When Carter selected Barbara Babcock to serve in the Justice Department, reporters asked her how it felt to get her job "because she was a woman." She replied that it felt a whole lot better than not getting the job because she was a woman. Wisconsin Supreme Court Justice Shirley Abrahamson addressed this conundrum in her address to the National Association of Women Judges in 1984. Abrahamson was the first woman appointed to serve on the Wisconsin Supreme Court. Reporters asked her whether she was appointed because she was a woman. Replying that she was confident she was appointed on the basis of merit (she graduated first in her class), she commented, "Had I anticipated the question, I would have realized how obvious it was, given society's expectation that a woman could not make it on her own merit."[91] The questions continued—Was she a token? Did she represent women? Would women judges make a difference? Abrahamson concluded:

> Naturally, I want to have all these wonderful traits attributed to me. It may be useful for me to claim that women have a different perceptual capacity they can bring to the bench. But do I believe that? I have spent a lifetime fighting society's urge to stereotype both men and women. I believe, and I have often said, that men and women are more alike than different, and that there should be equal opportunity for all. We must look not at gender but at the individual, judging each on his or her own merits.[92]

Abrahamson humorously opined that since judges were overworked and underpaid, perhaps judging was women's work. She suggested that governors might have thought so too, and hurriedly drawn up lists of eligible women, and had appointed Abrahamson—along with Ruth Abrams in Massachusetts and Rose Bird in California—because their names had come first alphabetically on their respective lists.[93] More seriously, she declared what other women judges have repeatedly said: that women, like men, bring all their life experiences to their judging, and that decisions are better when more diverse groups of people deliberate.[94] Being a woman, being a lawyer, being a child of immigrants, being a product of the New York public school system, and being the traumatized parent of a teenager who insisted on using his driver's license were all experiences she brought to judging.[95]

My experiences as a feminist and an emerging feminist scholar in the United States and the United Kingdom that I described in Chapter 1 led me to write this book. I have been troubled by how judicial scholars ignore gender and women, and by how activists and those who study women and politics ignore the judiciary. I have also had the privilege of meeting and knowing inspiring women judges. The humor of Chief Justice Shirley Abrahamson or Justice Ruth Bader Ginsburg's reference to the "handy maxim" of sexist assumptions speaks powerfully to me in print, much as having heard Justice Rosalie Wahl recount Koryne Horbal saying, "Thank you for being ready" still touches my heart. As one who has long studied sex discrimination, the experiences Rose Bird endured in her workplace pained, horrified, and scared me as a woman leader. I loved celebrating Sonia Sotomayor's ascendancy to the bench with a cadre of ecstatic Minnesota Latinas. Reading books such as *Crows over a Wheatfield* and *The Appeal* remind me of the issue's importance.

Women, as a group, may not decide cases differently from men, as a group, but excluding a majority of the population from higher judicial office unduly narrows the pool of talent. Perhaps President Obama had it right in his valorization of empathy rather than experience. Whoever is judging, they will have to pass judgment on those different from themselves. For justice to be done, and to be seen to be done, and for women not forever to be relegated to second-class citizenship, we need to draw more widely among our population in choosing judges. As the judiciary becomes even more visible and powerful, and as judicial selection continues to be highly contested in the United States, the representativeness of the judiciary will likely only grow in importance.

Gender is Not a Proxy for Feminist: We Need Both Represented on the Bench

The campaign to establish a gender-diverse International Criminal Court offers some insight into how to accomplish a gender-diverse bench and why it matters. Since the 1993 Vienna Conference, and strengthened by the Beijing Conference, feminist international human rights activists have fought to make rape in war a crime against humanity and to prosecute it vigorously in both the Yugoslavian and Rwandan war crimes tribunals. The campaigners drew from their experience with the women members of those other two war crimes tribunals to suggest that it was the women judges who pressed for recognition of the harm of rape.[96] So they insisted that the Rome Statute of the International Criminal Court specify that the composition of the court have a fair representation of women. They succeeded, as seven of the eighteen judges were women, an enormous breakthrough for either domestic or international tribunals. They also insisted that one criterion for prosecutors and judges be that they have experience in prosecuting sex crimes and are sensitive to gender issues. Just as President Carter required that his women appointees must have a demonstrable commitment to equal justice under law, the campaign for gender justice did not rely merely on the gender of the judges as a proxy for knowledge and interest in women's experience of sexual assault. Lastly, they have maintained an active vigilance on all aspects of the ICC through organizing and communication, not assuming that the treaty is self-executing or that women on the bench in and of itself produces social change.[97]

Whether it is a United Nations Security Council resolution calling for the International Criminal Tribunal for the former Yugoslavia to include women judges, or a requirement from the Council of Europe that member state nominations to the European Court of Human Rights include women on the shortlists (as long as exceptions are allowed for), or proposals to the Kenyan Constitution that no branch of government has more than two-thirds members of one sex,[98] the continued exclusion of women from legal institutions grossly disproportionate to their representation in the legal profession and the population is likely to be challenged. Powerful arguments support women serving as judges. Gender matters. But the best arguments do not rely on difference. We need to recommit ourselves to the goal of a diverse and representative bench and to mobilize rather than assume gender parity will happen naturally or inevitably. Judicial selection systems remain infected with gender bias, and we have made little progress. If we want to reach our goal of equal representation, we need to organize, mobilize, and recast our arguments.

Women's experiences and feminist consciousness both matter, although the quest to find sex differences and the coherence of a singular women's perspective are misguided. We need more feminists on the bench,[99] including men—whom I believe can be feminists—and we need women on the bench irrespective of whether they are feminists. Sex discrimination is not acceptable if the women are conservatives or anti feminists. Particularly on collegiate courts, I think there is a strong case to be made for including people with experiences of all sorts, rather than using "woman" as a proxy for feminist, liberal, or compassionate attitudes toward the downtrodden.

CONCLUSION

Throughout this book, I have argued that it can be useful to use sex as a variable. We can see if one method of selection is more likely to produce greater numbers of women than another (it is not). We can see if women take longer to confirm, or are less likely to be confirmed (sometimes). We can compare women's representation in the qualified labor pool and their likelihood of being selected as judges (women are underrepresented). We can see if they are more or less likely to be chosen for feeder statuses, such as Queen's Counsel or law clerk (less likely). We can track their numbers, and the reversals. Simply by counting women, we can learn a great deal.

Using sex as a variable, however, is unhelpful if it leads us to magnify differences or tendencies or to claim differences exist when they do not. In Chapter 2, I analyzed the data on sex differences in judging and found little support for difference, apart from a greater likelihood of women on US appellate courts to find for sex discrimination plaintiffs and influence their colleagues on panels to do so, too. Individuals, however, do matter. Justice Ginsburg provides a ringing voice championing the cause of women and criticizing the Supreme Court's treatment of young girls,[100] women managers who are paid less than men, or Wal-Mart employees who are not seen to be a class. Justice O'Connor joined her at times, but not always, and Justices Marshall, Brennan, Blackmun, and Breyer have done so as well. Judge Pillay brought the issue of rape as a war crime into deliberations, and Lady Hale cut through stereotypes about rape victims' behavior.[101] Justice L'Heureux-Dubé writes as a feminist; other women jurists refuse the label. I would like to see more judges like all of them on the bench.

In Chapter 2, I criticized the framing of women judges as adjudicating differently from men. First, the claim of difference often rests on studies with small numbers or conducted over a short period of time. Second, sex differences emerge for some kinds of cases but not others. Researchers, for example, find differences in sex discrimination cases but not sexual harassment cases,[102] or they find women supreme court justices more likely than men to vote for the woman in divorce cases (that likelihood diminishes if two women serve on the panel, but not if three serve). In other words, the likelihood that women will vote for women is extremely variable in ways that contradict essentialist assumptions.[103] They show little consistency over time, across jurisdiction, or in category of case. Third, by treating sex as a variable rather than exploring gender as a social process, they often assume rather than interrogate women's supposed and essential difference from men. Most troubling of all is the way the repeated finding of no or few sex differences does nothing to disrupt the conviction that such differences exist. Instead, researchers come to the conclusion that their studies have merely inexplicably failed to unearth them. Finally, women judges themselves largely reject this framing of difference.[104]

By contrast, looking at women judges through the lens of gender illuminates far more than simply analyzing sex as a variable. Women's studies scholars have shown repeatedly that when you place women at the center of analysis, your understandings change, from when the welfare state began to how children reason about moral dilemmas. When we add race, and think intersectionally, our understandings of the civil rights movement change by placing black women at the center of our analysis. Even more powerful is to move beyond women and analyze gender. Looking at the case of Rosalie Wahl in Minnesota, as I did in Chapter 3, reveals how social movements and candidates use emotions to connect with voters and mobilize activists. Looking at a case of a woman, but more importantly understanding how Rosalie Wahl "did" gender and was gendered, leads us to shift our understandings of social movement mobilization and the electoral process. Not all women candidates are the same, or mean the same thing. Social movement scholars need to bring emotions and emotion work back into the equation to understand mobilization. And women and politics scholars need to understand the fragility and the variability of women voters' connections to women candidates. Looking at a case of a judicial election also helps remove the blind spots social movement scholars and political scientists have about the third branch of government.

In Chapter 4, I looked at how President Carter came to appoint more women to the federal bench than all previous presidents combined and how he linked his commitment to women in government to merit selection of judges. Until recently, most feminist scholars saw women engaging the state as compromised sell-outs and did not count them as feminists at all. Interest groups and social movement scholars focus on pressure politics, looking at strategies and indicators of strength. But I argue policy implementation occurred because of the efforts of a strategically positioned feminist insider who worked in close collaboration with outside groups. Those who want to understand policy success and policy implementation would do well to pay attention to gender, women, and feminism in their case studies. Feminist scholars should pay more attention to the judicial branch and to women insiders. Both are engaged in meaning making as part of social change.

In Chapter 5, I showed how looking at the case of women judges can improve our understanding of agenda-setting. It is often the case that women's reform is promoted, and ultimately deemed acceptable, as being instrumental to some other goal. If we give public assistance to women, they can feed their children. If we pass married women's property acts, they will shield some property from creditors, providing a form of debtor's relief. If we pay attention to women's reproductive health in the workplace, men are safer. If we stop excluding women, we can show that Britain has modernized its judiciary. Tying women's inclusion to the case of modernization enabled the UK to appoint its first woman to its highest appellate court and reform its judicial selection process, but it has yet to mobilize public support behind a diverse and representative judiciary, which is necessary for further progress.

In Chapter 6, I showed what we can learn about the concept of representation by looking at courts as representative institutions and gender as an identity that merits representation. I showed how representative discourse is nothing new to courts. Closer scrutiny of how courts need to be representative in order to be legitimate reveals that legislators are often more like judges than the other way around, even though they are politically accountable to their constituents in a way that would be inconsistent with judicial independence. The European Court of Justice provides a great location for examining this question as representation is built into its practices, the European Union has a deep discourse about women and decision-making that has not been fully extended to courts, and lawyers struggle to wrest control of judicial selection from politicians.

In Chapter 7, looking at the case of Rose Bird in California showed a sharp contrast to Rosalie Wahl in Minnesota, despite many similarities. Once again, we can learn some things from using sex as a variable and from counting, but we learn much more when we combine that with a gender analysis. The core concept of backlash has been applied in a gender context and is useful to understanding Bird's demise. Her case, analyzed in conjunction with Wahl, further refutes the "too far, too fast" argument. It sheds light on why women's progress has been so slow and links heretofore isolated incidents to identify reversals and obstacles. Moreover, the case reveals the shortcomings of an all-or-nothing way of thinking about gender, rather than seeing gender as an important part, if not the decisive part, of an explanation. It provides an example of how to do a gender analysis and figure out whether gender helps explain events. This analysis is different from the approach of using sex as a variable.

Lastly, looking at the arguments about women's exclusion from juries provides insight as we develop arguments to support increasing the number of women in the judiciary. Courts wrestled with two values compromised by women's exclusion: equality and the right to a fair trial. Although courts could not always decide whether women were a "flavor" or whether they were different from men and that difference warranted their exclusion or made their inclusion all the more necessary, they ultimately developed a compelling case about why legal deliberations should not be done solely by men.

Although I have been critical of using sex as a variable, I believe it has its place, just as quantitative analysis can tell us a great deal. Whether women decide cases differently from men, however, should not be our only question. Nor should we understand a gender analysis to be exhausted by the search for essential sex differences. Instead, I have tried to argue that gender, understood as a social process, provides a rich conceptual tool to investigate other concepts, such as policy diffusion and emotions and social movement mobilization, backlash, insider–outsider partnerships for policy implementation, agenda-setting, and representation. Finally, I have argued that we should make the case for women judges without relying on claims about sex differences. And it is imperative that we mobilize for that task.

NOTES

1 INTRODUCTION

1 Barack Obama, "Remarks by the President in Nominating Judge Sonia Sotomayor to the United States Supreme Court," The White House, May 26, 2009, http://www.whitehouse.gov/the_press_office/Remarks-by-the-President-in-Nominating-Judge-Sonia-Sotomayor-to-the-United-States-Supreme-Court/, accessed July 27, 2011.

2 "Neither she [Elena's mother], nor Elena's father, lived to see this day. But I think her mother would relish this moment. I think she would relish—as I do—the prospect of three women taking their seat on the nation's highest Court for the first time in history. A Court that would be more inclusive, more representative, more reflective of us as a people than ever before." Barack Obama, "Remarks by the President and Solicitor General Elena Kagan at the Nomination of Solicitor General Elena Kagan to the Supreme Court," The White House, May 10, 2010, http://www.whitehouse. gov/the-press-office/remarks-president-and-solicitor-general-elena-kagan-nomination-solicitor-general-el, accessed July 27, 2011.

3 Dahlia Lithwick, "The Female Factor: Will Three Women Really Change the Court?" Newsweek, August 30, 2010, http://www.newsweek.com/2010/08/30/can-three-women-really-change-the-supreme-court.print.html, accessed January 25, 2011.

4 The more than 130 scholars from 17 countries that make up the Law and Society Association's Collaborative Research Network on Gender and Justice are an exception. http://genderandjudging.com/, accessed September 25, 2011.

5 The different voice refers to Carol Gilligan's landmark book *In a Different Voice: Psychological Theory and Women's Development* (Cambridge, MA: Harvard University Press, 1982). In the book, Gilligan did three things: she critiqued theories of moral development developed only by studying boys; she suggested that moral reasoning could include an ethic of care, not just an ethic of justice, something she discovered by giving

a hypothetical moral dilemma to boys and girls; and she noted that women who self-described their decisions to have an abortion as agonizing reasoned about the decision based on a web of connection to others. Although Gilligan never said the ethic of care and web of connection that she found (the different voice) was exclusively and distinctively women's voice, many others took her work as standing for that proposition.

6   *Groundhog Day*, directed by Harold Ramis, is a 1993 American comedy film starring Bill Murray about a self-absorbed TV weatherman who finds himself repeating the same day over and over again.

7   Sally J. Kenney, "Women, Feminism, Gender, and Law in Political Science: Ruminations of a Feminist Academic," *Women & Politics* 15, no. 3 (1995): 43–69.

8   Judith Taylor, "Imperfect Intimacies: The Problem of Women's Sociality in Contemporary North American Feminist Memoir," *Gender & Society* 22, no. 6 (2008): 705–727.

9   Martha Chamallas, *Introduction to Feminist Legal Theory*, 2nd edn (New York: Aspen, 2003).

10   Herma Hill Kay and Geraldine Sparrow, "Workshop on Judging: Does Gender Make a Difference?" *Wisconsin Women's Law Journal* 16, no. 1 (2001): 6.

11   Christina Boyd, Lee Epstein, and Andrew D. Martin, "Untangling the Causal Effects of Sex on Judging," *American Journal of Political Science* 54, no. 2 (2010): 389–411.

12   Deborah Solomon, "Case Closed: Questions for Sandra Day O'Connor," *New York Times Magazine*, March 22, 2009, 14.

13   Emily Bazelon, "The Place of Women on the Court," *New York Times Magazine*, July 12, 2009, 22. See also Ruth Bader Ginsburg, "Some Thoughts on the 1980s Debate over Special versus Equal Treatment for Women," *Law and Inequality* 4, no. 1 (1986): 143–151, where she said: "I am fearful, or suspicious, of generalizations about the way women or men are. My life's experience indicates that they cannot guide me reliably in making decisions about particular individuals" (148). The highest-ranking jurist in the United Kingdom, Lady Brenda Hale, declared: "Women do not want to claim that they look at things differently from men, partly because this would be manifestly inaccurate in many cases, and partly because it would make them less well qualified to be judges" ("Equality and the Judiciary: Why Should We Want More Women Judges?" *Public Law* Autumn (2001): 489–504). She thought that her academic career, reforming tendencies, and tendency to go native would be more important in explaining her judicial decisions than her gender (Hale 2001, 500).

14   Elaine Martin, "Judicial Role Models: A Women Judges' Network," paper presented at the Midwest Political Science Association annual meeting, April 18–20, 1991.

15   Elaine Martin, "The Representative Role of Women Judges," *Judicature* 77, no. 3 (1993): 171–172. Other women judges have written about the difference women will make. Madame Justice Bertha Wilson ("Will Women Judges Really Make a Difference?" *Osgoode Hall Law Journal* 28, no. 3 (1990): 507–522) was sympathetic to the possibility there might be some cases where women judges would correct male bias.

16   Kathryn Werdegar, "Why a Woman on the Bench?" *Wisconsin Women's Law Journal* 16, no. 1 (2001): 31–40, 39.

17 Werdegar 2001, 40.

18 Susan M. Hartmann, *From Margin to Mainstream: American Women and Politics since 1960* (New York: Alfred A. Knopf, 1989); Catharine A. MacKinnon, *Feminism Unmodified: Discourses on Life and Law* (Cambridge, MA: Harvard University Press, 1987).

19 Mary Katzenstein, *Faithful and Fearless: Moving Feminist Protest inside the Church and Military* (Princeton, NJ: Princeton University Press, 1998).

20 Susan M. Hartmann, *The Other Feminists: Activists in the Liberal Establishment* (New Haven, CT: Yale University Press, 1998a).

21 Catherine E. Rymph, *Republican Women: Feminism and Conservatism from Suffrage through the Rise of the New Right* (Chapel Hill: University of North Carolina Press, 2006).

22 Mary Jane Mossman, *The First Women Lawyers: A Comparative Study of Gender, Law and the Legal Professions* (Portland, OR: Hart, 2006); Sally J. Kenney, "Julia C. Addington from Stacyville, Iowa: First Woman Elected to Public Office in the United States? The World?" *Women/Politics* 21, no. 1 (2010): 12; Albie Sachs and Joan Hoff Wilson, *Sexism and the Law: A Study of Male Beliefs and Judicial Bias* (Oxford: Martin Robertson and Co., 1978).

23 Ellen Lewin, *Recognizing Ourselves: Ceremonies of Lesbian and Gay Commitment* (New York: Columbia University Press, 1998).

24 Lewin 1998, 86.

25 Lewin 1998, 54.

26 Lewin 1998, 242.

27 Lewin 1998, 31.

28 Joan Wallach Scott, *Parité! Sexual Equality and the Crisis of French Universalism* (Chicago: University of Chicago Press, 2005).

29 Scott 2005, 5.

30 Scott 2005, 54.

31 Derrick Bell, *Faces at the Bottom of the Well: The Permanence of Racism* (New York: Basic Books, 1992).

32 Elisabeth Israels Perry, "Rhetoric, Strategy, and Politics in the New York Campaign for Women's Jury Service, 1917–1975," *New York History* 82, no. 1 (2001): 53–78, 59; Gretchen Ritter, "Jury Service and Women's Citizenship before and after the Nineteenth Amendment," *Law and History Review* 20, no. 3 (2002): 479–515; Melissa S. Williams, *Voice, Trust, and Memory: Marginalized Groups and the Failings of Liberal Representation* (Princeton, NJ: Princeton University Press, 1998).

33 Linda Gordon, *Pitied but Not Entitled: Single Mothers and the History of Welfare, 1890–1935* (New York: The Free Press, 1994).

34 Holly J. McCammon, Courtney Sanders Muse, Harmony D. Newman, and Teresa M. Terrell, "Movement Framing and Discursive Opportunity Structures: The Political Successes of the US Women's Jury Movements," *American Sociological Review* 72, no. 5 (2007): 725–749; Perry 2001; Ritter 2002.

35 MacKinnon 1987.

36 Martha L. Minow, *Making All the Difference: Inclusion, Exclusion, and American Law* (Ithaca, NY: Cornell University Press, 1990).

37   Sally J. Kenney, *For Whose Protection? Reproductive Hazards and Exclusionary Policies in the United States and Britain* (Ann Arbor: University of Michigan Press, 1992).

38   Patricia Yancey Martin, John R. Reynolds, and Shelley Keith, "Gender Bias and Feminist Consciousness among Judges and Attorneys: A Standpoint Theory Analysis," *Signs: Journal of Women in Culture and Society* 27, no. 3 (2002): 665–701.

39   Rosemary Hunter, "The High Price of Success: The Backlash against Women Judges in Australia," in *Calling for Change: Women, Law, and the Legal Profession*, eds. Elizabeth Sheehy and Sheila McIntyre (Ottawa: University of Ottawa Press, 2006), 282–301.

40   Sonia Sotomayor, "A Latina Judge's Voice," *Berkeley La Raza Law Journal* 13, no. 1 (2002): 87–93.

41   Carol J. Greenhouse, "Judgment and the Justice: An Ethnographic Reading of the Sotomayor Confirmation Hearings," *Law, Culture and the Humanities*, November 25, 2010, http://lch.sagepub.com/content/early/2010/11/12/1743872110374916, accessed November 23, 2011.

42   Nancy Maveety, "Difference in Judicial Discourse," *Politics & Gender* 6, no. 3 (2010): 452–465.

43   Brenda Hale, "Foreword," in *Feminist Judgments: From Theory to Practice*, ed. Rosemary Hunter, Clare McGlynn, and Erika Rackley (Oxford: Hart, 2010).

44   Sally J. Kenney, "Britain Appoints First Woman Law Lord," *Judicature* 87, no. 4 (2004): 189–190.

45   Sarah Childs and Mona Lena Krook, "Critical Mass Theory and Women's Political Representation," *Political Studies* 56, no. 3 (2008): 725–736.

46   Elaine Martin and Barry Pyle, "Gender, Race, and Partisanship on the Michigan Supreme Court," *Albany Law Review* 63, no. 4 (2000): 1205–1236. See also Elaine Martin and Barry Pyle, "State High Courts and Divorce: The Impact of Judicial Gender," *University of Toledo Law Review* 36, no. 4 (2005): 923-948.

47   Sally J. Kenney, "Domestic Violence Intervention Program: Unconditional Shelter?" *Nonprofit Management and Leadership* 16, no. 2 (2005): 221–243, http://www.hhh.umn.edu/centers/wpp/pdf/case_studies/dvip/DVIP_case.pdf, accessed November 28, 2011.

48   Ginsburg 1986, 144, citing Cynthia Fuchs Epstein, *Women in Law*, 2nd edn (Urbana: University of Illinois Press, 1993).

49   Corinna Barnard, "Wal-Mart Ruling Puts Big Chill on Female Workers," *Women's eNews*, June 25, 2011, http://www.womensenews.org/story/in-the-courts/110624/wal-mart-ruling-puts-big-chill-female-workers, accessed August 12, 2011.

50   Theda Skocpol, *Protecting Soldiers and Mothers: The Political Origins of Social Policy in the United States* (Cambridge, MA: Belknap Press of Harvard University Press, 1992).

51   Herbert Jacob, *Silent Revolution: The Transformation of Divorce Law in the United States* (Chicago: University of Chicago Press, 1988).

52   Mary Joe Frug, "Progressive Feminist Legal Scholarship: Can We Claim 'A Different Voice'?" *Harvard Women's Law Journal* 15 (1992): 37–64; Gilligan 1982.

53   Joan Kelly, "Did Women Have a Renaissance?" in *Women, History, and Theory: The Essays of Joan Kelly* (Chicago: University of Chicago Press, 1984).

54 Carol Pateman, *The Sexual Contract* (Stanford, CA: Stanford University Press, 1988).

55 Belinda Robnett, *How Long? How Long? African American Women in the Struggle for Civil Rights* (New York: Oxford University Press, 1997).

56 Benita Roth, *Separate Roads to Feminism: Black, Chicana, and White Feminist Movements in America's Second Wave* (Cambridge: Cambridge University Press, 2004).

57 Boyd, Epstein, and Martin 2010.

2 GENDER, JUDGING, AND DIFFERENCE

1 I presented an earlier version of this chapter to the International Meeting of the Law and Society Association in Berlin in 2007, which was published in the *International Journal of the Legal Profession* 15, nos. 1–2 (2008): 87–110. I would like to thank Myra Marx Ferree and Patricia Yancey Martin for their helpful comments, and Amber Shipley and Lura Barber for research assistance. Thanks, too, for the helpful comments from the Gender and Judging Collaborative Research Network of the Law and Society Association.

2 Martha Chamallas, *Introduction to Feminist Legal Theory*, 2nd edn (New York: Aspen, 2003).

3 Sally J. Kenney, "New Research on Gendered Political Institutions," *Political Research Quarterly* 49, no. 2 (1996a): 445–466.

4 Eugene Borgida and Susan T. Fiske, *Beyond Common Sense: Psychological Science in the Courtroom* (Oxford: Wiley-Blackwell, 2008); Linda Hamilton Krieger, "The Content of Our Categories: A Cognitive Bias Approach to Discrimination and Equal Employment Opportunity," *Stanford Law Review* 47, no. 6 (1995): 1161–1248.

5 Kate Malleson, "Diversity in the Judiciary: The Case for Positive Action," *Journal of Law and Society* 36, no. 3 (2009): 376–402.

6 Beverly Blair Cook, "Women Judges: The End of Tokenism," in *Women in the Courts*, eds. Winifred L. Hepperle and Laura Crites (Williamsburg, VA: National Center for State Courts, 1978b), 84–105.

7 Cook 1978b.

8 Beverly Blair Cook, "Women Judges: A Preface to Their History," *Golden Gate University Law Review* 14, no. 3 (1984a): 573–610.

9 Cook 1984a.

10 Cook 1984a, 606.

11 Nicholas O. Alozie, "Selection Methods and the Recruitment of Women to State Courts of Last Resort," *Social Science Quarterly* 77, no. 1 (1996): 110–126; Kathleen A. Bratton and Rorie L. Spill, "Existing Diversity and Judicial Selection: The Role of the Appointment Method in Establishing Gender Diversity in State Supreme Courts," *Social Science Quarterly* 83, no. 2 (2002): 504–518; Elaine Martin and Barry Pyle, "Gender and Racial Diversification of State Supreme Courts," *Women & Politics* 24, no. 2 (2002): 35–52; Mark S. Hurwitz and Drew Noble Lanier, "Explaining Judicial

Diversity: The Differential Ability of Women and Minorities to Attain Seats on State Supreme and Appellate Courts," *State Politics and Policy Quarterly* 3, no. 4 (2003): 329–352; Malia Reddick, Michael J. Nelson, and Rachel Paine Caufield, "Explaining Diversity on State Courts," paper presented at the Midwest Political Science Association annual meeting, Chicago, April 2–5, 2009a; Malia Reddick, Michael J. Nelson, and Rachel Paine Caufield, "Racial and Gender Diversity on State Courts: An AJS Study," *Judges' Journal* 48, no. 3 (2009b): 28–32; Margaret Williams, "Women's Representation on State Trial and Appellate Courts," *Social Science Quarterly* 88, no. 5 (2007): 1192–1204.

12   Cook 1984a, 589.

13   Cynthia L. Cooper, "Women Supreme Court Clerks Striving for 'Commonplace,'" *Perspectives: The Quarterly Magazine of the American Bar Association Commission on Women in the Profession* 17, no. 1 (2008): 18–22.

14   Beverly Blair Cook, "Women as Supreme Court Candidates: From Florence Allen to Sandra O'Connor," *Judicature* 65, no. 6 (1982): 314–326; Beverly Blair Cook, "Women as Judges," in *Women in the Judicial Process*, eds. Beverly Blair Cook, Leslie F. Goldstein, Karen O'Connor, and Susette M. Talarico (Washington, D.C.: American Political Science Association, 1988); Susan B. Haire, "Rating the Ratings of the American Bar Association Standing Committee on Federal Judiciary," *Justice System Journal* 22, no. 1 (2001): 1–17; Susan Ness, "A Sexist Selection Process Keeps Qualified Women off the Bench," *Washington Post*, March 26, 1978; Elliot Slotnick, "The ABA Standing Committee on Federal Judiciary: A Contemporary Assessment—Part 1," *Judicature* 66, no. 7 (1983a): 349–362; Elliot Slotnick, "The ABA Standing Committee on Federal Judiciary: A Contemporary Assessment—Part 2," *Judicature* 66, no. 8 (1983b): 385–393.

15   A recent study found that men were 12.3 percent more likely to receive a "Well-Qualified" rating than women. See Richard L. Vining, Amy Steigerwalt, and Susan Navarro Smelcer, "Bias and the Bar: Evaluating the ABA Ratings of Federal Judicial Nominees," paper presented at the Midwest Political Science Association annual meeting, Chicago, April 2009.

16   Cook 1982, 325.

17   Patrick Winston Dunn, "Judicial Election and the Missouri Plan," in *Courts, Law, and Judicial Processes*, ed. S. Sidney Ulmer (New York: Free Press, 1981), 105–110; Beth Henschen, Robert Moog, and Steven Davis, "Judicial Nominating Commissioners: A National Profile," *Judicature* 73, no. 6 (1990): 328–334, 343.

18   Beverly Blair Cook, "Women on the State Bench: Correlates of Access," in *Political Women: Current Roles in State and Local Government*, ed. Janet A. Flammang (Beverly Hills, CA: Sage, 1984b), 209.

19   Dermot Feenan, *Applications by Women for Silk and Judicial Office in Northern Ireland* (Newtownabbey, UK: University of Ulster, 2005).

20   Beatriz Kohen, "Family Law Judges in the City of Buenos Aires: A View from Within," *International Journal of the Legal Profession* 15, nos. 1–2 (2008): 111–122.

21   Sally J. Kenney, "Equal Employment Opportunity and Representation: Extending the Frame to Courts," *Social Politics* 11, no. 1 (2004): 86–116.

22 Elaine Martin, "Women on the Federal Bench: A Comparative Profile," *Judicature* 65, no. 6 (1982): 306–313, 308.

23 Martin 1982, 309–310.

24 Elliot Slotnick, "Lowering the Bench or Raising It Higher? Affirmative Action and Judicial Selection during the Carter Administration," *Yale Law and Policy Review* 1, no. 2 (1983c): 270–298.

25 Phyllis D. Coontz, "Gender Bias in the Legal Profession: Women 'See' It, Men Don't," *Women & Politics* 15, no. 2 (1995): 1–22; Patricia Yancey Martin, John R. Reynolds, and Shelley Keith, "Gender Bias and Feminist Consciousness among Judges and Attorneys: A Standpoint Theory Analysis," *Signs: Journal of Women in Culture and Society* 27, no. 3 (2002): 665–701.

26 Jennifer L. Lawless and Richard Logan Fox, *It Takes a Candidate: Why Women Don't Run for Office* (Cambridge: Cambridge University Press, 2005).

27 Beverly Blair Cook, "The Path to the Bench: Ambitions and Attitudes of Women in the Law," *Trial* 19, no. 8 (1983): 49–55.

28 Margaret Williams, "Ambition, Gender, and the Judiciary," *Political Research Quarterly* 61, no. 1 (2008): 68–78.

29 Williams 2008.

30 Jennifer M. Jensen and Wendy L. Martinek, "The Effects of Race and Gender on the Judicial Ambitions of State Trial Court Judges," *Political Research Quarterly* 62, no. 2 (2009): 379–392.

31 Sally J. Kenney, "Which Judicial Selection Systems Generate the Most Women Judges? Lessons from the United States," in *Gender and Judging*, eds. Ulrike Schultz and Gisela Shaw (Oxford: Hart, forthcoming).

32 M. L. Henry, Estajo Koslow, Joseph Soffer, and John Furey, *The Success of Women and Minorities in Achieving Judicial Office: The Selection Process* (New York: The Fund for Modern Courts, 1985); R. Warden, T. Schlesinger, and J. Kearney, *Women, Blacks and Merit Selection of Judges* (Chicago: Committee on Courts and Justice, 1979).

33 Philip Dubois, "The Influence of Selection System and Region on the Characteristics of a Trial Court Bench: The Case of California," *Justice System Journal* 8, no. 1 (1983): 59–87.

34 Susan Carbon, Pauline Holden, and Larry Berkson, "Women on the State Bench: Their Characteristics and Attitudes about Judicial Selection," *Judicature* 65, no. 6 (1982): 294–305. See also Susan Carbon, "Judicial Retention Elections: Are They Serving Their Intended Purpose?" *Judicature* 64, no. 5 (1980): 210–233.

35 Beverly Blair Cook, "Women as Judges," in *Women in the Judicial Process*, eds. Beverly Blair Cook, Leslie F. Goldstein, Karen O'Connor, and Susette M. Talarico (Washington, D.C.: American Political Science Association, 1988), 9–24.

36 Karen Tokarz, "Women Judges and Merit Selection under the Missouri Plan," *Washington University Law Quarterly* 64, no. 3 (1986): 903, 927–928.

37 Nicholas O. Alozie, "Distribution of Women and Minority Judges: The Effects of Judicial Selection Methods," *Social Science Quarterly* 71, no. 2 (1990): 315–325; Kevin M. Esterling and Seth S. Andersen, "Diversity and the Judicial Merit Selection Process: A Statistical Report," in *Research on Judicial Selection 1999*, ed. Hunter Center for Judicial Selection (Chicago: American Judicature Society, 2000), 4–39, http://www.judicialselection.us/uploads/documents/Diversity_and_the_Judicial_Merit_Se_9C486

3118945B.pdf, accessed November 23, 2011; Lisa M. Holmes and Jolly A. Emrey, "Court Diversification: Staffing the State Courts of Last Resort through Interim Appointments," *Justice System Journal* 27, no. 1 (2006): 7; Mark S. Hurwitz and Drew Noble Lanier, "Women and Minorities on State and Federal Appellate Benches, 1985 and 1999," *Judicature* 85, no. 2 (2001): 84–92; Martin and Pyle 2002; Reddick, Nelson, and Caufield 2009b.

38 Marianne Githens, "Getting Appointed to the State Court: The Gender Dimension," *Women & Politics* 15, no. 4 (1995): 1–24.

39 Traciel V. Reid, "Women Candidates and Judicial Elections: Telling an Untold Story," *Politics & Gender* 6, no. 3 (2010): 465–474.

40 Ciara Torres-Spelliscy, Monique Chase, and Emma Greenman, "Improving Judicial Diversity," Brennan Center for Justice (2008), http://brennan.3cdn.net/31e6c0fa3c2e920910_ppm6ibehe.pdf, accessed November 23, 2011.

41 Torres-Spelliscy, Chase, and Greenman 2008.

42 Peter H. Russell, *Interim Report: Judicial Appointments Advisory Committee* (Toronto: Judicial Appointments Advisory Committee, 1990).

43 Judicial Appointments Advisory Committee, *2006 Annual Report* (2007), http://www.ontariocourts.on.ca/jaac/en/annualreport/2006.pdf, accessed November 28, 2011.

44 Peter H. Russell, personal correspondence with the author, July 6, 2009. See also Maryka Omatsu, "The Fiction of Judicial Impartiality," *Canadian Journal of Women and Law* 9, no. 1 (1997): 1–16.

45 Russell 1990, 10.

46 Fiona Mackay, "Gender and Diversity Review: Critical Reflections on Judicial Appointments in Scotland," report for the Judicial Appointments Board for Scotland and Scottish Executive Justice Department (2005), 3.

47 Alan Paterson, "The Scottish Judicial Appointments Board: New Wine in Old Bottles?" in *Appointing Judges in an Age of Judicial Power: Critical Perspectives from around the World*, eds. Kate Malleson and Peter H. Russell (Toronto: University of Toronto Press, 2006), 31.

48 Ruth B. Cowan, "Women's Representation on the Courts in the Republic of South Africa," *University of Maryland Law Journal of Race, Religion, Gender, and Class* 6, no. 2 (2006): 291–317, 303.

49 Herbert M. Kritzer and Thomas M. Uhlman, "Sisterhood in the Courtroom: Sex of Judge and Defendant as Factors in Criminal Case Disposition," *Social Science Journal* 14, no. 2 (1977): 77–88; Barbara Palmer, "Women in the American Judiciary: Their Influence and Impact," *Women & Politics* 23, no. 3 (2001): 91–101.

50 John Gruhl, Cassia Spohn, and Susan Welch, "Women as Policymakers: The Case of Trial Judges," *American Journal of Political Science* 25, no. 2 (1981): 308–322.

51 Gruhl, Spohn, and Welch 1981, 314.

52 Beverly Blair Cook, "Will Women Judges Make a Difference in Women's Legal Rights? A Prediction from Attitudes and Simulated Behavior," in *Women, Power, and Political Systems*, ed. Margherita Rendel (New York: St. Martin's Press, 1981), 216.

53 Cook 1981, 217.

54 Martin, Reynolds, and Keith 2002.

55 Cook 1981, 229.

56 Jon Gottschall, "Carter's Judicial Appointments: The Influence of Affirmative Action and Merit Selection on Voting on the US Courts of Appeals," *Judicature* 67, no. 4 (1983): 165–173.

57 Thomas Walker and Deborah Barrow, "The Diversification of the Federal Bench: Policy and Process Ramifications," *Journal of Politics* 47, no. 2 (1985): 596–617.

58 David Allen and Diane Wall, "The Behavior of Women State Supreme Court Justices: Are They Tokens or Outsiders?" *Justice System Journal* 12, no. 2 (1987): 232–245.

59 Elaine Martin, "Judicial Role Models: A Women Judges' Network," paper presented at the Midwest Political Science Association annual meeting, Chicago, April 18–20, 1991.

60 Martin et al. 2002, 669.

61 Martin et al. 2002.

62 Sue Davis, "Do Women Judges Speak 'In a Different Voice?' Carol Gilligan, Feminist Theory, and the Ninth Circuit," *Wisconsin Women's Law Journal* 8, no. 1 (1992–1993): 143–173.

63 Sue Davis, "The Voice of Sandra Day O'Connor," *Judicature* 77, no. 3 (1993): 134–139.

64 Donald R. Songer, Sue Davis, and Susan Haire, "A Reappraisal of Diversification in the Federal Courts: Gender Effects in the Courts of Appeal," *Journal of Politics* 56, no. 2 (1994): 425–439.

65 Songer, Davis, and Haire 1994.

66 Songer, Davis, and Haire 1994.

67 Theresa Beiner, "The Elusive (but Worthwhile) Quest for a Diverse Bench in the New Millennium," *University of California Davis Law Review* 36, no. 3 (2003): 610.

68 Jennifer Segal, "Representative Decision Making on the Federal Bench: Clinton's District Court Appointees," *Political Research Quarterly* 53, no. 1 (2000): 137–150.

69 Nancy Crowe, "Diversity on the US Courts of Appeals: How the Sexual and Racial Composition of Panels Affects Decision Making," paper prepared for the American Political Science Association annual meeting, Atlanta, September 2–5, 1999.

70 Jennifer Peresie, "Female Judges Matter: Gender and Collegial Decisionmaking in the Federal Appellate Courts," *Yale Law Journal* 114, no. 7 (2005): 1759–1790.

71 Elaine Martin and Barry Pyle, "State High Courts and Divorce: The Impact of Judicial Gender," *University of Toledo Law Review* 36, no. 4 (2005): 923–948.

72 Elaine Martin and Barry Pyle, "Gender, Race, and Partisanship on the Michigan Supreme Court," *Albany Law Review* 63, no. 4 (2000): 1205–1236, 1225.

73 Martin and Pyle 2005. Martin and Pyle examined whether women judges were more supportive of plaintiffs filing complaints under the Family Medical Leave Act (FMLA) but did not find consistent linear sex differences in the direction Martin had hypothesized. Elaine Martin and Barry Pyle, "Judicial Gender Perspectives in Resolving Family and Medical Leave Act Conflicts," paper presented at the Law and Society Association annual meeting, Chicago, May 27–30, 2010.

74 Rosabeth Moss Kanter, *Men and Women of the Corporation* (New York: Basic Books, 1977).

75 Ruth Bader Ginsburg, "Some Thoughts on the 1980s Debate over Special versus Equal Treatment for Women," *Law and Inequality* 4, no. 1 (1986): 148.

76 Beverly Blair Cook, "The Burger Court and Women's Rights, 1971–1977," in *Women in the Courts*, eds. Winifred L. Hepperle and Laura Crites (Williamsburg, VA: National Center for State Courts, 1978a), 54–55.

77 Cook 1978a, 78.

78 Cook 1982, 326.

79 Davis 1993, 136.

80 Suzanna Sherry, "Civic Virtue and the Feminine Voice in Constitutional Adjudication," *Virginia Law Review* 72, no. 3 (1986): 543–616.

81 Susan Behuniak-Long, "Justice Sandra Day O'Connor and the Power of Maternal Legal Thinking," *Review of Politics* 54, no. 3 (1992): 417–444; Patricia A. Sullivan and Steven R. Goldzwig, "Abortion and Undue Burdens: Justice Sandra Day O'Connor and Judicial Decision-Making," *Women & Politics* 16, no. 3 (1996): 27–54.

82 Davis 1993.

83 Jilda Aliotta, "Justice O'Connor and the Equal Protection Clause: A Feminine Voice?" *Judicature* 78, no. 5 (1995): 232–235.

84 Nancy Maveety, "Difference in Judicial Discourse," *Politics & Gender* 6, no. 3 (2010): 452–465.

85 Davis 1993, 139.

86 Sandra Day O'Connor, "Portia's Progress," *New York University Law Review* 66, no. 6 (1991): 1546–1558.

87 Cook 1988, 12.

88 Cook 1988, 15.

89 Beverly Blair Cook, "Justice Sandra Day O'Connor: Transition to a Republican Court Agenda," in *The Burger Court: Political and Judicial Profiles*, eds. Charles M. Lamb and Stephen C. Halpern (Urbana: University of Illinois Press, 1991), 238–275.

90 Cook 1991, 272–273 (emphasis added).

91 Karen O'Connor and Jeffrey Segal, "Justice Sandra Day O'Connor and the Supreme Court's Reaction to Its First Female Member," *Women & Politics* 10, no. 2 (1990): 95–104.

92 Sally J. Kenney, "The Constitutional Status of the Family and Medical Leave Act," paper presented at the Afterbirth Conference, Humphrey Institute of Public Affairs, Minneapolis, October 1, 2004, http://www.hhh.umn.edu/centers/wpp/afterbirth/pdf/kenney.pdf, accessed August 22, 2008.

93 Barbara Palmer, "Justice Ruth Bader Ginsburg and the Supreme Court's Reaction to Its Second Female Member," *Women & Politics* 24, no. 1 (2002): 1–23.

94 Martin and Pyle 2005.

95 Carol Gilligan, *In a Different Voice: Psychological Theory and Women's Development* (Cambridge, MA: Harvard University Press, 1982); Carrie Menkel-Meadow, "Asylum in a Difference Voice? Judging Immigration Claims and Gender," in *Refugee Roulette: Disparities in Asylum Adjudication and Proposals for Reform*, eds. Jaya Ramji-Nogales,

Andrew I. Schoenholtz, and Philip G. Schrag (New York: New York University Press, 2009), 202.

96 Menkel-Meadow 2009, 206.

97 Menkel-Meadow 2009, 206.

98 Menkel-Meadow 2009, 218.

99 Christina Boyd, Lee Epstein, and Andrew D. Martin, "Untangling the Causal Effects of Sex on Judging," *American Journal of Political Science* 54, no. 2 (2010): 389–411.

100 Boyd, Epstein, and Martin 2010, 410.

101 Peresie 2005.

102 Martin and Pyle 2005; Martin, Reynolds, and Keith 2002.

103 Martin and Pyle 2005.

104 Martin, Reynolds, and Keith 2002.

105 Sherrilyn Ifill, "Racial Diversity on the Bench: Beyond Role Models and Public Confidence," *Washington and Lee Law Review* 57, no. 2 (2000): 405–495.

106 Boyd, Epstein, and Martin 2010.

107 Boyd, Epstein, and Martin 2010, 396.

108 Gilligan 1982.

109 Boyd, Epstein, and Martin 2010, 391.

110 Sherry 1986.

111 Gilligan 1982.

112 Beiner 2003.

113 Boyd, Epstein, and Martin 2010, 390 n. 4.

114 Boyd, Epstein, and Martin 2010, 389.

115 Drude Dahlerup, ed., *Women, Quotas, and Politics* (New York: Routledge, 2006).

116 Rosalind Dixon, "Female Justices, Feminism, and the Politics of Judicial Appointment: A Re-Examination," *Yale Journal of Law and Feminism* 21, no. 2 (2010): 292–338.

117 Dixon 2010, 324.

118 Beiner 2003; Elaine Martin, "Differences in Men and Women Judges: Perspectives on Gender," *Journal of Political Science* 17, nos. 1–2 (1989): 74–85.

119 Cook drew attention to this issue early on: Justice Brennan generally refused to hire women clerks; Justices O'Connor and Marshall made it a priority; Justice Ginsburg's record was not as good as some of the men. Justice Blackmun hired more women law clerks than all the sitting justices combined, and during his last ten years on the Supreme Court, a majority of his clerks were women. See Linda Greenhouse, *Becoming Justice Blackmun: Harry Blackmun's Supreme Court Journey* (New York: Times Books, 2005), 208.

120 Martin 1989.

121 Judith Resnik, "On the Bias: Feminist Reconsiderations of the Aspirations for Our Judges," *Southern California Law Review* 61, no. 6 (1988): 1877–1944.

122 Robert Turner and Beau Breslin, "The Impact of Female State Chief Judges on the Administration of State Judiciaries," paper presented at the American Political Science Association annual meeting, Philadelphia, August 28–31, 2003.

123 Greenhouse 2005.

3 MOBILIZING EMOTIONS

1 Thanks to Ron Aminzade, Susan Bandes, Karlyn Kohrs Campbell, Harriet Lansing, Kathleen Laughlin, Mary Lay Schuster, Patricia Yancey Martin, David Meyer, Mary Jane Mossman, Joe Soss, and Judith Taylor for their helpful comments on the many drafts of this paper as well as those who critiqued drafts of the public policy teaching case, Kathryn Sikkink, Barbara Frey, and Cheryl Thomas. Thanks, too, to Lura Barber, Rachel Estroff, Rebecca Moskow, Amber Shipley, and Jaquilyn Waddell Boie for their research assistance. I benefited enormously from the opportunity to present early versions of this paper at Washington University, New York University, the Law and Society Association annual meeting in St. Louis, and the Western Political Science Association annual meeting in Las Vegas.

2 For more details, two longer earlier versions of this paper have been published. See Sally J. Kenney, "Thank You for Being Ready: Rosalie Wahl Holds Her Place on the Minnesota Supreme Court," Center on Women and Public Policy Case Study Program, Humphrey Institute of Public Affairs, University of Minnesota, 2001, http://www.hhh.umn.edu/centers/wpp/pdf/case_studies/rosalie_wahl/wahl_case.pdf, accessed July 12, 2011; and Sally J. Kenney, "Mobilizing Emotions to Elect Women: The Symbolic Meaning of Minnesota's First Woman Supreme Court Justice," *Mobilization* 15, no. 2 (2010c): 135–158.

3 Determining the degree to which gender was salient in a given state's choice of its first woman is possible to operationalize. If the process were an appointive one, we can locate what the governor said when announcing the nomination, and whether she promised first to appoint a woman before designating who that woman would be, as was the case for Governor Perpich in Minnesota. If the system were an elective one, we can investigate whether the woman argued in her campaign materials that voters should vote for her because the court currently had no women members. For example, Rose Spector, the first woman elected to the Texas Supreme Court, circulated materials with photos of the all-male court and the caption, "What's wrong with this picture?" Republican Harriet O'Neill defeated Spector in 1998. Megan McCarthy, "Judicial Campaigns: What Can They Tell Us about Gender on the Bench?" *Wisconsin Women's Law Journal* 16, no. 1 (2001): 87–112, 98.

4 At the time of writing, in 2011, 27 percent of all state court judges were women. But, again, states vary enormously in the proportion of women serving. Vermont ranks first with 40 percent; Idaho ranks last with 11 percent. See "Women in Federal and State-Level Judgeships," report of the Center for Women in Government and Civil Society, Rockefeller College of Public Affairs and Policy, University at Albany, SUNY, Spring 2011, http://www.albany.edu/news/images/judgeship_report_partII.pdf, accessed July 11, 2011.

5 Martha Finnemore and Kathryn Sikkink, "International Norm Dynamics and Political Change," *International Organization* 52, no. 4 (1998): 887–917, 891.

6 Minnesota's system is somewhat unusual in that judges have no partisan designation but the ballots do designate whether they are incumbents.

7 "Judicial Selection Methods in the States," American Judicature Society, 2009, http://www.ajs.org/selection/sel_state-select-map.asp, accessed November 9, 2011.

8 Nicholas O. Alozie, "Distribution of Women and Minority Judges: The Effects of Judicial Selection Methods," *Social Science Quarterly* 71, no. 2 (1990): 314–325; Nicholas O. Alozie, "Selection Methods and the Recruitment of Women to State Courts of Last Resort," *Social Science Quarterly* 77, no. 1 (1996): 110–126; Gary S. Brown, "Characteristics of Elected versus Merit-Selected New York City Judges, 1992–1997," report (New York: Fund for Modern Courts, 1998); Susan Carbon, Pauline Houlden, and Larry Berkson, "Women on the State Bench: Their Characteristics and Attitudes about Judicial Selection," *Judicature* 65, no. 6 (1982): 294–305; Beverly Blair Cook, "Women as Judges," in *Women in the Judicial Process*, eds. Beverly B. Cook, Leslie F. Goldstein, Karen O'Connor, and Susette M. Talarico (Washington, D.C.: American Political Science Association, 1988), 9–24; Kevin M. Esterling and Seth S. Andersen, "Diversity and the Judicial Merit Selection Process: A Statistical Report," in *Research on Judicial Selection 1999*, ed. Hunter Center for Judicial Selection (Chicago: American Judicature Society, 2000), http://www.judicial selection.us/uploads/documents/Diversity_and_the_Judicial_Merit_Se_9C48631189 45B.pdf, accessed November 23, 2011, 4–39; Elaine Martin and Barry Pyle, "Gender and Racial Diversification of State Supreme Courts," *Women & Politics* 24, no. 2 (2002): 35–52; Mark S. Hurwitz and Drew Noble Lanier, "Explaining Judicial Diversity: The Differential Ability of Women and Minorities to Attain Seats on State Supreme and Appellate Courts," *State Politics and Policy Quarterly* 3, no. 4 (2003): 329–352; Mark S. Hurwitz and Drew Noble Lanier, "Diversity in State and Federal Appellate Courts: Change and Continuity across 20 Years," *Justice System Journal* 29, no. 1 (2008): 47–70; Lisa M. Holmes and Jolly A. Emrey, "Court Diversification: Staffing the State Courts of Last Resort through Interim Appointments," *Justice System Journal* 27, no. 1 (2006): 1–13; Malia Reddick, Michael J. Nelson, and Rachel Paine Caufield, "Explaining Diversity on State Courts," paper presented at the Midwest Political Science Association annual meeting, Chicago, April 2–5, 2009a; Sally J. Kenney, "Which Judicial Selection Systems Generate the Most Women Judges? Lessons from the United States," in *Gender and Judging*, eds. Ulrike Schultz and Gisela Shaw (Oxford: Hart, forthcoming); Karen L. Tokarz, "Women Judges and Merit Selection under the Missouri Plan," *Washington University Law Quarterly* 64, no. 3 (1986): 903–951.

9 Erin Graham, Charles R. Shipan, and Craig Volden, "The Diffusion of Policy Diffusion Research," paper presented at the American Political Science Association annual meeting, Boston, August 2008.

10 Daniel J. Elazar, *American Federalism: A View from the States*, 3rd edn (New York: Harper and Row, 1984).

11 Religion may well be another factor. Large numbers of Catholics, for example, may make divorce reform or abortion liberalization more difficult, if not unlikely. See Herbert Jacob, *Silent Revolution: The Transformation of Divorce Law in the United States* (Chicago: University of Chicago Press, 1988); and Myra Marx Ferree, William Anthony Gamson, Jürgen Gerhards, and Dieter Rucht, *Shaping Abortion Discourse: Democracy and the Public Sphere in Germany and the United States* (Cambridge: Cambridge University Press, 2002).

12 Jason Windett argues that some state cultures are more supportive of women running for governor than others: "Understanding Female Candidates and Campaigns for Governor," Ph.D. dissertation, University of North Carolina at Chapel Hill, 2011.

13 Sally J. Kenney, Kathryn Pearson, Debra Fitzpatrick, and Elizabeth Sharrow, "Are We Progressing toward Equal Representation for Women in the Minnesota Legislature? New Evidence Offers Mixed Results," *Center for Urban and Regional Affairs (CURA) Reporter*, Fall/Winter (2009): 39–47.

14 Beverly Blair Cook, "Women on the State Bench: Correlates of Access," in *Political Women: Current Roles in State and Local Government*, ed. Janet A. Flammang (Beverly Hills, CA: Sage, 1984b), 191–218, 203.

15 Minnesota Supreme Court Task Force for Gender Fairness in the Courts, "Final Report," 1989.

16 Carbon, Houlden, and Berkson 1982, 298.

17 Beverly Blair Cook, "Political Culture and Selection of Women Judges in Trial Courts," in *Women in Local Politics*, ed. Debra W. Stewart (Metuchen, NJ: Scarecrow Press, 1980b), 53.

18 Beverly Blair Cook, "Women Judges: The End of Tokenism," in *Women in the Courts*, eds. Winifred L. Hepperle and Laura Crites (Williamsburg, VA: National Center for State Courts, 1978b), 98. Cook found a significant but weak relationship between a state population's answer to the Gallup Poll question of whether you would vote for a woman for president and the number of women judges in that state.

19 Alozie 1996.

20 Kathleen A. Bratton and Rorie L. Spill, "Existing Diversity and Judicial Selection: The Role of the Appointment Method in Establishing Gender Diversity in State Supreme Courts," *Social Science Quarterly* 83, no. 2 (2002): 504–518, 515.

21 Margaret Williams, "Women's Representation on State Trial and Appellate Courts," *Social Science Quarterly* 88, no. 5 (2007): 1192–1204, 1198.

22 Rorie L. Spill Solberg and Kathleen A. Bratton, "Diversifying the Federal Bench: Presidential Patterns," *Justice System Journal* 26, no. 2 (2005): 119–133, 130.

23 Mark Curriden, "Tipping the Scales: In the South, Women Have Made Huge Strides in the State Judiciaries," *ABA Journal*, July 1, 2010, http://www.abajournal.com/magazine/article/tipping_the_scales/, accessed July 15, 2011.

24 International and comparative scholars were equally split on what domestic factors determined a country's adoption of gender egalitarian policies. In their study of the diffusion of gender mainstreaming, True and Mintrom found that democratic openness and women's representation in the executive branch had some explanatory power. But they were struck by how little explanatory power any of the other variables had, such as the percentage of women in the paid workforce, the percentage of women in parliament, and whether the country had ratified the Convention on the Elimination of All Forms of Discrimination against Women (CEDAW). On an international level, we can see that some countries adopt policies as a result of their participation in regional blocs, such as the European Union. See Jacqui True and Michael Mintrom, "Transnational Networks and Policy Diffusion: The Case of Gender Mainstreaming," *International Studies Quarterly* 45, no. 1 (2001): 27–57.

25 James M. Lutz, "Regional Leadership Patterns in the Diffusion of Public Policies," *American Politics Quarterly* 15, no. 3 (1987): 387–398.

26 Jack L. Walker, "The Diffusion of Innovations among the American States," *American Political Science Review* 63, no. 3 (1969): 880–899.

27 Virginia Gray, "Innovation in the States: A Diffusion Study," *American Political Science Review* 67, no. 4 (1973): 1174–1185.

28 True and Mintrom 2001, 40.

29 Ferree et al. 2002.

30 Judith Adler Hellman, *Journeys among Women: Feminism in Five Italian Cities* (New York: Oxford University Press, 1987); Raka Ray, *Fields of Protest: Women's Movements in India* (Minneapolis: University of Minnesota Press, 1999).

31 Jacob 1988.

32 Finnemore and Sikkink 1998.

33 Jon B. Gould, *Speak No Evil: The Triumph of Hate Speech Regulation* (Chicago: Chicago University Press, 2005).

34 Susan A. Bandes, "The Heart Has Its Reasons: Examining the Strange Persistence of the American Death Penalty," *Studies in Law, Politics, and Society* 42, no. 1 (2008): 21–52.

35 In later works, Murray Edelman clarifies that symbolic politics is more than the process by which politicians trick the masses into thinking the government has solved their problems. In fact, much as they may try, politicians cannot effectively control the symbolic meanings of political events, which are fluid and multiple. See *Politics as Symbolic Action: Mass Arousal and Quiescence* (Madison, WI: Institute for Research on Poverty, 1971) and *Constructing the Political Spectacle* (Chicago: University of Chicago Press, 1988).

36 Rebecca E. Klatch, "Of Meanings and Masters: Political Symbolism and Symbolic Action," *Polity* 21, no. 1 (1988): 137–154, 140.

37 John W. Dean, *The Rehnquist Choice: The Untold Story of the Nixon Appointment that Redefined the Supreme Court* (New York: Free Press, 2001), 113.

38 Nancy Scherer, *Scoring Points: Politicians, Activists, and the Lower Federal Court Appointment Process* (Stanford, CA: Stanford University Press, 2005).

39 Mary L. Clark, "Changing the Face of the Law: How Women's Advocacy Groups Put Women on the Federal Judicial Appointments Agenda," *Yale Journal of Law and Feminism* 14, no. 2 (2002): 243–254; Elaine Martin, "Gender and Presidential Judicial Selection," *Women & Politics* 26, nos. 3–4 (2004): 109–129.

40 Suzanne Staggenborg, "Critical Events and the Mobilization of the Pro-Choice Movement," *Research in Political Sociology* 6 (1993): 319–345, 321. Our theories would benefit from more cross-fertilization between social movement scholars who study the significance of emotions, and political scientists who study the role of emotions in campaigns and elections.

41 Feminists have led the way in calling on social movement scholars and political scientists to take seriously emotions such as anger, pain, and joy in understanding mass mobilization and policy change. See, for instance, Ron Aminzade and Doug McAdam, "Emotions and Contentious Politics," in *Silence and Voice in the Study of Contentious*

Politics, eds. Ron Aminzade et al. (New York: Cambridge University Press, 2001), 14–50; Susan A. Bandes, "Introduction," in *The Passions of Law*, ed. Susan A. Bandes (New York: New York University Press, 1999), 1–15; Charles D. Elder and Roger W. Cobb, *The Political Uses of Symbols* (New York: Longman, 1983), 147; Amitai Etzioni, *The Moral Dimension: Toward a New Economics* (New York: Free Press, 1988), 89–113; Deborah B. Gould, "Life during Wartime: Emotions and the Development of ACT UP," *Mobilization* 7, no. 2 (2002): 177–200; Jeff Goodwin, James M. Jasper, and Francesca Polletta, "The Return of the Repressed: The Fall and Rise of Emotions in Social Movement Theory," *Mobilization* 5, no. 1 (2000): 65–84, 74; Jeff Goodwin, James M. Jasper, and Francesca Polletta, eds., *Passionate Politics: Emotions and Social Movements* (Chicago: University of Chicago Press, 2001), 9; and Martha C. Nussbaum, *Upheavals of Thought: The Intelligence of Emotions* (New York: Cambridge University Press, 2001). Indeed, the importance of emotion is a feminist insight. The dichotomy of reason and emotion contains a gendered hierarchy, with reason upheld as the appropriate guide of action. Women, the working class (J.M. Barbalet, "Secret Voting and Polical Emotions," *Mobilization* 7, no. 2 (2002): 129–140), or the non-legally trained (Mary Lay Schuster and Amy Propen, "Degrees of Emotion: Judicial Responses to Victim Impact Statements," *Law, Culture and the Humanities* 6, no. 1 (2010): 75–104) act on emotion and, in this sense, in an inferior way, politically speaking. Perhaps because of the larger denigration of emotions, social movement scholars have long neglected emotions, though social movements recognize emotions as key components of mobilization. Criminologists, too, are reexamining the importance of emotions (Susanne Karstedt, "Handle with Care: Emotions, Crime and Justice," in *Emotions, Crime and Justice*, eds. Susanne Karstedt, Ian Loader, and Heather Strange (Portland, OR: Hart, 2011), 1–19).

42 Aminzade and McAdam 2001, 28–29. They, for example, argue that the shift in the 1960s from civil rights to Black Power was as much a shift in emotional tone as ideological orientation. See also Goodwin et al. 2000, 73.

43 Sandra Morgen, "It Was the Best of Times, It Was the Worst of Times: Emotional Discourse in the Work Cultures of Feminist Health Clinics," in *Feminist Organizations: Harvest of the New Women's Movement*, eds. Myra Marx Ferree and Patricia Yancey Martin (Philadelphia, PA: Temple University Press, 1995), 234–247.

44 Aminzade and McAdam 2001; Elizabeth A. Armstrong and Suzanna M. Crage, "Movements and Memory: The Making of the Stonewall Myth," *American Sociological Review* 71, no. 5 (2006): 724–751; Sally J. Kenney, "Where Is Gender in Agenda Setting?" *Women & Politics* 25, nos. 1–2 (2003): 179–207; Thomas R. Rochon, *Culture Moves: Ideas, Activism, and Changing Values* (Princeton, NJ: Princeton University Press, 1998); William H. Sewell, "Historical Events as Transformations of Structures: Inventing Revolution at the Bastille," *Theory and Society* 25, no. 6 (1996): 841–881; Staggenborg 1993.

45 Political scientists who study emotions in electoral politics recognize that campaigns call forth different emotional responses and appeal to different emotions (George E. Marcus and Michael MacKuen, "Anxiety, Enthusiasm, and the Vote: The Emotional Underpinnings of Learning and Involvement during Presidential Campaigns," *American Political Science Review* 87, no. 3 (1993): 672–685). Schuster

and Propen (2010) documented how judges respond differently to different emotional appeals in victim impact statements—grief, anger, or compassion—and how the emotions of battered women are suspect while those of sexual assault victims more readily accepted. See also Patricia Yancey Martin, Douglas Schrock, Margaret Leaf, and Carmen Von Rohr, "Rape Work: Emotional Dilemmas in Work with Victims," in *The Emotional Organization: Passion and Power*, ed. Steve Fineman (London: Blackwell, 2007), 44–60.

46 Gould 2002; Mary Katzenstein, *Faithful and Fearless: Moving Feminist Protest inside the Church and Military* (Princeton, NJ: Princeton University Press, 1998); Verta Taylor, "Social Movement Continuity: The Women's Movement in Abeyance," *American Sociological Review* 54, no. 5 (1989): 761–775; Verta Taylor, "Watching for Vibes: Bringing Emotions into the Study of Feminist Organizations," in *Feminist Organizations: Harvest of the New Women's Movement*, eds. Myra Marx Ferree and Patricia Yancey Martin (Philadelphia, PA: Temple University Press, 1995), 223–233; Verta Taylor and Leila Rupp, "Loving Internationalism: The Emotion Culture of Transnational Women's Organizations, 1888–1945," *Mobilization* 7, no. 2 (2002): 141–158; Verta Taylor and Nancy Whittier, "Analytical Approaches to Social Movement Culture: The Culture of the Women's Movement," in *Social Movements and Culture*, eds. Hank Johnston and Bert Klandermans (Minneapolis: University of Minnesota Press, 1995), 163–187.

47 Bandes 2008.

48 Joseph R. Gusfield, *Symbolic Crusade: Status Politics and the American Temperance Movement*, 2nd edn (Urbana: University of Illinois Press, 1986).

49 Murray Edelman, *The Symbolic Uses of Politics* (Urbana: University of Illinois Press, 1967).

50 DeLysa Burnier, "Constructing Political Reality: Language, Symbols, and Meaning in Politics," *Political Research Quarterly* 47, no. 1 (1994): 239–253.

51 Laura Flanders, *Bushwomen: Tales of a Cynical Species* (New York: Verso, 2004).

52 Allison Stevens, "Filibuster Storm Brews over Judicial Nominations," *Women's eNews*, April 19, 2005, http://oldsite.womensenews.org/article.cfm/dyn/aid/2262/context/archive, accessed August 5, 2011.

53 Gusfield 1986.

54 Ellen Lewin, *Recognizing Ourselves: Ceremonies of Lesbian and Gay Commitment* (New York: Columbia University Press, 1998).

55 Francesca Polletta, "'It Was Like a Fever . . .': Narrative and Identity in Social Protest," *Social Problems* 45, no. 2 (1998): 137–159; Francesca Polletta, *It Was Like a Fever: Storytelling in Protest and Politics* (Chicago: University of Chicago Press, 2006); Virginia Sapiro and Joe Soss, "Spectacular Politics, Dramatic Interpretations: Multiple Meanings in the Thomas/Hill Hearings," *Political Communication* 16, no. 3 (1999): 285–314.

56 Daniel Elazar, Virginia Gray, and Wy Spano, *Minnesota Politics and Government* (Lincoln: University of Nebraska Press, 1999).

57 Betty Wilson, *Rudy! The People's Governor* (Minneapolis: Nodin Press, 2005).

58 Wilson 2005, 38.

59 Laura K. Auerbach, *Worthy to Be Remembered: A Political History of the Minnesota Democratic–Farmer–Labor Party, 1944–1984* (Minneapolis, MN: Democratic–Farmer–Labor Party of Minnesota, 1984), 67; Ellen Boneparth, "Women in Campaigns: From Lickin' and Stickin' to Strategy," *American Politics Quarterly* 5, no. 3 (1977): 289–300; Jo Freeman, *A Room at a Time: How Women Entered Party Politics* (New York: Rowman and Littlefield, 2000); Catherine Rymph, *Republican Women: Feminism and Conservatism from Suffrage through the Rise of the New Right* (Chapel Hill: University of North Carolina Press, 2006).

60 Esther Wattenberg, "Women in the DFL . . . A Preliminary Report: Present but Powerless," report for Democratic–Farmer–Labor Party Feminist Caucus, 1971.

61 Carol Lacey, "Women Wept, Cheered at Wahl's Appointment," *St. Paul Dispatch*, January 16, 1977, A1.

62 Oral history of Rosalie E. Wahl, Associate Justice, Minnesota Supreme Court, interviewed August 17, 1994 by Laura Cooper, transcript edited and annotated by Laura J. Cooper and Stacy Doepner-Hove, Rosalie Wahl Papers, Minnesota Historical Society, St. Paul, 45; Martin 2004; Lynn Hecht Schafran, "Not from Central Casting: The Amazing Rise of Women in the American Judiciary," *University of Toledo Law Review* 36, no. 4 (2005): 953–975. The Minnesota Historical Society holds Justice Wahl's papers, including a transcript of her oral history: http://www.mnhs.org/library/findaids/00430.xml, accessed December 10, 2011. William Mitchell's Law Library and the University of Minnesota's Law Library both hold copies: http://prime2.oit.umn.edu/primo_library/libweb/action/display.do?tabs=detailsTab&ct=display&fn=search&doc=umn_aleph003584850&indx=2&recIds=umn_aleph003584850&recIdxs=1&elementId=1&renderMode=poppedOut&displayMode=full&frbrVersion=&dscnt=1&scp.scps=scope%3A(tcsearch)&frbg=&tab=default_tab&dstmp=1323536678599&srt=rank&vl(263033741UI1)=all_items&mode=Basic&dum=true&tb=t&vl(1UIStartWith0)=contains&vl(13244018UI0)=any&vl(freeText0)=Rosalie Wahl&vid=TWINCITIES, accessed December 10, 2011. The University of Minnesota's Law Library also has a compilation of clippings and memorabilia from her appointment and campaigns: http://prime2.oit.umn.edu/primo_library/libweb/action/display.do?tabs=detailsTab&ct=display&fn=search&doc=umn_aleph003584580&indx=3&recIds=umn_aleph003584580&recIdxs=2&elementId=2&renderMode=poppedOut&displayMode=full&frbrVersion=&dscnt=0&scp.scps=scope%3A(tcsearch)&frbg=&tab=default_tab&dstmp=1323536793371&srt=rank&vl(263033741UI1)=all_items&mode=Basic&dum=true&tb=t&vl(1UIStartWith0)=contains&vl(13244018UI0)=any&vl(freeText0)=RosalieWahl&vid=TWINCITIES, accessed December 10, 2011.

63 Ruth Bader Ginsburg, "The Progression of Women in the Law," *Valparaiso University Law Review* 28, no. 4 (1994): 1161–1182; Lani Guinier, "Of Gentlemen and Role Models," in *Critical Race Feminism*, ed. Adrien Wing (New York: New York University Press, 2003), 228–249.

64 Carol Connolly, "How Rosalie Wahl Got to Be Queen," *Law & Politics* 2 (1994): 20–21.

65 Philip Kronebusch, "Minnesota Courts: Basic Structures, Processes, and Policies," in *Perspectives on Minnesota Government and Politics*, eds. Steve Hoffman, Homer

Williamson, and Kay Wolsborn, 4th edn (St. Paul, MN: Burgess Publishing, 1998), 91–123.

66   Roger M. Klaphake, "Minnesota Court System," in *Perspectives on Minnesota Government and Politics*, eds. Carolyn M. Shrewsbury and Homer E. Williamson, 3rd edn (St. Paul, MN: Burgess Publishing, 1993), 205–221; Lisa Larson and Deborah K. McKnight, "Judicial Selection and Retention: Minnesota and Other States," report to the Minnesota Legislature, St. Paul, 1988; Lawrence R. Yetka and Christopher H. Yetka, "The Selection and Retention of Judges in Minnesota," *Hamline Journal of Public Law and Policy* 15, no. 2 (1994): 169–179. Some women were appointed and held their seats without challenge: Lenore Prather, the first woman Mississippi Supreme Court justice, stood unopposed three times before being defeated in 2000; Carol Hunstein, the second woman on the Georgia Supreme Court; Betty Roberts (Oregon); and Linda Copple Trout (Idaho) (McCarthy 2001, 91 n. 25).

67   In 1992, Governor Cecil Andrus of Idaho announced he would appoint a woman as long as he could find a qualified candidate, and he appointed Linda Copple Trout. After the first woman, Betty Roberts, left the Oregon Supreme Court, Governor Neil Goldschmidt said he wanted to appoint a woman. An unprecedented number, nine women, applied for the vacant seat. Governor Brereton Jones had long promised to put a woman on the Kentucky Supreme Court and appointed Sara Combs in 1993 (McCarthy 2001, 97, n. 64).

68   Oral history of Rosalie E. Wahl 1994, 47.

69   The birth of her fifth child caused her to miss a week of classes during her second year.

70   Oral history of Rosalie E. Wahl 1994, 22; Bonnie Watkins and Nina Rothchild, *In the Company of Women: Voices from the Women's Movement* (St. Paul: Minnesota Historical Society, 1996), 176–179.

71   As recalled by Judith Oakes in email correspondence with the author, December 12, 2011.

72   *State v. Willis*, 269 N.W.2d 355 (Minn. 1978).

73   Cook 1978b, 102–103.

74   Christine Krueger, *Three Paths to Leadership: A Study of Women on the Minnesota Supreme Court* (St. Paul, MN: Hamline University Press, 1994), 13.

75   Carla E. Molette-Ogden, "Female Jurists: The Impact of Their Increased Presence on the Minnesota Supreme Court," Ph.D. dissertation, Washington University, 1998.

76   Jane Larson, "The Jurisprudence of Justice Rosalie Wahl," in *The Social Justice, Legal and Judicial Career of Rosalie Erwin Wahl*, eds. Marvin Roger Anderson and Susan K. Larson (St. Paul: Minnesota State Law Library, 2000), 9.

77   Watkins and Rothchild 1996, 178.

78   Herbert M. Kritzer, "Law Is the Mere Continuation of Politics by Different Means: American Judicial Selection in the Twenty-first Century," *DePaul Law Review* 56, no. 2 (2007): 423–467.

79   Mary Jane Mossman, *The First Women Lawyers: A Comparative Study of Gender, Law and the Legal Professions* (Portland, OR: Hart, 2006), 277–289; Carol Sanger,

"Curriculum Vitae (Feminae): Biography and Early American Women Lawyers," *Stanford Law Review* 46, no. 5 (1994): 1245–1281; Mary L. Volcansek, "Introduction," in *Women in Law: A Bio-bibliographical Sourcebook*, ed. Rebecca Mae Salokar and Mary L. Volcansek (Westport, CT: Greenwood Press, 1996), 12.

80 Pippa Norris, "Women Leaders Worldwide: A Splash of Color in the Photo Op," in *Women, Media, and Politics*, ed. Pippa Norris (New York: Oxford University Press, 1997), 149–165, 161.

81 Karlyn Kohrs Campbell, personal communication with author, November 30, 2006.

82 Beverly Blair Cook, "Women as Supreme Court Candidates: From Florence Allen to Sandra O'Connor," *Judicature* 65, no. 6 (1982): 314–326; Beverly Blair Cook, "Justice Sandra Day O'Connor: Transition to a Republican Court Agenda," in *The Burger Court: Political and Judicial Profiles*, eds. Charles M. Lamb and Stephen C. Halpern (Urbana: University of Illinois Press, 1991), 238–275.

83 Sewell 1996, 845, 865.

84 Armstrong and Crage 2006.

85 Marcus and MacKuen 1993, 672.

86 Aminzade and McAdam 2001, 34–35.

87 Harriet Lansing, "A Tribute to Rosalie E. Wahl: Rosalie E. Wahl and the Jurisprudence of Inclusivity," *William Mitchell Law Review* 21, no. 1 (1995): 11–12.

88 "Judy" to Rosalie Wahl, June 12, 1977. This and the following cited letters are in Justice Rosalie Wahl's papers, on file with the Minnesota Historical Society, St. Paul, http://www.mnhs.org/library/findaids/00430.xml, accessed December 10, 2011.

89 "Judy," June 12, 1977.

90 Elin Malmquist Skinner, MWPC, to Rosalie Wahl, June 4, 1977.

91 Linda Thirkelsen to Rosalie Wahl, n.d.

92 Rachel Tooker to Rosalie Wahl, n.d.

93 Marily Vogel to Rosalie Wahl, June 7, 1977.

94 Mary Ann Mattoon to Rosalie Wahl, June 22, 1977.

95 Margaret Perisho to Rosalie Wahl, October 2, 1977. Such reactions were not exclusive to Wahl. After *People Magazine* ran a story on North Dakota Justice Beryl Levine, the first woman on the court, one woman wrote in, "As a middle-aged mother of two who suffers bouts of frustration, I found Levine's story encouraging. Greatness is still within my grasp" (McCarthy 2001, 106–107, n. 126).

96 Aristide R. Zolberg, "Moments of Madness," *Politics and Society* 2, no. 2 (1972): 183–207.

97 Guobin Yang, "Emotional Events and the Transformation of Collective Action: The Chinese Student Movement," in *Emotions and Social Movements*, eds. Helena Flam and Debra King (New York: Routledge, 2005), 79–98, 81.

98 Sewell 1996, 866.

99 As Governor, Timothy Pawlenty surpassed the number of women appointments Governor Ventura had made. Sally J. Kenney, "Women in Minnesota," in *With Equal Right: The Official Publication of Minnesota Women Lawyers* (July 2009b), http://www.

mwlawyers.org/displaycommon.cfm?an=1&subarticlenbr=84, accessed December 10, 2011.

100   Amy Erdman Farrell, *Yours in Sisterhood:* Ms. *Magazine and the Promise of Popular Feminism* (Chapel Hill: University of North Carolina Press, 1998).

101   Farrell 1998, 159.

102   Goodwin et. al. 2001, 7.

103   James M. Jasper, *The Art of Moral Protest: Culture, Biography, and Creativity in Social Movements* (Chicago: University of Chicago Press, 1997), 186.

104   Coontz argued that Betty Friedan made the emotional connection between discrimination against women and the fact that women were hurting in the *Feminine Mystique*, which was one reason why it was such an important book. Stephanie Coontz, *A Strange Stirring:* The Feminine Mystique *and American Women at the Dawn of the 1960s* (New York: Basic Books, 2011).

105   Aminzade and McAdam 2001, 32.

106   Marion Just, Ann N. Crigler, and Todd L. Belt, "Don't Give up Hope: Emotions, Candidate Appraisals, and Votes," in *The Affect Effect: Dynamics of Emotion in Political Thinking and Behavior*, eds. W. Russell Neuman, George E. Marcus, Ann N. Crigler, and Michael MacKuen (Chicago: University of Chicago Press, 2007), 231–259, 247.

107   Sharon Begley, "When It's Head versus Heart, the Heart Wins," *Newsweek*, February 11, 2008, 36.

108   Begley 2008, 36.

109   Anne E. Kornblut, *Notes from the Cracked Ceiling: Hillary Clinton, Sarah Palin, and What It Will Take for a Woman to Win* (New York: Crown, 2009), 61.

110   Kornblut 2009, 62.

111   Women judges differed enormously about how much they emphasized their gender in the electoral campaigns for state supreme court (McCarthy 2001, 95).

112   Susan J. Carroll, "Reflections on Gender and Hillary Clinton's Presidential Campaign: The Good, the Bad, and the Misogynic," *Politics & Gender* 5, no. 1 (2009): 1–20; and Susan Morrison, ed., *Thirty Ways of Looking at Hillary* (New York: HarperCollins, 2008).

113   Kornblut 2009, 64–65.

114   Margaret Perisho in a letter to Rosalie Wahl, October 2, 1977, describing what one person said to her after Wahl gave a talk to the AAUW (Rosalie Wahl Papers, Minnesota Historical Society, St. Paul).

115   Armstrong and Crage 2006, 742.

116   Rickie Solinger, *Wake up Little Susie: Single Pregnancy and Race before* Roe v. Wade (New York: Routledge, 1992).

117   Virginia Sapiro, "The Political Uses of Symbolic Women: An Essay in Honor of Murray Edelman," *Political Communication* 10, no. 2 (1993): 141–154.

4 STRATEGIC PARTNERSHIPS AND WOMEN ON THE FEDERAL BENCH

1   I received a Grant-in-Aid grant from the University of Minnesota Graduate School to spend a week at the Carter Presidential Library in Atlanta to begin this research. I presented earlier versions of this paper at the 2007 Law and Society Conference in Berlin and the 2009 European Conference on Politics and Gender in Belfast and benefited from the comments during the panels, especially from Lee Ann Banaszak and Celia Valiente. I also presented it to the Gender and Women's Studies Program at the University of Texas, Austin. Margaret McKenna, Barbara Babcock, Patricia Wald, Virginia Kerr, Phyllis Segal, Nancy Stanley, Rachel Brand, and Eleanor Acheson all provided helpful information, as did Sheldon Goldman, Rorie Solberg, and Elliot Slotnick. Elizabeth Meehan, Mary Lee Clark, Kathleen Laughlin, Susan Hartmann, Cynthia Harrison, Lynn Hecht Schafran, Marian Sawer, Elizabeth Beaumont, and Dara Strolovitch all made helpful comments on drafts. Thanks, too, to Piyali Dalal, Lura Barber, Stephanie Short, and Laura Wolford for research assistance.
2   Elaine Martin, "Gender and Presidential Judicial Selection," *Women & Politics* 26, nos. 3–4 (2004): 109–129.
3   David Allen and Diane Wall, "The Behavior of Women State Supreme Court Justices: Are they Tokens or Outsiders?" *Justice System Journal* 12, no. 2 (1987): 232–245.
4   Mary L. Clark, "Changing the Face of the Law: How Women's Advocacy Groups Put Women on the Federal Judicial Appointments Agenda," *Yale Journal of Law and Feminism* 14, no. 2 (2002): 243–254; Beverly Blair Cook, "Political Culture and Selection of Women Judges in Trial Courts," in *Women in Local Politics*, ed. Debra W. Stewart (Metuchen, NJ: Scarecrow Press, 1980), 42–60; Elaine Martin, "Women on the Federal Bench: A Comparative Profile," *Judicature* 65, no. 6 (1982): 306–313.
5   For the very few who are not Patrick O'Brian fans, Captain Jack Aubrey, who becomes an admiral in the eighteenth novel, commands British ships during the Napoleonic naval wars.
6   Sally J. Kenney, "Where Are the Women in Public Policy Cases?" *Women's Policy Journal of Harvard, John F. Kennedy School of Government* 1 (2001b): 87–98; Sally J. Kenney, "Where Is Gender in Agenda Setting?" *Women & Politics* 25, nos. 1–2 (2003): 179–207; Sally J. Kenney, "Gender, the Public Policy Enterprise, and Case Teaching," *Journal of Policy Analysis and Management* 23, no. 1 (2004d): 159–178.
7   Louise A. Chappell, *Gendering Government: Feminist Engagement with the State in Australia and Canada* (Vancouver: University of British Columbia Press, 2002); Johanna Kantola, *Feminists Theorize the State* (New York: Palgrave Macmillan, 2006); Johanna Kantola and Joyce Outshoorn, "Changing State Feminism," in *Changing State Feminism*, eds. Joyce Outshoorn and Johanna Kantola (New York: Palgrave Macmillan, 2007), 1–19, 3–4; Joyce Outshoorn, "Administrative Accommodation in the Netherlands: The Department for the Coordination of Equality Policy," in *Comparative State Feminism*, eds. Dorothy McBride Stetson and Amy Mazur (Thousand Oaks, CA: Sage, 1995), 168–185; Joyce Outshoorn, "Incorporating Feminism: The Women's Policy

Network in the Netherlands," in *Sex Equality Policy in Western Europe*, ed. Frances Gardiner (New York: Routledge, 1997), 109–126; Benita Roth, "Gender Inequality and Feminist Activism in Institutions: Challenges of Marginalization and Feminist 'Fading,'" in *The Politics of Women's Interests: New Comparative Perspectives*, eds. Louise Chappell and Lisa Hill (New York: Routledge, 2006), 157–174; Georgina Waylen, "Gender, Feminism, and the State: An Overview," in *Gender, Politics, and the State*, eds. Vicky Randall and Georgina Waylen (London: Routledge, 1998), 1–17. Catharine MacKinnon developed this argument in the 1980s when she published her dissertation and other works: "Feminism, Marxism, Method, and the State: An Agenda for Theory," *Signs: Journal of Women in Culture and Society* 7, no. 3 (1982): 515–544; "Feminism, Marxism, Method, and the State: Toward Feminist Jurisprudence," *Signs: Journal of Women in Culture and Society* 8, no. 4 (1983): 635–658; and *Toward a Feminist Theory of the State* (Cambridge, MA: Harvard University Press, 1989). Paradoxically, MacKinnon herself engaged the state in seeking to pass a right of civil action for those harmed by pornography in league with far-right anti-feminists.

8   Audre Lorde, *Sister Outsider: Essays and Speeches* (Berkeley, CA: The Crossing Press, 1984), 110–114.

9   Susan Hartmann, "Liberal Feminism and the Reshaping of the New Deal Order," in *Making Sense of American Liberalism: Taking the Pulse of the Left in Contemporary Politics*, eds. Jonathan Bell and Timothy Stanley (Urbana: University of Illinois Press, forthcoming).

10   Judith Allen, "Does Feminism Need a Theory of 'The State'?" in *Playing the State: Australian Feminist Interventions*, ed. Sophie Watson (Sydney: Allen and Unwin, 1990), 21–38; Hester Eisenstein, *Contemporary Feminist Thought* (London: Unwin, 1984).

11   Lee Ann Banaszak, Karen Beckwith, and Dieter Rucht, eds., *Women's Movements Facing the Reconfigured State* (Cambridge: Cambridge University Press, 2003).

12   Janine Parry, "Women's Policy Agencies, the Women's Movement, and Representation in the USA," in *State Feminism and Political Representation*, ed. Joni Lovenduski (Cambridge, Cambridge University Press, 2005), 239–259; Roberta Spalter-Roth and Ronnee Schreiber, "Outsider Issues and Insider Tactics: Strategic Tensions in the Women's Policy Network during the 1980s," in *Feminist Organizations: Harvest of the New Women's Movement*, eds. Myra Marx Ferree and Patricia Yancey Martin (Philadelphia, PA: Temple University Press, 1995), 105–127.

13   Patricia Gagné, *Battered Women's Justice: The Movement for Clemency and the Politics of Self-Defense* (New York: Twayne, 1998).

14   Chappell 2002; Hester Eisenstein, *Gender Shock: Practicing Feminism on Two Continents* (Boston: Beacon, 1991); Hester Eisenstein, *Inside Agitators: Australian Femocrats and the State* (Philadelphia, PA: Temple University Press, 1996); Suzanne Franzway, Diane Court, and R.W. Connell, *Staking a Claim: Feminism, Bureaucracy and the State* (Sydney: Allen and Unwin, 1989); Marian Sawer, *Sisters in Suits: Women and Public Policy in Australia* (Sydney: Allen and Unwin, 1990); Marian Sawer, "'Femocrats in Glass Towers?' The Office of the Status of Women in Australia," in *Comparative State Feminism*, eds. Dorothy McBride Stetson and Amy Mazur (Thousand Oaks, CA: Sage, 1995), 22–39; Marian Sawer, "Australia: The Fall of the Femocrat," in *Changing*

State Feminism, ed. Joyce Outshoorn and Johanna Kantola (New York: Palgrave Macmillan, 2007), 20–40; Anna Yeatman, *Bureaucrats, Technocrats, Femocrats: Essays on the Contemporary Australian State* (Sydney: Allen and Unwin, 1990).

15 "An Interview with Eleanor Dean Acheson," *Court Review* 35, no. 2 (1998): 6–13; Georgia Duerst-Lahti, "The Government's Role in Building the Women's Movement," *Political Science Quarterly* 104, no. 2 (1989): 249–268; Kathleen Laughlin, *Women's Work and Public Policy: A History of the Women's Bureau, US Department of Labor, 1945–1970* (Boston: Northeastern University Press, 2000); Shirin M. Rai, *Mainstreaming Gender, Democratizing the State? Institutional Mechanisms for the Advancement of Women* (Manchester: United Nations, 2003); Dorothy McBride Stetson and Amy Mazur, eds., *Comparative State Feminism* (Thousand Oaks, CA: Sage, 1995); Judith Taylor, "Who Manages Feminist-Inspired Reform? An In-Depth Look at Title IX Coordinators in the United States," *Gender & Society* 19, no. 3 (2005): 358–375.

16 See the complete issue of *Feminist Legal Studies* 10, nos. 3–4 (2002).

17 Franzway, Court, and Connell 1989; Lynne Haney, "Homeboys, Babies, Men in Suits: The State and the Reproduction of Male Dominance," *American Sociological Review* 61, no. 5 (1996): 759–778.

18 Myra Marx Ferree and Patricia Yancey Martin, eds., *Feminist Organizations: Harvest of the New Women's Movement* (Philadelphia, PA: Temple University Press, 1995).

19 Joni Lovenduski, "Sex Equality and the Rules of the Game," in *Sex Equality Policy in Western Europe*, ed. Frances Gardiner (New York: Routledge, 1997), 87–103, 107.

20 Vicky Randall, "Gender and Power: Women Engage the State," in *Gender, Politics, and the State*, eds. Vicky Randall and Georgina Waylen (London: Routledge, 1998), 185–205.

21 Charles Tilly, *From Mobilization to Revolution* (Reading, MA: Addison-Wesley, 1978).

22 Lee Ann Banaszak, *The Women's Movement Inside and Outside the State* (Cambridge: Cambridge University Press, 2010), 2.

23 Banaszak 2010, 5–6.

24 Banaszak 2010, 30.

25 Duerst-Lahti 1989; David S. Meyer and Deana A. Rohlinger, "Big Books and Social Movements: A Myth of Ideas and Social Change," *Social Problems* 59, no. 1 (2012): 136–153.

26 Banaszak 2010, 135. I join these scholars in advocating for a new way of understanding feminist insiders. See Mary Katzenstein, *Faithful and Fearless: Moving Feminist Protest inside the Church and Military* (Princeton, NJ: Princeton University Press, 1998). Insiders' power and influence stems directly from the strength of an outside movement and the quality of their connection to it. Activists move between insider and outsider roles over a career, and other insiders often see feminists inside the government as outsiders rather than team players due to their gender policy allegiances (Eisenstein 1991, 1996). We should probably abandon the nomenclature of insiders and outsiders altogether, since insiders are participants in, rather than merely allies of, a movement.

Because I want to focus on the work feminists do inside government, however, I shall keep the nomenclature for the time being.

27 Dolores Korman Sloviter, "Personal Reflections," *University of Toledo Law Review* 36, no. 4 (2005): 855–861, 857.

28 Carter was grooming Ninth Circuit judge Shirley Hufstedler, who served as his secretary of education, for a Supreme Court appointment. Had Carter not been expected to name a woman to the Supreme Court for the next vacancy, "it is questionable whether Ronald Reagan would have made his pledge to appoint a woman to the Supreme Court during the fall 1980 presidential campaign" (Sheldon Goldman, "Book Review of *Pursuit of Justices: Presidential Politics and the Selection of Supreme Court Nominees* by David Alistair Yalof," *American Political Science Review* 96, no. 1 (2002): 222–223, 223). Similarly, Gerald Ford nominated his one woman to the federal bench, Mary Anne Reimann Richey, after candidate Jimmy Carter had promised to appoint more women to the bench. See Mary L. Clark, "One Man's Token Is Another Woman's Breakthrough? The Appointment of the First Women Federal Judges," *Villanova Law Review* 49, no. 3 (2004): 487–549, 533.

29 Martin 2004, 117.

30 Jennifer Diascro and Rorie Spill Solberg, "George W. Bush's Legacy on the Federal Bench: Policy in the Face of Diversity," *Judicature* 92, no. 6 (2009): 289–301, 292.

31 Eugene Bardach, *The Implementation Game: What Happens after a Bill Becomes Law* (Cambridge, MA: MIT Press, 1977); John W. Kingdon, *Agendas, Alternatives, and Public Policies* (New York: HarperCollins, 1995).

32 Janet M. Martin, "Women Who Govern: The President's Appointments," in *The Other Elites: Women, Politics, and Power in the Executive Branch*, eds. MaryAnne Borrelli and Janet M. Martin (Boulder, CO: Lynne Rienner, 1997), 51–72, 63.

33 Amy G. Mazur, *Theorizing Feminist Policy* (Oxford: Oxford University Press, 2002).

34 Banaszak, Beckwith, and Rucht 2003; Joni Lovenduski, ed., *State Feminism and Political Representation* (Cambridge: Cambridge University Press, 2005); Stetson and Mazur 1995.

35 Mieke Verloo, ed., *Multiple Meanings of Gender Equality: A Critical Frame Analysis of Gender Policies in Europe* (Budapest: CEU Press, 2007).

36 Virginia Vargas and Saskia Wieringa, "The Triangle of Empowerment: Processes and Actors in the Making of Public Policy for Women," in *Women's Movements and Public Policy in Western Europe, Latin America, and the Caribbean*, eds. Geertje Lycklama à Nijeholt, Virginia Vargas, and Saskia Wieringa (New York: Garland, 1998).

37 For Eisenstein, the term "femocrat" includes political appointees (1991, 1996).

38 Once the President makes a nomination, the chair of the Senate Judiciary Committee sends out blue slips to the two senators from the nominee's home state. If either senator returns the slip with the mark "objection," traditionally no hearing on the nomination is scheduled. If both senators return the slip marked "no objection," the subcommittee and then full committee proceed to hearings. Senators who object to a choice may simply fail to return the blue slip altogether, delaying the process without having to take responsibility for opposing the nomination.

39 Jeffrey Toobin, *The Nine: Inside the Secret World of the Supreme Court* (New York: Doubleday, 2007); Stephen B. Burbank, "Politics, Privilege, and Power: The Senate's Role in the Appointment of Federal Judges," *Judicature* 86, no. 1 (2002): 24–27; Hendrik Hertzberg, "Filibluster," *New Yorker*, June 13, 2005, 63–64; Nancy Scherer, *Scoring Points: Politicians, Activists, and the Lower Federal Court Appointment Process* (Stanford, CA: Stanford University Press, 2005); Elliot Slotnick, "A Historical Perspective on Federal Judicial Selection," *Judicature* 86, no. 1 (2002): 13–16.

40 American Bar Association, "Statement of H. Thomas Wells Jr., President, American Bar Association Re: The American Bar Association Standing Committee on the Federal Judiciary" (March 17, 2009), http://www.americanbar.org/content/dam/aba/migrated/scfedjud/wellsstatement.authcheckdam.pdf, accessed December 11, 2011. President Obama reinstated the role of the ABA to prescreen candidates.

41 Elliot Slotnick, "Federal Judicial Recruitment and Selection Research: A Review Essay," *Judicature* 71, no. 6 (1988): 317–324.

42 Clark 2004; Martin 1982.

43 Susan Ness, "A Sexist Selection Process Keeps Qualified Women off the Bench," *Washington Post*, March 26, 1978, 48. The committee currently has five women members out of fifteen: http://www.abanet.org/scfedjud/roster.html, accessed November 10, 2011.

44 Dolores Korman Sloviter, "Personal Reflections," *University of Toledo Law Review* 36, no. 4 (2005): 855–861, 858.

45 Sheldon Goldman, *Picking Federal Judges: Lower Court Selection from Roosevelt through Reagan* (New Haven, CT: Yale University Press, 1997), 261.

46 Scherer 2005. Although he appointed no women to the federal bench, recent evidence suggests that President Eisenhower may have been more engaged in judicial appointments than previous historians had thought and sought Republican judges in the South who may have been more amenable to racial integration. See Michael S. Mayer, "Civil Rights and the Politics of Judicial Nomination: The Haynsworth Confirmation Battle (and Not the One You Think)," paper presented at Teacher, Scholar, Citizen: Conference in Honor of Stan Katz, Princeton, February 23, 2007.

47 President Nixon embraced some versions of affirmative action and brought Barbara Franklin into the White House staff to recruit women. She is reported to have asked why only three of the first 200 appointments went to women (Janet M. Martin, *The Presidency and Women: Promise, Performance, and Illusion* (College Station: Texas A & M University Press, 2003), 143). However, she had few powerful feminist interest groups supporting her proposals. Nixon's example supports my claim that femocrats without connections to a strong feminist movement enjoy little policy success.

48 Anne N. Costain, *Inviting Women's Rebellion: A Political Process Interpretation of the Women's Movement* (Baltimore: Johns Hopkins University Press, 1992).

49 David S. Meyer and Debra C. Minkoff, "Conceptualizing Political Opportunity," *Social Forces* 82, no. 4 (2004): 1457–1492.

50 Mary L. Clark, "Carter's Groundbreaking Appointment of Women to the Federal Bench: His Other 'Human Rights' Record," *American University Journal of Gender, Social Policy, and the Law* 11, no. 3 (2003): 1131–1163, 1133.

51 Martin 2004, 111.

52 Staff Secretary 4, January 28, 1977, Carter Papers, Carter Presidential Library, Atlanta.

53 Goldman 1997.

54 Although I examined the original documents in the Carter Presidential Library that Goldman cited, this entire section is heavily indebted to his research, analysis, and written account (Goldman 1997, 236–283). Unless I cite otherwise, Goldman is my source for information in this section.

55 McKenna recounts that she tried race and not sex discrimination cases because, although Title VII included a prohibition against sex discrimination, no one, including the Equal Employment Opportunities Commission, took sex discrimination seriously until well into the 1970s (Margaret McKenna, telephone interview with the author, June 25, 2007).

56 In 1980, McKenna became Deputy Under-Secretary of Education. She would go on to become president of Lesley College when she was thirty-nine and nine months pregnant with her second son. McKenna transformed Lesley and significantly diversified its faculty. Tracy Jan, "Bigger, More Diverse Lesley University: Leader Who Reinvented School Will Step Down," *Boston Globe*, December 28, 2006.

57 Margaret McKenna, telephone interview with the author, June 25, 2007. Babcock reaches a similar conclusion, telling Judge LaDoris Cordell on March 2, 2006, as part of an oral history: "Leadership is what you really need. Even though Carter himself didn't know from day to day what was going on, he sent out this order: I want to appoint women, see that it gets done. And it gets done."

58 Barbara Babcock, interview by Sarah Wilson, May 19, 1995, from "Diversifying the Judiciary: An Oral History of Women Federal Judges," Federal Judicial Center, 5.

59 Barbara Babcock, email correspondence with the author, June 30, 2007. Babcock laments that so little of what they did left a paper trail: "in the dark ages it was all phone calls and meetings."

60 Babcock 1995, 6.

61 Other scholars have documented the work feminist groups have done to secure judicial appointments for women, beginning with Beverly Blair Cook's analysis of efforts to appoint Florence Allen to the US Supreme Court ("Women as Supreme Court Candidates: From Florence Allen to Sandra O'Connor," *Judicature* 65, no. 6 (1982): 314–326) and various analyses of the Carter Administration. See Clark 2002; Beverly Blair Cook, "Will Women Judges Make a Difference in Women's Legal Rights? A Prediction from Attitudes and Simulated Behavior," in *Women, Power, and Political Systems*, ed. Margherita Rendel (New York: St. Martin's Press, 1981), 216–239; Arvonne Fraser, "Insiders and Outsiders: Women in the Political Arena," in *Women in Washington: Advocates for Public Policy*, ed. Irene Tinker (Beverly Hills, CA: Sage, 1983), 120–139; and Elaine Martin, "Gender and Judicial Selection: A Comparison of the Reagan and Carter Administrations," *Judicature* 71, no. 3 (1987): 136–142.

62 Clark 2002, 246; see also Susan Ness and Fredrica Wechsler, "Women Judges: Why So Few?" *Graduate Woman* 73, no. 6 (1979): 10–12, 46–49, 49.

63 Virginia Kerr, interview and email correspondence with the author, February 2007,

February 2009; Liz Carpenter, "What's Wrong with This Picture? Isn't It Time to Have a Woman on the Supreme Court?" *Redbook*, October 27, 1979. See Sally J. Kenney, "Nixon Gaffe Sparks Era of Judicial Advance," *Women's eNews* (May 4, 2009a), http://www.womensenews.org/article.cfm/dyn/aid/3999, accessed December 12, 2011.

64 Clark 2002, 246.

65 Kerr 2009.

66 Goldman 1997, 253.

67 Clark 2002, 247.

68 Ness and Wechsler 1979, 46–47. Ginsburg's difficulty getting nominated for a federal judgeship in New York may have stemmed from the fact that Senator Jacob K. Javits's six-member judicial selection panel of eight years had no woman member and Senator Daniel Patrick Moynihan's new ten-member panel included only one woman, a non-lawyer (Ness 1978). Ironically, the difficulties Ginsburg had being nominated in New York led to her appointment to the D.C. Circuit Court of Appeals, positioning her well so that President Clinton could then appoint her to the US Supreme Court.

69 Ness and Wechsler 1979, 10.

70 Letter from Charles Halpern, Judicial Selection Project, to Robert Lipshutz, December 4, 1978, WHCF FG 164 FG 46 1/20/77-1/20/81, Carter Papers, Carter Presidential Library, Atlanta.

71 Ness and Wechsler 1979, 48.

72 Ness and Wechsler 1979, 48.

73 Clark 2002, 250; Lynn C. Rossman, "Women Judges Unite: A Report from the Founding Convention of the National Association of Women Judges," *Golden Gate University Law Review* 10, no. 3 (1980): 1237–1265.

74 Arvonne Fraser, *She's No Lady: Politics, Family, and International Feminism* (Minneapolis: Nodin Press, 2007), 138.

75 Babcock 1995, 3.

76 Egan had been the minority leader of the Georgia House when Jimmy Carter was Governor. Michael Egan, "Remarks on Judicial Selection," paper presented at the Lloyd N. Cutler Conference on White House Counsel, Miller Center, University of Virginia, November 10, 2006.

77 Whether Bell would or did indeed create such a firewall is disputed, and was raised during his confirmation hearings.

78 Burton I. Kaufman, *Presidential Profiles: The Carter Years* (New York: Facts on File, 2006), 290.

79 Perhaps the strongest written piece of evidence of McKenna's role is a draft memo she wrote on October 16, 1978, which was never sent and required special permission for the Carter Presidential Library to release. In this memo, McKenna speaks frankly about their travails with the Justice Department and the credit they deserve for pressing the affirmative action agenda.

80 Bell had been a friend of Carter since childhood and was a distant cousin of Rosalynn. Bell joined the prestigious law firm of King and Spaulding and chaired John F. Kennedy's presidential campaign in Georgia. President Kennedy appointed him a

judge on the Fifth Circuit Court of Appeals, where he voted to force the University of Mississippi to admit James Meredith, its first black student, but opposed busing to integrate schools. Like many of his contemporaries, Bell held membership in two segregated social clubs (Kaufman 2006, 41–42). As Patricia Wald, who worked in the Justice Department at the time, commented, Attorney General Griffin Bell would have loyally carried out President Carter's policy injunction to seek out qualified women and minority men, but it would not have been his passion (Patricia Wald, interview with the author, August 2002). As a former judge and a moderate, not a liberal, Democrat, Attorney General Bell had a very narrow definition of merit. He frowned on advocacy of any kind, preferred elite law school graduates, and valorized working for a big law firm. The problem was, however, as with the ABA criteria, that the large law firms openly discriminated against the few women, such as Sandra Day O'Connor, Ruth Bader Ginsburg, or Bella Abzug, who were in this cohort of law school graduates. When Bell left office, he said, "I would suggest that the time is approaching when the affirmative action can be terminated and the selection process returned to the normal method of selecting the best person available without regard to race, creed, or ethnicity" (quoted in Ness and Wechsler 1979, 49).

81 Kaufman 2006, 291.

82 Carter had promised women at the 1976 Democratic National Convention that he would appoint women to the judiciary (Ness and Wechsler 1979, 10).

83 Ness, however, criticized the fact that only 36 percent of the women members were attorneys and no panel was chaired by a woman (Ness 1978).

84 Goldman 1997, 271.

85 McKenna (2007) recalls that the magnitude of making a lifetime appointment made the panels, even the lay members, more conservative in their choices. Without a strong presidential injunction to include women and minority men on the lists, McKenna feels the panels never would have done so.

86 Kravitch ran against two men to become the first woman superior court judge in Georgia in January 1977. A graduate of Goucher College and then the University of Pennsylvania Law School (one of two women in her graduating class and a member of the Law Review), Kravitch was dismayed to discover that no large firm would consider hiring her and her gender prevented her from clerking for a Supreme Court justice. Kravitch went home to Savannah to share a practice with her father, a flamboyant lawyer who had championed the cause of civil rights and was a member of the Legal Aid Society. Lee Giffen's article about her in the *Atlanta Journal and Constitution Magazine* reassures readers that Kravitch was not the darling of "women's liberationists" and that she would be the first judge to wear a size-four robe (Lee Giffen, "Her Honor, the Judge," *Atlanta Journal and Constitution Magazine*, December 12, 1976).

87 "The most severe criticisms to date of this Administration's judicial appointments have come from women's groups, who are distressed that none of the 12 circuit judges nominated to date have been women. In part, this has been caused by the failure of many nominating panels to include women in the list of candidates submitted to us. In this case, however, both the panels have included women among their nominees ... We believe that these two appointments should be announced simultaneously and

that they can be politically beneficial by emphasizing your commitment to increase the number of well qualified minority and women judges." Carter checked his approval for Kravitch and Jones and wrote on the memo: "Handle p.r. Senate relations with care. J" (Memorandum for the President from Bob Lipshutz, Tim Kraft, and Frank Moore, "Appointments to Vacancies on the Courts of Appeals for the 5th and 6th Circuits (Georgia and Ohio)," October 10, 1978, Box 165, FG 52#5, Carter Papers, Carter Presidential Library, Atlanta).

88 On a note to "R" from "m" dated September 21, 1978, it states: "Carol tells me you plan to do the lobbying for Judge Kravitch yourself, so I'm returning all we have on her nomination." On the bottom is a handwritten note: "Jimmy, I hope you can appoint Phyllis Kravitch" (Box 165, Folder FG 52#5, Carter Papers, Carter Presidential Library, Atlanta). Clark also reports that Bell said, "Phyllis Kravitch was strongly supported by Mrs. Carter" (Clark 2002, 245).

89 Griffin B. Bell, *Taking Care of the Law* (New York: William Morrow, 1982), 40–41.

90 Goldman 1997, 240, n. 11b.

91 McKenna 2007. See also Robert J. Lipshutz and Douglas B. Huron, "Achieving a More Representative Federal Judiciary," *Judicature* 62, no. 10 (1978–1979): 483–485.

92 Ness and Wechsler 1979, 12.

93 Ness 1978.

94 Even liberal senators like Alan Cranston, who had many distinguished women lawyers to choose from in the State of California, submitted lists with one or no women (Ness and Wechsler 1979, 10). Robert Byrd's commission recommended only white men; Georgia Senators Nunn and Talmadge recommended six men, one of whom was black. Illinois Senator Adlai Stevenson recommended three white men (Goldman 1997, 262).

95 Ness and Wechsler 1979, 47. Third Circuit Federal Judge Dolores Sloviter reported being asked discriminatory questions by the district panel. She wrote that the nominating commissions the senators established were very different from the circuit court panels President Carter established (Sloviter 2005, 859).

96 Women's groups noted with dismay the double standard between Krauskopf and J. Harvie Wilkinson III, whom President Reagan nominated straight from the legal academy onto the Fourth Circuit Court of Appeals.

97 Ness and Wechsler 1979, 48.

98 Goldman 1997, 268.

99 Goldman 1997, 267.

100 Goldman 1997, 249.

101 Stanley was an officer in NOW.

102 Babcock recalls that she can "take some credit" for Seymour and Ginsburg but struck out with other women nominees. She recalls it not being so much men against women but, with the Democrats having been out of office for so long, a case of a "woman versus a specific well-qualified man who had done a huge amount for the Party and having thus far been denied what he had worked most of his career for" (Barbara Babcock, email correspondence with the author, July 2, 2007).

103 Lipshutz said, "So, the president had me go to speak with the Standing Committee. And frankly, we just had to be rather blunt and tell them if they did not

cooperate with us by modifying these requirements [thirteen years of practice, extensive trial experience] that we would start ignoring the Standing Committee and the American Bar and go directly to the process" (Robert J. Lipshutz, "Remarks on Judicial Selection," paper presented at the Lloyd N. Cutler Conference on White House Counsel, Miller Center, University of Virginia, November 10, 2006). A document I had to petition for release summarized a meeting with Michael Egan, Robert Lipshutz, and the ABA Standing Committee at the White House on November 16, 1978.

104 Lynn Hecht Schafran, email communication with the author, May 13, 2007.

105 Elliot Slotnick, "Lowering the Bench or Raising It Higher? Affirmative Action and Judicial Selection during the Carter Administration," *Yale Law and Policy Review* 1, no. 2 (1983c): 270–298, 294–297.

106 Patricia M. Wald, "Six Not-So-Easy Pieces: One Woman Judge's Journey to the Bench and Beyond," *University of Toledo Law Review* 36, no. 4 (2005): 979–993.

107 Jo Freeman, *A Room at a Time: How Women Entered Party Politics* (New York: Rowman and Littlefield, 2000); Kira Sanbonmatsu, *Democrats, Republicans, and the Politics of Women's Place* (Ann Arbor: University of Michigan Press, 2002); Sheila Tobias, *Faces of Feminism: An Activist's Reflections on the Women's Movement* (Boulder, CO: Westview Press, 1997); Lisa Young, *Feminists and Party Politics* (Ann Arbor: University of Michigan Press, 2000).

108 Susan Hartmann, "Feminism, Public Policy, and the Carter Administration," in *The Carter Presidency: Policy Choices in the Post-New Deal Era*, eds. Gary M. Fink and Hugh Davis Graham (Lawrence: University of Kansas Press, 1998b), 224–243.

109 Carter supported the legalization of abortion, but not public funding for abortion.

110 Costain 1992, 93–99.

111 Toni Carabillo, Judith Meuli, and June Bundy Csida, *Feminist Chronicles, 1953–1993* (Los Angeles: Women's Graphics, 1993), 91.

112 Freeman 2000; Tobias 1997, 109. As 20,000 women gathered in Houston for the conference, it became clear that a feminist backlash was organizing. Approximately 20 percent of the women who gathered were anti-feminists.

113 "The President's Remarks to the National Advisory Committee for Women," McKenna Box 136, Carter Papers, Carter Presidential Library, Atlanta.

114 Martin 2003, 235. Abzug was not the first prominent woman whom Carter fired. His first political adviser was Midge Costanza, whom he fired allegedly for overstating his support for gay rights. See Suzanne Braun Levine and Mary Thom, *Bella Abzug: How One Tough Broad from the Bronx Fought Jim Crow and Joe McCarthy, Pissed Off Jimmy Carter, Battled for the Rights of Women and Workers, Rallied against War and for the Planet, and Shook Up Politics along the Way* (New York: Farrar, Straus, and Giroux, 2007), 214–228.

115 Martin 2003, 225.

116 Martin 2003, 245.

117 President Carter took seriously his pledge to ensure women served at high levels of government departments. For example, he sent a handwritten note to Energy

Secretary James Schlesinger saying he had reports of no women in his top fifty appointments and demanding an immediate accounting of those positions.

118 Clark 2002.

119 Governor Jimmy Carter, "Speech Given before the US National Women's Agenda Conference, October 2, 1976, Washington, D.C.," Carter Papers, Carter Presidential Library, Atlanta.

120 Hamilton Jordan, "Memorandum to the President re: Judicial Appointment to the First Circuit Court of Appeals," July 14, 1977, Box Staff Secretary 38 7/18/77 [3], Carter Papers, Carter Presidential Library, Atlanta. Ultimately, the panel recommended five people, including one woman from Rhode Island—Florence Murray.

121 McKenna 2007.

122 McKenna 2007.

123 Slotnick 1983c, 277.

124 Apparently, no one at the White House had thought to ask a woman's Bar group to conduct similar reviews for qualified women candidates (Ness 1978). Indeed, it was women's groups themselves who proposed to Griffin Bell that they take on this task. Bell agreed but then ignored their work.

125 Staff Secretary 4, 1/28/1977, Carter Papers, Carter Presidential Library, Atlanta.

126 Sloviter 2005, 859.

127 WHCF FG 164 FG 46, Carter Papers, Carter Presidential Library, Atlanta.

128 His prepared answers for the debate support my argument about how Carter saw the issue. Carter emphasized the importance of an independent judiciary and pointed to the importance in the South of the federal judiciary's enforcement of *Brown*. See Lloyd Cutler, "Memorandum to the President," October 20, 1980, Counsel File Cutler, Box 96, Folder Judges 9/11/80, Carter Papers, Carter Presidential Library, Atlanta.

129 At least since Eleanor Roosevelt, first ladies have championed the appointment of women to the federal bench, but Hillary Clinton had far greater capacity for influence than any of her predecessors.

130 MaryAnne Borrelli, "Gender, Politics, and Change in the United States Cabinet: The Madeleine Korbel Albright and Janet Reno Appointments," in *Gender and American Politics: Women, Men, and the Political Process*, eds. Sue Tolleson-Rinehart and Jyl J. Josephson (New York: M.E. Sharpe, 2000), 185–204.

131 Lou Chibbaro, "Task Force to Expand Its Federal Profile," March 4, 2005, http://www.expressgaynews.com, accessed June 15, 2007.

132 Sheldon Goldman, Elliot Slotnick, Gerard Gryski, and Gary Zuk, "Clinton's Judges: Summing up the Legacy," *Judicature* 84, no. 5 (2001): 228–254, 234.

133 Sheldon Goldman and Elliot Slotnick, "Clinton's Second Term Judiciary: Picking Judges under Fire," *Judicature* 82, no. 6 (1999): 264–284, 269.

134 Goldman et al. 2001, 234.

135 Nan Aron, director of the Alliance for Justice, was especially vocal when identifying and quantifying what she argued was a clear double standard (Goldman et al. 2001, 236). Others argued it was "merely" a case of women having few friends with clout to lobby for them and senators "profiling" women and minority men as more likely to be liberal.

136 Sarah Wilson, "Appellate Judicial Appointments during the Clinton Presidency: An Inside Perspective," *Journal of Appellate Practice and Process* 5, no. 1 (2003): 29–47, 43.

137 Carl Tobias, "Leaving a Legacy on the Federal Courts," *University of Miami Law Review* 53, no. 2 (1999): 315–332, 321–322.

138 Tobias 1999, 324.

139 Tobias 1999, 324.

140 Jan Crawford Greenburg, *Supreme Conflict: The Inside Story of the Struggle for Control of the United States Supreme Court* (New York: Penguin, 2007), 257.

141 Toobin 2007, 184–197.

142 Diascro and Spill Solberg 2009, 292.

143 Jeffrey Toobin, "Diverse Opinions," *New Yorker*, June 8 and 15, 2009, 37–38.

144 "Women in the Federal Judiciary: Still a Long Way to Go," National Women's Law Center, October 18, 2011, http://www.nwlc.org/resource/women-federal-judiciary-still-long-way-go-1, accessed September 25, 2011.

145 See Sally J. Kenney, "Critical Perspectives on Gender and Judging," *Politics & Gender* 6, no. 3 (2010a): 433–441, and other essays in the "Critical Perspectives on Gender and Judging" section of that volume of *Politics & Gender*.

146 Steven M. Teles, *The Rise of the Conservative Legal Movement: The Battle for Control of the Law* (Princeton, NJ: Princeton University Press, 2008); Toobin 2007.

5 GENDER ON THE AGENDA

1 I enjoyed the generous support of the British Government in the form of an Atlantic Fellowship in 2002 and a Fulbright Fellowship in 2005 to work on this project. I also benefited from the comments at presentations before New York University's Law and Society Faculty, University of Minnesota College of Law, the Humphrey Institute of Public Affairs, Queen's University Faculty of Law, the Midwest Law and Society Retreat, and the Atlantic Fellows. I would like to thank Ed Goetz, David Meyer, Kate Malleson, Brice Dickson, Debra Fitzpatrick, K.T. Albiston, and Myra Marx Ferree for their helpful comments on drafts. Thanks to the research assistance of Natalie Elkan, Sarah Taylor-Nanista, Jaquilyn Waddell Boie, Amber Shipley, Emily Warren, and Renee Klitzke. Thanks to Norman Foster for help with data analysis and preparing the figures. Earlier iterations of this work have appeared as "Gender on the Agenda: How the Paucity of Women Judges Became an Issue," *Journal of Politics* 70, no. 3 (2008a): 717–735; and "Equal Employment Opportunity and Representation: Extending the Frame to Courts," *Social Politics* 11, no. 1 (2004c): 86–116.

2 The United Kingdom of Great Britain and Northern Ireland is made up of four parts: Scotland, England, Northern Ireland, and Wales. Scotland maintains a separate judicial system and reformed its judicial selection process before the rest of the UK. I use the term "British" as the inclusive term for the whole, but in other places, I refer to the English judicial system to denote its distinctiveness from the Scottish judiciary.

3   Scholars refer to the process by which ideas or issues spread from state to state or country to country as "diffusion." See Frances Stokes Berry and William D. Berry, "State Lottery Adoptions as Policy Innovations: An Event History Analysis," *American Political Science Review* 84, no. 2 (1990): 395–415; Frances Stokes Berry and William D. Berry, "Tax Innovation in the States: Capitalizing on Political Opportunity," *American Journal of Political Science* 36, no. 3 (1992): 715–742; Robert Eyestone, "Confusion, Diffusion, and Innovation," *American Political Science Review* 71, no. 2 (1977): 441–447; Virginia Gray, "Innovation in the States: A Diffusion Study," *American Political Science Review* 67, no. 4 (1973): 1174–1185; Virginia Gray, "Competition, Emulation, and Policy Innovation," in *New Perspectives on American Politics*, eds. Lawrence C. Dodd and Calvin Jillson (Washington, D.C.: CQ Press, 1994), 230–248; Scott P. Hays, "Influences on Reinvention during the Diffusion of Innovations," *Political Research Quarterly* 49, no. 3 (1996): 631–650; Michael Mintrom and Sandra Vergari, "Policy Networks and Innovation Diffusion: The Case of State Education Reforms," *Journal of Politics* 60, no. 1 (1998): 126–148; Jack L. Walker, "The Diffusion of Innovations among the American States," *American Political Science Review* 63, no. 3 (1969): 880–889.

4   Frank R. Baumgartner and Bryan D. Jones, *Agendas and Instability in American Politics* (Chicago: University of Chicago Press, 1993); Roger W. Cobb and Charles D. Elder, *Participation in American Politics: The Dynamics of Agenda-Building* (Boston: Allyn and Bacon, 1972); John W. Kingdon, *Agendas, Alternatives, and Public Policies* (New York: HarperCollins, 1995).

5   Thomas R. Rochon, *Culture Moves: Ideas, Activism, and Changing Values* (Princeton, NJ: Princeton University Press, 1998).

6   Mary Katzenstein, *Faithful and Fearless: Moving Feminist Protest inside the Church and Military* (Princeton, NJ: Princeton University Press, 1998).

7   Jane J. Mansbridge, "What is the Feminist Movement?" in *Feminist Organizations: Harvest of the New Women's Movement*, eds. Myra Marx Ferree and Patricia Yancey Martin (Philadelphia, PA: Temple University Press, 1995), 27–34.

8   Katzenstein 1998, 107.

9   Kingdon 1995.

10 Baumgartner and Jones 1993.

11 Myra Marx Ferree et al., *Shaping Abortion Discourse: Democracy and the Public Sphere in Germany and the United States* (Cambridge: Cambridge University Press, 2002).

12 Murray Edelman, *The Symbolic Uses of Politics* (Urbana: University of Illinois Press, 1967); Deborah Stone, "Causal Stories and the Formation of Policy Agendas," *Political Science Quarterly* 104, no. 2 (1989): 281–300; Deborah Stone, *Policy Paradox: The Art of Political Decision Making* (New York: Norton, 2002).

13 Feminists, for example, disappointed with either the failure to enact policies or the failure of enacted policies to produce social change on issues such as rape, domestic violence, unequal pay, or sexual harassment, often point to setting the agenda as itself a social movement success, presuming it to be the necessary first step in the chain producing change. See Maria Bevacqua, *Rape on the Public Agenda: Feminism and the Politics of Sexual Assault* (Boston: Northeastern University Press, 2000); Janet C. Gornick and David S. Meyer, "Changing Political Opportunity: The Anti-Rape Movement and

Public Policy," *Journal of Policy History* 10, no. 4 (1998): 367–398; David S. Meyer and Deana A. Rohlinger, "Big Books and Social Movements: A Myth of Ideas and Social Change," *Social Problems* 59, no. 1 (2012), 136–153; Nancy Matthews, *Confronting Rape: The Feminist Anti-Rape Movement and the State* (New York: Routledge, 1994).

14 The direction of change in this case has occurred in other instances. The creation of the right to special education, for example, was a catalyst for the movement rather than a policy response to it; see R. Shep Melnick, "Separation of Powers and the Strategy of Rights: The Expansion of Special Education," in *The New Politics of Public Policy*, eds. Marc Landy and Martin A. Levin (Baltimore: Johns Hopkins University Press, 1995), 23–46. Other examples abound. The campaign for redress for Japanese Americans and/or comparable worth may well have been precipitated by government actions rather than by merely responding to group demands. See Calvin Naito and Esther Scott, "Against All Odds: The Campaign in Congress for Japanese American Redress," Case Program, John F. Kennedy School of Government, Harvard University, 1990, http://www.ksgcase.harvard.edu/casetitle.asp?caseNo=1006.0, accessed February 28, 2008; Michael McCann, *Rights at Work: Pay Equity Reform and the Politics of Legal Mobilization* (Chicago: University of Chicago Press, 1994); Margaret Keck and Kathryn Sikkink, *Activists beyond Borders: Advocacy Networks in International Politics* (Ithaca, NY: Cornell University Press, 1998); Gray 1994.

15 Kingdon 1995.

16 This method of tracking newspaper article coverage of issues follows Baumgartner and Jones, Ferree et al., and John. See Peter John, "Explaining Policy Change: The Impact of the Media, Public Opinion, and Political Violence on Urban Budgets in England," *Journal of European Public Policy* 13, no. 7 (2006): 1053–1068. Beginning in 1987, I searched the major national newspapers for the terms "Lord Chancellor" (and the names of the individual Lord Chancellors), "judicial selection," "judges," "House of Lords (Appellate Committee)," and "women judges."

17 The nomenclature can be confusing since the House of Lords was used interchangeably for the legislative and judicial bodies. Before constitutional reform, the highest appellate court in the United Kingdom was the Appellate Committee of the House of Lords (and the Judicial Committee of the Privy Council). Judges were eligible to participate in the legislative functions of that body, but members of the House of Lords more generally were not eligible to hear cases. In 2009, Parliament created the Supreme Court and transferred jurisdiction, creating a clear separation of legislative and judicial functions.

18 Robert Stevens, *The Independence of the Judiciary: The View from the Lord Chancellor's Office* (Oxford: Oxford University Press, 1993).

19 The legal profession is bifurcated into two groups. Solicitors interact directly with clients while barristers are the oral advocates in the higher courts. Although Parliament removed the barrier to the appointment of solicitors to the bench by passing the Courts and Legal Services Act 1990, solicitors with judicial aspirations face many obstacles and few are appointed to high judicial office.

20 A committee now selects Queen's Counsel based on applications (and a fee). The number of women applicants, number of successful women applicants, and percentage of successful women applicants compared to men varies wildly and has garnered media

attention. Queen's Counsel Appointments, "88 Queen's Counsel Appointed in 2011–12 Competition," 2012, http://www.qcappointments.org/wp-content/uploads/2012/02/ QCA-Press-Release-2011-12.doc, accessed March 14, 2012. See also Helena Kennedy, *Eve Was Framed: Women and British Justice* (London: Vintage, 1993), 59.

21 Lizzie Barmes and Kate Malleson, "The Legal Profession as Gatekeeper to the Judiciary: Design Faults in Measures to Enhance Diversity," *Modern Law Review* 74, no. 2 (2011): 245–271, 254; Brenda Hale, "Equality and the Judiciary: Why Should We Want More Women Judges?" *Public Law* Autumn (2001): 489–504, 493–496; Kate Malleson, "Justifying Gender Equality on the Bench: Why Difference Won't Do," *Feminist Legal Studies* 11, no. 1 (2003): 1–24; Kate Malleson, "Prospects for Parity: The Position of Women in the Judiciary in England and Wales," in *Women in the World's Legal Profession*, eds. Ulrike Schultz and Gisela Shaw (Oxford: Hart, 2003), (175–189).

22 Judiciary of England and Wales, "Gender Statistics," 2010, http://www.judiciary. gov.uk/publications-and-reports/statistics/diversity-stats-and-gen-overview/gender-statistics/gender-statistics-judges-in-post-2010, accessed November 10, 2011.

23 The Bar Council Records Office, "Self-Employed Bar QCs by Ethnicity and Gender," December 23, 2010, http://www.barcouncil.org.uk/assets/documents/Table_ 3_Self%20Employed%20QCs%20by%20Ethnicity%20and%20Gender.pdf, accessed July 5, 2011. Lady Hale explained: "The most obvious barrier to the progression of women in the judiciary is that high judicial office has been reserved to those with successful careers as barristers. The Bar is the least family friendly profession in the world" (Dan Tench and Laura Coogan, "An Exclusive Interview with Lady Hale," *United Kingdom Supreme Court Blog*, September 16, 2010, http://ukscblog.com/an-exclusive-interview-with-lady-hale, accessed November 10, 2011). See also Frances Gibb, "QC Reprieve: Shrewd Move or Missed Opportunity?" *The Times* (London), June 1, 2004.

24 In 2010, 1 of 11 Supreme Court justices was a woman, while 3 of 37 Court of Appeal Justices and 16 of 108 High Court judges were women, for a percentage of 10.7. See Judiciary of England and Wales 2010.

25 UK Supreme Court, "The Supreme Court," 2011, http://www.supremecourt.gov. uk/about/the-supreme-court.html, accessed June 30, 2011.

26 J.A.G. Griffith, *The Politics of the Judiciary* (Manchester: Manchester University Press, 1977).

27 The June 2001 election saw a slight drop in that number to 118. After the 2010 election, 143 women served in Parliament (22 percent) (House of Commons Information Office, "Women in the House of Commons," June 2010, http://www.parliament.uk/ documents/commons-information-office/m04.pdf, accessed June 30, 2011).

28 Lucy Ward, "Learning from the 'Babe' Experience: How the Finest Hour Becomes a Fiasco," in *New Gender Agenda: Why Women Still Want More*, ed. Anna Coote (London: Institute for Public Policy Research, 2000), 23–32.

29 Marcel Berlins and Clare Dyer, *The Law Machine* (London: Penguin, 2000), 71; Hazel Genn, *Paths to Justice: What People Do and Think about Going to Law* (Oxford: Hart, 1999), 240; Clare Dyer, "News in Brief," *Guardian* (London), January 27, 1995.

30 *R v Bow Street Metropolitan Stipendiary Magistrate and others ex parte Pinochet Ugarte* [1998] 3 WLR 1456.

31 Grant Hammond, *Judicial Recusal: Principles, Process and Problems* (Oxford: Hart, 2009), 3; Kate Malleson, "Judicial Bias and Disqualifications after *Pinochet (No. 2),*" *Modern Law Review* 63, no. 1 (2000): 119.

32 Anthony Lester and David Pannick, *Human Rights Law and Practice* (London: Butterworths, 2004), ch. 1. See also Robert Stevens, "Judges, Politics, Politicians, and the Confusing Role of the Judiciary," in *The Human Face of Law*, ed. Keith Hawkins (Oxford: Clarendon Press, 1997), 245–289.

33 Labour Research Department, "Judging Labour on the Judges," *Labour Research* June (1999): 13–14.

34 Kate Malleson, "The New Judicial Appointments Commission in England and Wales: New Wine in New Bottles?" in *Appointing Judges in an Age of Judicial Power: Critical Perspectives from around the World*, eds. Kate Malleson and Peter H. Russell (Toronto: University of Toronto Press, 2006a), 39–55.

35 Lester and Pannick 2004, 43, 69.

36 Many speculated that the timing of Lord Irvine's departure had more to do with his conflicts with Home Secretary David Blunkett and less to do with a desire on the part of Prime Minister Blair to accelerate the speed of constitutional reform and the appointment of women. Blunkett had antagonized judges by openly criticizing them and proposing legislation to withdraw asylum cases from judicial review. Speculation at the time suggested that Irvine's departure represented Blair backing Blunkett over Irvine on the asylum issue.

37 The Council of Europe and the European Union were enlarging their membership and it became increasingly hypocritical to require progress toward gender equality and separation of powers in new member states but not existing member states. See Kate Malleson, "Modernising the Constitution: Completing the Unfinished Business," *Legal Studies* 24, nos. 1–2 (2004b): 130. The European Council recommends that member states use judicial commissions to select judges, which appears to be an emerging European norm. See Erik Jurgens, "Oral Evidence to the Lord Chancellor's Department Select Committee," minutes of evidence (March 27, 2003), http://www.publications.parliament.uk/pa/cm200203/cmselect/cmlcd/ 584/3032701.htm, accessed December 12, 2011. The UK did follow a strict procedure of advertising and interviews for its last appointment to the European Court of Human Rights, and the nominee faced interrogation from a legislative committee concerned about diversity. Perhaps the most significant pressure that the Council of Europe brought to bear on the UK, however, was over separation of powers issues and the Lord Chancellor. Should the Lord Chancellor have exercised his power to sit as a judge, the European Court of Human Rights would surely have struck it down as a failure to constitute an impartial tribunal. Erik Jurgens, a Dutch member of the Council of Europe Parliamentary Assembly and Rapporteur of the Committee on Legal Affairs and Human Rights, had issued a report highly critical of the Lord Chancellor in 2002.

38 "Commissioner for Judicial Appointments," *The Lawyer*, March 19, 2001.

39 Lord Derry Irvine, "Judicial Appointments Annual Report 2000–2001," October 2001, http://www.dca.gov.uk/judicial/ja_arep2001/00fore.htm, accessed February 27, 2008. See also Kate Malleson, "Another Nail in the Coffin?" *New Law Journal* 152, no. 7052 (2002): 1573–1577.

40 Kate Malleson, "Creating a Judicial Appointments Commission: Which Model Works Best?" *Public Law* Spring (2004a): 102–121.

41 Frances Gibb, "Revealed: The Radical New QC Selection System," *The Times* (London), July 19, 2005.

42 The Bar Council Records Office 2010; Barmes and Malleson 2011, 253.

43 Andrew Le Sueur, *Building the UK's New Supreme Court: National and Comparative Perspectives* (Oxford: Oxford University Press, 2004).

44 Judith L. Maute, "English Reforms to Judicial Selection: Comparative Lessons for American States," *Fordham Urban Law Journal* 34, no. 1 (2007): 419–422; "Trading Places," *The Times* (London), October 11, 2005, 15.

45 Clare McGlynn, *The Woman Lawyer: Making the Difference* (London: Butterworths, 1998), 95.

46 Hilary Sommerlad, Lisa Webley, Liz Duff, Daniel Musio, and Jennifer Tomlinson, *Diversity in the Legal Profession in England and Wales: A Qualitative Study of Barriers and Individual Choices* (London: Legal Services Board, 2010), 6, http://www.legal servicesboard.org.uk/what_we_do/Research/Publications/pdf/lsb_diversity_in_the_leg al_profession_final_rev.pdf, accessed July 1, 2011; Jennifer Sauboorah, "Bar Barometer: Trends in the Barristers' Profession," Bar Council Research Department, March 1, 2011, http://www.legalservicesboard.org.uk/what_we_do/consultations/closed/pdf/ annex_b.pdf, accessed August 9, 2011.

47 "More Women and Ethnic Minority Solicitors," *Equal Opportunities Review* 84 (1999): 9.

48 Caroline Walker, "Advancing and Retaining Women in the Legal Profession," Ark Group, 2009, http://www.ark-group.com/Downloads/advancingwomenTOC.pdf, accessed July 1, 2011; Hilary Sommerlad and Peter Sanderson, *Gender, Choice, and Commitment: Women Solicitors in England and Wales and the Struggle for Equal Status* (Aldershot, UK: Ashgate/Dartmouth, 1998).

49 "Sex Discrimination (Gender Reassignment) Regulations: An *EOR* Guide," *Equal Opportunities Review* 85 (1999): 8–9.

50 Berlins and Dyer 2000, 41; Kennedy 1993, 32–64.

51 Malleson 2003a, 3.

52 Rochon 1998, 24.

53 Sally J. Kenney, *For Whose Protection? Reproductive Hazards and Exclusionary Policies in the United States and Britain* (Ann Arbor: University of Michigan Press, 1992).

54 Ironically, the incremental changes the Lord Chancellor's Department made to the process of selecting lower court judges—such as advertising the posts, writing job descriptions, using strict criteria to solicit comments on candidates, and conducting interviews—affirmed the idea that modern employment practices should apply to judicial selection. Criticizing the former secretive process for judicial selection, then chair of the Association of Women Barristers, Barbara Hewson, declared: "It's a ludicrous way of going about things. You wouldn't appoint the chair of British Gas this way" ("Suffering from 'Institutional Schizophrenia,'" *The Lawyer*, November 28, 1995).

55 Elizabeth Davidson, ". . . And Will Duck Question Session at Law Soc Conference," *The Lawyer*, October 14, 1997.

56 Robert Verkaik, "Law: The Case of the Judges' Guilty Secret; The System of 'Secret Soundings' to Appoint Judges and QCs Is under Fire, but Is the Lord Chancellor Ready to Implement Wholesale Reform?" *Independent* (London), November 16, 1999.

57 *Coker and Osamor v Lord Chancellor and Lord Chancellor's Department* [1999] IRLR 396, 403.

58 *Coker and Osamor v Lord Chancellor* [1999], 403.

59 *Coker and Osamor v Lord Chancellor* [1999], 403.

60 The Commission for Racial Equality supported Osamor. See "Sex Inequality Still Deeply Rooted," *Equal Opportunities Review* 95 (2001): 5–6.

61 "Lord Chancellor's Sex Discrimination Appeal – EOC to Support Coker and Asomar," Equal Opportunities Commission press release, November 6, 2000.

62 *Coker and Osamor v Lord Chancellor and Lord Chancellor's Department* [2001] IRLR 116.

63 The Court of Appeal (*Coker and Osamor v Lord Chancellor and Lord Chancellor's Department* [2002] IRLR 80), in turn, criticized the EOC and CRE for sponsoring Coker and Osamor. The Lord Chancellor did not discriminate indirectly because the pool he considered consisted of just one person, Garry Hart: "Sometimes an employer will create a post in order to employ a specific individual . . . In such circumstances no 'vacancy' ever exists, no selection for a post ever occurs and there is no question of any requirement or condition being applied to anyone else . . . May it not have been that the Lord Chancellor decided to appoint a Special Adviser only because he thought that Mr. Hart would be of value to him in that role?" The Court of Appeal concluded that, because the Lord Chancellor considered only one person, he did not recruit by word of mouth, and so did not discriminate against women.

64 "Arrangements Not Indirectly Discriminatory," *Equal Opportunities Review* 96 (2001): 48–49.

65 Rosabeth Moss Kanter, *Men and Women of the Corporation* (New York: Basic Books, 1977), 68.

66 Committee on Legal Affairs and Human Rights, "Office of the Lord Chancellor in the Constitutional System of the United Kingdom," Parliamentary Assembly, Council of Europe, Doc. 9798 (April 28, 2003), 4.

67 Since the beginning of the second wave of feminism, writers such as Albie Sachs and Joan Hoff Wilson (*Sexism and the Law: A Study of Male Beliefs and Judicial Bias* (Oxford: Martin Robertson and Co., 1978)), Polly Pattullo (*Judging Women: A Study of Attitudes that Rule Our Legal System* (Nottingham, UK: Russell Press, 1983)), and Helena Kennedy (1993) have documented the sexism of judges.

68 Advisory Panel on Judicial Diversity, "The Report of the APJD 2010," 2010, http://www.justice.gov.uk/publications/docs/advisory-panel-judicial-diversity-2010.pdf, accessed July 1, 2011, 14–15.

69 Josephine Hayes and Daphne Loebl, "Childbirth and the Law," *The Times* (London), October 4, 1996.

70 Paul Harris and Gaby Hinsliff, "Cherie Booth Attacks Sexist Judges," *Observer* (London), May 26, 2002, http://www.guardian.co.uk/politics/2002/may/26/uk.cherieblair, accessed December 4, 2011.

71 Frances Gibb, "Women Have Every Chance to Be Judges," *The Times* (London), May 27, 2002.

72 Steve Doughty, "Harman Humiliated over 'Unfair' Judges," *Daily Mail* (London), October 23, 1997.

73 Polly Newton, "Harman is Rebuked for Women Judges Slip," *The Times* (London), October 23, 1997.

74 Robert Shrimsley, "Irvine Jumps to Defence of Male Judges," *Daily Telegraph* (London), October 23, 1997.

75 Doughty 1997.

76 Clare Dyer, "Crown Prosecutors Could Win Right to Become Judges: Move to Widen Mix on White, Male, Public School Educated Bench," *Guardian* (London), June 5, 2002.

77 Tench and Coogan 2010.

78 Frances Gibb, "Lady Justice Arden: Not Enough Women Judges," *The Times* (London), June 4, 2008; Association of Women Barristers, "The Rt Hon Lady Justice Arden DBE Address to the Association of Women Barristers' Annual General Meeting" (June 3, 2008), http://www.judiciary.gov.uk/Resources/JCO/Documents/Speeches/lja_add_assoc_women_barristers_agm_0608.pdf, accessed December 12, 2011.

79 The Fawcett Society is a nonpartisan group campaigning for women's equality. It has concentrated its efforts on securing women's representation in Parliament and in public bodies generally, coordinates a Women's Budget Group, and most recently has worked with the Home Office as part of an advisory group on Women and Criminal Justice policy (http://www.fawcettsociety.org.uk). It has increasingly championed the cause of a gender diverse judiciary.

80 *R v A*, [2001] 3 All ER 1, 40.

81 *R v A*, [2001] 3 All ER 1, 42.

82 Genn 1999, 240.

83 Erika Rackley, "Difference in the House of Lords," *Social & Legal Studies* 15, no. 2 (2006): 163–185.

84 Elaine Martin, "The Representative Role of Women Judges," *Judicature* 77, no. 3 (1993): 166–173.

85 Brenda Hale, "Judging Women/Women Judging," *Counsel* August (2002): 10–12.

86 Hale 2001.

87 UK Association of Women Judges, http://www.ukawj.org/index.html, accessed July 1, 2011.

88 "Equal Justices Initiative," Queen Mary, University of London, School of Law, July 4, 2011, http://www.law.qmul.ac.uk/eji/index.html, accessed November 10, 2011.

89 Rochon 1998, 178–179. Nor should one neglect the role of academics in the creation of critical communities. Just as Beverly Blair Cook's pioneering work on women judges sparked the creation of the National Association of Women Judges and legitimated an entire field of inquiry in public law, committed legal academics have championed this issue. Most notable is Professor Kate Malleson, who conducts research reports for the Lord Chancellor's Department, submits testimony to Parliament, works

with the UK Association of Women Judges, and gathered academics to found the Equal Justices Initiative.

90 The policy literature recognizes that significant change, particularly important social shifts, are most likely during times of upheaval, such as the Progressive Movement, the 1960s, or during times of partisan realignment. See Gray 1973; Rochon 1998, 10.

91 Kingdon 1995, 168–169.

92 Catherine Barnard, "A European Litigation Strategy: The Case of the Equal Opportunities Commission," in *New Legal Dynamics of the European Union*, eds. Jo Shaw and Gillian More (Oxford: Clarendon Press, 1995), 253–272.

93 A criticism leveled by Marc Galanter, "The Radiating Effects of Courts," in *Empirical Theories about Courts*, eds. Keith O. Boyum and Lynn Mather (New York: Longman, 1983), 117–142; Bryant G. Garth and Austin Sarat, eds., *How Does Law Matter?* (Evanston, IL: Northwestern University Press, 1998); McCann 1994; Michael W. McCann, "How Does Law Matter for Social Movements?" in *How Does Law Matter?*, eds. Bryant G. Garth and Austin Sarat (Evanston, IL: Northwestern University Press, 1998), 76–108.

94 Scholars will want to pay more attention to the international aspects of domestic public policy. The cross-national campaign to appoint women to the International Criminal Court may have bolstered the campaign to appoint women to domestic courts and helped to extend the discourse on representation to courts. See Pam Spees, "Women's Advocacy in the Creation of the International Criminal Court: Changing the Landscapes of Justice and Power," *Signs: Journal of Women in Culture and Society* 28, no. 4 (2003): 1233–1254.

95 Comparative research on women and public policy warns us that even when feminist policies emerge from feminist actors, their implementation by state bureaucracies does not always yield feminists results, most notably in the field of gender mainstreaming. See Amy G. Mazur, "Drawing Comparative Lessons from France and Germany," *Review of Policy Research* 20, no. 3 (2003): 493–523; Dorothy McBride Stetson and Amy G. Mazur, "Women's Movements and the State: Job-Training Policy in France and the US," *Political Research Quarterly* 53, no. 3 (2000): 597–623; Mieke Verloo, ed., *Multiple Meanings of Gender Equality: A Critical Frame Analysis of Gender Policies in Europe* (Budapest: CEU Press, 2007). We should pay close attention to how this policy unfolds in practice.

96 Equal Justices Initiative, "Evidence to House of Lords Select Committee on the Constitution Inquiry into the Judicial Appointments Process," June 2011, http://www.law.qmul.ac.uk/eji/docs/EJI%20submisson%20INQUIRY%20INTO%20THE%20JUDICIAL%20APPOINTMENTS%20PROCESS.pdf, accessed July 5, 2011; Barmes and Malleson 2011.

97 Advisory Panel on Judicial Diversity 2010.

98 House of Lords Select Committee on the Constitution, "The Judicial Appointments Process: Call for Evidence," May 13, 2011b, http://www.parliament.uk/documents/lords-committees/constitution/JAP/FinalCFE130511.pdf, accessed July 5, 2011.

99 Judicial Appointments Commission, "Examination of Witnesses (Questions 1–38)," September 7, 2010, http://www.publications.parliament.uk/pa/cm201011/

cmsclect/cmjust/449-i/10090702.htm, accessed July 5, 2011. Member of the Judicial Appointments Commission Jonathan Sumption opined that, as the quality of women applicants was increasing, he was hopeful more appointments could be made, implying that the only thing holding back women in the past had been their own abilities. Although Kenneth Clarke could not recall how many women were on the Supreme Court (one), he maintained that it was a priority, and that gender discrimination was a thing of the past (House of Lords Select Committee on the Constitution, "Inquiry on Annual Meeting with the Lord Chancellor," unrevised transcript of Evidence Session No. 1 (Questions 1–37), January 19, 2011a, http://www.parliament.uk/documents/lords-committees/constitution/LordChancellor/ucCNST190111LC.pdf, accessed July 5, 2011, 21–23).

100 Sally J. Kenney, "Which Judicial Selection Systems Generate the Most Women Judges? Lessons from the United States," in *Gender and Judging*, eds. Ulrike Schultz and Gisela Shaw (Oxford: Hart, forthcoming).

101 Kingdon 1995, 168–170.

6 A CASE FOR REPRESENTATION

1 I published an earlier version of this paper: "Breaking the Silence: Gender Mainstreaming and the Composition of the European Court of Justice," *Feminist Legal Studies* 10, nos. 3–4 (2002): 257–270. Thanks to the Atlantic Fellowship in Public Policy for funding. Thanks to Caroline Naome, Fionuala Connolly, Judge Ninon Colneric, and Advocate General Christine Stix-Hackl for interviews and Diana Faber, Carol Harlow, Kate Malleson, and the editors of *Feminist Legal Studies* for comments. Thanks to Andrew Mowbray, who read a more recent version, and to Noreen Burrows, Rosa Greaves, Susan Millns, Ann Stewart, Antoine Vauchez, and Erik Voeten for sharing work in progress and information. Thanks to Ann Towns for translating the Swedish legal opinions into English. Thanks, too, to the many research assistants who have worked on this project over the years, most recently Laura Wolford and Stephanie Short.

2 Under the Treaty of Lisbon, the entire judicial system of the European Union is known as the Court of Justice of the European Union, made up of three courts: the Court of Justice, the General Court, and the Civil Service Tribunal. I continue the convention of referring to the Court of Justice as the European Court of Justice or the ECJ. Similar changes in nomenclature affect what we call the body of law, for many years known as Community law, or EC law. I refer to it in this chapter as EU law.

3 The former Chief Justice of Australia, on the occasion of the opening of the Queensland Supreme Court Library's Rare Books Room, Brisbane, denounced the very idea that courts should be more broadly representative as "heresy" and warned of the damage an unqualified judge could do, linking the efforts at gender diversity to a diminution in the quality of judges (Sir Harry Gibbs, "Oration Delivered at the Opening of the Supreme Court Library's Rare Books Room," February 11, 2000, http://archive.sclqld.org.au/lectures/rare_books/speech.pdf, accessed August 17, 2011). See Chapter 3.

4   Catherine Barnard, "A European Litigation Strategy: The Case of the Equal Opportunities Commission," in *New Legal Dynamics of the European Union*, eds. Jo Shaw and Gillian More (Oxford: Clarendon Press, 1995), 253–272; Rachel A. Cichowski, *The European Court and Civil Society: Litigation, Mobilization and Governance* (Cambridge: Cambridge University Press, 2007); Catherine Hoskyns, *Integrating Gender: Women, Law and Politics in the European Union* (London: Verso, 1996); Susanne Burri and Sacha Prechal, "Comparative Approaches to Gender Equality and Non-discrimination within Europe," in *European Union Non-discrimination Law: Comparative Perspectives on Multidimensional Equality Law*, eds. Dagmar Schiek and Victoria Chege (London: Routledge, 2009), 215–247; Christine Stix-Hackl, "The Future of European Law from Women Lawyers' Perspective," speech delivered at the opening of the 6th Congress of the European Women Lawyers Association, Budapest, May 19–20, 2006, http://www.ewla. org/modules/files/file_group_76/Congresses/ Budapest%202006/Papers/speech.Stix-Hackl.pdf, accessed August 19, 2006. For a more critical view, see Evelyn Ellis, "The Recent Jurisprudence of the Court of Justice in the Field of Sex Equality," *Common Market Law Review* 37, no. 6 (2000): 1403–1426.

5   Susan Millns, "Gender Equality, Citizenship, and the EU's Constitutional Future," *European Law Journal* 13, no. 2 (2007): 218–237. See also Jo Shaw, "Gender and the Court of Justice," in *The European Court of Justice*, eds. Gráinne de Búrca and Joseph H.H. Weiler (Oxford: Oxford University Press, 2001), 87-142, and Jo Shaw, "The European Union and Gender Mainstreaming: Constitutionally Embedded or Comprehensively Marginalised?" *Feminist Legal Studies* 10, no. 3 (2002): 213–226.

6   Jan Linehan, "Women and Public International Litigation," background paper prepared for the seminar held by the Project on International Courts and Tribunals and Matrix Chambers, London, July 13, 2001.

7   Members include judges and advocates general. One advocate general is assigned to each case and sits with the judges and may ask questions during oral argument. The advocate general writes an opinion recommending how the ECJ should rule. The advocate general's opinion sometimes reads more like a brief, with policy arguments about why the precedent should develop in a particular direction. The ECJ's singular collegiate decision often reads more like a pronouncement of an answer to a legal question more akin to civil law judgments and may be a vague lowest common denominator of agreement among the judges on the panel. Member states sometimes appoint advocates general as judges and more occasionally judges as advocates general. See Iyiola Solanke, "Diversity and Independence in the European Court of Justice," *Columbia Journal of European Law* 15, no. 1 (2008): 89–121.

8   For efforts to secure women judges between 1920 and 1970, see Beverly Blair Cook, "Women Judges in the Opportunity Structure," in *Women, the Courts, and Equality*, eds. Laura L. Crites and Winifred L. Hepperle (Newbury Park, CA: Sage, 1987), 143–174; and Mary L. Clark, "One Man's Token Is Another Woman's Breakthrough? The Appointment of the First Women Federal Judges," *Villanova Law Review* 49, no. 3 (2004): 487–549.

9   Gráinne de Búrca, "Introduction," in *The European Court of Justice*, eds. Gráinne de Búrca and Joseph H.H. Weiler (Oxford: Oxford University Press, 2001), 1–8.

10 Werner Feld, "The Judges of the Court of Justice of the European Communities," *Villanova Law Review* 9, no. 1 (1963): 37–58, n. 68.

11 The Council of Europe amended its process for the selection of judges in 1998. Member states are less free than previously to select judges. They now submit a slate of three ranked candidates to the Council. See Erik Voeten, "The Politics of International Judicial Appointments: Evidence from the European Court of Human Rights," *International Organization* 61, no. 4 (2007): 669–701.

12 Antonin Cohen, "Scarlet Robes, Dark Suits: The Social Recruitment of the European Court of Justice," Robert Schuman Centre for Advanced Studies, European University Institute, Florence, 2008. EUI working paper, RSCAS 2008/35.http://cadmus.eui.eu/bitstream/handle/1814/10029/EUI_RSCAS_2008_35.pdf, accessed December 12, 2011.

13 Solanke 2008, 102.

14 Solanke 2008; Noreen Burrows, "The Lisbon Treaty and the Revised Appointments Process of the Advocate General," paper presented at the University Association for Contemporary European Studies annual conference, Bruges, September 2010.

15 Hazel Cameron, "Establishment of the European Union Civil Service Tribunal," *The Law & Practice of International Courts and Tribunals* 5, no. 2 (2006): 273–283, 276.

16 Voeten 2007, 676. See also Feld 1963; Sally J. Kenney, "Beyond Principals and Agents: Seeing Courts as Organizations by Comparing *Référendaires* at the European Court of Justice and Law Clerks at the US Supreme Court," *Comparative Political Studies* 33, no. 5 (2000): 593–625; Stuart A. Scheingold, *The Rule of Law in European Integration: The Path of the Schuman Plan* (New Haven, CT and London: Yale University Press, 1965); Solanke 2008.

17 Kate Malleson, *The New Judiciary: The Effects of Expansion and Activism* (Aldershot, UK: Ashgate/Dartmouth, 1999), 79–155.

18 Solanke 2008, 104.

19 See Fidelma Macken and Joseph Weiler, "To Be a European Constitutional Court Judge," Distinguished Fellow Lecture Series, Hauser Global Law School Program, NYU School of Law, September 4, 2003, centers.law.nyu.edu/jeanmonnet/hauser/Macken_script.rtf, accessed May 23, 2011, 10–13. I interviewed members in 1994.

20 Solanke 2008, 91, quoting Renaud Dehousse, *The European Court of Justice: The Politics of Judicial Integration* (London: Macmillan, 1998), 14. See also Sally J. Kenney, "The Members of the Court of Justice of the European Communities," *Columbia Journal of European Law* 5, no. 1 (1998): 101–133.

21 Quoted in Sionaidh Douglas-Scott, *Constitutional Law of the European Union* (Harlow, UK: Pearson, 2002), 201.

22 Martin Shapiro and Alec Stone Sweet, *On Law, Politics, and Judicialization* (New York: Oxford University Press, 2002), 136, n. 2.

23 Alec Stone Sweet, *The Birth of Judicial Politics in France: The Constitutional Council in Comparative Perspective* (New York: Oxford University Press, 1992).

24 Donald P. Kommers, *The Constitutional Jurisprudence of the Federal Republic of Germany* (Durham, NC: Duke University Press, 1997).

25 Susan Sterett, *Creating Constitutionalism? The Politics of Legal Expertise and Administrative Law in England and Wales* (Ann Arbor: University of Michigan Press, 1997).

26 Louise Chappell, "'Women's Interests' as 'Women's Rights': Developments at the UN Criminal Tribunals and the International Criminal Court," in *The Politics of Women's Interests: New Comparative Perspectives*, eds. Louise Chappell and Lisa Hill (London: Routledge, 2006), 217–236; Louise Chappell, "Women's Rights and Religious Opposition: The Politics of Gender at the International Criminal Court," in *Gendering the National State: Canadian Comparative Perspectives*, ed. Yasmeen Abu-Laban (Vancouver: University of British Columbia Press, 2008), 139–161; Louise Chappell, "Gender and Judging at the International Criminal Court," *Gender & Politics* 6, no. 3 (2010): 484–495. For a comprehensive analysis of these changes, see Kate Malleson and Peter Russell, *Appointing Judges in an Age of Judicial Power: Critical Perspectives from around the World* (Toronto: University of Toronto Press, 2006).

27 Joseph H.H. Weiler, "Epilogue: The Judicial Après Nice," in *The European Court of Justice*, ed. Gráinne de Búrca and Joseph H.H. Weiler (Oxford: Oxford University Press, 2001), 215–226.

28 Cohen 2008; Kenney 2000.

29 Solanke 2008, 103.

30 Voeten 2007, 695; see also Karen Alter, "Who Are the 'Masters of the Treaty'? European Governments and the European Court of Justice," *International Organization* 52, no. 1 (1998): 121–147, 139, n. 62.

31 Burrows 2010, 9. The other scholars include: Antonin Cohen, "Constitutionalism without Constitution: Transnational Elites between Political Mobilization and Legal Expertise in the Making of a Constitution for Europe, 1940s–1960s," *Law & Social Inquiry* 32, no. 1 (2007): 109–135; Cohen 2008; Ruth Mackenzie, Kate Malleson, Penny Martin, and Philippe Sands, *Selecting International Judges: Principle, Process, and Politics* (Oxford: Oxford University Press, 2010); Solanke 2008; and Antoine Vauchez, "Keeping the Dream Alive: The European Court of Justice and the Transnational Fabric of Integrationist Jurisprudence," *European Political Science Review* (June 14, 2011), http://journals.cambridge.org/action/displayAbstract?fromPage=online&aid=8306565, accessed December 14, 2011.

32 Sarah Helm, "Judge Accused of Cover-up in Cools Murder Case," *Independent* (London), September 13, 1996, 11; Agence Europe, Reuter Textline, "EC: Mr. Goppel Criticizes the EP Report on the Court of Justice," Brussels, October 5, 1993, 2.

33 Solanke 2008, 103.

34 Working Party for the European Commission, "Report by the Working Party on the Future of the European Communities' Court System," January 2000, 51.

35 Cameron 2006.

36 Cameron 2006, 280.

37 Rosa Greaves, "Reforming Some Aspects of the Role of Advocates General," in *A Constitutional Order of States: Essays in EU Law in Honour of Alan Dashwood*, eds. Anthony Arnull, Catherine Barnard, Michael Dougan, and Eleanor Spaventa (Oxford: Hart, 2011), 161–178.

38   Council of the European Union (Mr. V. Skouris, President of the Court of Justice of the European Union to Mr. Miguel Angel Moratinos, President of the Council of the European Union), "Recommendation Concerning the Composition of the Panel Provided for in Article 255 TFEU," 5932/10, February 2, 2010.

39   EU Law Blog, "Judicial Appointments in the General Court and Court of Justice" (July 8, 2010), http://eulaw.typepad.com/eulawblog/2010/07/judicial-appointments-in-the-general-court-and-court-of-justice.html, accessed December 12, 2011.

40   Pescatorius, "Transparency at the ECJ: A Reflection after API," *Adjudicating Europe Blog*, December 12, 2010, http://adjudicatingeurope.eu/blog/?p=520, accessed November 11, 2011.

41   Court of Justice of the European Communities, *Formal Sittings of the Court of Justice of the European Communities, 1980 and 1981* (1982), 76. Sionaidh Douglas-Scott observed, "Unfortunately Madame Rozès is still referred to throughout CELEX, the EU's official full text legal database, as *Mr.* Advocate General Rozès" (Douglas-Scott 2002, 202, n. 22).

42   Anne Boigeol, "Male Strategies in the Face of the Feminisation of a Profession: The Case of the French Judiciary," in *Women in the World's Legal Profession*, eds. Ulrike Schultz and Gisela Shaw (Oxford: Hart, 2003), 401–418.

43   Brick Court Chambers, "Business and the Law: New Faces on the Bench: European Court," *Financial Times* (London), October 11, 1994, 13.

44   Mona Hickey, email correspondence with the author, February 1, 2002.

45   "Her Turn," *Financial Times* (London), September 28, 1999, 17.

46   Macken and Weiler 2003.

47   Macken and Weiler 2003, 11.

48   Macken and Weiler 2003, 12.

49   Macken and Weiler 2003, 22. The UK judge on the ECJ, Konrad Schiemann, made a similar point: "The differences between us have less to do with countries than with temperament and résumé. A professor thinks differently than a former politician and the administrative official thinks that everything should be functional. Everything is different here than at the English court, where everyone has gone through the same career path" (Joachim Fritz-Vannahme, "In the End Is the Word: The European Court of Justice Guards the Ideals of Europe if the EU Commission Fails," *Zeit Online*, May 4, 2006).

50   Macken and Weiler 2003, 24.

51   Fritz-Vannahme 2006.

52   Stix-Hackl 2006.

53   Stix-Hackl 2006, 2.

54   Stix-Hackl 2006, 3.

55   "Court of Justice: Report on Future of European Legal System," *Europolitics*, December 8, 1999.

56   "Slovenia's Appointments," in BBC, *BBC Summary of World Broadcasts*, May 20, 2004.

57   "First Women Judges for Court of Justice," *Herald Sun* (Melbourne), January 11, 1995.

58 "Women's Day: A Year of Living Dangerously," *Guardian* (London), March 6, 1995.

59 Sybil Nolan, "Sydney Women Win Fight to Keep Single-Sex Pool," *Age* (Australia), March 10, 1995.

60 "European Court of Justice: Four New Bulgarian and Romanian Judges in Luxembourg," *Europe-East*, January 25, 2007.

61 Rex Wockner, "Austria, Ireland Propose Civil-Union Laws," *San Francisco Bay Times*, November 8, 2007.

62 Susanne Burri, "The European Network of Legal Experts in the Field of Gender Equality," *European Anti-Discrimination Law Review* 6/7 (2008): 11–12.

63 Cohen 2007, 2008.

64 Sacha Prechal, "'Non-Discrimination Does Not Fall Down from Heaven': The Context and Evolution of Non-Discrimination in EU Law," Eric Stein Working Paper No. 4, Czech Society for European and Comparative Law, 2009, www.ericsteinpapers. eu/images/doc/eswp-2009-04-prechal.pdf, accessed November 11, 2011.

65 John Carvel, "Europe's Shadowy Arbiters of Power," *Guardian* (London), June 28, 1992, F:27.

66 Agence Europe 1993.

67 "Biased Referee? European Court of Justice," *The Economist*, May 17, 1997, 59–60.

68 Martin Westlake, *A Modern Guide to the European Parliament* (London and New York: Pinter, 1994), 106–109.

69 Donald W. Jackson, "Judging Human Rights: The Formative Years of the European Court of Human Rights, 1959–1989," *Windsor Yearbook of Access to Justice* 13 (1993): 217–236, 220; Linehan 2001.

70 Centre for Research on European Women, *CREW Report No. 52*, March 4, 2002, 1–2.

71 Thordis Ingadottir, "The International Criminal Court Nomination and Election of Judges," ICC Discussion Paper No. 4, Project on International Courts and Tribunals, June 2002, http://www.pict-pcti.org/publications/ICC_paprs/election.pdf, accessed November 11, 2011, 17; Mark A. Pollack and Emilie M. Hafner-Burton, "Mainstreaming Gender in the European Union," *Journal of European Public Policy* 7, no. 3 (2000): 432–456; Emilie M. Hafner-Burton and Mark A. Pollack, "Mainstreaming Gender in the European Union: Getting the Incentives Right," *Comparative European Politics* 7, no. 1 (2009): 114–138; Jacqui True and Michael Mintrom, "Transnational Networks and Policy Diffusion: The Case of Gender Mainstreaming," *International Studies Quarterly* 45, no. 1 (2001): 27–57.

72 Miriam Anasagasti and Nathalie Wuiame, *Women and Decision-Making in the Judiciary in the European Union* (Luxembourg: Office for Official Publications of the European Communities, 1999); Sonia Mazey, "Introduction: Integrating Gender—Intellectual and 'Real World' Mainstreaming," *Journal of European Public Policy* 7, no. 3 (2000): 342; Jo Shaw, "European Union Governance and the Question of Gender: A Critical Comment," in *Mountain or Molehill? A Critical Appraisal of the Commission White Paper on Governance*, eds. Christian Joerges, Yves Mény, and Joseph H.H. Weiler,

Jean Monnet Working Paper No. 6, Brussels, July 25, 2001a, 153–162, http://www.jeanmonnet program.org/papers/01/010601.html, accessed November 11, 2011.

73 United Nations, "Report of the Fourth World Conference on Women," Beijing, U.N. Doc. A/CONF.177/20, September 4–15, 1995, paragraph 142b, http://www.un.org/womenwatch/daw/beijing/pdf/Beijing%20full%20report%20E.pdf, accessed November 11, 2011.

74 *The Fourth Action Programme for Equal Opportunities for Women and Men, 1996–2000* (Brussels: European Commission, 1996), 3.

75 *The Fourth Action Programme* 1996, 7.

76 Fiona Beveridge and Sue Nott, "Mainstreaming: A Case for Optimism and Cyncism," *Feminist Legal Studies* 10, no. 3 (2002): 299–311; Hafner-Burton and Pollack 2009; True and Mintrom, Mazey 2000, 37; Teresa Rees, *Mainstreaming Equality in the European Union: Education, Training and Labour Market Policies* (London: Routledge, 1998); Jo Shaw, "Importing Gender: The Challenge of Feminism and the Analysis of the EU Legal Order," *Journal of European Public Policy* 7, no. 3 (2000): 406–431.

77 Beverly Blair Cook, "Women as Judges," in *Women in the Judicial Process*, eds. Beverly Blair Cook, Leslie F. Goldstein, Karen O'Connor, and Susette M. Talarico (Washington, D.C.: American Political Science Association, 1988), 9–24.

78 Malleson 1999; Clare McGlynn, "Judging Women Differently: Gender, the Judiciary, and Reform," in *Feminist Perspectives on Public Law*, eds. Susan Millns and Noel Whitty (London: Cavendish, 1999), 87–106.

79 Sandra Fredman, "After *Kalanke* and *Marschall*: Affirming Affirmative Action," in *The Cambridge Yearbook of European Legal Studies*, eds. Alan Dashwood and Angela Ward (Cambridge: Hart, 1998), 199–215.

80 Ninon Colneric, "Making Equality Law More Effective: Lessons from the German Experience," *Cardozo Women's Law Journal* 3, no. 2 (1996): 229–250, 249.

81 *Kalanke v. Land Bremen*, Case C-450/93 [1995] ECR I-3051.

82 Three British women challenged the Lord Chancellor's appointment of a special adviser without a search, arguing that selecting on the criterion of being well known to the Lord Chancellor constituted indirect discrimination. The case attracted attention because, if the courts had held that employment discrimination forbade such a practice, selecting judges by "secret soundings" would be further discredited as contrary to equality law, even if that law did not extend to judicial appointments. One settled and the other two lost at the Court of Appeal, despite having the sponsorship of the Equal Opportunities Commission (Sally J. Kenney, "Equal Employment Opportunity and Representation: Extending the Frame to Courts," *Social Politics* 11, no. 1 (2004c): 86–116). Moreover, as I discuss in Chapter 3, members from the private sector on the Judicial Appointments Commission looked askance at the employment practices of the Lord Chancellor's Department.

83 Ann E. Towns, *Women and States: Norms and Hierarchies in International Society* (Cambridge: Cambridge University Press, 2010).

84 I rely on correspondence with Sundberg-Weitman for details of the case and a Swedish translation of the two opinions, provided by Ann Towns. Because neither Swedish court referred the case to the ECJ, the opinions exist only in Swedish.

85 Odile Quintin letter to Linda Steneberg, "Ms. Brita Sundberg-Weitman's Law Suit towards the Swedish State," Brussels, V/D/DM/siD(98)45803, September 16, 1998.

86 Mackenzie et al. 2010, 47–49.

87 Ingadottir 2002, 18.

88 Marie-Bénédicte Dembour, *Who Believes in Human Rights? Reflections on the European Convention* (Cambridge: Cambridge University Press, 2006); INTERIGHTS (International Centre for the Legal Protection of Human Rights), *Judicial Independence: Law and Practice of Appointments to the European Court of Human Rights* (London: Lancaster House, 2003), 26; Alastair Mowbray, "The Consideration of Gender in the Process of Appointing Judges to the European Court of Human Rights," *Human Rights Law Review* 8, no. 3 (2008): 549–559.

89 The ECHR invited contracting parties to supply written details of any domestic rules designed to ensure the presence of women or the under-represented gender on their highest national courts. The ECHR received thirty-seven replies. Only three had legislation requiring egalitarian procedures: Austria, Belgium, and Latvia (Mowbray 2008).

90 Ingadottir 2002, 19.

91 Mowbray 2008, 558.

92 Association of Women Barristers, "Memorandum," *House of Commons Home Affairs Committee Third Report, Judicial Appointments Procedures*, Volume III: *Minutes of Evidence and Appendices*, June 5, 1996, 191–197; Association of Women Solicitors, "Memorandum," *House of Commons Home Affairs Committee Third Report, Judicial Appointments Procedures*, Volume III: *Minutes of Evidence and Appendices*, June 5, 1996, 198–200; Equal Opportunities Commission, "Memorandum," *House of Commons Home Affairs Committee Third Report, Judicial Appointments Procedures*, Volume III: *Minutes of Evidence and Appendices*, June 5, 1996, 210–215.

93 "Equal Justices Initiative," Queen Mary, University of London, School of Law, July 4, 2011, http://www.law.qmul.ac.uk/eji/index.html, accessed November 10, 2011.

94 Birgit Schmidt am Busch, "European Institutions: Strategies for Exerting More Influence," paper presented at the European Women Lawyers Association annual congress, Berlin, March 17–19, 2000.

95 European Women Lawyers Association, "EWLA Statement on the Obligation to Name Women for Top Positions in the European Union," November 9, 2009, www.curioweb.is/webs/ewla.org/modules/files/file_group_76/2009_Statement_on_the_ Obligation_to_Name_Women_for_Top_Positions_in_the_EU.pdf, accessed November 11, 2011.

96 Sally J. Kenney, "New Research on Gendered Political Institutions," *Political Research Quarterly* 49, no. 2 (1996a): 445–466.

97 Hanna Fenichel Pitkin, *The Concept of Representation* (Berkeley: University of California Press, 1967).

98 Barbara Perry, *A "Representative" Supreme Court? The Impact of Race, Religion, and Gender on Appointments* (Westport, CT: Greenwood Press, 1991).

99 Helm 1996; Brenda Hale, "Equality and the Judiciary: Why Should We Want More Women Judges?" *Public Law* Autumn (2001): 489–504, 493.

100 Solanke 2008, 92.

101 Weiler 2001, 219.

102 Anthony Arnull, "Judicial Architecture or Judicial Folly? The Challenge Facing the European Union," *European Law Review* 24, no. 5 (1999): 516–524; Walter van Gerven, "The Role and Structure of the European Judiciary Now and in the Future," *European Law Review* 21, no. 3 (1996): 217–219; Weiler 2001.

103 Lord Alexander Mackenzie Stuart, "The Court of Justice: A Personal View," in *In Memoriam J.D.B. Mitchell*, eds. St. John Bates, Wilson Finnie, John A. Usher, and Hans Wildberg, European Governmental Studies (London: Sweet and Maxwell, 1983), 118–127, 126 (emphasis added).

104 Mary L. Volcansek and Jacqueline Lucienne Lafon, *Judicial Selection: The Cross-Evolution of French and American Practices* (Westport, CT: Greenwood Press, 1987), 15–41.

105 Dan Tench and Laura Coogan, "An Exclusive Interview with Lady Hale," *United Kingdom Supreme Court Blog*, September 16, 2010, http://ukscblog.com/an-exclusive-interview-with-lady-hale, accessed November 10, 2011; Kate Malleson, "Rethinking the Merit Principle in Judicial Selection," *Journal of Law and Society* 33, no. 1 (2006b): 126–140.

106 Professor Rosa Greaves (2011), for example, has called for abandoning the requirement that the court have one judge for each member state, as other international courts have done.

107 Jane Mansbridge, "Should Blacks Represent Blacks and Women Represent Women? A Contingent 'Yes,'" *Journal of Politics* 61, no. 3 (1999): 628–657, 629, quoting J. Roland Pennock, *Democratic Political Theory* (Princeton: Princeton University Press, 1979), 314.

108 Weiler 2001, 221, 224.

109 Solanke 2008, 105.

110 Solanke 2008, 107.

111 Solanke 2008.

112 Solanke 2008, 92, n. 23.

113 Working Party for the European Commission 2000, 51.

114 Solanke 2008, 108–110.

115 Alexander M. Bickel, *The Least Dangerous Branch: The Supreme Court at the Bar of Politics* (Indianapolis, IN: Bobbs-Merrill, 1962).

116 Jane Mansbridge, "Rethinking Representation," *American Political Science Review* 97, no. 4 (2003): 515–528, 515.

117 Mansbridge 2003, 515.

118 Mansbridge 2003, 520.

119 Howard Gillman, *The Votes that Counted: How the Court Decided the 2000 Presidential Election* (Chicago: University of Chicago Press, 2001).

120 Anne Phillips, "Democracy and Representation: Or, Why Should It Matter Who Our Representatives Are?" in *Feminism and Politics*, ed. Anne Phillips (Oxford: Oxford University Press, 1998), 224–240.

121 Virginia Sapiro, "Research Frontier Essay: When Are Interests Interesting? The Problem of Political Representation of Women," *American Political Science Review* 75, no. 3 (1981): 701–716.

122 Mansbridge 1999, 630.

123 Mansbridge 1999, 639.

124 Mansbridge 1999, 635.

125 Phillips 1998, 236.

126 Mansbridge 1999, 644.

127 Brenda Hale, "Foreword," in *Feminist Judgments: From Theory to Practice*, eds. Rosemary Hunter, Clare McGlynn, and Erika Rackley (Oxford: Hart, 2010).

7 BACKLASH AGAINST WOMEN JUDGES

1 Thanks to Michael Bernstein, Linda Greenhouse, Thomas Hilbink, Harriet Lansing, Sarudzayi Matambanadzo, Clare Pastore, Traciel Reid, Judith Resnik, Reva Siegel, Esther Tomljanovich, Margaret Thornton, and Janice Yoder for their helpful comments on this chapter. I presented earlier versions of this paper at the 2010 Law and Society annual meeting in Chicago, at the 2011 Southern Political Science Association's annual meeting in New Orleans, and at a faculty workshop of the Tulane University Law School, where I received helpful comments. Thanks to Lura Barber, Rosalind Cook, Stephanie Short, Libby Sharrow, and Laura Wolford for research assistance.

2 Stephanie Francis Ward, "Female Judicial Candidates Are Held to Different Standards, Sotomayor Tells Students," *ABA Journal*, March 8, 2011, http://www.aba journal.com/news/article/female_judicial_candidates_are_held_to_different_standards_ sotomayor_tells_/, accessed August 4, 2011.

3 Carol J. Greenhouse, "Judgment and the Justice: An Ethnographic Reading of the Sotomayor Confirmation Hearings," *Law, Culture and the Humanities*, November 25, 2010, http://lch.sagepub.com/content/early/2010/11/12/1743872110374916.full.pdf, accessed November 23, 2011.

4 Tracy Clark-Flory, "Elena Kagan, Cross Your Legs!" *Salon*, May 24, 2010, http://www.salon.com/2010/05/24/kagan_clothing_givhan/, accessed November 15, 2011.

5 "Fat?" you ask. Compared to Justices Thomas and Scalia? Yes, it is true. See Megan Carpentier, "Women Too Stupid to Stay Thin Are Not Smart Enough for Supreme Court," *Jezebel*, May 5, 2009, http://jezebel.com/5241128/women-too, accessed August 4, 2011; and Paul Campos, "Fat Judges Need Not Apply," *The Daily Beast*, May 4, 2009, http://www.thedailybeast.com/articles/2009/05/04/fat-judges-need-not-apply.html, accessed August 4, 2011.

6 Susan Faludi, *Backlash: The Undeclared War against American Women* (New York: Crown, 1991).

7 I am heavily indebted to Rosemary Hunter's analysis in "The High Price of Success: The Backlash against Women Judges in Australia," in *Calling for Change: Women, Law, and the Legal Profession*, eds. Elizabeth Sheehy and Sheila McIntyre (Ottawa: University of Ottawa Press, 2006), 281–301; and to Constance Backhouse, who describes what women encounter upon becoming a judge as a "chilly climate" ("The Chilly Climate for Women Judges: Reflections on the Backlash from the *Ewanchuk* Case," *Canadian Journal of Women and the Law* 15, no. 1 (2003): 167–193).

8 E.J. Graff, "The Opt-Out Myth," *Columbia Journalism Review*, 45, no. 6 (2007): 51–54, http://www.brandeis.edu/investigate/gender/optoutmyth.html, accessed January 2, 2012.

9 Mary Hawkesworth, "Analyzing Backlash: Feminist Standpoint Theory as Analytical Tool," *Women's Studies International Forum* 22, no. 2 (1999): 135–155.

10 Martha Chamallas, *Introduction to Feminist Legal Theory*, 2nd edn (New York: Aspen, 2003).

11 Vicki Schultz, "Reconceptualizing Sexual Harassment," *Yale Law Journal* 107, no. 6 (1998): 1683–1805.

12 Reva B. Siegel, "Constitutional Culture, Social Movement Conflict and Constitutional Change: The Case of the de facto ERA," *California Law Review* 94, no. 5 (2006): 1323–1419, 1362–1363.

13 Felice A. Stern, "Backlash," *American Speech* 40, no. 2 (1965): 156–157.

14 Jane Mansbridge and Shauna L. Shames, "Toward a Theory of Backlash: Dynamic Resistance and the Central Role of Power," *Politics & Gender* 4, no. 4 (2008): 623–634, 624. They, in turn, draw on Seymour Martin Lipset and Earl Raab, *The Politics of Unreason: Right-Wing Extremism in America, 1790–1970* (New York: Harper and Row, 1973). See also Robert Post and Reva Siegel, "*Roe* Rage: Democratic Constitutionalism and Backlash," *Harvard Civil Rights–Civil Liberties Law Review* 42, no. 2 (2007): 373–433, 389.

15 Myra Marx Ferree, "Soft Repression: Ridicule, Stigma, and Silencing in Gender-Based Movements," in *Authority in Contention: Research in Social Movements, Conflicts and Change*, vol. 25, eds. Daniel J. Myers and Daniel M. Cress (Amsterdam: Elsevier, 2004), 85–101.

16 Paula Giddings, *Ida: A Sword among Lions* (New York: HarperCollins, 2008); Mansbridge and Shames 2008, 626.

17 Clarence Y.H. Lo, "Countermovements and Conservative Movements in the Contemporary US," *Annual Review of Sociology* 8 (1982): 107–134; Mayer N. Zald, "Culture, Ideology, and Strategic Framing," in *Comparative Perspectives on Social Movements: Political Opportunities, Mobilizing Structures, and Cultural Framings*, eds. Doug McAdam, John D. McCarthy, and Mayer N. Zald (Cambridge: Cambridge University Press, 1996), 261–274; Siegel 2006; David S. Meyer and Suzanne Staggenborg, "Movements, Countermovements, and the Structure of Political Opportunity," *American Journal of Sociology* 101, no. 6 (1996): 1628–1660; Mayer Zald and Bert Useem, "Movement and Countermovement Interaction: Mobilization, Tactics, and State Involvement," in *Social Movements in an Organizational Society*, eds. Mayer N. Zald and John D. McCarthy (New Brunswick, NJ: Transaction, 1987), 247–271.

18 Linda Greenhouse and Reva B. Siegel, "Before (and after) *Roe v. Wade*: New Questions about Backlash," *Yale Law Journal* 120, no. 8 (2011): 2028–2087, 2078, n. 175.

19 Mansbridge and Shames 2008.

20 Joseph R. Gusfield, *Symbolic Crusade: Status Politics and the American Temperance Movement* (Urbana: University of Illinois Press, 1986).

21 Often the "too far, too fast" argument is intertwined with the separate point that courts cannot bring about social change alone or that litigation is always

counterproductive. See Gerald Rosenberg, *The Hollow Hope: Can Courts Bring about Social Change?* (Chicago: University of Chicago Press, 1991; and 2nd edn 2008) and Michael J. Klarman, "*Brown*, Racial Change, and the Civil Rights Movement," *Virginia Law Review* 80, no. 1 (1994): 7–150. Greenhouse and Siegel (2011, 2028) argue, "The backlash narrative suggests that turning to courts to vindicate rights is too often counter-productive, and that adjudication is to be avoided at all costs. We are not ready to accept this grim diagnosis at face value, and we urge further research into the dynamics of conflict in the decades after *Roe*. The stakes in understanding this history are high." See also Post and Siegel 2007.

22 Kira Sanbonmatsu, "Gender Backlash in American Politics?" *Politics & Gender* 4, no. 4 (2008): 634–642, 635.

23 See Carol Jenkins, "Media Justice for Sotomayor," Women's Media Center, July 10, 2009, http://womensmediacenter.com/wordpress/?p=857, accessed July 29, 2009; and Women's Media Center's video "Sexism Sells, but We're Not Buying It" on the media's treatment of Hillary Clinton, May 23, 2008, http://www.womensmediacenter. com/blog/2008/05/sexism-might-sell-but-were-not-buying-it/, accessed November 12, 2011. See also Susan J. Carroll, "Reflections on Gender and Hillary Clinton's Presidential Campaign: The Good, the Bad, and the Misogynic," *Politics & Gender* 5, no. 1 (2009): 1–20, as well as the Critical Perspectives section, "Race and Gender in the 2008 Democratic Presidential Nominations Process," in the same issue.

24 Kathleen A. Bratton operationalizes backlash narrowly as support for a policy agenda or opposition to it and separates out whites or men simply letting blacks or women shoulder the burden for legislation versus increased opposition to sponsored legislation as a result of legislative diversity ("The Effect of Legislative Diversity on Agenda-Setting: Evidence from Six State Legislatures," *American Politics Research* 30, no. 2 (2002): 115–142). Lyn Kathlene, however, found resistance to women legislators in legislative debates and in frequent interruptions ("Power and Influence in State Legislative Policymaking: The Interaction of Gender and Position in Committee Hearing Debates," *American Political Science Review* 88, no. 3 (1994): 560–576). Donald P. Haider-Markel found LGBT state legislators did introduce more pro-gay legislation, but their presence increased the likelihood that legislators would introduce and pass anti-gay legislation ("Representation and Backlash: The Positive and Negative Influence of Descriptive Representation," *Legislative Studies Quarterly* 32, no. 1 (2007): 107–133).

25 Janice D. Yoder, "Rethinking Tokenism: Looking beyond Numbers," *Gender & Society* 5, no. 2 (1991): 178–192.

26 Yoder 1991, 184.

27 Margaret Thornton, "'Otherness' on the Bench: How Merit Is Gendered," *Sydney Law Review* 29, no. 3 (2007): 391–413, 411.

28 Cynthia Fuchs Epstein, *Women in Law* (New York: Basic Books, 1981), 194.

29 Cynthia Cockburn, *In the Way of Women: Men's Resistance to Sex Equality in Organizations* (Ithaca, NY: ILR Press, 1991); Sally J. Kenney, "New Research on Gendered Political Institutions," *Political Research Quarterly* 49, no. 2 (1996a): 445–466; Kenney 1996; Janice D. Yoder, "Context Matters: Understanding Tokenism Processes

and Their Impact on Women's Work," *Psychology of Women Quarterly* 26, no. 1 (2002): 1–8.

30 Sanbonmatsu 2008.

31 Rosabeth Moss Kanter, *Men and Women of the Corporation* (New York: Basic Books, 1977).

32 Rosabeth Moss Kanter, *Men and Women of the Corporation*, 2nd edn (New York: Basic Books, 1993), 316.

33 Cockburn 1991.

34 Backhouse 2003.

35 Meredith Reid Sarkees and Nancy E. McGlen, "Misdirected Backlash: The Evolving Nature of Academia and the Status of Women in Political Science," *PS: Political Science & Politics* 32, no. 1 (1999): 100–108.

36 Melissa Harris-Perry analyzes the savage response to feminists on Duke's campus for suggesting there may be a campus culture of condoning rape, irrespective of whether its lacrosse players had raped anyone (*Sister Citizen: Shame, Stereotypes, and Black Women in America* (New Haven, CT: Yale University Press, 2011)).

37 Kate Zernike, "Gains, and Drawbacks, for Female Professors," *New York Times*, March 21, 2011.

38 Thornton 2007, 398.

39 Thornton 2007, 399.

40 Thomas Keck, "Beyond Backlash: Assessing the Impact of Judicial Decisions on LGBT Rights," *Law & Society Review* 43, no. 1 (2009): 151–186.

41 Keck 2009, 152.

42 Post and Siegel 2007.

43 Greenhouse and Siegel 2011.

44 Looking at the likely outcome of the next battleground state, Pennsylvania, Rosemary Nossiff shows that pro-life forces were already much better organized and situated than pro-choice groups ("Why Justice Ginsburg Is Wrong about States Expanding Abortion Rights," *PS: Political Science & Politics* 27, no. 2 (1994): 227–231). Scott Lemieux argues legislative attempts to reform abortion laws sparked backlash to the same degree as litigation ("Constitutional Politics and the Political Impact of Abortion Litigation: Judicial Power and Judicial Independence in Comparative Perspective," Ph.D. dissertation, University of Washington, 2004).

45 Greenhouse and Siegel 2011, 2031.

46 Faludi 1991, xx.

47 Derrick Bell, *Faces at the Bottom of the Well: The Permanence of Racism* (New York: Basic Books, 1992).

48 Sue Thomas, "'Backlash' and Its Utility to Political Scientists," *Politics & Gender* 4, no. 4 (2008): 615–623, 620.

49 Hawkesworth 1999.

50 Hunter 2006, 295. Hunter offers a theoretically sophisticated analysis of backlash rich with examples from Australia, with some additional observations from Canada, although she does not directly connect her examples with broader arguments about backlash outside of the legal profession. See also Barbara Hamilton, "The Law Council

of Australia Policy 2001 on the Process of Judicial Appointments: Any Good News for Future *Female* Judicial Appointees?" *Queensland University of Technology Law and Justice Journal* 1, no. 2 (2001): 223–240.

51 Bryna Bogoch, "Courtroom Discourse and the Gendered Construction of Professional Identity," *Law & Social Inquiry* 24, no. 2 (1999): 329–375; Judith Resnik, "Now Is the WRONG Time to Stop Courts' Self-Study," *New Jersey Law Journal* 142, no. 6 (1995): 27–39.

52 John W. Dean, *The Rehnquist Choice: The Untold Story of the Nixon Appointment that Redefined the Supreme Court* (New York: Free Press, 2001), 111–116, 144–146. Federal District Judge Nancy Gertner, interview by Linda Greenhouse, "Gender and the Law: Unintended Consequences, Unsettled Questions," Radcliffe Institute for Advanced Study, Harvard University, March 12–13, 2009, http://www.radcliffe.edu/events/calendar_2009law.aspx, accessed September 23, 2011.

53 Joan Biskupic, "Politics Snares Court Hopes of Minorities and Women," *USA Today*, August 22, 2000; Lauren Cohen Bell, "Senatorial Discourtesy: The Senate's Use of Delay to Shape the Federal Judiciary," *Political Research Quarterly* 55, no. 3 (2002): 589–607; Roger E. Hartley, "A Look at Race, Gender, and Experience," *Judicature* 84, no. 4 (2001): 191–197; Amy Steigerwalt, *Battle over the Bench: Senators, Interest Groups, and Lower Court Confirmations* (Charlottesville: University of Virginia Press, 2010).

54 Allison Stevens, "Filibuster Storm Brews over Judicial Nominations," *Women's eNews*, April 19, 2005, http://oldsite.womensenews.org/article.cfm/dyn/aid/2262/context/archive, accessed August 5, 2011.

55 Bell 2002, 602.

56 David Ingram, "Grassley Critiques Qualifications of Four Judicial Nominees," *Blog of Legal Times*, June 8, 2011, http://legaltimes.typepad.com/blt/2011/06/grassley-questions-qualifications-of-four-judicial-nominees-.html, accessed September 23, 2011.

57 Manu Raju, "Patrick Leahy: GOP Males It In," *Politico*, July 20, 2010, www.politico.com/news/stories/0710/39941.html, accessed August 5, 2010.

58 "Judicial Nomination Materials: 111th Congress," United States Senate Committee on the Judiciary, 2010, http://judiciary.senate.gov/nominations/Materials111thCongress.cfm, accessed November 12, 2011.

59 In the context of race, scholars have labeled these phenomena "microaggressions."

60 Beverly Blair Cook, "Florence Allen," in *Notable American Women: The Modern Period: A Biographical Dictionary*, eds. Barbara Sicherman and Carol Hurd Green (Cambridge, MA: Harvard University Press, 1980a), 11–13, 12; Beverly Blair Cook, "Women as Supreme Court Candidates: From Florence Allen to Sandra O'Connor," *Judicature* 65, no. 6 (1982): 314–326; Sally J. Kenney, "Critical Perspectives on Gender and Judging," *Politics & Gender* 6, no. 3 (2010a): 433–441; Joan Ellen Organ, "Sexuality as a Category of Historical Analysis: A Study of Judge Florence E. Allen, 1884–1966," Ph.D. dissertation, Case Western Reserve University, 1998; Jeanette E. Tuve, *First Lady of the Law: Florence Ellinwood Allen* (Lanham, MD: University Press of America, 1984).

61 Florence Allen, *To Do Justly* (Cleveland, OH: Western Reserve University Press, 1965), 95.

62 Tuve 1984, 116, 135. Former Minnesota Supreme Court Justice Esther Tomljanovich had this to say about Judge Florence Allen's solitary meals: "I was in her chambers in Cincinnati some years ago, a woman Judge Kennedy now occupies the chambers. She showed me a small marble-topped table that she said Judge Allen had used to hold a hot plate where she heated soup for her lunch, because the men judges lunched at the exclusive men's club where women were not admitted. That marble table represents to me how early professional women were treated. The worst part is that I have Judge Allen's autobiography where she says that her men colleagues were supportive of her. That too is typical; we smiled a lot and ignored a lot" (personal communication with the author, January 11, 2011).

63 Backhouse 2003, 176–77.

64 Backhouse 2003, 177.

65 Claire L'Heureux-Dubé, "Outsiders on the Bench: The Continuing Struggle for Equality," *Wisconsin Women's Law Journal* 16, no. 1 (2001): 15–30, 15.

66 Betty Medsger, *Framed: The New Right Attack on Chief Justice Rose Bird and the Courts* (New York: Pilgrim Press, 1983). See also Winifred L. Hepperle, "Review of *Framed: The New Right Attack on Chief Justice Rose Bird and the Courts. By Betty Medsger*," *Golden Gate University Law Review* 14, no. 3 (1984): 505–517.

67 Hunter 2006, 282, drawing on Margaret Thornton, *Dissonance and Distrust: Women in the Legal Profession* (Melbourne: Oxford University Press, 1996), 208.

68 Mary L. Clark, "One Man's Token Is Another Woman's Breakthrough? The Appointment of the First Women Federal Judges," *Villanova Law Review* 49, no. 3 (2004): 487–549, 524, 499.

69 Clark 2004, 499.

70 Hunter 2006, 282.

71 Hunter 2006, 283, quoting the Honorable Rob Hulls, MP, "Welcome to Chief Justice Warren," *Australian Law Journal* 78, no. 2 (2004): 79.

72 Sally J. Kenney, "Britain Appoints First Woman Law Lord," *Judicature* 87, no. 4 (2004a): 189–190, 190.

73 Backhouse 2003, 172–175.

74 Backhouse 2003, 175.

75 Mona Harrington, *Women Lawyers: Rewriting the Rules* (New York: Alfred A. Knopf, 1994); Lynn Hecht Schafran, "Documenting Gender Bias in the Courts: The Task Force Approach," *Judicature* 70, no. 5 (1987): 280–290; Judith Resnik, "Asking about Gender in Courts," *Signs: Journal of Women in Culture and Society* 21, no. 4 (1996): 952–990; Andrea Stepnick and James D. Orcutt, "Conflicting Testimony: Judges' and Attorneys' Perceptions of Gender Bias in Legal Settings," *Sex Roles* 34, nos. 7–8 (1996): 567–579; Patricia Van Voorhis, Joanne Belknap, Karen Welch, and Amy Stichman, "Gender Bias in Courts: The Findings and Recommendations of the Task Forces," paper presented at the American Society of Criminology annual meeting, Phoenix, October 1993; Norma J. Wikler, "Water on Stone: A Perspective on the Movement to Eliminate Gender Bias in the Courts," *Court Review* 26, no. 3 (1989): 6–13.

76 Bogoch 1999, 341.

77 Bogoch 1999, 342.

78   In the mock oral argument before a panel of women judges from different countries at the 2002 meeting of the International Association of Women Judges, judges considered a case of statutory rape. The first motion of the defendant's lawyer was to ask the women to recuse themselves for bias on the grounds of sex, suggesting that such challenges to objectivity exist cross-nationally.

79   In *Caperton v. Massey* (556 U.S. ___ (2009)), the US Supreme Court held that massive campaign contributions to a West Virginia Supreme Court justice by one of the parties before him raised such fundamental questions of impartiality that he could not be allowed to refuse to recuse himself. For a call on states to update recusal requirements, see Peter Hardin, "*NY Times* Recusal Editorial Cites JAS and Partner," *GavelGrab*, June 16, 2011, http://www.gavelgrab.org/?p=21712, accessed July 5, 2011.

80   Canadian Bar Association, Task Force on Gender Equality in the Legal Profession, *Touchstones for Change: Equality, Diversity, Accountability* (1993), http://www.cba.org/cba/equity/main/pubs.aspx, 192–194, accessed December 12, 2011; Herma Hill Kay and Geraldine Sparrow, "Workshop on Judging: Does Gender Make a Difference?" *Wisconsin Women's Law Journal* 16, no. 1 (2001): 1–14; L'Heureux-Dubé 2001, 22.

81   Constance Baker Motley, "Reflections," *Columbia Law Review* 102, no. 6 (2002): 1449–1450.

82   *Pennsylvania v. Local Union*, 388 F. Supp. 155 (E.D. Pa. 1974). Judge Higginbotham eloquently demanded the exposure of "the instinct for double standards" (181).

83   Bell 1992, 113.

84   William Horne, "Judging Tadic," *American Lawyer*, September 1995, http://unconqueredbosnia.tripod.com/McDonald1.html, accessed August 5, 2011. McDonald went on to be a judge on the International Criminal Tribunal for the former Yugoslavia and eventually its president. She then served as an arbitrator on the Iran–US Claims Tribunal.

85   Marlise Simons, "Then It Was the Klan: Now It's the Balkan Agony," *New York Times*, January 13, 1999, A4.

86   Constance Backhouse, "Bias in Canadian Law: A Lopsided Precipice," *Canadian Journal of Women and the Law* 10, no. 1 (1998): 170–183, 181.

87   Maura Dolan, "Gay Judge Wasn't Required to Remove Himself from Same-Sex Marriage Case, US Judge Rules," *Los Angeles Times*, June 15, 2011, http://articles.latimes.com/2011/jun/15/local/la-me-0615-gay-judge-20110616, accessed August 5, 2011.

88   Jena Recer and Penny Anderson, "Texas Judge Resigns Citing Political Harassment," *National NOW Times*, November 1995, http://www.now.org/nnt/11-95/reed.html, accessed November 12, 2011.

89   The lawyer, State Representative John Longoria, and Judge Reed had a history of conflicts stemming from Longoria's Operation Rescue, whose members were charged with trespassing at abortion clinics.

90   Rita Mayer and Ilene Whitworth, "Judge Handcuffed and Jailed for Trying Wife-Beater," *National NOW Times*, May 1995, http://www.now.org/nnt/05-95/judge.html, accessed September 23, 2011.

91 A similar scenario played out in Australia. Hunter (2006, 281) argues Queensland Chief Magistrate Diane Fingleton was convicted of retaliating against a witness and jailed for what she says could be described, at best, as workplace bullying. Hunter (2006, 290) suggests other judges resented Fingleton for issuing an apology to indigenous people as a concession toward reconciliation (the Chief Justice of Queensland openly reproached her for doing so) and resented the administrative power she had over other magistrates and her forthright manner (Thornton 2007, 400). Moreover, Fingleton was from a working-class background with a record as a fierce campaigner for social justice causes (Hunter 2006, 294). Hunter (2006, 292) observes that "women judges who attempt to defend themselves or their colleagues by taking the attack up to the attackers tend to find themselves in an even worse position than before. It is inconceivable that any let alone all of this would have happened to a man." As evidence, she notes that Fingleton's successor's attempt to bully a newly appointed indigenous female magistrate led to his quiet retirement with pension, rather than jail time, after the magistrate successfully challenged the reassignment (Hunter 2006, 292).

92 *R. v. R.D.S.* [1997] 3 S.C.R. 484.

93 Backhouse 2003, 180.

94 Backhouse 2003, 180, quoting Ellen Anderson, *Judging Bertha Wilson: Law as Large as Life* (Toronto: University of Toronto Press, 2001), 349.

95 Hunter 2006, 296. The response to Justice Wilson's survey is echoed in the move of a group of conservative senators to shut down the gender-bias taskforce movement. In 1995, five senators asked the General Accounting Office to investigate the federal funds spent on such taskforces and recommended that Congress not allow any further spending. Although some of these taskforce reports, like the one from the Eighth Circuit, hardly touched on the lack of gender diversity in the judiciary, others did call for opening up the judicial selection process and reported sexist treatment toward women judges as well as toward women lawyers and plaintiffs. The thirteen-year run from 1982 to when opponents shut it down in 1995 was wildly successful in documenting the absence of judicial impartiality in certain areas of case law, most notably domestic violence, but also in the treatment of women (and minority men in the case of the race-bias studies). Anticipating the response to Justice Sotomayor, in 1995 opponents effectively framed those pointing at gender bias as lacking impartiality and judicial temperament and engaging in sex discrimination. The shutdown of the gender-bias taskforce movement was part of a backlash and a reaction to its success. Those who wanted to challenge gender bias in the courts were on notice that they would face not only opposition but stiff counter-attacks.

96 Jennifer Lucas, "Is Justice Blind? Gender and Voting in Judicial Elections," paper presented at the Midwest Political Science Association annual meeting, Chicago, April 2007.

97 Traciel V. Reid, "The Competitiveness of Female Candidates in Judicial Elections: An Analysis of the North Carolina Trial Court Races," *Albany Law Review* 67, no. 3 (2004b): 829–842, 834. See also Traciel V. Reid, "The Role of Gender in Judicial Campaigns: North Carolina Trial Court Races," *Southeastern Political Review* 28, no. 3 (2000b): 551–584; and Traciel V. Reid, "Assessing the Impact of a Candidate's Sex

in Judicial Campaigns and Elections in North Carolina," *Justice System Journal* 25, no. 2 (2004a): 183–207.

98 Traciel V. Reid, "The Politicization of Judicial Retention Elections: The Defeat of Justices Lanphier and White," in *Research on Judicial Selection 1999*, ed. Hunter Center for Judicial Selection (Chicago: American Judicature Society, 2000a), http://www.judicialselection.us/uploads/documents/Diversity_and_the_Judicial_Merit_Se_9C486 3118945B.pdf, 43–71, accessed November 23, 2011; Traciel V. Reid, "Women Candidates and Judicial Elections: Telling an Untold Story," *Politics & Gender* 6, no. 3 (2010): 465–474.

99 Stephanie B. Goldberg, "Women Fight to Retain State Supreme Court Seats," American Bar Association, Commission on Women in the Profession, *Perspectives* Winter (2008): 4–7.

100 Paul Reidinger, "The Politics of Judging," *ABA Journal*, April 1, 1987, 52–58, 56.

101 Rebecca Easley, quoted in Traciel V. Reid, "The Politicization of Retention Elections: Lessons from the Defeat of Justices Lanphier and White," *Judicature* 83, no. 2 (1999): 68–77, 51.

102 Reid 1999.

103 Goldberg 2008, 4.

104 Goldberg 2008, 6.

105 In Australia, for example, women leaving the bench have not been replaced by women. Both Hunter and Thornton describe the determination not to replace Mary Gaudron on the Australian High Court in 2003 with a woman (Hunter 2006, 285; Thornton 2007, 395).

106 Beverly Blair Cook, "Women Judges: The End of Tokenism," in *Women in the Courts*, eds. Winifred L. Hepperle and Laura Crites (Williamsburg, VA: National Center for State Courts, 1978b), 84–105, 96.

107 Rorie L. Spill and Kathleen A. Bratton, "Clinton and Diversification of the Federal Judiciary," *Judicature* 84, no. 2 (2001): 256–261, 258.

108 Kathleen A. Bratton and Rorie L. Spill, "Existing Diversity and Judicial Selection: The Role of the Appointment Method in Establishing Gender Diversity in State Supreme Courts," *Social Science Quarterly* 83, no. 2 (2002): 504–518.

109 Hunter 2006, 295–296; Kenney 2010a.

110 Deirdre English, "The Ordeal of Rose Bird," *Ms. Magazine*, November 1986, 71–75.

111 English 1986.

112 Todd S. Purdum, "Rose Bird, Once California's Chief Justice, Is Dead at 63," *New York Times*, December 6, 1999, B18.

113 John H. Culver and John T. Wold, "Rose Bird and the Politics of Judicial Accountability in California," *Judicature* 70, no. 2 (1986): 81–89, 87; John H. Culver and John T. Wold, "The Defeat of the California Justices: The Campaign, the Electorate, and the Issue of Judicial Accountability," *Judicature* 70, no. 6 (1987): 348–355.

114 Preble Stolz, *Judging Judges: The Investigation of Rose Bird and the California Supreme Court* (New York: The Free Press, 1981), 121.

115 Culver and Wold 1987, 354.

116 Culver and Wold 1986, 87.

117 Patrick K. Brown, "The Rise and Fall of Rose Bird: A Career Killed by the Death Penalty," Master's essay, California State University, 2007.

118 English 1986, 72.

119 Bestselling author John Grisham's novel *The Appeal* (New York: Doubleday, 2008) features a campaign to unseat a woman judge. In it, business interests concerned about tort liability target a woman on the Mississippi Supreme Court in an echo of the campaign that was waged against Rose Bird. The judge's opponents diagnose her as the weakest sitting justice and the easiest to beat precisely because she is a woman. Her gender makes it easier to tar her as liberal, activist, and anti-business.

120 Erin Adrian, "Rose Elizabeth Bird: Choosing to Be Just," student paper for course on Women in the Legal Profession, Stanford University, April 5, 2002, 3, http://womenslegalhistory.stanford.edu/papers/BirdR-Adrian02.pdf, accessed November 12, 2011. See also Beverly Blair Cook, "Rose Bird," *American Biography Online* (2001) http://www.amb.org.floyd.lib.umn.edu/articles/11/11-01013-print.html, accessed July 1, 2009.

121 "Rose Elizabeth Bird," *Current Biography* 45 (1984): 26–29; Adrian 2002.

122 Bob Schmidt, "Beyond Bird: In Deciding the Political Fate of Chief Justice Rose Bird, Can a Balance Be Struck between the Need for an Independent Judiciary and the Public Demand that Judges Be Accountable to the Voters?" *Golden State Report* 2, no. 1 (1986): 13–18.

123 Medsger 1983, 14.

124 Culver and Wold 1986, 83.

125 Larry D. Hatfield and Anastasia Hendrix, "Rose Bird Recalled as Brilliant Legal Trailblazer," *San Francisco Examiner*, December 6, 1999, A1; Adrian 2002.

126 Hatfield and Hendrix 1999.

127 Hatfield and Hendrix 1999.

128 Now that these jobs are no longer closed to them, women are finding that working as a prosecutor is a better path to elective and judicial office than working as a public defender. See Anne E. Kornblut, *Notes from the Cracked Ceiling: Hillary Clinton, Sarah Palin, and What It Will Take for a Woman to Win* (New York: Crown, 2009).

129 Bob Schmidt, "Looking Ahead with Rose Bird," *San Jose Mercury News*, March 20, 1977; Adrian 2002.

130 "Rose Bird," *State Net California Journal*, November 1, 1999.

131 Purdum, 1999.

132 Quoted in Harriet Chiang and Joan Ryan, "Bird's Passion for Principles Recalled," *San Francisco Chronicle*, December 6, 1999, http://articles.sfgate.com/1999-12-06/news/17709325_1_california-justices-justices-joseph-grodin-chief-justice/4, accessed December 7, 2011.

133 As evidence of his open disdain for the judiciary, Brown refused to appoint replacements for the first seventy vacancies that occurred during his tenure as Governor, and he gave speeches in his first year saying that judges were lazy and did not deserve a raise (Medsger 1983, 9).

134 Medsger 1983, 9.

135 Brown 2007, 6–7.

136 Medsger 1983, 10.

137 *State Net* 1999.

138 Culver and Wold 1986, 83; Deborah Ruble Round, "Gender Bias in the Judicial System," *Southern California Law Review* 61, no. 6 (1987–1988): 2193–2220, 2197.

139 Lynn Hecht Schafran, "California: First as Usual," *Women's Rights Law Reporter* 22, no. 2 (2001): 159–167.

140 English 1986, 71.

141 Medsger 1983, 9–10.

142 Adrian 2002, 11.

143 *State Net* 1999, 2.

144 Medsger 1983, 13.

145 Medsger 1983, 11.

146 Culver and Wold 1986, 87; Culver and Wold 1987, 351. See also Michael Farrell, "Obituary: Chief Justice Rose Bird," *ACLU News* (January/February, 2002).

147 Medsger 1983, 40.

148 Culver and Wold 1986, 82.

149 Medsger 1983, 40.

150 Medsger (1983) and Stolz (1981) analyze the hearings in great detail.

151 Clark's loyalty to Reagan would later earn him the position of National Security Advisor, although he shamed himself before the Foreign Relations Committee during his confirmation hearings for being unable to name world leaders, identify pressing foreign policy issues, or define the terms "*détente*" and "Third World" (Medsger 1983, 33).

152 Culver and Wold 1986, 82.

153 Susan B. Carbon, "Judicial Retention Elections: Are They Serving Their Intended Purpose?" *Judicature* 64, no. 5 (1980): 221–223.

154 Mike Weiss, "Goodbye to a Rose that Thrived in Every Climate," *San Francisco Chronicle*, December 6, 1999, A2.

155 English 1986, 74.

156 Culver and Wold 1987, 350.

157 Culver and Wold 1986, 88.

158 Daniel M. Weintraub, "Board to 'Invite' Duffy to Meet: Lawsuit over Post Cards for Chief Justice at Issue," *Los Angeles Times*, February 21, 1985, 1.

159 Culver and Wold 1986, 86; Purdum 1999.

160 Culver and Wold 1986, 87.

161 Medsger 1983, 55.

162 Medsger 1983, 59.

163 Medsger 1983, 67.

164 Medsger 1983, 72.

165 Medsger 1983, 63.

166 Purdum 1999.

167 Meredith May, "Rose Bird Tribute Honors Ex-Justice as Humanitarian," *San Francisco Chronicle*, January 17, 2000, A15.

168 A journalist alleged that the only job offer Bird received after she left the court, reportedly from feminist Gloria Allred's Los Angeles firm in 1986, was rescinded because of Bird's poor temperament, although the article making that allegation does not provide any evidence (Joel Sappell, "Death Penalty Controversy Trails Bird," *Los Angeles Times*, May 14, 1990, A1, in Adrian 2002).

169 Reidinger 1987, 52; Culver and Wold 1987, 350.

170 Reidinger 1987, 54.

171 Nadine Strossen, "The Leadership Role of the Legal Community in Promoting both Civil Liberties and National Security Post-9/11," paper presented at the Minnesota Women Lawyers' Annual Rosalie Wahl Leadership Lecture, Minneapolis, February 13, 2003.

172 When asked, she replied, "I haven't married because the right man hasn't asked me" (Eric Levin, "The New Look in Old Maids," *People*, March 31, 1986, 28, in Adrian 2002).

173 Margaret Thornton analyzes corporealizing the body of the "other" as a significant mechanism for denying rationality, autonomy, and authority to women ("Authority and Corporeality: The Conundrum for Women in Law," *Feminist Legal Studies* 6, no. 2 (1998): 147–170).

174 Lee Sigelman, Carol K. Sigelman, and Christopher A. Fowler, "A Bird of a Different Feather? An Experimental Investigation of Physical Attractiveness and the Electability of Female Candidates," *Social Psychology Quarterly* 50, no. 1 (1987): 32–43.

175 Sigelman et al. 1987, 37. Women students were more likely to support Bird (an 11 percent difference), and, since women were less supportive of the death penalty, that factor made the difference even more pronounced.

176 Likewise, studies of orchestra tryouts (Claudia Goldin and Cecilia Rouse, "Orchestrating Impartiality: The Impact of 'Blind' Auditions on Female Musicians," *American Economic Review* 90, no. 4 (2000): 715–741) and evaluations of identical résumés with the gender of names switched testify to the fact that men and women who express no conscious hostility to women or belief in their inferiority routinely devalue women's attributes, even if the women's credentials are superior or identical to men's. Recent studies of women producers choosing to produce few women playwrights (Emily Glassberg Sands, "Opening the Curtain on Playwright Gender: An Integrated Economic Analysis of Discrimination in American Theater," Master's thesis, Princeton University, 2009, http://graphics8.nytimes.com/packages/pdf/theater/Openingthe curtain.pdf, accessed August 5, 2011; Sheri Wilner and Julia Jordan, "Discrimination and the Female Playwright," *GIA Reader* 21, no. 1 (2010), http://www.giarts.org/article/discrimination-and-female-playwright, accessed August 5, 2011) and young women's lack of enthusiasm for Hillary Clinton's campaign (Kornblut 2009) suggest that the problem of devaluing women is not restricted to a few sexist men but is ubiquitous.

177 See Tali Mendelberg's research on implicit racial appeals in *The Race Card: Campaign Strategy, Implicit Messages, and the Norm of Equality* (Princeton, NJ: Princeton University Press, 2001).

178   Rose Elizabeth Bird, "State of the Judiciary, 1986," *Guild Practitioner* 43, no. 3 (1986): 91–93, 93.

179   Reidinger 1987, 52.

180   Backhouse 2003, quoting Judith Resnik, "Asking about Gender in Courts," *Signs: Journal of Women in Culture and Society* 21, no. 4 (1996): 952-990.

181   Backhouse 2003, 189.

182   Kornblut 2009; Regina G. Lawrence and Melody Rose, *Hillary Clinton's Race for the White House: Gender Politics and the Media on the Campaign Trail* (Boulder, CO: Lynne Rienner, 2010).

183   Chris W. Bonneau and Melinda Gann Hall, *In Defense of Judicial Elections* (New York: Routledge, 2009); James L. Gibson and Gregory A. Caldeira, *Citizens, Courts, and Confirmations: Positivity Theory and the Judgments of the American People* (Princeton, NJ: Princeton University Press, 2009). Reid's (2010) methods uncover more sex differences, and she critiques previous work for hiding sex differences.

184   Schultz 1998.

8 CONCLUSION

1   I presented earlier versions of the paper to the International Conference on Women in the Legal Professions, Law Faculty, University of Buenos Aires, Argentina; as a Leadership Lecture at Gustavus Adolphus College; at the Indianapolis meeting of the National Association of Women Judges; to the 8th Annual Workshop of the Justice at Stake Campaign; to a Women and the Law class, University of Texas at Austin; to the Center for German and European Studies, Gender and Women's Studies, and the Department of Sociology, University of Wisconsin-Madison; and to the Law and Public Affairs Program at Princeton University. Special thanks to Myra Marx Ferree and Aili Tripp for their comments and to Lura Barber for research assistance.

2   "Women in Federal and State-Level Judgeships," report of the Center for Women in Government and Civil Society, Rockefeller College of Public Affairs and Policy, University at Albany, SUNY, Spring 2011, http://www.albany.edu/news/images/judgeship_report_partII.pdf, accessed July 11, 2011; "Women in the Federal Judiciary: Still a Long Way to Go," National Women's Law Center, October 18, 2011, http://www.nwlc.org/resource/women-federal-judiciary-still-long-way-go-1, accessed November 16, 2011.

3   Karen O'Connor and Alixandra B. Yanus, "Judging Alone: Reflections on the Importance of Women on the Court," *Politics & Gender* 6, no. 3 (2010): 441–452.

4   Kathy Bonk et al., *Strategic Communications for Nonprofits: A Step-by-Step Guide to Working with the Media* (San Francisco: Jossy-Bass, 2008); George Lakoff, *Don't Think of an Elephant! Know Your Values and Frame the Debate* (White River Junction, VT: Chelsea Green, 2004).

5   Myra Marx Ferree, "An American Road Map? Framing Feminist Goals in a Liberal Landscape," in *Gender Equality: Transforming Family Divisions of Labor*, eds. Janet Gornick and Marcia Meyers (London: Verso, 2009) 283–315.

6 Patricia Yancey Martin, John R. Reynolds, and Shelley Keith, "Gender Bias and Feminist Consciousness among Judges and Attorneys: A Standpoint Theory Analysis," *Signs: Journal of Women in Culture and Society* 27, no. 3 (2002): 665–701.

7 Sherrilyn Ifill, "Racial Diversity on the Bench: Beyond Role Models and Public Confidence," *Washington and Lee Law Review* 57, no. 2 (2000): 405–495.

8 Tania Tetlow makes a similar argument: "Finally, group associations can matter to government decision-making, because group associations matter to citizens themselves when they participate in government. It ignores human experience to pretend that race is not a potentially valuable predictor of certain beliefs, which are, after all, often the result of common experience" ("How *Batson* Spawned *Shaw*: Requiring the Government to Treat Citizens as Individuals When It Cannot," *Loyola Law Review* 49, no. 1 (2003): 133–169, 136).

9 Leonie Huddy and Tony E. Carey Jr., "Group Politics Redux: Race and Gender in the 2008 Democratic Presidential Primaries," *Politics & Gender* 5, no. 1 (2009): 81–96.

10 Theresa M. Beiner, "The Elusive (but Worthwhile) Quest for a Diverse Bench in the New Millennium," *University of California Davis Law Review* 36, no. 3 (2003): 597–615; Theresa M. Beiner, "What Will Diversity on the Bench Mean for Justice?" *Michigan Journal of Gender & Law* 6, no. 1 (1999): 113–152; Theresa M. Beiner, "Female Judging," *University of Toledo Law Review* 36, no. 4 (2005): 821–847.

11 Linda Kerber, *No Constitutional Right to be Ladies: Women and the Obligations of Citizenship* (New York: Hill and Wang, 1998), 143; Holly J. McCammon et al., "Movement Framing and Discursive Opportunity Structures: The Political Successes of the US Women's Jury Movements," *American Sociological Review* 72, no. 5 (2007): 725–749, 727; Elisabeth Israels Perry, "Rhetoric, Strategy, and Politics in the New York Campaign for Women's Jury Service, 1917–1975," *New York History* 82, no. 1 (2001): 53–78; Gretchen Ritter, "Jury Service and Women's Citizenship before and after the Nineteenth Amendment," *Law and History Review* 20, no. 3 (2002): 479–515.

12 Barbara Allen Babcock, "A Place in the Palladium: Women's Rights and Jury Service," *University of Cincinnati Law Review* 61, no. 4 (1993): 1139–1180, 1169; Perry 2001.

13 In premodern England, a mixed jury was established when the senses of justice of two difference communities were at issue. See Marianne Constable, *The Law of the Other: The Mixed Jury and Changing Conceptions of Citizenship, Law, and Knowledge* (Chicago: University of Chicago Press, 1994). The matron's jury was called to establish whether a woman condemned to death was pregnant. It was to find the facts, and under close supervision. The matron's jury was also occasionally called on to identify bodily marks that indicated witchcraft. See Ritter 2002, 493–494. Oregon passed a law in 1921 instituting a law mandating that criminal cases involving a minor must have a jury with half of its members women. It had to abandon this law when so few women voluntarily registered for jury service. See Ritter 2002, 511.

14 McCammon et al. 2007, 740.

15 Susan Hartmann, "Feminism, Public Policy, and the Carter Administration," in *The Carter Presidency: Policy Choices in the Post-New Deal Era*, eds. Gary M. Fink and

Hugh Davis Graham (Lawrence: University of Kansas Press, 1998b), 224–243; Kerber 1998.

16 Babcock 1993.

17 Perry 2001, 68. Congress codified this with the Civil Rights Act of 1957, declaring women competent to serve on federal juries regardless of state law. See Lucy Fowler, "Gender and Jury Deliberations: The Contributions of Social Science," *William & Mary Journal of Women and the Law* 12, no. 1 (2005): 1–48, 3.

18 Babcock 1993, 1169.

19 *Ballard v. United States*, 329 U.S. 187 (1946), 191–2.

20 *Ballard v. United States* (1946), 193.

21 *Ballard v. United States* (1946), 193–194 (emphasis added).

22 *Ballard v. United States* (1946), 195.

23 Kerber 1998, 148–151.

24 Kerber 1998, 155. Campaigners for women's right to serve on juries made an alleged case of infanticide a rallying cry in 1936 in New York. Women argued only mothers would appreciate the strength it would take to give birth alone, unaided, without making a sound, and understand the desperation a young woman might feel bearing a child out of wedlock. See Perry 2001, 55.

25 Kerber 1998, 156.

26 *Hoyt v. State*, 119 So. 2nd 691 (1959), 700–702.

27 Kerber 1998, 169.

28 *Hoyt v. Florida*, 368 U.S. 57 (1961), 59.

29 *Hoyt v. Florida* (1961), 62.

30 *Hoyt v. Florida* (1961), 68.

31 Kerber 1998, 188.

32 Kerber 1998, 191.

33 *White v. Crook*, 251 F. Supp. 401 (1966).

34 In her confirmation hearings, Ginsburg would mention *Hoyt* as one of the cases with the most meaning to her (see Kerber 1998, 217). She represented Healy. See Ruth Bader Ginsburg, "The Supreme Court: A Place for Women," *Southwestern University Law Review* 32, no. 2 (2003): 189–199.

35 *Healy v. Edwards*, 363 F. Supp. 1110, 1115 (1973).

36 *Healy v. Edwards* (1973) (emphasis added).

37 *Taylor v. Louisiana*, 419 U.S. 522 (1975), 527.

38 *Taylor v. Louisiana* (1975), 529.

39 *Taylor v. Louisiana* (1975), 530.

40 *Taylor v. Louisiana* (1975), 531.

41 *Taylor v. Louisiana* (1975), n. 12.

42 *Peters v. Kiff*, 407 U.S. 493 (1972), 503.

43 *Taylor v. Louisiana* (1975), n. 12.

44 *Peters v. Kiff* (1972), 542.

45 Ruth Bader Ginsburg, "Women at the Bar: A Generation of Change," *University of Puget Sound Law Review* 2, no. 1 (1978): 1–14, 9.

46 *J.E.B. v. Alabama*, 511 U.S. 127 (1994).

47 *J.E.B. v. Alabama* (1994), 138–139.

48 *J.E.B. v. Alabama* (1994), 140–142.

49 *J.E.B. v. Alabama* (1994), 145 (emphasis added).

50 *J.E.B. v. Alabama* (1994), 138, n. 9.

51 *J.E.B. v. Alabama* (1994), 149, n. 14.

52 *J.E.B. v. Alabama* (1994), 149.

53 *J.E.B. v. Alabama* (1994), 156.

54 Kerber 1998, 174, 178. Wisconsin Supreme Court Justice Shirley Abrahamson added a new twist to this longstanding concern that, if women served on juries, dinner would go unmade. When she was impaneled on a jury, she had the clerk of court call her husband with instructions on the recipe for the dish she had promised to bring to a party that evening. She would be unable to prepare the dish or attend because she would be serving on a jury. In a remarkable breakthrough for women's rights, with the help of the clerk, her husband was able to make the dish and go without her while she served.

55 "When [the prosecutor] announced, 'The People will excuse and thank Juror Number 9, Mrs. Hemphill,' there were murmurs . . . and hisses . . . We all knew she was going to be excused. She knew it too. We were all embarrassed and saddened that Mrs. Janie Hemphill had to suffer another insult" (Mary Timothy, *Jury Woman: The Story of the Trial of Angela Y. Davis* (Palo Alto, CA: Emty Press, 1974), 27–29, quoted in Babcock 1993, 1160).

56 Susan L. McCoin, "Sex Discrimination in the *Voir Dire* Process: The Rights of Prospective Female Jurors," *Southern California Law Review* 58, no. 5 (1985): 1239, discussing *People v. Mims*; Jean Montoya, "'What's so Magic(al) about Black Women?' Peremptory Challenges at the Intersection of Race and Gender," *Michigan Journal of Gender & Law* 3, no. 2 (1996): 369–419.

57 Shirley S. Abrahamson, "Justice and Juror," *Georgia Law Review* 20, no. 2 (1986b): 278–287.

58 Abrahamson 1986b, 280; McCoin 1985, 1227.

59 Abigail Rury, "All Things Being Equal, Women Lose: Investigating the Lack of Diversity among the Recent Appointments to the Iowa Supreme Court," paper presented at the Southern Political Science Association annual meeting, New Orleans, January 12–14, 2012.

60 Abrahamson made the point earlier (1986b, 286).

61 One problem with the difference arguments is that they put the studies finding differences in the main body of the text and the studies finding no differences, in this case in rape cases, in the footnotes. See Fowler 2005, 22, n. 175.

62 Babcock 1993, 1145, n. 14.

63 Babcock 1993, 1146.

64 Babcock 1993, 1174, naming Elizabeth Holtzman, Marcia Greenberger, and others.

65 Rhonda Copelon, Elizabeth M. Schneider, and Nancy Stearns, "Constitutional Perspectives on Sex Discrimination in Jury Selection," *Women's Rights Law Reporter* 2, no. 4 (1975): 3–12.

66 Joanna L. Grossman, "Women's Jury Service: Right of Citizenship or Privilege of Difference?" *Stanford Law Review* 46, no. 5 (1994): 1115–1160, 1116.

67 Shirley S. Abrahamson, "A View from the Other Side of the Bench," *Marquette Law Review* 69, no. 4 (1986a): 463–493, 477; Jeffrey Abramson, *We, the Jury: The Jury System and the Ideal of Democracy* (Cambridge, MA: Harvard University Press, 2000), 158.

68 Despite this evidence, Abramson (2000, 162) concludes "[t]he myth of scientific jury selection was unstoppable." And, later, he notes we have moved from stereotypes to polls, but the difficulty of applying small differences in the general to the particular remains.

69 Sean G. Overland, *The Juror Factor: Race and Gender in America's Civil Courts* (El Paso, TX: LFB Scholarly, 2009), 11–12. Like Boyd et al. (Christina Boyd, Lee Epstein, and Andrew D. Martin, "Untangling the Causal Effects of Sex on Judging,"*American Journal of Political Science* 54, no. 2 (2010): 389-411), Overland criticizes (2009, 39) the unsophisticated statistical analyses for leading researchers to incorrect conclusions about sex differences.

70 Cameron McGowan Currie and Aleta M. Pillick, "Sex Discrimination in the Selection and Participation of Female Jurors: A Post-*J.E.B.* Analysis," *Judges' Journal* 35, no. 1 (1996): 2–6, 38–42, 4. Reviewing the studies of gender differences among jurors before 1996, Currie and Pillick find few differences in outcomes, other than women's greater propensity to convict in rape trials and to oppose the death penalty, but they do find women less likely to be chosen as foreperson, less likely to speak, etc. (40–41). Sandra Benlevy embraces the difference argument, but reports the opposite in rape cases ("Venus and Mars in the Jury Deliberation Room: Exploring the Differences that Exist among Male and Female Jurors during the Deliberation Process," *Southern California Review of Law and Women's Studies* 9, no. 2 (2000): 445–477, 469).

71 Sally J. Kenney, *For Whose Protection? Reproductive Hazards and Exclusionary Policies in the United States and Britain* (Ann Arbor: University of Michigan Press, 1992).

72 Perry 2001, 78.

73 Perry 2001, 64.

74 Ritter 2002.

75 Perry 2001, 78.

76 Joshua Gamson, "Must Identity Movements Self-Destruct? A Queer Dilemma," *Social Problems* 42, no. 3 (1995): 390–407.

77 Joan Wallach Scott, *Parité! Sexual Equality and the Crisis of French Universalism* (Chicago: University of Chicago Press, 2005); see also Valerie Hoekstra, "Increasing the Gender Diversity of High Courts: A Comparative View," *Politics & Gender* 6, no. 3 (2010): 474–484.

78 Many others have made eloquent arguments that parallel mine, and also diverge from it in important ways, most notably on the argument from difference. See Paula Monopoli, "Gender and Justice: Parity and the United States Supreme Court," *Georgetown Journal of Gender and the Law* 8, no. 1 (2007): 43–65.

79 Anne Phillips, *The Politics of Presence* (Oxford: Oxford University Press, 1995), 112.

80 Kristi Andersen, *After Suffrage: Women in Partisan and Electoral Politics before the*

New Deal (Chicago: University of Chicago Press, 1996); Freeman 2000; Ritter 2002, 480.

81 Abramson 2000, 101.

82 Abrahamson 1986a, 491; Abrahamson 1986b, 297.

83 Grossman 1994.

84 Robert Barnes, "High-Court Divide Has a New Dynamic," *Washington Post*, October 3, 2010, A15. North Dakota Supreme Court Justice Beryl Levine made what McCarthy calls the "role-model argument": "We get lots of children, lots of visitors. Just seeing a woman among the men helps alter consciousness" (Megan McCarthy, "Judicial Campaigns: What Can They Tell Us about Gender on the Bench?" *Wisconsin Women's Law Journal* 16, no. 1 (2001): 87–111, 106).

85 Ritter 2002, 495.

86 Ritter 2002, 495.

87 The UK's Advisory Panel on Judicial Diversity stressed equal opportunity, democracy, diversity of experiences, and representativeness in making its arguments ("The Report of the APJD 2010," 2010, http://www.justice.gov.uk/publications/docs/advisory-panel-judicial-diversity-2010.pdf, accessed July 1, 2011). Deborah Goldberg, director of the Democracy Program at the Brennan Center for Justice at New York University Law School, emphasized how the quality of judging and its legitimacy are improved by diversity, and it is necessary for fair and impartial justice ("Testimony of Deborah Goldberg," Public Forum: A Lasting Blueprint for Judicial Diversity, Brennan Center for Justice, March 1, 2007, http://www.brennancenter.org/content/resource/a_lasting_blueprint_for_judicial_diversity_testimony_of_deborah_goldberg/, accessed August 12, 2011). The Equal Justices Initiative's evidence to the House of Lords Select Committee on the Constitution recently stressed how diversity was necessary for democratic legitimacy ("Evidence to House of Lords Select Committee on the Constitution Inquiry into the Judicial Appointments Process," June 2011, http://www.law.qmul.ac.uk/eji/docs/EJI%20submisson%20INQUIRY%20INTO%20THE%20JUDICIAL%20APPOINTMENTS%20PROCESS.pdf, accessed July 5, 2011).

88 Perry 2001; Jeffrey Toobin, "Diverse Opinions," *New Yorker*, June 8 and 15, 2009, 37–38; Mary L. Volcansek, "Introduction," in *Women in Law: A Bio-bibliographical Sourcebook*, eds. Rebecca Mae Salokar and Mary L. Volcansek (Westport, CT: Greenwood Press, 1996), 1–13.

89 Congress recently passed a statute requiring one judge from each state in a circuit, but that does not solve the issue of how to allocate the remaining seats. In the Eighth Circuit, for example, there are eleven seats and seven states.

90 Graycar makes a similar point about how we only ask questions about difference of non-dominant groups. She queries why we never have panels entitled "Men's Judgments: Can They Make a Difference?" See Regina Graycar, "The Gender of Judgments: An Introduction," in *Public and Private: Feminist Legal Debates*, ed. Margaret Thornton (Oxford: Oxford University Press, 1995), 262–282, 264.

91 Shirley S. Abrahamson, "The Woman Has Robes: Four Questions," *Golden Gate University Law Review* 14, no. 3 (1984): 489–503, 490.

92 Abrahamson 1984, 492.

93 Abrahamson 1984, 491.

94 Bradley Blackburn, "Justices Ruth Bader Ginsburg and Sandra Day O'Connor on Life and the Supreme Court," *ABC World News*, October 26, 2010, http://abcnews.go.com/WN/diane-sawyer-interviews-maria-shriver-sandra-day-oconnor/story?id=119 77195, accessed August 12, 2011.

95 Abrahamson 1984, 493.

96 Barbara Frey, "A Fair Representation: Advocating for Women's Rights in the International Criminal Court," Case Study for Center on Women and Public Policy, University of Minnesota, 2004, http://www.hhh.umn.edu/centers/wpp/pdf/case_studies/fair_representation/fair_representation.pdf, accessed November 12, 2011.

97 Louise Chappell, "'Women's Interests' as 'Women's Rights': Developments at the UN Criminal Tribunals and the International Criminal Court," in *The Politics of Women's Interests: New Comparative Perspectives*, eds. Louise Chappell and Lisa Hill (London: Routledge, 2006), 217–236; Louise Chappell, "Women's Rights and Religious Opposition: The Politics of Gender at the International Criminal Court," in *Gendering the National State: Canadian and Comparative Perspectives*, ed. Yasmeen Abu-Laban (Vancouver: University of British Columbia Press, 2008), 139–161; Louise Chappell, "Gender and Judging at the International Criminal Court," *Politics & Gender* 6, no. 3 (2010): 484–495.

98 Maria Nzomo and Patricia Kameri-Mbote, "Gender Issues in the Draft Bill of the Constitution of Kenya: An Analysis," Contribution for the Constitution Review Commission of Kenya, International Environmental Law Research Centre Working Paper, 2003, http://www.ielrc.org/content/w0301.pdf, accessed November 12, 2011.

99 Brenda Hale, "Foreword," in *Feminist Judgments: From Theory to Practice*, eds. Rosemary Hunter, Clare McGlynn, and Erika Rackley (Oxford: Hart, 2010), v–vi.

100 Ruth Bader Ginsburg, interview by Linda Greenhouse, "Gender and the Law: Unintended Consequences, Unsettled Questions," Radcliffe Institute for Advanced Study, Harvard University, March 12–13, 2009, http://www.radcliffe.edu/events/calendar_2009law.aspx, accessed August 19, 2009.

101 Erika Rackley, "Difference in the House of Lords," *Social & Legal Studies* 15, no. 2 (2006): 163–185.

102 Jennifer Peresie, "Female Judges Matter: Gender and Collegial Decisionmaking in the Federal Appellate Courts," *Yale Law Journal* 114, no. 7 (2005): 1759–1790.

103 Elaine Martin and Barry Pyle, "State High Courts and Divorce: The Impact of Judicial Gender," *University of Toledo Law Review* 36, no. 4 (2005): 923–948.

104 Neil A. Lewis, "Debate on Whether Female Judges Decide Differently Arises Anew," *New York Times*, June 3, 2009.

BIBLIOGRAPHY

Abrahamson, Shirley S. 1984. "The Woman Has Robes: Four Questions." *Golden Gate University Law Review* 14, no. 3: 489–503.

Abrahamson, Shirley S. 1986a. "A View from the Other Side of the Bench." *Marquette Law Review* 69, no. 4: 463–493.

Abrahamson, Shirley S. 1986b. "Justice and Juror." *Georgia Law Review* 20, no. 2: 257–298.

Abramson, Jeffrey. 2000. *We, the Jury: The Jury System and the Ideal of Democracy.* Cambridge, MA: Harvard University Press.

Adrian, Erin. 2002. "Rose Elizabeth Bird: Choosing to Be Just." Student paper for course on Women in the Legal Profession, Stanford University, April 5. http://womenslegalhistory.stanford.edu/papers/BirdR-Adrian02.pdf. Accessed November 12, 2011.

Advisory Panel on Judicial Diversity. 2010. "The Report of the APJD 2010." http://www.justice.gov.uk/publications/docs/advisory-panel-judicial-diversity-2010.pdf. Accessed July 1, 2011.

Agence Europe. 1993. "EC: Mr. Goppel Criticizes the EP Report on the Court of Justice." Reuter Textline, Brussels. October 5.

Aliotta, Jilda. 1995. "Justice O'Connor and the Equal Protection Clause: A Feminine Voice?" *Judicature* 78, no. 5: 232–235.

Allen, David and Diane Wall. 1987. "The Behavior of Women State Supreme Court Justices: Are They Tokens or Outsiders?" *Justice System Journal* 12, no. 2: 232–245.

Allen, Florence. 1965. *To Do Justly.* Cleveland, OH: Western Reserve University Press.

Allen, Judith. 1990. "Does Feminism Need a Theory of 'The State'?" In *Playing the State: Australian Feminist Interventions*, ed. Sophie Watson. Boston: Allen and Unwin.

Alozie, Nicholas O. 1990. "Distribution of Women and Minority Judges: The Effects of Judicial Selection Methods." *Social Science Quarterly* 71, no. 2: 315–325.

Alozie, Nicholas O. 1996. "Selection Methods and the Recruitment of Women to State Courts of Last Resort." *Social Science Quarterly* 77, no. 1: 110–126.

Alter, Karen. 1998. "Who Are the 'Masters of the Treaty'? European Governments and the European Court of Justice." *International Organization* 52, no. 1: 121–147.

American Bar Association. 2009. "Statement of H. Thomas Wells Jr., President, American Bar Association Re: The American Bar Association Standing Committee on the Federal Judiciary." March 17. http://www.americanbar.org/content/dam/aba/migrated/scfedjud/wellsstatement.authcheckdam.pdf. Accessed December 11, 2011.

American Judicature Society. 2009. "Judicial Selection Methods in the States." http://www.ajs.org/selection/sel_state-select-map.asp. Accessed November 9, 2011.

Aminzade, Ron and Doug McAdam. 2001. "Emotions and Contentious Politics." In *Silence and Voice in the Study of Contentious Politics*, eds. Ronald R. Aminzade, Jack A. Goldstone, Doug McAdam, Elizabeth J. Perry, William H. Sewell Jr., Sidney Tarrow, and Charles Tilley. New York: Cambridge University Press.

Anasagasti, Miriam and Nathalie Wuiame. 1999. *Women and Decision-Making in the Judiciary in the European Union*. Luxembourg: Office for Official Publications of the European Communities.

Andersen, Kristi. 1996. *After Suffrage: Women in Partisan and Electoral Politics before the New Deal*. Chicago: University of Chicago Press.

Anderson, Ellen. 2001. *Judging Bertha Wilson: Law as Large as Life*. Toronto: University of Toronto Press.

"An Interview with Eleanor Dean Acheson." 1998. *Court Review* 35, no. 2: 6–13.

Armstrong, Elizabeth A. and Suzanna M. Crage. 2006. "Movements and Memory: The Making of the Stonewall Myth." *American Sociological Review*, 71, no. 5: 724–751.

Arnull, Anthony. 1999. "Judicial Architecture or Judicial Folly? The Challenge Facing the European Union." *European Law Review* 24, no. 5: 516–524.

"Arrangements Not Indirectly Discriminatory." 2001. *Equal Opportunities Review* 96: 47–49.

Association of Women Barristers. 1996. "Memorandum." *House of Commons Home Affairs Committee Third Report, Judicial Appointments Procedures, Volume III: Minutes of Evidence and Appendices*. June 5.

Association of Women Barristers. 2008. "The Rt Hon Lady Justice Arden DBE Address to the Association of Women Barristers' Annual General Meeting." June 3. http://www.judiciary.gov.uk/Resources/JCO/Documents/Speeches/lja_add_assoc_women_barristers_agm_0608.pdf. Accessed December 12, 2011.

Association of Women Solicitors. 1996. "Memorandum." *House of Commons Home Affairs Committee Third Report, Judicial Appointments Procedures,* Volume III: *Minutes of Evidence and Appendices.* June 5.

Auerbach, Laura K. 1984. *Worthy to Be Remembered: A Political History of the Minnesota Democratic–Farmer–Labor Party, 1944–1984.* Minneapolis: Democratic–Farmer–Labor Party of Minnesota.

Babcock, Barbara Allen. 1993. "A Place in the Palladium: Women's Rights and Jury Service." *University of Cincinnati Law Review* 61, no. 4: 1139–1180.

Babcock, Barbara. 1995. Interview by Sarah Wilson, May 19. From "Diversifying the Judiciary: An Oral History of Women Federal Judges." Federal Judicial Center.

Backhouse, Constance. 1998. "Bias in Canadian Law: A Lopsided Precipice." *Canadian Journal of Women and the Law* 10, no. 1: 170–183.

Backhouse, Constance. 2003. "The Chilly Climate for Women Judges: Reflections on the Backlash from the *Ewanchuk* Case." *Canadian Journal of Women and the Law* 15, no. 1: 167–193.

Ballard v. United States, 1946. 329 U.S. 187 (1946).

Banaszak, Lee Ann. 2010. *The Women's Movement Inside and Outside the State.* Cambridge: Cambridge University Press.

Banaszak, Lee Ann, Karen Beckwith, and Dieter Rucht, eds. 2003. *Women's Movements Facing the Reconfigured State.* Cambridge: Cambridge University Press.

Bandes, Susan A. 1999. "Introduction." In *The Passions of Law,* ed. Susan A. Bandes. New York: New York University Press.

Bandes, Susan A. 2008. "The Heart Has Its Reasons: Examining the Strange Persistence of the American Death Penalty." *Studies in Law, Politics, and Society* 42, no. 1: 21–52.

Bar Council Records Office. 2010. "Self-Employed Bar QCs by Ethnicity and Gender." December 23. http://www.barcouncil.org.uk/assets/documents/Table_3_Self%20Employed%20QCs%20by%20Ethnicity%20and%20Gender.pdf. Accessed July 5, 2011.

Barbalet, J.M. 2002. "Secret Voting and Political Emotions." *Mobilization* 7, no. 2: 129–140.

Bardach, Eugene. 1977. *The Implementation Game: What Happens after a Bill Becomes Law.* Cambridge, MA: MIT Press.

Barmes, Lizzie and Kate Malleson. 2011. "The Legal Profession as Gatekeeper to the Judiciary: Design Faults in Measures to Enhance Diversity." *Modern Law Review* 74, no. 2: 245–271.

Barnard, Catherine. 1995. "A European Litigation Strategy: The Case of the Equal Opportunities Commission." In *New Legal Dynamics of the European Union,* eds. Jo Shaw and Gillian More. Oxford: Clarendon Press.

Barnard, Corinna. 2011. "Wal-Mart Ruling Puts Big Chill on Female Workers." *Women's eNews.* June 25. http://www.womensenews.org/story/in-the-courts/

110624/wal-mart-ruling-puts-big-chill-female-workers. Accessed August 12, 2011.

Barnes, Robert. 2010. "High-Court Divide Has a New Dynamic." *Washington Post.* October 3.

Baumgartner, Frank R. and Bryan D. Jones. 1993. *Agendas and Instability in American Politics.* Chicago: University of Chicago Press.

Bazelon, Emily. 2009. "The Place of Women on the Court." *New York Times Magazine.* July 12.

BBC. 2004. "Slovenia's Appointments." In *BBC Summary of World Broadcasts.* May 20.

Begley, Sharon. 2008. "When It's Head versus Heart, the Heart Wins." *Newsweek.* February 11.

Behuniak-Long, Susan. 1992. "Justice Sandra Day O'Connor and the Power of Maternal Legal Thinking." *Review of Politics* 54, no. 3: 417–444.

Beiner, Theresa M. 1999. "What Will Diversity on the Bench Mean for Justice?" *Michigan Journal of Gender & Law* 6, no. 1: 113–152.

Beiner, Theresa M. 2003. "The Elusive (but Worthwhile) Quest for a Diverse Bench in the New Millennium." *University of California Davis Law Review* 36, no. 3: 597–617.

Beiner, Theresa M. 2005. "Female Judging." *University of Toledo Law Review* 36, no. 4: 821–847.

Bell, Derrick. 1992. *Faces at the Bottom of the Well: The Permanence of Racism.* New York: Basic Books.

Bell, Griffin B. 1982. *Taking Care of the Law.* New York: William Morrow.

Bell, Lauren Cohen. 2002. "Senatorial Discourtesy: The Senate's Use of Delay to Shape the Federal Judiciary." *Political Research Quarterly* 55, no. 3: 589–607.

Benlevy, Sandra. 2000. "Venus and Mars in the Jury Deliberation Room: Exploring the Differences that Exist among Male and Female Jurors during the Deliberation Process." *Southern California Review of Law and Women's Studies* 9, no. 2: 445–477.

Berlins, Marcel and Clare Dyer. 2000. *The Law Machine.* London: Penguin.

Berry, Frances Stokes and William D. Berry. 1990. "State Lottery Adoptions as Policy Innovations: An Event History Analysis." *American Political Science Review* 84, no. 2: 395–415.

Berry, Frances Stokes and William D. Berry. 1992. "Tax Innovation in the States: Capitalizing on Political Opportunity." *American Journal of Political Science* 36, no. 3: 715–742.

Bevacqua, Maria. 2000. *Rape on the Public Agenda: Feminism and the Politics of Sexual Assault.* Boston: Northeastern University Press.

Beveridge, Fiona and Sue Nott. 2002. "Mainstreaming: A Case for Optimism and Cynicism." *Feminist Legal Studies* 10, no. 3: 299–311.

"Biased Referee? European Court of Justice." 1997. *The Economist.* May 17. 59–60.

Bickel, Alexander M. 1962. *The Least Dangerous Branch: The Supreme Court at the Bar of Politics.* Indianapolis, IN: Bobbs-Merrill.

Bird, Rose Elizabeth. 1986. "State of the Judiciary, 1986." *Guild Practitioner* 43, no. 3: 91–93.

Biskupic, Joan. 2000. "Politics Snares Court Hopes of Minorities and Women." *USA Today.* August 22.

Blackburn, Bradley. 2010. "Justices Ruth Bader Ginsburg and Sandra Day O'Connor on Life and the Supreme Court." *ABC World News.* October 26. http://abcnews.go.com/WN/diane-sawyer-interviews-maria-shriver-sandra-day-oconnor/story?id=11977195. Accessed August 12, 2011.

Bogoch, Bryna. 1999. "Courtroom Discourse and the Gendered Construction of Professional Identity." *Law & Social Inquiry* 24, no. 2: 329–375.

Boigeol, Anne. 2003. "Male Strategies in the Face of the Feminisation of a Profession: The Case of the French Judiciary." In *Women in the World's Legal Profession,* eds. Ulrike Schultz and Gisela Shaw. Oxford: Hart.

Boneparth, Ellen. 1977. "Women in Campaigns: From Lickin' and Stickin' to Strategy." *American Politics Quarterly* 5, no. 3: 289–300.

Bonk, Kathy, Emily Tynes, Henry Griggs, and Phil Sparks. 2008. *Strategic Communications for Nonprofits: A Step-by-Step Guide to Working with the Media.* San Francisco: Jossey-Bass.

Bonneau, Chris W. and Melinda Gann Hall. 2009. *In Defense of Judicial Elections.* New York: Routledge.

Borgida, Eugene and Susan T. Fiske. 2008. *Beyond Common Sense: Psychological Science in the Courtroom.* Oxford: Wiley-Blackwell.

Borrelli, MaryAnne. 2000. "Gender, Politics, and Change in the United States Cabinet: The Madeleine Korbel Albright and Janet Reno Appointments." In *Gender and American Politics: Women, Men, and the Political Process,* eds. Sue Tolleson-Rinehart and Jyl J. Josephson. New York: M.E. Sharpe.

Boyd, Christina, Lee Epstein, and Andrew D. Martin. 2010. "Untangling the Causal Effects of Sex on Judging." *American Journal of Political Science* 54, no. 2: 389–411.

Bratton, Kathleen A. 2002. "The Effect of Legislative Diversity on Agenda-Setting: Evidence from Six State Legislatures." *American Politics Research* 30, no. 2: 115–142.

Bratton, Kathleen A. and Rorie L. Spill. 2002. "Existing Diversity and Judicial Selection: The Role of the Appointment Method in Establishing Gender Diversity in State Supreme Courts." *Social Science Quarterly* 83, no. 2: 504–518.

Brown, Gary S. 1998. "Characteristics of Elected versus Merit-Selected New York City Judges, 1992–1997." Report. New York: Fund for Modern Courts.

Brown, Patrick K. 2007. "The Rise and Fall of Rose Bird: A Career Killed by the Death Penalty." Master's essay. California State University.

Burbank, Stephen B. 2002. "Politics, Privilege, and Power: The Senate's Role in the Appointment of Federal Judges." *Judicature* 86, no. 1: 24–27.

Burnier, DeLysa. 1994. "Constructing Political Reality: Language, Symbols, and Meaning in Politics." *Political Research Quarterly* 47, no. 1: 239–253.

Burri, Susanne. 2008. "The European Network of Legal Experts in the Field of Gender Equality." *European Anti-Discrimination Law Review* 6/7: 11–12.

Burri, Susanne and Sacha Prechal. 2009. "Comparative Approaches to Gender Equality and Non-Discrimination within Europe." In *European Union Non-Discrimination Law: Comparative Perspectives on Multidimensional Equality Law*, eds. Dagmar Schiek and Victoria Chege. London: Routledge.

Burrows, Noreen. 2010. "The Lisbon Treaty and the Revised Appointments Process of the Advocate General." Paper presented at the University Association for Contemporary European Studies annual conference, Bruges, September.

Cameron, Hazel. 2006. "Establishment of the European Union Civil Service Tribunal." *The Law & Practice of International Courts and Tribunals* 5, no. 2: 273–283.

Campos, Paul. 2009. "Fat Judges Need Not Apply." *The Daily Beast*. May 4. http://www.thedailybeast.com/articles/2009/05/04/fat-judges-need-not-apply.html. Accessed August 4, 2011.

Canadian Bar Association, Task Force on Gender Equality in the Legal Profession. 1993. *Touchstones for Change: Equality, Diversity, Accountability.* http://www.cba.org/cba/equity/main/pubs.aspx. Accessed December 12, 2011.

Caperton v. Massey. 556 U.S. ___(2009).

Carabillo, Toni, Judith Meuli, and June Bundy Csida. 1993. *Feminist Chronicles, 1953–1993.* Los Angeles: Women's Graphics.

Carbon, Susan. 1980. "Judicial Retention Elections: Are They Serving Their Intended Purpose?" *Judicature* 64, no. 5: 210–233.

Carbon, Susan, Pauline Houlden, and Larry Berkson. 1982. "Women on the State Bench: Their Characteristics and Attitudes about Judicial Selection." *Judicature* 65, no. 6: 294–305.

Carpenter, Liz. 1979. "What's Wrong with This Picture? Isn't It Time to Have a Woman on the Supreme Court?" *Redbook*. October 27.

Carpentier, Megan. 2009. "Women Too Stupid to Stay Thin Are Not Smart Enough for Supreme Court." *Jezebel*. May 5. http://jezebel.com/5241128/women-too. Accessed August 4, 2011.

Carroll, Susan J. 2009. "Reflections on Gender and Hillary Clinton's Presidential Campaign: The Good, the Bad, and the Misogynic." *Politics & Gender* 5, no. 1: 1–20.

Carvel, John. 1992. "Europe's Shadowy Arbiters of Power." *Guardian* (London). June 28.

Center for Women in Government and Civil Society. 2011. "Women in Federal and State-Level Judgeships." Rockefeller College of Public Affairs and Policy, University at Albany, SUNY. http://www.albany.edu/news/images/judgeship_report_partII.pdf. Accessed July 11, 2011.

Centre for Research on European Women. 2002. *CREW Report No. 52.* March 4.

Chamallas, Martha. 2003. *Introduction to Feminist Legal Theory.* Second edition. New York: Aspen.

Chappell, Louise A. 2002. *Gendering Government: Feminist Engagement with the State in Australia and Canada.* Vancouver: University of British Columbia Press.

Chappell, Louise A. 2006. "'Women's Interests' as 'Women's Rights': Developments at the UN Criminal Tribunals and the International Criminal Court." In *The Politics of Women's Interests: New Comparative Perspectives*, ed. Louise Chappell and Lisa Hill. London: Routledge.

Chappell, Louise A. 2008. "Women's Rights and Religious Opposition: The Politics of Gender at the International Criminal Court." In *Gendering the Nation State: Canadian and Comparative Perspectives*, ed. Yasmeen Abu-Laban. Vancouver: University of British Columbia Press.

Chappell, Louise A. 2010. "Gender and Judging at the International Criminal Court." *Politics & Gender* 6, no. 3: 484–495.

Chiang, Harriet and Joan Ryan. 1999. "Bird's Passion for Principles Recalled." *San Francisco Chronicle.* December 6. http://articles.sfgate.com/1999-12-06/news/17709325_1_california-justices-justices-joseph-grodin-chief-justice/4. Accessed December 7, 2011.

Chibbaro, Lou. 2005. "TaskForce to Expand Its Federal Profile." March 4. http://www.expressgaynews.com. Accessed June 15, 2007.

Childs, Sarah and Mona Lena Krook. 2008. "Critical Mass Theory and Women's Political Representation." *Political Studies* 56, no. 3: 725–736.

Cichowski, Rachel A. 2007. *The European Court and Civil Society: Litigation, Mobilization and Governance.* Cambridge: Cambridge University Press.

Clark, Mary L. 2002. "Changing the Face of the Law: How Women's Advocacy Groups Put Women on the Federal Judicial Appointments Agenda." *Yale Journal of Law and Feminism* 14, no. 2: 243–254.

Clark, Mary L. 2003. "Carter's Groundbreaking Appointment of Women to the Federal Bench: His Other 'Human Rights' Record." *American University Journal of Gender, Social Policy, and the Law* 11, no. 3: 1131–1163.

Clark, Mary L. 2004. "One Man's Token Is Another Woman's Breakthrough? The Appointment of the First Women Federal Judges." *Villanova Law Review* 49, no. 3: 487–549.

Clark-Flory, Tracy. 2010. "Elena Kagan, Cross Your Legs!" *Salon.* May 24. http://www.salon.com/2010/05/24/kagan_clothing_givhan/. Accessed November 15, 2011.

Cobb, Roger W. and Charles D. Elder. 1972. *Participation in American Politics: The Dynamics of Agenda-Building.* Boston: Allyn and Bacon.

Cockburn, Cynthia. 1991. *In the Way of Women: Men's Resistance to Sex Equality in Organizations.* Ithaca, NY: ILR Press.

Cohen, Antonin. 2007. "Constitutionalism without Constitution: Transnational Elites between Political Mobilization and Legal Expertise in the Making of a Constitution for Europe, 1940s–1960s." *Law & Social Inquiry* 32, no. 1: 109–135.

Cohen, Antonin. 2008. "Scarlet Robes, Dark Suits: The Social Recruitment of the European Court of Justice," Robert Schuman Centre for Advanced Studies, European University Institute, Florence. EUI working paper, RSCAS 2008/35. http://cadmus.eui.eu/bitstream/handle/1814/10029/EUI_RSCAS_2008_35.pdf. Accessed December 12, 2011.

Coker and Osamor v Lord Chancellor and Lord Chancellor's Department [1999] IRLR 396, [2001] IRLR 116, [2002] IRLR 80.

Colneric, Ninon. 1996. "Making Equality Law More Effective: Lessons from the German Experience." *Cardozo Women's Law Journal* 3, no. 2: 229–250.

"Commissioner for Judicial Appointments." 2004. *The Lawyer*. March 19.

Committee on Legal Affairs and Human Rights, Parliamentary Assembly, Council of Europe. 2003. *Office of the Lord Chancellor in the Constitutional System of the United Kingdom.* Doc. 9798. April 28.

Connolly, Carol. 1994. "How Rosalie Wahl Got to Be Queen." *Law & Politics* 2: 20–21.

Constable, Marianne. 1994. *The Law of the Other: The Mixed Jury and Changing Conceptions of Citizenship, Law, and Knowledge.* Chicago: University of Chicago Press.

Cook, Beverly Blair. 1978a. "The Burger Court and Women's Rights, 1971–1977." In *Women in the Courts*, eds. Winifred L. Hepperle and Laura Crites. Williamsburg, VA: National Center for State Courts.

Cook, Beverly Blair. 1978b. "Women Judges: The End of Tokenism." In *Women in the Courts*, eds. Winifred L. Hepperle and Laura Crites. Williamsburg, VA: National Center for State Courts.

Cook, Beverly Blair. 1980a. "Florence Allen." In *Notable American Women: The Modern Period—A Biographical Dictionary*, eds. Barbara Sicherman and Carol Hurd Green. Cambridge, MA: Harvard University Press.

Cook, Beverly Blair. 1980b. "Political Culture and Selection of Women Judges in Trial Courts." In *Women in Local Politics*, ed. Debra W. Stewart. Metuchen, NJ: Scarecrow Press.

Cook, Beverly Blair. 1981. "Will Women Judges Make a Difference in Women's Legal Rights? A Prediction from Attitudes and Simulated Behavior." In *Women, Power, and Political Systems*, ed. Margherita Rendel. New York: St. Martin's Press.

Cook, Beverly Blair. 1982. "Women as Supreme Court Candidates: From Florence Allen to Sandra O'Connor." *Judicature* 65, no. 6: 314–326.

Cook, Beverly Blair. 1983. "The Path to the Bench: Ambitions and Attitudes of Women in the Law." *Trial* 19, no. 8: 49–55.

Cook, Beverly Blair. 1984a. "Women Judges: A Preface to Their History." *Golden Gate University Law Review* 14, no. 3: 573–610.

Cook, Beverly Blair. 1984b. "Women on the State Bench: Correlates of Access." In *Political Women: Current Roles in State and Local Government*, ed. Janet A. Flammang. Beverly Hills, CA: Sage.

Cook, Beverly Blair. 1987. "Women Judges in the Opportunity Structure." In *Women, the Courts, and Equality*, ed. Laura L. Crites and Winifred L. Hepperle. Newbury Park, CA: Sage.

Cook, Beverly Blair. 1988. "Women as Judges." In *Women in the Judicial Process*, eds. Beverly Blair Cook, Leslie F. Goldstein, Karen O'Connor, and Susette M. Talarico. Washington, D.C.: American Political Science Association.

Cook, Beverly Blair. 1991. "Justice Sandra Day O'Connor: Transition to a Republican Court Agenda." In *The Burger Court: Political and Judicial Profiles*, eds. Charles M. Lamb and Stephen C. Halpern. Urbana: University of Illinois Press.

Cook, Beverly Blair. 2001. "Rose Bird." *American Biography Online*. http://www.amb.org.floyd.lib.umn.edu/articles/11/11-01013-print.html. Accessed July 1, 2009.

Coontz, Phyllis D. 1995. "Gender Bias in the Legal Profession: Women 'See' It, Men Don't." *Women & Politics* 15, no. 2: 1–22.

Coontz, Stephanie. 2011. *A Strange Stirring: The Feminine Mystique and American Women at the Dawn of the 1960s*. New York: Basic Books.

Cooper, Cynthia L. 2008. "Women Supreme Court Clerks Striving for 'Commonplace.'" *Perspectives: The Quarterly Magazine of the American Bar Association Commission on Women in the Profession* 17, no. 1: 18–19, 22.

Copelon, Rhonda, Elizabeth M. Schneider, and Nancy Stearns. 1975. "Constitutional Perspectives on Sex Discrimination in Jury Selection." *Women's Rights Law Reporter* 2, no. 4: 3–12.

Costain, Anne N. 1992. *Inviting Women's Rebellion: A Political Process Interpretation of the Women's Movement*. Baltimore: Johns Hopkins University Press.

Council of the European Union. 2010. "Recommendation concerning the composition of the panel provided for in Article 255 TFEU." 5932/10. February 2. V. Skouris, President of the Court of Justice of the European Union, to Miguel Angel Moratinos, President of the Council of the European Union.

Court Chambers, Brick. 1994. "Business and the Law: New Faces on the Bench—European Court." *Financial Times* (London). October 11.

Court of Justice of the European Communities. 1982. *Formal Sittings of the Court of Justice of the European Communities, 1980 and 1981*.

"Court of Justice: Report on Future of European Legal System." 1999. *Europolitics*. December 8.

Cowan, Ruth B. 2006. "Women's Representation on the Courts in the Republic of South Africa." *University of Maryland Law Journal of Race, Religion, Gender, and Class* 6, no. 2: 291–317.

Crowe, Nancy E. 1999. "Diversity on the US Courts of Appeals: How the

Sexual and Racial Composition of Panels Affects Decision Making." Paper prepared for the American Political Science Association annual meeting, Atlanta, September 2-5.

Culver, John H. and John T. Wold. 1986. "Rose Bird and the Politics of Judicial Accountability in California." *Judicature* 70, no. 2: 81–89.

Culver, John H. and John T. Wold. 1987. "The Defeat of the California Justices: The Campaign, the Electorate, and the Issue of Judicial Accountability." *Judicature* 70, no. 6: 348–355.

Curriden, Mark. 2010. "Tipping the Scales: In the South, Women Have Made Huge Strides in the State Judiciaries." *ABA Journal*. July 1. http://www.abajournal.com/magazine/article/tipping_the_scales/. Accessed July 15, 2011.

Currie, Cameron McGowan and Aleta M. Pillick. 1996. "Sex Discrimination in the Selection and Participation of Female Jurors: A Post-*J.E.B.* Analysis." *Judges' Journal* 35, no. 1: 2–6, 38–42.

Dahlerup, Drude, ed. 2006. *Women, Quotas, and Politics.* New York: Routledge.

Davidson, Elizabeth. 1997. ". . . And Will Duck Question Session at Law Soc Conference." *The Lawyer*. October 14.

Davis, Sue. 1992–1993. "Do Women Judges Speak 'In a Different Voice?' Carol Gilligan, Feminist Legal Theory, and the Ninth Circuit." *Wisconsin Women's Law Journal* 8, no. 1: 143–173.

Davis, Sue. 1993. "The Voice of Sandra Day O'Connor." *Judicature* 77, no. 3: 134–139.

de Búrca, Gráinne. 2001. "Introduction." In *The European Court of Justice*, eds. Gráinne de Búrca and Joseph H.H. Weiler. Oxford: Oxford University Press.

Dean, John W. 2001. *The Rehnquist Choice: The Untold Story of the Nixon Appointment that Redefined the Supreme Court.* New York: Free Press.

Dehousse, Renaud. 1998. *The European Court of Justice: The Politics of Judicial Integration.* London: Macmillan.

Dembour, Marie-Bénédicte. 2006. *Who Believes in Human Rights? Reflections on the European Convention.* Cambridge: Cambridge University Press.

Diascro, Jennifer Segal and Rorie Spill Solberg. 2009. "George W. Bush's Legacy on the Federal Bench: Policy in the Face of Diversity." *Judicature* 92, no. 6: 289–301.

Dixon, Rosalind. 2010. "Female Justices, Feminism, and the Politics of Judicial Appointment: A Re-Examination." *Yale Journal of Law and Feminism* 21, no. 2: 297–338.

Dolan, Maura. 2011. "Gay Judge Wasn't Required to Remove Himself from Same-Sex Marriage Case, US Judge Rules." *Los Angeles Times.* June 15. http://articles.latimes.com/2011/jun/15/local/la-me-0615-gay-judge-20110616. Accessed August 5, 2011.

Doughty, Steve. 1997. "Harman Humiliated over 'Unfair' Judges." *Daily Mail* (London). October 23.

Douglas-Scott, Sionaidh. 2002. *Constitutional Law of the European Union.* Harlow, UK: Pearson.

Dubois, Philip. 1983. "The Influence of Selection System and Region on the Characteristics of a Trial Court Bench: The Case of California." *Justice System Journal* 8, no. 1: 59–87.

Duerst-Lahti, Georgia. 1989. "The Government's Role in Building the Women's Movement." *Political Science Quarterly* 104, no. 2: 249–268.

Dunn, Patrick Winston. 1981. "Judicial Election and the Missouri Plan." In *Courts, Law, and Judicial Processes*, ed. S. Sidney Ulmer. New York: Free Press.

Dyer, Clare. 1995. "News in Brief." *Guardian* (London). January 27.

Dyer, Clare. 2002. "Crown Prosecutors Could Win Right to Become Judges: Move to Widen Mix on White, Male, Public School Educated Bench." *Guardian* (London). June 5.

Edelman, Murray. 1967. *The Symbolic Uses of Politics.* Urbana: University of Illinois Press.

Edelman, Murray. 1971. *Politics as Symbolic Action: Mass Arousal and Quiescence.* Madison, WI: Institute for Research on Poverty.

Edelman, Murray. 1988. *Constructing the Political Spectacle.* Chicago: University of Chicago Press.

Egan, Michael. 2006. "Remarks on Judicial Selection." Paper presented at the Lloyd N. Cutler Conference on White House Counsel, Miller Center, University of Virginia, November 10.

Eisenstein, Hester. 1984. *Contemporary Feminist Thought.* London: Unwin.

Elazar, Daniel J. 1984. *American Federalism: A View from the States.* Third edition. New York: Harper and Row.

Elazar, Daniel, Virginia Gray, and Wy Spano. 1999. *Minnesota Politics and Government.* Lincoln: University of Nebraska Press.

Elder, Charles D. and Roger W. Cobb. 1983. *The Political Uses of Symbols.* New York: Longman.

Ellis, Evelyn. 2000. "The Recent Jurisprudence of the Court of Justice in the Field of Sex Equality." *Common Market Law Review* 37, no. 6: 1403–1426.

English, Deirdre. 1986. "The Ordeal of Rose Bird." *Ms. Magazine.* November.

Epstein, Cynthia Fuchs. 1981. *Women in Law.* New York: Basic Books.

Epstein, Cynthia Fuchs. 1993. *Women in Law.* Second edition. Urbana: University of Illinois Press.

Equal Justices Initiative. 2011. "Equal Justices Initiative." Queen Mary, University of London, School of Law. July 4. http://www.law.qmul.ac.uk/eji/index.html. Accessed November 10, 2011.

Equal Justices Initiative. 2011. "Evidence to House of Lords Select Committee on the Constitution Inquiry into the Judicial Appointments Process." June. http://www.law.qmul.ac.uk/eji/docs/EJI%20submisson%20INQUIRY%20INTO%20THE%20JUDICIAL%20APPOINTMENTS%20PROCESS.pdf. Accessed July 5, 2011.

Equal Opportunities Commission. 1996. "Memorandum." *House of Commons Home Affairs Committee Third Report, Judicial Appointments Procedures,* Volume III: *Minutes of Evidence and Appendices.* June 5.

Equal Opportunities Commission. 2000. "Lord Chancellor's Sex Discrimination Appeal: EOC to Support Coker and Osamor." Press release. November 6. London: Equal Opportunities Commission.

Esterling, Kevin Michael and Seth S. Andersen. 2000. "Diversity and the Judicial Merit Selection Process: A Statistical Report." In *Research on Judicial Selection 1999,* ed. Hunter Center for Judicial Selection. Chicago: American Judicature Society. http://www.judicialselection.us/uploads/documents/Diversity_and_the_Judicial_Merit_Se_9C4863118945B.pdf. Accessed November 23, 2011.

Etzioni, Amitai. 1988. *The Moral Dimension: Toward a New Economics.* New York: Free Press.

EU Law Blog. 2010. "Judicial Appointments in the General Court and Court of Justice." July 8. http://eulaw.typepad.com/eulawblog/2010/07/judicial-appointments-in-the-general-court-and-court-of-justice.html. Accessed December 12, 2011.

"European Court of Justice: Four New Bulgarian and Romanian Judges in Luxembourg." 2007. *Europe-East.* January 25.

European Women Lawyers Association. 2009. "EWLA Statement on the Obligation to Name Women for Top Positions in the European Union." November 9. www.curioweb.is/webs/ewla.org/modules/files/file_group_76/2009_Statement_on_the_Obligation_to_Name_Women_for_Top_Positions_in_the_EU.pdf. Accessed November 11, 2011.

Evans, Sara. 2003. *Tidal Wave: How Women Changed America at Century's End.* New York: The Free Press.

Eyestone, Robert. 1977. "Confusion, Diffusion, and Innovation." *American Political Science Review* 71, no. 2: 441–447.

Faludi, Susan. 1991. *Backlash: The Undeclared War against American Women.* New York: Crown.

Farrell, Amy Erdman. 1998. *Yours in Sisterhood:* Ms. *Magazine and the Promise of Popular Feminism.* Chapel Hill: University of North Carolina Press.

Farrell, Michael. 2002. "Obituary: Chief Justice Rose Bird." *ACLU News.* January/February.

Feenan, Dermot. 2005. *Applications by Women for Silk and Judicial Office in Northern Ireland.* Newtownabbey, UK: University of Ulster.

Feld, Werner. 1963. "The Judges of the Court of Justice of the European Communities." *Villanova Law Review* 9, no. 1: 37–58.

Ferree, Myra Marx. 2004. "Soft Repression: Ridicule, Stigma, and Silencing in Gender-Based Movements." In *Authority in Contention: Research in Social Movements, Conflicts and Change,* eds. Daniel J. Myers and Daniel M. Cress. Volume 25. Amsterdam: Elsevier.

Ferree, Myra Marx. 2009. "An American Road Map? Framing Feminist Goals in a Liberal Landscape." In *Gender Equality: Transforming Family Divisions of Labor*, ed. Janet Gornick and Marcia Meyers. London: Verso.

Ferree, Myra Marx and Patricia Yancy Martin, eds. 1995. *Feminist Organizations: Harvest of the New Women's Movement*. Philadelphia, PA: Temple University Press.

Ferree, Myra Marx, William Anthony Gamson, Jürgen Gerhards, and Dieter Rucht. 2002. *Shaping Abortion Discourse: Democracy and the Public Sphere in Germany and the United States*. Cambridge: Cambridge University Press.

Finnemore, Martha and Kathryn Sikkink. 1998. "International Norm Dynamics and Political Change." *International Organization* 52, no. 4: 887–917.

"First Women Judges for Court of Justice." 1995. *Herald Sun* (Melbourne). January 11.

Flanders, Laura. 2004. *Bushwomen: Tales of a Cynical Species*. New York: Verso.

Fourth Action Programme for Equal Opportunities for Women and Men, 1996–2000. 1996. Brussels: European Commission.

Fowler, Lucy. 2005. "Gender and Jury Deliberations: The Contributions of Social Science." *William & Mary Journal of Women and the Law* 12, no. 1: 1–48.

Franzway, Suzanne, Diane Court, and R.W. Connell. 1989. *Staking a Claim: Feminism, Bureaucracy and the State*. Sydney: Allen and Unwin.

Fraser, Arvonne. 1983. "Insiders and Outsiders: Women in the Political Arena." In *Women in Washington: Advocates for Public Policy*, ed. Irene Tinker. Beverly Hills, CA: Sage.

Fraser, Arvonne. 2007. *She's No Lady: Politics, Family, and International Feminism*. Minneapolis: Nodin Press.

Fredman, Sandra. 1998. "After *Kalanke* and *Marschall*: Affirming Affirmative Action." In *The Cambridge Yearbook of European Legal Studies*, eds. Alan Dashwood and Angela Ward. Cambridge: Hart.

Freeman, Jo. 2000. *A Room at a Time: How Women Entered Party Politics*. New York: Rowman and Littlefield.

Frey, Barbara. 2004. "A Fair Representation: Advocating for Women's Rights in the International Criminal Court." Case Study for Center on Women and Public Policy, University of Minnesota. http://www.hhh.umn.edu/centers/wpp/pdf/case_studies/fair_representation/fair_representation.pdf. Accessed November 12, 2011.

Fritz-Vannahme, Joachim. 2006. "In the End Is the Word: The European Court of Justice Guards the Ideals of Europe if the EU Commission Fails." *Zeit Online*. May 4.

Frug, Mary Joe. 1992. "Progressive Feminist Legal Scholarship: Can We Claim 'A Different Voice'?" *Harvard Women's Law Journal* 15: 37–64.

Gagné, Patricia. 1998. *Battered Women's Justice: The Movement for Clemency and the Politics of Self-Defense*. New York: Twayne.

Galanter, Marc. 1983. "The Radiating Effects of Courts." In *Empirical Theories about Courts*, eds. Keith O. Boyum and Lynn Mather. New York: Longman.

Gamson, Joshua. 1995. "Must Identity Movements Self-Destruct? A Queer Dilemma." *Social Problems* 42, no. 3: 390–407.

Garth, Bryant G. and Austin Sarat, eds. 1998. *How Does Law Matter?* Evanston, IL: Northwestern University Press.

Genn, Hazel. 1999. *Paths to Justice: What People Do and Think about Going to Law.* Oxford: Hart.

Gertner, Nancy. 2009. Interview by Linda Greenhouse at "Gender and the Law: Unintended Consequences, Unsettled Questions," Radcliffe Institute for Advanced Study, Harvard University, March 12–13. http://www.radcliffe.edu/events/calendar_2009law.aspx. Accessed September 23, 2011.

Gibb, Frances. 2002. "Women Have Every Chance to Be Judges." *The Times* (London). May 27.

Gibb, Frances. 2004. "QC Reprieve: Shrewd Move or Missed Opportunity?" *The Times* (London). June 1.

Gibb, Frances. 2005. "Revealed: The Radical New QC Selection System." *The Times* (London). July 19.

Gibb, Frances. 2008. "Lady Justice Arden: Not Enough Women Judges." *The Times* (London). June 4.

Gibbs, Sir Harry. 2000. "Oration Delivered at the Opening of the Supreme Court Library's Rare Books Room." Speech at the Supreme Court of Queensland, Brisbane, February 11. http://archive.sclqld.org.au/lectures/rare_books/speech.pdf. Accessed August 17, 2011.

Gibson, James L. and Gregory A. Caldeira. 2009. *Citizens, Courts, and Confirmations: Positivity Theory and the Judgments of the American People.* Princeton, NJ: Princeton University Press.

Giddings, Paula. 2008. *Ida: A Sword among Lions.* New York: HarperCollins.

Giffen, Lee. 1976. "Her Honor, the Judge." *Atlanta Journal and Constitution Magazine.* December 12.

Gilligan, Carol. 1982. *In a Different Voice: Psychological Theory and Women's Development.* Cambridge, MA: Harvard University Press.

Gillman, Howard. 2001. *The Votes that Counted: How the Court Decided the 2000 Presidential Election.* Chicago: University of Chicago Press.

Ginsburg, Ruth Bader. 1978. "Women at the Bar: A Generation of Change." *University of Puget Sound Law Review* 2, no. 1: 1–14.

Ginsburg, Ruth Bader. 1986. "Some Thoughts on the 1980s Debate over Special versus Equal Treatment for Women." *Law and Inequality* 4, no. 1: 143–151.

Ginsburg, Ruth Bader. 1994. "The Progression of Women in the Law." *Valparaiso University Law Review* 28, no. 4: 1161–1182.

Ginsburg, Ruth Bader. 2003. "The Supreme Court: A Place for Women." *Southwestern University Law Review* 32, no. 2: 189–199.

Ginsburg, Ruth Bader. 2009. Interview by Linda Greenhouse at "Gender and the Law: Unintended Consequences, Unsettled Questions," Radcliffe Institute for Advanced Study, Harvard University, March 12–13.

http://www.radcliffe.edu/events/calendar_2009law.aspx. Accessed August 19, 2009.

Githens, Marianne. 1995. "Getting Appointed to the State Court: The Gender Dimension." *Women & Politics* 15, no. 4: 1–24.

Goldberg, Deborah. 2007. "Testimony of Deborah Goldberg." Public Forum: A Lasting Blueprint for Judicial Diversity, Brennan Center for Justice, March 1. http://www.brennancenter.org/content/resource/a_lasting_blueprint_for_judicial_diversity_testimony_of_deborah_goldberg/. Accessed August 12, 2011.

Goldberg, Stephanie B. 2008. "Women Fight to Retain State Supreme Court Seats." American Bar Association, Commission on Women in the Profession, *Perspectives* Winter: 4–7.

Goldin, Claudia and Cecilia Rouse. 2000. "Orchestrating Impartiality: The Impact of 'Blind' Auditions on Female Musicians." *American Economic Review* 90, no. 4: 715–741.

Goldman, Sheldon. 1997. *Picking Federal Judges: Lower Court Selection from Roosevelt through Reagan.* New Haven, CT: Yale University Press.

Goldman, Sheldon. 2002. "Book Review of *Pursuit of Justices: Presidential Politics and the Selection of Supreme Court Nominees* by David Alistair Yalof." *American Political Science Review* 96, no. 1: 222–223.

Goldman, Sheldon and Elliot Slotnick. 1999. "Clinton's Second Term Judiciary: Picking Judges under Fire." *Judicature* 82, no. 6: 264–284.

Goldman, Sheldon, Elliot Slotnick, Gerard Gryski, and Gary Zuk. 2001. "Clinton's Judges: Summing up the Legacy." *Judicature* 84, no. 5: 228–254.

Goodwin, Jeff, James M. Jasper, and Francesca Polletta. 2000. "The Return of the Repressed: The Fall and Rise of Emotions in Social Movement Theory." *Mobilization* 5, no. 1: 65–83.

Goodwin, Jeff, James M. Jasper, and Francesca Polletta, eds. 2001. *Passionate Politics: Emotions and Social Movements.* Chicago: University of Chicago Press.

Gordon, Linda. 1994. *Pitied but Not Entitled: Single Mothers and the History of Welfare, 1890–1935.* New York: The Free Press.

Gornick, Janet C. and David S. Meyer. 1998. "Changing Political Opportunity: The Anti-Rape Movement and Public Policy." *Journal of Policy History* 10, no. 4: 367–398.

Gottschall, Jon. 1983. "Carter's Judicial Appointments: The Influence of Affirmative Action and Merit Selection on Voting on the U.S. Courts of Appeals." *Judicature* 67, no. 4: 165–173.

Gould, Deborah B. 2002. "Life during Wartime: Emotions and the Development of ACT UP." *Mobilization* 7, no. 2: 177–200.

Gould, Jon B. 2005. *Speak No Evil: The Triumph of Hate Speech Regulation.* Chicago: Chicago University Press.

Graff, E.J. 2007. "The Opt-Out Myth." *Columbia Journalism Review* 45, no.

6: 51–54. http://www.brandeis.edu/investigate/gender/optoutmyth.html. Accessed January 2, 2012.

Graham, Erin, Charles R. Shipan, and Craig Volden. 2008. "The Diffusion of Policy Diffusion Research." Paper presented at the American Political Science Association annual meeting, Boston, August 28-31.

Gray, Virginia. 1973. "Innovation in the States: A Diffusion Study." *American Political Science Review* 67, no. 4: 1174–1185.

Gray, Virginia. 1994. "Competition, Emulation, and Policy Innovation." In *New Perspectives on American Politics*, eds. Lawrence C. Dodd and Calvin Jillson. Washington, D.C.: CQ Press.

Graycar, Regina. 1995. "The Gender of Judgments: An Introduction." In *Public and Private: Feminist Legal Debates*, ed. Margaret Thornton. Oxford: Oxford University Press.

Greaves, Rosa. 2011. "Reforming Some Aspects of the Role of Advocates General." In *A Constitutional Order of States: Essays in EU Law in Honour of Alan Dashwood*, eds. Anthony Arnull, Catherine Barnard, Michael Dougan, and Eleanor Spaventa. Oxford: Hart.

Greenburg, Jan Crawford. 2007. *Supreme Conflict: The Inside Story of the Struggle for Control of the United States Supreme Court.* New York: Penguin.

Greenhouse, Carol J. 2010. "Judgment and the Justice: An Ethnographic Reading of the Sotomayor Confirmation Hearings." *Law, Culture and the Humanities.* November 25. http://lch.sagepub.com/content/early/2010/11/12/1743872110374916. Accessed November 23, 2011.

Greenhouse, Linda. 2005. *Becoming Justice Blackmun: Harry Blackmun's Supreme Court Journey.* New York: Times Books.

Greenhouse, Linda and Reva B. Siegel. 2011. "Before (and after) *Roe v. Wade*: New Questions about Backlash." *Yale Law Journal* 120, no. 8: 2028–2087.

Griffith, J.A.G. 1977. *The Politics of the Judiciary.* Manchester: Manchester University Press.

Grisham, John. 2008. *The Appeal.* New York: Doubleday.

Grossman, Joanna L. 1994. "Women's Jury Service: Right of Citizenship or Privilege of Difference?" *Stanford Law Review* 46, no. 5: 1115–1160.

Gruhl, John, Cassia Spohn, and Susan Welch. 1981. "Women as Policymakers: The Case of Trial Judges." *American Journal of Political Science* 25, no. 2: 308–322.

Guinier, Lani. 2003. "Of Gentlemen and Role Models." In *Critical Race Feminism*, ed. Adrien Wing. New York: New York University Press.

Gusfield, Joseph R. 1986. *Symbolic Crusade: Status Politics and the American Temperance Movement.* Second edition. Urbana: University of Illinois Press.

Hafner-Burton, Emilie M. and Mark A. Pollack. 2009. "Mainstreaming Gender in the European Union: Getting the Incentives Right." *Comparative European Politics* 7, no. 1: 114–138.

Haider-Markel, Donald P. 2007. "Representation and Backlash: The Positive and Negative Influence of Descriptive Representation." *Legislative Studies Quarterly* 32, no. 1: 107–133.

Haire, Susan B. 2001. "Rating the Ratings of the American Bar Association Standing Committee on Federal Judiciary." *Justice System Journal* 22, no. 1: 1–17.

Hale, Brenda. 2001. "Equality and the Judiciary: Why Should We Want More Women Judges?" *Public Law* Autumn: 489–504.

Hale, Brenda. 2002. "Judging Women/Women Judging." *Counsel* August: 10–12.

Hale, Brenda. 2010. "Foreword." In *Feminist Judgments: From Theory to Practice*, eds. Rosemary Hunter, Clare McGlynn, and Erika Rackley. Oxford: Hart.

Hamilton, Barbara. 2001. "The Law Council of Australia Policy 2001 on the Process of Judicial Appointments: Any Good News for Future *Female* Judicial Appointees?" *Queensland University of Technology Law and Justice Journal* 1, no. 2: 223–240.

Hammond, Grant. 2009. *Judicial Recusal: Principles, Process and Problems*. Oxford: Hart.

Haney, Lynne. 1996. "Homeboys, Babies, Men in Suits: The State and the Reproduction of Male Dominance." *American Sociological Review* 61, no. 5: 759–778.

Hardin, Peter. 2011. "*NY Times* Recusal Editorial Cites JAS and Partner." *GavelGrab*. June 16. http://www.gavelgrab.org/?p=21712. Accessed July 5, 2011.

Harrington, Mona. 1994. *Women Lawyers: Rewriting the Rules*. New York: Alfred A. Knopf.

Harris, Paul and Gaby Hinsliff. 2002. "Cherie Booth Attacks Sexist Judges." *Observer* (London). May 26. http://www.guardian.co.uk/politics/2002/may/26/uk.cherieblair. Accessed December 4, 2011.

Harris-Perry, Melissa. 2011. *Sister Citizen: Shame, Stereotypes, and Black Women in America*. New Haven, CT: Yale University Press.

Hartley, Roger E. 2001. "A Look at Race, Gender, and Experience." *Judicature* 84, no. 4: 191–197.

Hartmann, Susan. 1989. *From Margin to Mainstream: American Women and Politics since 1960*. New York: Alfred A. Knopf.

Hartmann, Susan. 1998a. *The Other Feminists: Activists in the Liberal Establishment*. New Haven, CT: Yale University Press.

Hartmann, Susan. 1998b. "Feminism, Public Policy, and the Carter Administration." In *The Carter Presidency: Policy Choices in the Post-New Deal Era*, eds. Gary M. Fink and Hugh Davis Graham. Lawrence: University of Kansas Press.

Hartmann, Susan. Forthcoming. "Liberal Feminism and the Reshaping of the New Deal Order." In *Making Sense of American Liberalism: Taking the Pulse of the Left in Contemporary Politics*, eds. Jonathan Bell and Timothy Stanley. Urbana: University of Illinois Press.

Hatfield, Larry D. and Anastasia Hendrix. 1999. "Rose Bird Recalled as Brilliant Legal Trailblazer." *San Francisco Examiner*. December 6.

Hawkesworth, Mary. 1999. "Analyzing Backlash: Feminist Standpoint Theory as Analytical Tool." *Women's Studies International Forum* 22, no. 2: 135–155.

Hayes, Josephine and Daphne Loebl. 1996. "Childbirth and the Law." *The Times* (London). October 4.

Hays, Scott P. 1996. "Influences on Reinvention during the Diffusion of Innovations." *Political Research Quarterly* 49, no. 3: 631–650.

Healy v. Edwards, 363 F. Supp. 1110 (1973).

Hellman, Judith Adler. 1987. *Journeys among Women: Feminism in Five Italian Cities*. New York: Oxford University Press.

Helm, Sarah. 1996. "Judge Accused of Cover-up in Cools Murder Case." *Independent* (London). September 13.

Henry, M.L., Estajo Koslow, Joseph Soffer, and John Furey. 1985. *The Success of Women and Minorities in Achieving Judicial Office: The Selection Process*. New York: The Fund for Modern Courts.

Henschen, Beth, Robert Moog, and Steven Davis. 1990. "Judicial Nominating Commissioners: A National Profile." *Judicature* 73, no. 6: 328–334, 343.

Hepperle, Winifred L. 1984. "Review of *Framed: The New Right Attack on Chief Justice Rose Bird and the Courts*. By Betty Medsger." *Golden Gate University Law Review* 14, no. 3: 505–517.

"Her Turn." 1999. *Financial Times* (London). September 28.

Hertzberg, Hendrik. 2005. "Filibluster." *New Yorker*. June 13.

Hoekstra, Valerie. 2010. "Increasing the Gender Diversity of High Courts: A Comparative View." *Politics & Gender* 6, no. 3: 474–484.

Holmes, Lisa M. and Jolly A. Emrey. 2006. "Court Diversification: Staffing the State Courts of Last Resort through Interim Appointments." *Justice System Journal* 27, no. 1: 1–13.

Horne, William. 1995. "Judging Tadic." *American Lawyer*. September. http://unconqueredbosnia.tripod.com/McDonald1.html. Accessed August 5, 2011.

Hoskyns, Catherine. 1996. *Integrating Gender: Women, Law and Politics in the European Union*. London: Verso.

House of Commons Information Office. 2010. "Women in the House of Commons." June. http://www.parliament.uk/documents/commons-information-office/m04.pdf. Accessed June 30, 2011.

House of Lords Select Committee on the Constitution. 2011a. "Inquiry on Annual Meeting with the Lord Chancellor." Unrevised transcript of Evidence Session No. 1 (Questions 1–37). January 19. http://www.parliament.uk/documents/lords-committees/constitution/LordChancellor/ucCNST190111 LC.pdf. Accessed July 5, 2011.

House of Lords Select Committee on the Constitution. 2011b. "The Judicial Appointments Process: Call for Evidence." May 13. http://www.parliament. uk/documents/lords-committees/constitution/JAP/FinalCFE130511.pdf. Accessed July 5, 2011.

Hoyt v. Florida, 368 U.S. 57 (1961).

Hoyt v. State, 119 So. 2nd 691 (1959).

Huddy, Leonie and Tony E. Carey, Jr. 2009. "Group Politics Redux: Race and Gender in the 2008 Democratic Presidential Primaries." *Politics & Gender* 5, no. 1: 81–96.

Hulls, Rob. 2004. "Welcome to Chief Justice Warren." *Australian Law Journal* 78, no. 2: 79.

Hunter, Rosemary. 2006. "The High Price of Success: The Backlash against Women Judges in Australia." In *Calling for Change: Women, Law, and the Legal Profession*, eds. Elizabeth Sheehy and Sheila McIntyre. Ottawa: University of Ottawa Press.

Hurwitz, Mark S. and Drew Noble Lanier. 2001. "Women and Minorities on State and Federal Appellate Benches, 1985 and 1999." *Judicature* 85, no. 2: 84–92.

Hurwitz, Mark S. and Drew Noble Lanier. 2003. "Explaining Judicial Diversity: The Differential Ability of Women and Minorities to Attain Seats on State Supreme and Appellate Courts." *State Politics and Policy Quarterly* 3, no. 4: 329–352.

Hurwitz, Mark S. and Drew Noble Lanier. 2008. "Diversity in State and Federal Appellate Courts: Change and Continuity across 20 Years." *Justice System Journal* 29, no. 1: 47–70.

Ifill, Sherrilyn. 2000. "Racial Diversity on the Bench: Beyond Role Models and Public Confidence." *Washington and Lee Law Review* 57, no. 2: 405–495.

Ingadottir, Thordis. 2002. "The International Criminal Court Nomination and Election of Judges." ICC Discussion Paper No. 4. Project on International Courts and Tribunals. June. http://www.pict-pcti.org/publications/ICC_paprs/election.pdf. Accessed November 11, 2011.

Ingram, David. 2011. "Grassley Critiques Qualifications of Four Judicial Nominees." *Blog of Legal Times*. June 8. http://legaltimes.typepad.com/blt/2011/06/grassley-questions-qualifications-of-four-judicial-nominees-.html. Accessed September 23, 2011.

INTERIGHTS (International Centre for the Legal Protection of Human Rights). 2003. *Judicial Independence: Law and Practice of Appointments to the European Court of Human Rights*. London: Lancaster House.

Irvine, Lord Derry. 2001. "Judicial Appointments Annual Report 2000–2001." October. http://www.dca.gov.uk/judicial/ja_arep2001/00fore.htm. Accessed February 27, 2008.

J.E.B. v. Alabama, 511 U.S. 127 (1994).

Jackson, Donald W. 1993. "Judging Human Rights: The Formative Years of the European Court of Human Rights, 1959–1989." *Windsor Yearbook of Access to Justice* 13: 217–236.

Jacob, Herbert. 1988. *Silent Revolution: The Transformation of Divorce Law in the United States.* Chicago: University of Chicago Press.

Jan, Tracy. 2006. "Bigger, More Diverse Lesley University: Leader Who Reinvented School Will Step Down." *Boston Globe.* December 28.

Jasper, James M. 1997. *The Art of Moral Protest: Culture, Biography, and Creativity in Social Movements.* Chicago: University of Chicago Press.

Jenkins, Carol. 2009. "Media Justice for Sotomayor." *Women's Media Center.* July 10. http://womensmediacenter.com/wordpress/?p=857. Accessed July 29, 2009.

Jensen, Jennifer M. and Wendy L. Martinek. 2009. "The Effects of Race and Gender on the Judicial Ambitions of State Trial Court Judges." *Political Research Quarterly* 62, no. 2: 379–392.

John, Peter. 2006. "Explaining Policy Change: The Impact of the Media, Public Opinion and Political Violence on Urban Budgets in England." *Journal of European Public Policy* 13, no. 7: 1053–1068.

Judicial Appointments Advisory Committee. 2007. *2006 Annual Report.* http://www.ontariocourts.on.ca/jaac/en/annualreport/2006.pdf. Accessed November 28, 2011.

Judicial Appointments Commission. 2010. "Examination of Witnesses (Questions 1–38)." September 7. http://www.publications.parliament.uk/pa/cm201011/cmselect/cmjust/449-i/10090702.htm. Accessed July 5, 2011.

Judiciary of England and Wales. 2010. "Gender Statistics." http://www.judiciary.gov.uk/publications-and-reports/statistics/diversity-stats-and-gen-overview/gender-statistics/gender-statistics-judges-in-post-2010. Accessed November 10, 2011.

Jurgens, Erik. 2003. "Oral Evidence to the Lord Chancellor's Department Select Committee." Minutes of evidence. March 27. http://www.publications.parliament.uk/pa/cm200203/cmselect/cmlcd/584/3032701.htm. Accessed December 12, 2011.

Just, Marion, Ann N. Crigler, and Todd L. Belt. 2007. "Don't Give up Hope: Emotions, Candidate Appraisals, and Votes." In *The Affect Effect: Dynamics of Emotion in Political Thinking and Behavior,* eds. W. Russell Neuman, George E. Marcus, Ann N. Crigler, and Michael MacKuen. Chicago: University of Chicago Press.

Kalanke v. Land Bremen, Case C-450/93 [1995], ECR I-3051.

Kanter, Rosabeth Moss. 1977. *Men and Women of the Corporation.* New York: Basic Books.

Kanter, Rosabeth Moss. 1993. *Men and Women of the Corporation.* Second edition. New York: Basic Books.

Kantola, Johanna. 2006. *Feminists Theorize the State.* New York: Palgrave Macmillan.

Kantola, Johanna and Joyce Outshoorn. 2007. "Changing State Feminism." In *Changing State Feminism*, eds. Joyce Outshoorn and Johanna Kantola. New York: Palgrave Macmillan.

Karstedt, Susanne. 2011. "Handle with Care: Emotions, Crime and Justice." In *Emotions, Crime and Justice*, eds. Susanne Karstedt, Ian Loader, and Heather Strang. Portland, OR: Hart.

Kathlene, Lyn. 1994. "Power and Influence in State Legislative Policymaking: The Interaction of Gender and Position in Committee Hearing Debates." *American Political Science Review* 88, no. 3: 560–576.

Katzenstein, Mary. 1998. *Faithful and Fearless: Moving Feminist Protest inside the Church and Military*. Princeton, NJ: Princeton University Press.

Kaufman, Burton I. 2006. *Presidential Profiles: The Carter Years*. New York: Facts on File.

Kay, Herma Hill and Geraldine Sparrow. 2001. "Workshop on Judging: Does Gender Make a Difference?" *Wisconsin Women's Law Journal* 16, no. 1: 1–14.

Keck, Margaret and Kathryn Sikkink. 1998. *Activists beyond Borders: Advocacy Networks in International Politics*. Ithaca, NY: Cornell University Press.

Keck, Thomas. 2009. "Beyond Backlash: Assessing the Impact of Judicial Decisions on LGBT Rights." *Law & Society Review* 43, no. 1: 151–186.

Kelly, Joan. 1984. "Did Women Have a Renaissance?" In *Women, History, and Theory: The Essays of Joan Kelly*. Chicago: University of Chicago Press.

Kennedy, Helena. 1993. *Eve Was Framed: Women and British Justice*. London: Vintage.

Kenney, Sally J. 1992. *For Whose Protection? Reproductive Hazards and Exclusionary Policies in the United States and Britain*. Ann Arbor: University of Michigan Press.

Kenney, Sally J. 1995. "Women, Feminism, Gender, and Law in Political Science: Ruminations of a Feminist Academic." *Women & Politics* 15, no. 3: 43–69.

Kenney, Sally J. 1996. "New Research on Gendered Political Institutions." *Political Research Quarterly* 49, no. 2: 445–466.

Kenney, Sally J. 1998. "The Members of the Court of Justice of the European Communities." *Columbia Journal of European Law* 5, no. 1: 101–133.

Kenney, Sally J. 2000. "Beyond Principals and Agents: Seeing Courts as Organizations by Comparing *Référendaires* at the European Court of Justice and Law Clerks at the US Supreme Court." *Comparative Political Studies* 33, no. 5: 593–625.

Kenney, Sally J. 2001a. "Thank You for Being Ready: Rosalie Wahl Holds Her Place on the Minnesota Supreme Court." Center on Women and Public Policy Case Study Program, Humphrey Institute of Public Affairs, University of Minnesota. http://www.hhh.umn.edu/centers/wpp/pdf/case_studies/rosalie_wahl/wahl_case.pdf. Accessed July 12, 2011.

Kenney, Sally J. 2001b. "Where Are the Women in Public Policy Cases?" *Women's Policy Journal of Harvard, John F. Kennedy School of Government* 1: 87–98.

Kenney, Sally J. 2002. "Breaking the Silence: Gender Mainstreaming and the Composition of the European Court of Justice." *Feminist Legal Studies* 10, nos. 3–4: 257–270.

Kenney, Sally J. 2003. "Where Is Gender in Agenda Setting?" *Women & Politics* 25, nos. 1–2: 179–207.

Kenney, Sally J. 2004a. "Britain Appoints First Woman Law Lord." *Judicature* 87, no. 4: 189–190.

Kenney, Sally J. 2004b. "The Constitutional Status of the Family and Medical Leave Act." Paper presented at the Afterbirth Conference, Humphrey Institute of Public Affairs, Minneapolis, October 1. http://www.hhh.umn.edu/centers/wpp/afterbirth/pdf/kenney.pdf. Accessed August 22, 2008.

Kenney, Sally J. 2004c. "Equal Employment Opportunity and Representation: Extending the Frame to Courts." *Social Politics* 11, no. 1: 86–116.

Kenney, Sally J. 2004d. "Gender, the Public Policy Enterprise, and Case Teaching." *Journal of Policy Analysis and Management* 23, no. 1: 159–178.

Kenney, Sally J. 2005. "Domestic Violence Intervention Program: Unconditional Shelter?" *Nonprofit Management and Leadership* 16, no. 2: 221–243. http://www.hhh.umn.edu/centers/wpp/pdf/case_studies/dvip/DVIP_case.pdf. Accessed November 28, 2011.

Kenney, Sally J. 2008a. "Gender on the Agenda: How the Paucity of Women Judges Became an Issue." *Journal of Politics* 70, no. 3: 717–735.

Kenney, Sally J. 2008b. "Thinking about Gender and Judging." *International Journal of the Legal Profession* 15, nos. 1–2: 87–110.

Kenney, Sally J. 2009a. "Nixon Gaffe Sparks Era of Judicial Advance." *Women's eNews.* May 4. http://www.womensenews.org/article.cfm/dyn/aid/3999. Accessed December 12, 2011.

Kenney, Sally J. 2009b. "Women in Minnesota." *With Equal Right: The Official Publication of Minnesota Women Lawyers.* July. http://www.mwlawyers.org/displaycommon.cfm?an=1&subarticlenbr=84. Accessed December 10, 2011.

Kenney, Sally J. 2010a. "Critical Perspectives on Gender and Judging." *Politics & Gender* 6, no. 3: 433–441.

Kenney, Sally J. 2010b. "Julia C. Addington from Stacyville, Iowa: First Woman Elected to Public Office in the United States? The World?" *Women/Politics* 21, no. 1: 12.

Kenney, Sally J. 2010c. "Mobilizing Emotions to Elect Women: The Symbolic Meaning of Minnesota's First Woman Supreme Court Justice." *Mobilization* 15, no. 2: 135–158.

Kenney, Sally J. Forthcoming. "Which Judicial Selection Systems Generate the Most Women Judges? Lessons from the United States." In *Gender and Judging*, eds. Ulrike Schultz and Gisela Shaw. Oxford: Hart.

Kenney, Sally J., Kathryn Pearson, Debra Fitzpatrick, and Elizabeth Sharrow. 2009. "Are We Progressing Toward Equal Representation for Women in the Minnesota Legislature? New Evidence Offers Mixed Results." *Center for Urban and Regional Affairs (CURA) Reporter* Fall/Winter: 39–47.

Kerber, Linda K. 1998. *No Constitutional Right to Be Ladies: Women and the Obligations of Citizenship*. New York: Hill and Wang.

Kingdon, John W. 1995. *Agendas, Alternatives, and Public Policies*. New York: HarperCollins.

Klaphake, Roger M. 1993. "Minnesota Court System." In *Perspectives on Minnesota Government and Politics*, eds. Carolyn M. Shrewsbury and Homer E. Williamson. Third edition. St. Paul, MN: Burgess.

Klarman, Michael J. 1994. "*Brown*, Racial Change, and the Civil Rights Movement." *Virginia Law Review* 80, no. 1: 7–150.

Klatch, Rebecca E. 1988. "Of Meanings and Masters: Political Symbolism and Symbolic Action." *Polity* 21, no. 1: 137–154.

Kohen, Beatriz. 2008. "Family Law Judges in the City of Buenos Aires: A View from Within." *International Journal of the Legal Profession* 15, nos. 1–2: 111–122.

Kommers, Donald P. 1997. *The Constitutional Jurisprudence of the Federal Republic of Germany*. Durham, NC: Duke University Press.

Kornblut, Anne E. 2009. *Notes from the Cracked Ceiling: Hillary Clinton, Sarah Palin, and What It Will Take for a Woman to Win*. New York: Crown.

Krieger, Linda Hamilton. 1995. "The Content of Our Categories: A Cognitive Bias Approach to Discrimination and Equal Employment Opportunity." *Stanford Law Review* 47, no. 6: 1161–1248.

Kritzer, Herbert M. 2007. "Law Is the Mere Continuation of Politics by Different Means: American Judicial Selection in the Twenty-first Century." *DePaul Law Review* 56, no. 2: 423–467.

Kritzer, Herbert M. and Thomas M. Uhlman. 1977. "Sisterhood in the Courtroom: Sex of Judge and Defendant as Factors in Criminal Case Disposition." *Social Science Journal* 14, no. 2: 77–88.

Kronebusch, Philip. 1998. "Minnesota Courts: Basic Structures, Processes, and Policies." In *Perspectives on Minnesota Government and Politics*, eds. Steve Hoffman, Homer Williamson, and Kay Wolsborn. Fourth edition. St. Paul, MN: Burgess.

Krueger, Christine. 1994. *Three Paths to Leadership: A Study of Women on the Minnesota Supreme Court*. St. Paul, MN: Hamline University Press.

L'Heureux-Dubé, Claire. 2001. "Outsiders on the Bench: The Continuing Struggle for Equality." *Wisconsin Women's Law Journal* 16, no. 1: 15–30.

Labour Research Department. 1999. "Judging Labour on the Judges." *Labour Research* June: 13–14.

Lacey, Carol. 1977. "Women Wept, Cheered at Wahl's Appointment." *St. Paul Dispatch*. January 16.

Lakoff, George. 2004. *Don't Think of an Elephant! Know Your Values and Frame the Debate*. White River Junction, VT: Chelsea Green.

Lansing, Harriet. 1995. "A Tribute to Rosalie E. Wahl: Rosalie E. Wahl and the Jurisprudence of Inclusivity." *William Mitchell Law Review* 21, no. 1: 11–12.

Larson, Jane. 2000. "The Jurisprudence of Justice Rosalie Wahl." In *The Social Justice, Legal and Judicial Career of Rosalie Erwin Wahl*, eds. Marvin Roger Anderson and Susan K. Larson. St. Paul: Minnesota State Law Library.

Larson, Lisa and Deborah K. McKnight. 1988. *Judicial Selection and Retention: Minnesota and Other States.* Report to the Minnesota Legislature, St. Paul.

Laughlin, Kathleen. 2000. *Women's Work and Public Policy: A History of the Women's Bureau, US Department of Labor, 1945–1970.* Boston: Northeastern University Press.

Lawless, Jennifer L. and Richard Logan Fox. 2005. *It Takes a Candidate: Why Women Don't Run for Office.* Cambridge: Cambridge University Press.

Lawrence, Regina G. and Melody Rose. 2010. *Hillary Clinton's Race for the White House: Gender Politics and the Media on the Campaign Trail.* Boulder, CO: Lynne Rienner.

Le Sueur, Andrew, ed. 2004. *Building the UK's New Supreme Court: National and Comparative Perspectives.* Oxford: Oxford University Press.

Lemieux, Scott. 2004. "Constitutional Politics and the Political Impact of Abortion Litigation: Judicial Power and Judicial Independence in Comparative Perspective." Ph.D. dissertation, University of Washington.

Lester, Anthony and David Pannick. 2004. *Human Rights Law and Practice.* London: Butterworths.

Levin, Eric. 1986. "The New Look in Old Maids." *People.* March 31.

Levine, Suzanne Braun and Mary Thom. 2007. *Bella Abzug: How One Tough Broad from the Bronx Fought Jim Crow and Joe McCarthy, Pissed Off Jimmy Carter, Battled for the Rights of Women and Workers, Rallied against War and for the Planet, and Shook Up Politics along the Way.* New York: Farrar, Straus, and Giroux.

Lewin, Ellen. 1998. *Recognizing Ourselves: Ceremonies of Lesbian and Gay Commitment.* New York: Columbia University Press.

Lewis, Neil A. 2009. "Debate on whether Female Judges Decide Differently Arises Anew." *New York Times.* June 3.

Linehan, Jan. 2001. "Women and Public International Litigation." Background paper presented for the seminar held by the Project on International Courts and Tribunals and Matrix Chambers, London, July 13.

Lipset, Seymour Martin and Earl Raab. 1973. *The Politics of Unreason: Right-Wing Extremism in America, 1790–1970.* New York: Harper and Row.

Lipshutz, Robert J. 2006. "Remarks on Judicial Selection." Paper presented at the Lloyd N. Cutler Conference on White House Counsel, Miller Center, University of Virginia, November 10.

Lipshutz, Robert J. and Douglas B. Huron. 1978–1979. "Achieving a More Representative Federal Judiciary." *Judicature* 62, no. 10: 483–485.

Lithwick, Dahlia. 2010. "The Female Factor: Will Three Women Really Change the Court?" *Newsweek.* August 30. http://www.newsweek.com/2010/08/30/can-three-women-really-change-the-supreme-court.print.html. Accessed January 25, 2011.

Lo, Clarence Y.H. 1982. "Countermovements and Conservative Movements in the Contemporary US." *Annual Review of Sociology* 8: 107–134.

Lorde, Audre. 1984. *Sister Outsider: Essays and Speeches*. Berkeley, CA: The Crossing Press.

Lovenduski, Joni. 1997. "Sex Equality and the Rules of the Game." In *Sex Equality Policy in Western Europe*, ed. Frances Gardiner. New York: Routledge.

Lovenduski, Joni, ed. 2005. *State Feminism and Political Representation*. Cambridge: Cambridge University Press.

Lucas, Jennifer. 2007. "Is Justice Blind? Gender and Voting in Judicial Elections." Paper presented at the Midwest Political Science Association annual meeting, Chicago, April.

Lutz, James M. 1987. "Regional Leadership Patterns in the Diffusion of Public Policies." *American Politics Quarterly* 15, no. 3: 387–398.

Mackay, Fiona. 2005. "Gender and Diversity Review: Critical Reflections on Judicial Appointments in Scotland." Report for the Judicial Appointments Board for Scotland and Scottish Executive Justice Department.

Macken, Fidelma and Joseph Weiler. 2003. "To Be a European Constitutional Court Judge." Distinguished Fellow Lecture Series, Hauser Global Law School Program, NYU School of Law, September 4. centers.law.nyu.edu/jeanmonnet/hauser/Macken_script.rtf. Accessed May 23, 2011.

Mackenzie, Ruth, Kate Malleson, Penny Martin, and Philippe Sands. 2010. *Selecting International Judges: Principle, Process, and Politics*. Oxford: Oxford University Press.

Mackenzie Stuart, Lord Alexander. 1983. "The Court of Justice: A Personal View." In *In Memoriam J.D.B. Mitchell*, eds. St. John Bates, Wilson Finnie, John A. Usher, and Hans Wildberg. European Governmental Studies. London: Sweet and Maxwell.

MacKinnon, Catharine A. 1982. "Feminism, Marxism, Method, and the State: An Agenda for Theory." *Signs: Journal of Women in Culture and Society* 7, no. 3: 515–544.

MacKinnon, Catharine A. 1983. "Feminism, Marxism, Method, and the State: Toward Feminist Jurisprudence." *Signs: Journal of Women in Culture and Society* 8, no. 4: 635–658.

MacKinnon, Catharine A. 1987. *Feminism Unmodified: Discourses on Life and Law*. Cambridge, MA: Harvard University Press.

MacKinnon, Catharine A. 1989. *Toward a Feminist Theory of the State*. Cambridge, MA: Harvard University Press.

Malleson, Kate. 1999. *The New Judiciary: The Effects of Expansion and Activism*. Aldershot, UK: Ashgate/Dartmouth.

Malleson, Kate. 2000. "Judicial Bias and Disqualification after *Pinochet (No. 2)*." *Modern Law Review* 63, no. 1: 119–127.

Malleson, Kate. 2002. "Another Nail in the Coffin?" *New Law Journal* 152, no. 7052: 1573–1577.

Malleson, Kate. 2003a. "Justifying Gender Equality on the Bench: Why Difference Won't Do." *Feminist Legal Studies* 11, no. 1: 1–24.

Malleson, Kate. 2003b. "Prospects for Parity: The Position of Women in the Judiciary in England and Wales." In *Women in the World's Legal Profession*, eds. Ulrike Schultz and Gisela Shaw. Oxford: Hart.

Malleson, Kate. 2004a. "Creating a Judicial Appointments Commission: Which Model Works Best?" *Public Law* Spring, nos. 1–2: 102–121.

Malleson, Kate. 2004b. "Modernising the Constitution: Completing the Unfinished Business." *Legal Studies* 24, nos. 1–2: 119–133.

Malleson, Kate. 2006a. "The New Judicial Appointments Commission in England and Wales: New Wine in New Bottles?" In *Appointing Judges in an Age of Judicial Power: Critical Perspectives from around the World*, eds. Kate Malleson and Peter H. Russell. Toronto: University of Toronto Press.

Malleson, Kate. 2006b. "Rethinking the Merit Principle in Judicial Selection." *Journal of Law and Society* 33, no. 1: 126–140.

Malleson, Kate. 2009. "Diversity in the Judiciary: The Case for Positive Action." *Journal of Law and Society* 36, no. 3: 376–402.

Malleson, Kate and Peter Russell. 2006. *Appointing Judges in an Age of Judicial Power: Critical Perspectives from around the World*. Toronto: University of Toronto Press.

Mansbridge, Jane. 1995. "What Is the Feminist Movement?" In *Feminist Organizations: Harvest of the New Women's Movement*, eds. Myra Marx Ferree and Patricia Yancey Martin. Philadelphia, PA: Temple University Press.

Mansbridge, Jane. 1999. "Should Blacks Represent Blacks and Women Represent Women? A Contingent 'Yes.'" *Journal of Politics* 61, no. 3: 628–657.

Mansbridge, Jane. 2003. "Rethinking Representation." *American Political Science Review* 97, no. 4: 515–528.

Mansbridge, Jane and Shauna L. Shames. 2008. "Toward a Theory of Backlash: Dynamic Resistance and the Central Role of Power." *Politics & Gender* 4, no. 4: 623–634.

Marcus, George E. and Michael MacKuen. 1993. "Anxiety, Enthusiasm, and the Vote: The Emotional Underpinnings of Learning and Involvement during Presidential Campaigns." *American Political Science Review* 87, no. 3: 672–685.

Martin, Elaine. 1982. "Women on the Federal Bench: A Comparative Profile." *Judicature* 65, no. 6: 306–313.

Martin, Elaine. 1987. "Gender and Judicial Selection: A Comparison of the Reagan and Carter Administrations." *Judicature* 71, no. 3: 136–142.

Martin, Elaine. 1989. "Differences in Men and Women Judges: Perspectives on Gender." *Journal of Political Science* 17, nos. 1–2: 74–85.

Martin, Elaine. 1991. "Judicial Role Models: A Women Judges' Network." Paper presented at the Midwest Political Science Association annual meeting, Chicago, April 18–20.

Martin, Elaine. 1993. "The Representative Role of Women Judges." *Judicature* 77, no. 3: 166–173.

Martin, Elaine. 2004. "Gender and Presidential Judicial Selection." *Women & Politics* 26, nos. 3/4: 109–129.

Martin, Elaine and Barry Pyle. 2000. "Gender, Race, and Partisanship on the Michigan Supreme Court." *Albany Law Review* 63, no. 4: 1205–1236.

Martin, Elaine and Barry Pyle. 2002. "Gender and Racial Diversification of State Supreme Courts." *Women & Politics* 24, no. 2: 35–52.

Martin, Elaine and Barry Pyle. 2003. "Judicial Bias or Counterbalance? A Test of 'Representative Voice' Theory." Paper presented at the Midwest Political Science Association annual meeting, Chicago, April 3–6.

Martin, Elaine and Barry Pyle. 2005. "State High Courts and Divorce: The Impact of Judicial Gender." *University of Toledo Law Review* 36, no. 4: 923–948.

Martin, Elaine and Barry Pyle. 2010. "Judicial Gender Perspectives in Resolving Family and Medical Leave Act Conflicts." Paper presented at the Law and Society Association annual meeting, Chicago, May 27–30.

Martin, Janet M. 1997. "Women Who Govern: The President's Appointments." In *The Other Elites: Women, Politics, and Power in the Executive Branch*, eds. MaryAnne Borrelli and Janet M. Martin. Boulder, CO: Lynne Rienner.

Martin, Janet M. 2003. *The Presidency and Women: Promise, Performance, and Illusion.* College Station: Texas A & M University Press.

Martin, Patricia Yancey, Douglas Schrock, Margaret Leaf, and Carmen Von Rohr. 2007. "Rape Work: Emotional Dilemmas in Work with Victims." In *The Emotional Organization: Passion and Power*, ed. Steve Fineman. London: Blackwell.

Martin, Patricia Yancey, John R. Reynolds, and Shelley Keith. 2002. "Gender Bias and Feminist Consciousness among Judges and Attorneys: A Standpoint Theory Analysis." *Signs: Journal of Women in Culture and Society* 27, no. 3: 665–701.

Matthews, Nancy. 1994. *Confronting Rape: The Feminist Anti-Rape Movement and the State.* New York: Routledge.

Maute, Judith L. 2007. "English Reforms to Judicial Selection: Comparative Lessons for American States." *Fordham Urban Law Journal* 34, no. 1: 387–423.

Maveety, Nancy. 2010. "Difference in Judicial Discourse." *Politics & Gender* 6, no. 3: 452–465.

May, Meredith. 2000. "Rose Bird Tribute Honors Ex-Justice as Humanitarian." *San Francisco Chronicle.* January 17.

Mayer, Michael S. 2007. "Civil Rights and the Politics of Judicial Nomination: The Haynsworth Confirmation Battle (and Not the One You Think)." Paper presented at Teacher, Scholar, Citizen: Conference in Honor of Stan Katz, Princeton, February 23.

Mayer, Rita and Ilene Whitworth. 1995. "Judge Handcuffed and Jailed for

Trying Wife-Beater." *National NOW Times*. May. http://www.now.org/nnt/05-95/judge.html. Accessed September 23, 2011.

Mazey, Sonia. 2000. "Introduction: Integrating Gender—Intellectual and 'Real World' Mainstreaming." *Journal of European Public Policy* 7, no. 3: 333–345.

Mazur, Amy G. 2002. *Theorizing Feminist Policy*. Oxford: Oxford University Press.

Mazur, Amy G. 2003. "Drawing Comparative Lessons from France and Germany." *Review of Policy Research* 20, no. 3: 493–523.

McCammon, Holly J., Courtney Sanders Muse, Harmony D. Newman, and Teresa M. Terrell. 2007. "Movement Framing and Discursive Opportunity Structures: The Political Successes of the US Women's Jury Movements." *American Sociological Review* 72, no. 5: 725–749.

McCann, Michael W. 1994. *Rights at Work: Pay Equity Reform and the Politics of Legal Mobilization*. Chicago: University of Chicago Press.

McCann, Michael W. 1998. "How Does Law Matter for Social Movements?" In *How Does Law Matter?*, eds. Bryant G. Garth and Austin Sarat. Evanston, IL: Northwestern University Press.

McCarthy, Megan. 2001. "Judicial Campaigns: What Can They Tell Us about Gender on the Bench?" *Wisconsin Women's Law Journal* 16, no. 1: 87–111.

McCoin, Susan L. 1985. "Sex Discrimination in the *Voir Dire* Process: The Rights of Prospective Female Jurors." *Southern California Law Review* 58, no. 5: 1225–1259.

McGlynn, Clare. 1998. *The Woman Lawyer: Making the Difference*. London: Butterworths.

McGlynn, Clare. 1999. "Judging Women Differently: Gender, the Judiciary, and Reform." In *Feminist Perspectives on Public Law*, eds. Susan Millns and Noel Whitty. London: Cavendish.

Medsger, Betty. 1983. *Framed: The New Right Attack on Chief Justice Rose Bird and the Courts*. New York: The Pilgrim Press.

Melnick, R. Shep. 1995. "Separation of Powers and the Strategy of Rights: The Expansion of Special Education." In *The New Politics of Public Policy*, eds. Marc Landy and Martin A. Levin. Baltimore: Johns Hopkins University Press.

Mendelberg, Tali. 2001. *The Race Card: Campaign Strategy, Implicit Messages, and the Norm of Equality*. Princeton, NJ: Princeton University Press.

Menkel-Meadow, Carrie. 2009. "Asylum in a Difference Voice? Judging Immigration Claims and Gender." In *Refugee Roulette: Disparities in Asylum Adjudication and Proposals for Reform*, eds. Jaya Ramji-Nogales, Andrew I. Schoenholtz, and Philip G. Schrag. New York: New York University Press.

Meyer, David S. and Deana A. Rohlinger. 2012. "Big Books and Social Movements: A Myth of Ideas and Social Change." *Social Problems* 59, no. 1: 136–153.

Meyer, David S. and Debra C. Minkoff. 2004. "Conceptualizing Political Opportunity." *Social Forces* 82, no. 4: 1457–1492.

Meyer, David S. and Suzanne Staggenborg. 1996. "Movements, Counter-movements, and the Structure of Political Opportunity." *American Journal of Sociology* 101, no. 6: 1628–1660.

Millns, Susan. 2007. "Gender Equality, Citizenship, and the EU's Constitutional Future." *European Law Journal* 13, no. 2: 218–237.

Minnesota Supreme Court Task Force for Gender Fairness in the Courts. 1989. "Final Report."

Minow, Martha L. 1990. *Making All the Difference: Inclusion, Exclusion, and American Law*. Ithaca, NY: Cornell University Press.

Mintrom, Michael and Sandra Vergari. 1998. "Policy Networks and Innovation Diffusion: The Case of State Education Reforms." *Journal of Politics* 60, no. 1: 126–148.

Molette-Ogden, Carla E. 1998. "Female Jurists: The Impact of Their Increased Presence on the Minnesota Supreme Court." Ph.D. dissertation, Washington University.

Monopoli, Paula. 2007. "Gender and Justice: Parity and the United States Supreme Court." *Georgetown Journal of Gender and the Law* 8, no. 1: 43–65.

Montoya, Jean. 1996. "'What's so Magic(al) about Black Women?' Peremptory Challenges at the Intersection of Race and Gender." *Michigan Journal of Gender & Law* 3, no. 2: 369–419.

"More Women and Ethnic Minority Solicitors." 1999. *Equal Opportunities Review* 84: 9–10.

Morgen, Sandra. 1995. "It Was the Best of Times, It Was the Worst of Times: Emotional Discourse in the Work Cultures of Feminist Health Clinics." In *Feminist Organizations: Harvest of the New Women's Movement*, eds. Myra Marx Ferree and Patricia Yancey Martin. Philadelphia, PA: Temple University Press.

Morrison, Susan, ed. 2008. *Thirty Ways of Looking at Hillary*. New York: HarperCollins.

Mossman, Mary Jane. 2006. *The First Women Lawyers: A Comparative Study of Gender, Law and the Legal Professions*. Portland, OR: Hart.

Motley, Constance Baker. 2002. "Reflections." *Columbia Law Review* 102, no. 6: 1449–1450.

Mowbray, Alastair. 2008. "The Consideration of Gender in the Process of Appointing Judges to the European Court of Human Rights." *Human Rights Law Review* 8, no. 3: 549–559.

Naito, Calvin and Esther Scott. 1990. "Against All Odds: The Campaign in Congress for Japanese American Redress." Case program, John F. Kennedy School of Government, Harvard University. http://www.ksgcase.harvard.edu/casetitle.asp?caseNo=1006.0. Accessed February 28, 2008.

National Women's Law Center. 2011. "Women in the Federal Judiciary: Still a Long Way to Go." October 18. http://www.nwlc.org/resource/women-federal-judiciary-still-long-way-go-1. Accessed November 10, 2011.

Ness, Susan. 1978. "A Sexist Selection Process Keeps Qualified Women off the Bench." *Washington Post.* March 26.

Ness, Susan and Fredrica Wechsler. 1979. "Women Judges: Why So Few?" *Graduate Woman* 73, no. 6: 10–12, 46–49.

Newton, Polly. 1997. "Harman Is Rebuked for Women Judges Slip." *The Times* (London). October 23.

Nolan, Sybil. 1995. "Sydney Women Win Fight to Keep Single-Sex Pool." *The Age* (Australia). March 10.

Norris, Pippa. 1997. "Women Leaders Worldwide: A Splash of Color in the Photo Op." In *Women, Media, and Politics*, ed. Pippa Norris. New York: Oxford University Press.

Nossiff, Rosemary. 1994. "Why Justice Ginsburg Is Wrong about States Expanding Abortion Rights." *PS: Political Science & Politics* 27, no. 2: 227–231.

Nussbaum, Martha C. 2001. *Upheavals of Thought: The Intelligence of Emotions.* New York: Cambridge University Press.

Nzomo, Maria and Patricia Kameri-Mbote. 2003. "Gender Issues in the Draft Bill of the Constitution of Kenya: An Analysis." Contribution for the Constitution Review Commission of Kenya, International Environmental Law Research Centre Working Paper. http://www.ielrc.org/content/w0301. pdf. Accessed November 12, 2011.

Obama, Barack. 2009. "Remarks by the President in Nominating Judge Sonia Sotomayor to the United States Supreme Court." The White House. May 26. http://www.whitehouse.gov/the_press_office/Remarks-by-the-President-in-Nominating-Judge-SoniaSotomayor-to-the-United-States-Supreme-Court/. Accessed July 27, 2011.

Obama, Barack. 2010. "Remarks by the President and Solicitor General Elena Kagan at the Nomination of Solicitor General Elena Kagan to the Supreme Court." The White House. May 10. http://www.whitehouse.gov/the-press-office/remarks-president-and-solicitor-general-elena-kagan-nomination-solicitor-general-el. Accessed July 27, 2011.

O'Connor, Karen and Alixandra B. Yanus. 2010. "Judging Alone: Reflections on the Importance of Women on the Court." *Politics & Gender* 6, no. 3: 441–452.

O'Connor, Karen and Jeffrey Segal. 1990. "Justice Sandra Day O'Connor and the Supreme Court's Reaction to Its First Female Member." *Women & Politics* 10, no. 2: 95–104.

O'Connor, Sandra Day. 1991. "Portia's Progress." *New York University Law Review* 66, no. 6: 1546–1558.

Omatsu, Maryka. 1997. "The Fiction of Judicial Impartiality." *Canadian Journal of Women and the Law* 9, no. 1: 1–16.

Organ, Joan Ellen. 1998. "Sexuality as a Category of Historical Analysis: A Study of Judge Florence E. Allen, 1884–1966." Ph.D. dissertation, Case Western Reserve University.

Outshoorn, Joyce. 1995. "Administrative Accommodation in the Netherlands: The Department for the Coordination of Equality Policy." In *Comparative State Feminism*, eds. Dorothy McBride Stetson and Amy Mazur. Thousand Oaks, CA: Sage.

Outshoorn, Joyce. 1997. "Incorporating Feminism: The Women's Policy Network in the Netherlands." In *Sex Equality Policy in Western Europe*, ed. Frances Gardiner. New York: Routledge.

Overland, Sean G. 2009. *The Juror Factor: Race and Gender in America's Civil Courts*. El Paso, TX: LFB Scholarly.

Palmer, Barbara. 2001. "Women in the American Judiciary: Their Influence and Impact." *Women & Politics* 23, no. 3: 91–101.

Palmer, Barbara. 2002. "Justice Ruth Bader Ginsburg and the Supreme Court's Reaction to Its Second Female Member." *Women & Politics* 24, no. 1: 1–23.

Parry, Janine. 2005. "Women's Policy Agencies, the Women's Movement, and Representation in the USA." In *State Feminism and Political Representation*, ed. Joni Lovenduski. Cambridge: Cambridge University Press.

Pateman, Carol. 1988. *The Sexual Contract*. Stanford, CT: Stanford University Press.

Paterson, Alan. 2006. "The Scottish Judicial Appointments Board: New Wine in Old Bottles?" In *Appointing Judges in an Age of Judicial Power: Critical Perspectives from around the World*, eds. Kate Malleson and Peter H. Russell. Toronto: University of Toronto Press.

Pattullo, Polly. 1983. *Judging Women: A Study of Attitudes that Rule Our Legal System*. Nottingham, UK: Russell Press.

Pennock, J. Roland. 1979. *Democratic Political Theory*. Princeton, NJ: Princeton University Press.

Pennsylvania v. Local Union, 388 F. Supp. 155 (E.D. Pa. 1974).

Peresie, Jennifer. 2005. "Female Judges Matter: Gender and Collegial Decisionmaking in the Federal Appellate Courts." *Yale Law Journal* 114, no. 7: 1759–1790.

Perry, Barbara. 1991. *A "Representative" Supreme Court? The Impact of Race, Religion, and Gender on Appointments*. Westport, CT: Greenwood Press.

Perry, Elisabeth Israels. 2001. "Rhetoric, Strategy, and Politics in the New York Campaign for Women's Jury Service, 1917–1975." *New York History* 82, no. 1: 53–78.

Pescatorius. 2010. "Transparency at the ECJ: A Reflection after API." *Adjudicating Europe Blog*. December 12. http://adjudicatingeurope.eu/blog/?p=520. Accessed November 11, 2011.

Peters v. Kiff, 407 U.S. 493 (1972).

Phillips, Anne. 1995. *The Politics of Presence*. Oxford: Oxford University Press.

Phillips, Anne. 1998. "Democracy and Representation: Or, Why Should It Matter Who Our Representatives Are?" In *Feminism and Politics*, ed. Anne Phillips. Oxford: Oxford University Press.

Pitkin, Hanna Fenichel. 1967. *The Concept of Representation*. Berkeley: University of California Press.

Pollack, Mark A. and Emilie M. Hafner-Burton. 2000. "Mainstreaming Gender in the European Union." *Journal of European Public Policy* 7, no. 3: 432–456.

Polletta, Francesca. 1998. "'It Was Like a Fever . . .': Narrative and Identity in Social Protest." *Social Problems* 45, no. 2: 137–159.

Polletta, Francesca. 2006. *It Was Like a Fever: Storytelling in Protest and Politics.* Chicago: University of Chicago Press.

Post, Robert and Reva Siegel. 2007. "*Roe* Rage: Democratic Constitutionalism and Backlash." *Harvard Civil Rights–Civil Liberties Law Review* 42, no. 2: 373–433.

Prechal, Sacha. 2009. "'Non-Discrimination Does Not Fall Down from Heaven': The Context and Evolution of Non-Discrimination in EU Law." Eric Stein Working Paper No. 4. Czech Society for European and Comparative Law. http://www.ericsteinpapers.eu/images/doc/eswp-2009-04-prechal.pdf. Accessed November 11, 2011.

Purdum, Todd S. 1999. "Rose Bird, Once California's Chief Justice, Is Dead at 63." *New York Times.* December 6.

Queen's Counsel Appointments, 2012. "88 Queen's Counsel Appointed in 2011–12 Competition." http://www.qcappointments.org/wp-content/uploads/2012/02/QCA-Press-Release-2011-12.doc. Accessed March 14, 2012.

R. v. A. [2001] 3 All ER1.

R. v. Bow Street Metropolitan Stipendiary Magistrate and others ex parte Pinochet Ugarte [1998] 3 WLR 1456.

R. v. R.D.S. [1997] 3 S.C.R. 484.

Rackley, Erika. 2006. "Difference in the House of Lords." *Social & Legal Studies* 15, no. 2: 163–185.

Rai, Shirin M. 2003. *Mainstreaming Gender, Democratizing the State? Institutional Mechanisms for the Advancement of Women.* Manchester: United Nations.

Raju, Manu. 2010. "Patrick Leahy: GOP Males It In." *Politico.* July 20. http://www.politico.com/news/stories/0710/39941.html. Accessed August 5, 2010.

Randall, Vicky. 1998. "Gender and Power: Women Engage the State." In *Gender, Politics, and the State*, eds. Vicky Randall and Georgina Waylen. London: Routledge.

Ray, Raka. 1999. *Fields of Protest: Women's Movements in India.* Minneapolis: University of Minnesota Press.

Recer, Jena and Penny Anderson. 1995. "Texas Judge Resigns Citing Political Harassment." *National NOW Times.* November. http://www.now.org/nnt/11-95/reed.html. Accessed November 12, 2011.

Reddick, Malia, Michael J. Nelson, and Rachel Paine Caufield. 2009a. "Explaining Diversity on State Courts." Paper presented at the Midwest Political Science Association annual meeting, Chicago, April 2–5.

Reddick, Malia, Michael J. Nelson, and Rachel Paine Caufield. 2009b. "Racial and Gender Diversity on State Courts: An AJS Study." *Judges' Journal* 48, no. 3: 28–32.

Rees, Teresa L. 1998. *Mainstreaming Equality in the European Union: Education, Training and Labour Market Policies.* London: Routledge.

Reid, Traciel V. 1999. "The Politicization of Retention Elections: Lessons from the Defeat of Justices Lanphier and White." *Judicature* 83, no. 2: 68–77.

Reid, Traciel V. 2000a. "The Politicization of Judicial Retention Elections: The Defeat of Justices Lanphier and White." In *Research on Judicial Selection 1999*, ed. Hunter Center for Judicial Selection. Chicago: American Judicature Society. http://www.judicialselection.us/uploads/documents/Diversity_and_the_Judicial_Merit_Se_9C4863118945B.pdf. Accessed November 23, 2011.

Reid, Traciel V. 2000b. "The Role of Gender in Judicial Campaigns: North Carolina Trial Court Races." *Southeastern Political Review* 28, no. 3: 551–584.

Reid, Traciel V. 2004a. "Assessing the Impact of a Candidate's Sex in Judicial Campaigns and Elections in North Carolina." *Justice System Journal* 25, no. 2: 183–207.

Reid, Traciel V. 2004b. "The Competitiveness of Female Candidates in Judicial Elections: An Analysis of the North Carolina Trial Court Races." *Albany Law Review* 67, no. 3: 829–842.

Reid, Traciel V. 2010. "Women Candidates and Judicial Elections: Telling an Untold Story." *Politics & Gender* 6, no. 3: 465–474.

Reidinger, Paul. 1987. "The Politics of Judging." *ABA Journal* April 1: 52–58.

Resnik, Judith. 1988. "On the Bias: Feminist Reconsiderations of the Aspirations for Our Judges." *Southern California Law Review* 61, no. 6: 1877–1944.

Resnik, Judith. 1995. "Now Is the WRONG Time to Stop Courts' Self-Study." *New Jersey Law Journal* 142, no. 6: 27–39.

Resnik, Judith. 1996. "Asking about Gender in Courts." *Signs: Journal of Women in Culture and Society* 21, no. 4: 952–990.

Ritter, Gretchen. 2002. "Jury Service and Women's Citizenship before and after the Nineteenth Amendment." *Law and History Review* 20, no. 3: 479–515.

Robnett, Belinda. 1997. *How Long? How Long? African American Women in the Struggle for Civil Rights.* New York: Oxford University Press.

Rochon, Thomas R. 1998. *Culture Moves: Ideas, Activism, and Changing Values.* Princeton, NJ: Princeton University Press.

"Rose Bird." 1999. *State Net California Journal.* November 1.

"Rose Elizabeth Bird." 1984. *Current Biography* 45: 26–29.

Rosenberg, Gerald. 1991. *The Hollow Hope: Can Courts Bring about Social Change?* Chicago: University of Chicago Press.

Rosenberg, Gerald. 2008. *The Hollow Hope: Can Courts Bring about Social Change?* Second edition. Chicago: University of Chicago Press.

Rossman, Lynn C. 1980. "Women Judges Unite: A Report from the Founding Convention of the National Association of Women Judges." *Golden Gate University Law Review* 10, no. 3: 1237–1265.

Roth, Benita. 2004. *Separate Roads to Feminism: Black, Chicana, and White Feminist Movements in America's Second Wave.* Cambridge: Cambridge University Press.

Roth, Benita. 2006. "Gender Inequality and Feminist Activism in Institutions: Challenges of Marginalization and Feminist 'Fading.'" In *The Politics of Women's Interests: New Comparative Perspectives*, eds. Louise Chappell and Lisa Hill. New York: Routledge.

Round, Deborah Ruble. 1987–1988. "Gender Bias in the Judicial System." *Southern California Law Review* 61, no. 6: 2193–2220.

Rury, Abigail. 2012. "All Things Being Equal, Women Lose: Investigating the Lack of Diversity among the Recent Appointments to the Iowa Supreme Court." Paper presented at the Southern Political Science Association annual meeting, New Orleans, January 12-14.

Russell, Peter H. 1990. *Interim Report: Judicial Appointments Advisory Committee.* Toronto: Judicial Appointments Advisory Committee.

Rymph, Catherine. 2006. *Republican Women: Feminism and Conservatism from Suffrage through the Rise of the New Right.* Chapel Hill: University of North Carolina Press.

Sachs, Albie and Joan Hoff Wilson. 1978. *Sexism and the Law: A Study of Male Beliefs and Judicial Bias.* Oxford: Martin Robertson and Co.

Sanbonmatsu, Kira. 2002. *Democrats, Republicans, and the Politics of Women's Place.* Ann Arbor: University of Michigan Press.

Sanbonmatsu, Kira. 2008. "Gender Backlash in American Politics?" *Politics & Gender* 4, no. 4: 634–642.

Sands, Emily Glassberg. 2009. "Opening the Curtain on Playwright Gender: An Integrated Economic Analysis of Discrimination in American Theater." Master's thesis. Princeton University. http://graphics8.nytimes.com/packages/pdf/theater/Openingthecurtain.pdf. Accessed August 5, 2011.

Sanger, Carol. 1994. "Curriculum Vitae (Feminae): Biography and Early American Women Lawyers." *Stanford Law Review* 46, no. 5: 1245–1281.

Sapiro, Virginia. 1981. "Research Frontier Essay: When Are Interests Interesting? The Problem of Political Representation of Women." *American Political Science Review* 75, no. 3: 701–716.

Sapiro, Virginia. 1993. "The Political Uses of Symbolic Women: An Essay in Honor of Murray Edelman." *Political Communication* 10, no. 2: 141–154.

Sapiro, Virginia and Joe Soss. 1999. "Spectacular Politics, Dramatic Interpretations: Multiple Meanings in the Thomas/Hill Hearings." *Political Communication* 16, no. 3: 285–314.

Sappell, Joel. 1990. "Death Penalty Controversy Trails Bird." *Los Angeles Times*. May 14.

Sarkees, Meredith Reid and Nancy E. McGlen. 1999. "Misdirected Backlash: The Evolving Nature of Academia and the Status of Women in Political Science." *PS: Political Science & Politics* 32, no. 1: 100–108.

Sauboorah, Jennifer. 2011. "Bar Barometer: Trends in the Barristers' Profession." Bar Council Research Department. March 1. http://www.legalservicesboard.org.uk/what_we_do/consultations/closed/pdf/annex_b.pdf. Accessed August 9, 2011.

Sawer, Marian. 1990. *Sisters in Suits: Women and Public Policy in Australia*. Sydney: Allen and Unwin.

Sawer, Marian. 1995. "'Femocrats in Glass Towers?' The Office of the Status of Women in Australia." In *Comparative State Feminism*, eds. Dorothy McBride Stetson and Amy Mazur. Thousand Oaks, CA: Sage.

Sawer, Marian. 2007. "Australia: The Fall of the Femocrat." In *Changing State Feminism*, eds. Joyce Outshoorn and Johanna Kantola. New York: Palgrave Macmillan.

Schafran, Lynn Hecht. 1987. "Documenting Gender Bias in the Courts: The Task Force Approach." *Judicature* 70, no. 5: 280–290.

Schafran, Lynn Hecht. 2001. "California: First as Usual." *Women's Rights Law Reporter* 22, no. 2: 159–167.

Schafran, Lynn Hecht. 2005. "Not from Central Casting: The Amazing Rise of Women in the American Judiciary." *University of Toledo Law Review* 36, no. 4: 953–975.

Scheingold, Stuart A. 1965. *The Rule of Law in European Integration: The Path of the Schuman Plan*. New Haven, CT and London: Yale University Press.

Scherer, Nancy. 2005. *Scoring Points: Politicians, Activists, and the Lower Federal Court Appointment Process*. Stanford, CT: Stanford University Press.

Schmidt, Bob. 1977. "Looking ahead with Rose Bird." *San Jose Mercury News*. March 20.

Schmidt, Bob. 1986. "Beyond Bird: In Deciding the Political Fate of Chief Justice Rose Bird, Can a Balance Be Struck between the Need for an Independent Judiciary and the Public Demand that Judges Be Accountable to the Voters?" *Golden State Report* 2, no. 1: 13–18.

Schmidt am Busch, Birgit. 2000. "European Institutions: Strategies for Exerting More Influence." Paper presented at the European Women Lawyers Association annual congress, Berlin, March 17–19.

Schultz, Vicki. 1998. "Reconceptualizing Sexual Harassment." *Yale Law Journal* 107, no. 6: 1683–1805.

Schuster, Mary Lay and Amy Propen. 2010. "Degrees of Emotion: Judicial Responses to Victim Impact Statements." *Law, Culture and the Humanities* 6, no. 1: 75–104.

Scott, Joan Wallach. 2005. *Parité! Sexual Equality and the Crisis of French Universalism*. Chicago: University of Chicago Press.

Segal, Jennifer. 2000. "Representative Decision Making on the Federal Bench: Clinton's District Court Appointees." *Political Research Quarterly* 53, no. 1: 137–150.

Sewell, William H. 1996. "Historical Events as Transformations of Structures: Inventing Revolution at the Bastille." *Theory and Society* 25, no. 6: 841–881.

"Sex Discrimination (Gender Reassignment) Regulations: An *EOR* Guide." 1999. *Equal Opportunities Review* 85: 8–9.

"Sex Inequality Still Deeply Rooted." 2001. *Equal Opportunities Review* 95: 5–6.

Shapiro, Martin and Alec Stone Sweet. 2002. *On Law, Politics, and Judicialization*. New York: Oxford University Press.

Shaw, Jo. 2000. "Importing Gender: The Challenge of Feminism and the Analysis of the EU Legal Order." *Journal of European Public Policy* 7, no. 3: 406–431.

Shaw, Jo. 2001a. "European Union Governance and the Question of Gender: A Critical Comment." In *Mountain or Molehill? A Critical Appraisal of the Commission White Paper on Governance*, eds. Christian Joerges, Yves Mény, and Joseph H.H. Weiler. Jean Monnet Working Paper No. 6, Brussels, July 25. http://www.jeanmonnetprogram.org/papers/01/010601.html. Accessed November 11, 2011.

Shaw, Jo. 2001b. "Gender and the Court of Justice." In *The European Court of Justice*, eds. Gráinne de Búrca and Joseph H.H. Weiler. Oxford: Oxford University Press, 87-142

Shaw, Jo. 2002. "The European Union and Gender Mainstreaming: Constitutionally Embedded or Comprehensively Marginalised?" *Feminist Legal Studies* 10, no. 3: 213–226.

Sherry, Suzanna. 1986. "Civic Virtue and the Feminine Voice in Constitutional Adjudication." *Virginia Law Review* 72, no. 3: 543–616.

Shrimsley, Robert. 1997. "Irvine Jumps to Defence of Male Judges." *Daily Telegraph* (London). October 23.

Siegel, Reva B. 2006. "Constitutional Culture, Social Movement Conflict and Constitutional Change: The Case of the de facto ERA." *California Law Review* 94, no. 5: 1323–1419.

Sigelman, Lee, Carol K. Sigelman, and Christopher A. Fowler. 1987. "A Bird of a Different Feather? An Experimental Investigation of Physical Attractiveness and the Electability of Female Candidates." *Social Psychology Quarterly* 50, no. 1: 32–43.

Simons, Marlise. 1999. "Then It Was the Klan: Now It's the Balkan Agony." *New York Times*. January 13.

Skocpol, Theda. 1992. *Protecting Soldiers and Mothers: The Political Origins of Social Policy in the United States*. Cambridge, MA: Belknap Press of Harvard University Press.

Slotnick, Elliot. 1983a. "The ABA Standing Committee on Federal Judiciary: A Contemporary Assessment: Part 1." *Judicature* 66, no. 7: 349–362.

Slotnick, Elliot. 1983b. "The ABA Standing Committee on Federal Judiciary: A Contemporary Assessment: Part 2." *Judicature* 66, no. 8: 385–393.

Slotnick, Elliot. 1983c. "Lowering the Bench or Raising It Higher? Affirmative Action and Judicial Selection during the Carter Administration." *Yale Law and Policy Review* 1, no. 2: 270–298.

Slotnick, Elliot. 1988. "Federal Judicial Recruitment and Selection Research: A Review Essay." *Judicature* 71, no. 6: 317–324.

Slotnick, Elliot. 2002. "A Historical Perspective on Federal Judicial Selection." *Judicature* 86, no. 1: 13–16.

Sloviter, Dolores Korman. 2005. "Personal Reflections." *University of Toledo Law Review* 36, no. 4: 855–861.

Solanke, Iyiola. 2008. "Diversity and Independence in the European Court of Justice." *Columbia Journal of European Law* 15, no. 1: 89–121.

Solinger, Rickie. 1992. *Wake up Little Susie: Single Pregnancy and Race before* Roe v. Wade. New York: Routledge.

Solomon, Deborah. 2009. "Case Closed: Questions for Sandra Day O'Connor." *New York Times Magazine*. March 22.

Sommerlad, Hilary and Peter Sanderson. 1998. *Gender, Choice, and Commitment: Women Solicitors in England and Wales and the Struggle for Equal Status*. Aldershot, UK: Ashgate/Dartmouth.

Sommerlad, Hilary, Lisa Webley, Liz Duff, Daniel Musio, and Jennifer Tomlinson. 2010. *Diversity in the Legal Profession in England and Wales: A Qualitative Study of Barriers and Individual Choices*. London: Legal Services Board. http://www.legalservicesboard.org.uk/what_we_do/Research/Publications/pdf/lsb_diversity_in_the_legal_profession_final_rev.pdf. Accessed July 1, 2011.

Songer, Donald R., Sue Davis, and Susan Haire. 1994. "A Reappraisal of Diversification in the Federal Courts: Gender Effects in the Courts of Appeals." *Journal of Politics* 56, no. 2: 425–439.

Sotomayor, Sonia. 2002. "A Latina Judge's Voice." *Berkeley La Raza Law Journal* 13, no. 1: 87–93.

Spalter-Roth, Roberta and Ronnee Schreiber. 1995. "Outsider Issues and Insider Tactics: Strategic Tensions in the Women's Policy Network during the 1980s." In *Feminist Organizations: Harvest of the New Women's Movement*, eds. Myra Marx Ferree and Patricia Yancey Martin. Philadelphia, PA: Temple University Press.

Spees, Pam. 2003. "Women's Advocacy in the Creation of the International Criminal Court: Changing the Landscapes of Justice and Power." *Signs: Journal of Women in Culture and Society* 28, no. 4: 1233–1254.

Spill, Rorie L. and Kathleen A. Bratton. 2001. "Clinton and Diversification of the Federal Judiciary." *Judicature* 84, no. 2: 256–261.

Spill Solberg, Rorie L. and Kathleen A. Bratton. 2005. "Diversifying the

Federal Bench: Presidential Patterns." *Justice System Journal* 26, no. 2: 119–133.

Staggenborg, Suzanne. 1993. "Critical Events and the Mobilization of the Pro-Choice Movement." *Research in Political Sociology* 6: 319–345.

State v. Willis, 269 N.W.2d 355 (Minn. 1978).

Steigerwalt, Amy. 2010. *Battle over the Bench: Senators, Interest Groups, and Lower Court Confirmations.* Charlottesville: University of Virginia Press.

Stepnick, Andrea and James D. Orcutt. 1996. "Conflicting Testimony: Judges' and Attorneys' Perceptions of Gender Bias in Legal Settings." *Sex Roles* 34, nos. 7–8: 567–579.

Sterett, Susan. 1997. *Creating Constitutionalism? The Politics of Legal Expertise and Administrative Law in England and Wales.* Ann Arbor: University of Michigan Press.

Stern, Felice A. 1965. "Backlash." *American Speech* 40, no. 2: 156–157.

Stetson, Dorothy McBride and Amy G. Mazur. 2000. "Women's Movements and the State: Job-Training Policy in France and the US." *Political Research Quarterly* 53, no. 3: 597–623.

Stetson, Dorothy McBride and Amy Mazur, eds. 1995. *Comparative State Feminism.* Thousand Oaks, CA: Sage.

Stevens, Allison. 2005. "Filibuster Storm Brews over Judicial Nominations." *Women's eNews.* April 19. http://oldsite.womensenews.org/article.cfm/dyn/aid/2262/context/archive. Accessed August 5, 2011.

Stevens, Robert. 1993. *The Independence of the Judiciary: The View from the Lord Chancellor's Office.* Oxford: Oxford University Press.

Stevens, Robert. 1997. "Judges, Politics, Politicians, and the Confusing Role of the Judiciary." In *The Human Face of Law*, ed. Keith Hawkins. Oxford: Clarendon Press.

Stix-Hackl, Christine. 2006. "The Future of European Law from Women Lawyers' Perspective." Speech delivered at the opening of the Sixth Congress of the European Women Lawyers Association, Budapest, May 19–20. http://www.ewla.org/modules/files/file_group_76/Congresses/Budapest%202006/Papers/speech.Stix-Hackl.pdf. Accessed on August 19, 2006.

Stolz, Preble. 1981. *Judging Judges: The Investigation of Rose Bird and the California Supreme Court.* New York: The Free Press.

Stone, Deborah. 1989. "Causal Stories and the Formation of Policy Agendas." *Political Science Quarterly* 104, no. 2: 281–300.

Stone, Deborah. 2002. *Policy Paradox: The Art of Political Decision Making.* New York: Norton.

Stone Sweet, Alec. 1992. *The Birth of Judicial Politics in France: The Constitutional Council in Comparative Perspective.* New York: Oxford University Press.

Strossen, Nadine. 2003. "The Leadership Role of the Legal Community in Promoting both Civil Liberties and National Security Post-9/11." Paper presented at the Minnesota Women Lawyers' Annual Rosalie Wahl Leadership Lecture, Minneapolis, February 13.

"Suffering from 'Institutional Schizophrenia.'" 1995. *The Lawyer.* November 28.

Sullivan, Patricia A. and Steven R. Goldzwig. 1996. "Abortion and Undue Burdens: Justice Sandra Day O'Connor and Judicial Decision-Making." *Women & Politics* 16, no. 3: 27–54.

Taylor v. Louisiana, 419 U.S. 522 (1975).

Taylor, Judith. 2005. "Who Manages Feminist-Inspired Reform? An In-Depth Look at Title IX Coordinators in the United States." *Gender & Society* 19, no. 3: 358–375.

Taylor, Judith. 2008. "Imperfect Intimacies: The Problem of Women's Sociality in Contemporary North American Feminist Memoir." *Gender & Society* 22, no. 6: 705–727.

Taylor, Verta. 1989. "Social Movement Continuity: The Women's Movement in Abeyance." *American Sociological Review* 54, no. 5: 761–775.

Taylor, Verta. 1995. "Watching for Vibes: Bringing Emotions into the Study of Feminist Organizations." In *Feminist Organizations: Harvest of the New Women's Movement,* eds. Myra Marx Ferree and Patricia Yancey Martin. Philadelphia, PA: Temple University Press.

Taylor, Verta and Leila Rupp. 2002. "Loving Internationalism: The Emotion Culture of Transnational Women's Organizations, 1888–1945." *Mobilization* 7, no. 2: 141–158.

Taylor, Verta and Nancy Whittier. 1995. "Analytical Approaches to Social Movement Culture: The Culture of the Women's Movement." In *Social Movements and Culture,* eds. Hank Johnston and Bert Klandermans. Minneapolis: University of Minnesota Press.

Teles, Steven M. 2008. *The Rise of the Conservative Legal Movement: The Battle for Control of the Law.* Princeton, NJ: Princeton University Press.

Tench, Dan and Laura Coogan. 2010. "An Exclusive Interview with Lady Hale." *United Kingdom Supreme Court Blog.* September 16. http://ukscblog. com/an-exclusive-interview-with-lady-hale. Accessed November 10, 2011.

Tetlow, Tania. 2003. "How *Batson* Spawned *Shaw*: Requiring the Government to Treat Citizens as Individuals when It Cannot." *Loyola Law Review* 49, no. 1: 133–169.

Thomas, Sue. 2008. "'Backlash' and Its Utility to Political Scientists." *Politics & Gender* 4, no. 4: 615–623.

Thornton, Margaret. 1996. *Dissonance and Distrust: Women in the Legal Profession.* Melbourne: Oxford University Press.

Thornton, Margaret. 1998. "Authority and Corporeality: The Conundrum for Women in Law." *Feminist Legal Studies* 6, no. 2: 147–170.

Thornton, Margaret. 2007. "'Otherness' on the Bench: How Merit Is Gendered." *Sydney Law Review* 29, no. 3: 391–413.

Tilly, Charles. 1978. *From Mobilization to Revolution.* Reading, MA: Addison-Wesley.

Timothy, Mary. 1974. *Jury Woman: The Story of the Trial of Angela Y. Davis.* Palo Alto, CA: Emty Press.

Tobias, Carl. 1999. "Leaving a Legacy on the Federal Courts." *University of Miami Law Review* 53, no. 2: 315–332.

Tobias, Sheila. 1997. *Faces of Feminism: An Activist's Reflections on the Women's Movement.* Boulder, CO: Westview Press.

Tokarz, Karen L. 1986. "Women Judges and Merit Selection under the Missouri Plan." *Washington University Law Quarterly* 64, no. 3: 903–951.

Toobin, Jeffrey. 2007. *The Nine: Inside the Secret World of the Supreme Court.* New York: Doubleday.

Toobin, Jeffrey. 2009. "Diverse Opinions." *New Yorker.* June 8 and 15.

Torres-Spelliscy, Ciara, Monique Chase, and Emma Greenman. 2008. "Improving Judicial Diversity." Brennan Center for Justice. http://brennan. 3cdn.net/31e6c0fa3c2e920910_ppm6ibehe.pdf. Accessed November 23, 2011.

Towns, Ann E. 2010. *Women and States: Norms and Hierarchies in International Society.* Cambridge: Cambridge University Press.

"Trading Places." 2005. *The Times* (London). October 11.

True, Jacqui and Michael Mintrom. 2001. "Transnational Networks and Policy Diffusion: The Case of Gender Mainstreaming." *International Studies Quarterly* 45, no. 1: 27–57.

Turner, Robert C. and Beau Breslin. 2003. "The Impact of Female State Chief Judges on the Administration of State Judiciaries." Paper presented at the American Political Science Association annual meeting, Philadelphia, August 28–31.

Tuve, Jeanette E. 1984. *First Lady of the Law: Florence Ellinwood Allen.* Lanham, MD: University Press of America.

UK Supreme Court. 2011. "The Supreme Court." http://www.supremecourt. gov.uk/about/the-supreme-court.html. Accessed June 30, 2011.

United Nations. 1995. "Report of the Fourth World Conference on Women." Beijing, September 4–15. Doc.A/CONF.177/20.http://www.un.org/ womenwatch/ daw/beijing/pdf/Beijing%20full%20report%20E.pdf. Accessed November 11, 2011.

United States Senate Committee on the Judiciary. 2010. "Judicial Nomination Materials: 111th Congress." http://judiciary.senate.gov/nominations/ Materials111thCongress.cfm. Accessed November 12, 2011.

van Gerven, Walter. 1996. "The Role and Structure of the European Judiciary Now and in the Future." *European Law Review* 21, no. 3: 211–223.

Van Voorhis, Patricia, Joanne Belknap, Karen Welch, and Amy Stichman. 1993. "Gender Bias in Courts: The Findings and Recommendations of the Task Forces." Paper presented at the American Society of Criminology annual meeting, Phoenix, October.

Vargas, Virginia and Saskia Wieringa. 1998. "The Triangle of Empowerment: Processes and Actors in the Making of Public Policy for Women." In *Women's Movements and Public Policy in Western Europe, Latin America, and the Caribbean*, eds. Geertje Lycklama à Nijeholt, Virginia Vargas, and Saskia Wieringa. New York: Garland.

Vauchez, Antoine. 2011. "Keeping the Dream Alive: The European Court of Justice and the Transnational Fabric of Integrationist Jurisprudence." *European Political Science Review.* June 14. http://journals.cambridge.org/action/displayAbstract?fromPage=online&aid=8306565. Accessed December 14, 2011.

Verkaik, Robert. 1999. "Law: The Case of the Judges' Guilty Secret." *Independent* (London). November 16.

Verloo, Mieke, ed. 2007. *Multiple Meanings of Gender Equality: A Critical Frame Analysis of Gender Policies in Europe.* Budapest: CEU Press.

Vining, Richard L., Amy Steigerwalt, and Susan Navarro Smelcer. 2009. "Bias and the Bar: Evaluating the ABA Ratings of Federal Judicial Nominees." Paper presented at the Midwest Political Science Association annual meeting, Chicago, April.

Voeten, Erik. 2007. "The Politics of International Judicial Appointments: Evidence from the European Court of Human Rights." *International Organization* 61, no. 4: 669–701.

Volcansek, Mary L. 1996. "Introduction." In *Women in Law: A Bio-bibliographical Sourcebook*, eds. Rebecca Mae Salokar and Mary L. Volcansek. Westport, CT: Greenwood Press.

Volcansek, Mary L. and Jacqueline Lucienne Lafon. 1987. *Judicial Selection: The Cross-Evolution of French and American Practices.* Westport, CT: Greenwood Press.

Wahl, Rosalie. 1994. Oral history of Rosalie E. Wahl, Associate Justice, Minnesota Supreme Court. Interviewed August 17, 1994 by Laura Cooper. Transcript edited and annotated by Laura J. Cooper and Stacy Doepner-Hove. Rosalie Wahl Papers, Minnesota Historical Society, St. Paul.

Wald, Patricia. 2005. "Six Not-So-Easy Pieces: One Woman Judge's Journey to the Bench and Beyond." *University of Toledo Law Review* 36, no. 4: 979–993.

Walker, Caroline. 2009. "Advancing and Retaining Women in the Legal Profession." Ark Group. http://www.ark-group.com/Downloads/advancingwomenTOC.pdf. Accessed July 1, 2011.

Walker, Jack L. 1969. "The Diffusion of Innovations among the American States." *American Political Science Review* 63, no. 3: 880–899.

Walker, Thomas and Deborah Barrow. 1985. "The Diversification of the Federal Bench: Policy and Process Ramifications." *Journal of Politics* 47, no. 2: 596–617.

Ward, Lucy. 2002. "Learning from the 'Babe' Experience: How the Finest Hour Became a Fiasco." In *New Gender Agenda: Why Women Still Want More*, ed. Anna Coote. London: Institute for Public Policy Research.

Ward, Stephanie Francis. 2011. "Female Judicial Candidates Are Held to Different Standards, Sotomayor Tells Students." *ABA Journal.* March 8. http://www.abajournal.com/news/article/female_judicial_candidates_are

held_to_different_standards_sotomayor_tells_/. Accessed August 4, 2011.

Warden, R., T. Schlesinger, and J. Kearney. 1979. *Women, Blacks and Merit Selection of Judges.* Chicago: Committee on Courts and Justice.

Watkins, Bonnie and Nina Rothchild. 1996. *In the Company of Women: Voices from the Women's Movement.* St. Paul: Minnesota Historical Society.

Watson, Sophie, ed. 1990. *Playing the State: Australian Feminist Interventions.* Sydney: Allen and Unwin.

Wattenberg, Esther. 1971. "Women in the DFL . . . A Preliminary Report: Present but Powerless." Report for the Democratic–Farmer–Labor Party Feminist Caucus.

Waylen, Georgina. 1998. "Gender, Feminism, and the State: An Overview." In *Gender, Politics, and the State*, eds. Vicky Randall and Georgina Waylen. London: Routledge.

Weiler, Joseph H.H. 2001. "Epilogue: The Judicial Après Nice." In *The European Court of Justice*, eds. Gráinne de Búrca and Joseph H.H. Weiler. Oxford: Oxford University Press.

Weintraub, Daniel M. 1985. "Board to 'Invite' Duffy to Meet: Lawsuit over Post Cards for Chief Justice at Issue." *Los Angeles Times.* February 21.

Weiss, Mike. 1999. "Goodbye to a Rose that Thrived in Every Climate." *San Francisco Chronicle.* December 6.

Werdegar, Kathryn. 2001. "Why a Woman on the Bench?" *Wisconsin Women's Law Journal* 16, no. 1: 31–40.

Westlake, Martin. 1994. *A Modern Guide to the European Parliament.* London and New York: Pinter.

White v. Crook, 251 F. Supp. 401 (1966).

Wikler, Norma J. 1989. "Water on Stone: A Perspective on the Movement to Eliminate Gender Bias in the Courts." *Court Review* 26, no. 3: 6–13.

Williams, Margaret. 2007. "Women's Representation on State Trial and Appellate Courts." *Social Science Quarterly* 88, no. 5: 1192–1204.

Williams, Margaret. 2008. "Ambition, Gender, and the Judiciary." *Political Research Quarterly* 61, no. 1: 68–78.

Williams, Melissa S. 1998. *Voice, Trust, and Memory: Marginalized Groups and the Failings of Liberal Representation.* Princeton, NJ: Princeton University Press.

Wilner, Sheri and Julia Jordan. 2010. "Discrimination and the Female Playwright." *GIA Reader* 21, no. 1. http://www.giarts.org/article/discrimination-and-female-playwright. Accessed August 5, 2011.

Wilson, Bertha. 1990. "Will Women Judges Really Make a Difference?" *Osgoode Hall Law Journal* 28, no. 3: 507–522.

Wilson, Betty. 2005. *Rudy! The People's Governor.* Minneapolis, MN: Nodin Press.

Wilson, Sarah. 2003. "Appellate Judicial Appointments during the Clinton Presidency: An Inside Perspective." *Journal of Appellate Practice and Process* 5, no. 1: 29–47.

Windett, Jason. 2011. "Understanding Female Candidates and Campaigns for Governor." Ph.D. dissertation, University of North Carolina at Chapel Hill.

Wockner, Rex. 2007. "Austria, Ireland Propose Civil-Union Laws." *San Francisco Bay Times*. November 8.

"Women's Day: A Year of Living Dangerously." 1995. *Guardian* (London). March 6.

Women's Media Center. 2008. "Sexism Sells, but We're Not Buying It." May 23. http://www.womensmediacenter.com/blog/2008/05/sexism-might-sell-but-were-not-buying-it/. Accessed November 12, 2011.

Working Party for the European Commission. 2000. "Report by the Working Party on the Future of the European Communities' Court System." January.

Yang, Guobin. 2005. "Emotional Events and the Transformation of Collective Action: The Chinese Student Movement." In *Emotions and Social Movements*, eds. Helena Flam and Debra King. New York: Routledge.

Yeatman, Anna. 1990. *Bureaucrats, Technocrats, Femocrats: Essays on the Contemporary Australian State.* Sydney: Allen and Unwin.

Yetka, Lawrence R. and Christopher H. Yetka. 1994. "The Selection and Retention of Judges in Minnesota." *Hamline Journal of Public Law and Policy* 15, no. 2: 169–179.

Yoder, Janice D. 1991. "Rethinking Tokenism: Looking beyond Numbers." *Gender & Society* 5, no. 2: 178–192.

Yoder, Janice D. 2002. "Context Matters: Understanding Tokenism Processes and Their Impact on Women's Work." *Psychology of Women Quarterly* 26, no. 1: 1–8.

Young, Lisa. 2000. *Feminists and Party Politics.* Ann Arbor: University of Michigan Press.

Zald, Mayer N. 1996. "Culture, Ideology, and Strategic Framing." In *Comparative Perspectives on Social Movements: Political Opportunities, Mobilizing Structures, and Cultural Framings*, eds. Doug McAdam, John D. McCarthy, and Mayer N. Zald. Cambridge: Cambridge University Press.

Zald, Mayer and Bert Useem. 1987. "Movement and Countermovement Interaction: Mobilization, Tactics, and State Involvement." In *Social Movements in an Organizational Society*, eds. Mayer N. Zald and John D. McCarthy. New Brunswick, NJ: Transaction.

Zernike, Kate. 2011. "Gains, and Drawbacks, for Female Professors." *New York Times*. March 21.

Zolberg, Aristide R. 1972. "Moments of Madness." *Politics and Society* 2, no. 2: 183–207.

INDEX

Note: A justice or judge is indicated by 'J.' before the given name e.g. O'Connor, J. Sandra Day. Bold refers to tables or figures.

power of 2–3; as representative institutions 108–9, 184

Coyne, J. Jeanne 5

criminal procedure cases, impact of judges' gender on 30–1

critical communities 97–8, 104–7

cronyism 179 *see also* "secret soundings"

Culver, J.H. and Wold, J.T. 150

Daughters of the American Revolution (DAR) 73

Davis, Angela 171

Davis, Sue: analysis of O'Connor's "feminine" reasoning 34; feminine difference, impact on judgments 30–1; as pioneer of scholarly investigation of female judges 23

death penalty 150, 151–7

democracy: "democracy deficit" 119, 176; legislation and concept of 129, 130; participation all citizens in 132, 161, 163, 166, 171, 175–6

Democrats, voting patterns of 17, 31, 32, 39, 42, 47–8, 61–2, 85, 138, 140, 146, 156, 159

Denmark 126, 127

Department of Justice, role in judicial nominations 70, 165

DFL Feminist Caucus 52–3, 54, 56

difference theory: and gender diversity on juries 168, 164–74, 185; arguments 1, 6–9, 16–17, 24–5; in judges' decisions 28–39, 40; judges' rejection of 5–6, 121, 180; lack of evidence of from studies 28–33, 38, 175; limitations of arguments based on 3–4, 13–14, 22–3, 42, 132, 161–3, 183; *see also* essentialism

diffusion of innovation 47–50

discrimination: absence of women as 122–4; employment law applied to judicial selection 98, 136, 163, 170–1, 177; impact of judges' gender on 30–1, 78, 139, 143–4, 145, 162; indirect 25–6, 99; *see also* judicial selection process; sex discrimination cases

discursive politics 89

disparate impact 25–6, 78, 99, 121, 177

divorce cases: divorce reform 49, 52; impact of judges' gender on 19, 32–3, 41, 183

Dixon, Rosalind-39

Doolittle, John 149

Douglas, J. William O. 165–7

Due, J. Ole 112, 116

Dyer, Clare 104

Edelman, Murray 50, 51

Egan, Michael 72, 75, 81

emotions: and Rosalie Wahl campaign 57–60, 61, 62, 63, 183; and social mobilization 51; women and emotional connection with voters 44–5, 61–2

English, Deirdre 150

Epstein, Cynthia Fuchs 16, 137

Equal Employment Opportunity Commission (EEOC) 67, 68, 70

equality law, used to challenge exclusion of women 122–4, 133–4

Equal Justices Initiative 104, 106, 125

Equal Opportunities Commission (EOC) 99, 106, 125

Equal Protection Clause 50, 70, 164, 170, 177

Equal Rights Amendment 41, 70, 79, 174

essentialism: Davis' approach 30, 31; defined 1; dichotomy and 29–30; limitations of 17, 161–2, 175; and representativeness of judiciary 131–2, 133; and scholarly approach 23; tenacity of approach 43; underpinning Boyd, C. et al.*et al* 2010 39; *see also* difference theory

European Civil Service Tribunal, creation of 112

European Coal and Steel Community 110, 127

European Community: reforms to judicial selection process 129–30; The Treaty of Amsterdam 110, 121–2; The Treaty of Lisbon 113;

The Treaty of Rome 110, 122, 123, 126

European Court of Human Rights (ECHR): appointment process to 111–12, 133, 176; requires gender diversity 124–5, 181; as supranational judicial power 3, 93

European Court of Justice (ECJ): equality law used to challenge judicial selection process 122–4, 133–4; history of judicial appointments to 63, 108, 110–13; judicial independence 126, 130; national representation on 126–132; numbers of women on 109–10, 113–18; policy role of judges 129–30, 184; political aspect (personal) of appointments 111–12; reforms to judicial selection process 129–30; representativeness and gender 19, 20–1, 101, 128, 131–3, 176, 178, 184; resists involvement of European Parliament in judicial selection 118–19

European Parliament 109, 112–3, 118–9, 124

European Union: equality law 122–4; Equal Treatment Directive 122–3; gender mainstreaming 67, 101, 109, 116; 121–2

European Women-Lawyers Association 115, 125

exclusionary policies 8, 9, 14

Executive Order 11972 76

Executive Order 12059 76, 77

Falconer, J. Lord Charles Leslie, Baron Falconer of Thoroton 95, 96, 105, 106

Faludi, Susan (*Backlash*) 135, 138–9

Fawcett Society 101, 103–4, 106

Federation of Women Lawyers' Judicial Screening Panel 71, 74

feminism: continued search for sex differences 4, 6–9, 13–14, 39, 41, 43; engagement with the state 67–8; feminist consciousness 30, 41–2; French (feminism) 12–13; historical perspectives 6–9; in the 1970s 6, 23–4; lack of female solidarity within 4, 7–8, 173; liberal 7, 8, 9, 67; mainstreaming 67, 101, 109, 116, 122; maternalist 13, 162, 174; policy implementation through insider–outsider collaboration 66, 68–9, 74–5, 83, 86, 184; radical 9, 43, 67; rejects essentialism 23, 161–2; second-wave 68, 69; standpoint theory 14–15, 28, 30, 162; *see also* difference theory; essentialism

feminists: and appointment of Rosalie Wahl 51, 52–3, 54, 56–57, 60, 62; calls for representativeness on ECJ 110, 133; campaigns for women jurors 163, 165, 170–1, 174; commitment to Carter's policy of racially and gender-diverse bench 71, 73–5, 79–83; judges as 5, 6, 15, 22, 28–39, 41, 57–8, 63, 142–3, 178, 182–3; lack of lobbying of ECJ 125; men 14, 15, 17, 29, 39, 40, 83, 131, 173, 182; relationship with Carter 79–82

feminists, British: campaign for diverse and representative judiciary 101–2, 103–4, 106, 107; demands tied to diversity debates 100–1; demands tied to modernization debates 95, 96–7, 98, 105, 106–7, 184; and judicial selection process 88, 92, 94, 98, 105; links with European Union policy discussions 101; raise issues in the media 104–5

femocrats 67, 68

Ferree, M. and Martin, P. Yancey 67

Ferree, M. et al.et al 2002 49, 89

Finland 110, 114, 116–17, 120

'firsts' *see* women firsts

Flanders, Laura 51

focusing event 51, 60

Fourth World Conference on Women (Beijing) 7, 101, 110, 120, 181

framing 44, 49, 51; *see also* emotions

France 12–13, 111, 113, 174

Kennedy, J. Helena 102, 104, 106
Kenyon, Dorothy 166–7
Kerr, Virginia 73
Kingdon, John W. 69, 89, 90, 92, 105, 107
Kleps, Ralph 155
Kokott, J. Juliane 116
Krauskopf, Joan 77–8
Kravitch, J. Phyllis 76

Labour Party (UK): changes constitutional policy 20, 93; move to reduce power of Lord Chancellor 94–5, 102, 105; theme of modernization of the judiciary 88, 95, 98
Lane, J. Elizabeth 96
large-firm experience (law) 25, 26, 69–70, 151, 177
Lawless, J. and Fox, R. 26
Law Lords: 42, 96; selection process 92; role in deciding *R v. A* 103, 122; composition of 104, 105, 178
law school: impact on women's differences 31; women as graduates from 25, 53, 54, 57, 63, 66, 71, 83–4, 144, 167
legal system, need for legitimacy 30, 163, 165–6
legislature: compared to the judiciary 20–1, 109, 126, 129, 130–1, 133, 179, 184; women's access to 15, 26, 47–8, 131–2, 137
legitimacy of the judiciary: and exclusion of women and minorities 131, 163, 165–6, 171, 172, 173–4, 175, 181; representativeness and 88, 101, 103, 106, 120, 126–7, 134, 162, 179
Lewin, Ellen 10–11
Lewis, J. Rhoda 47
L'Heureux-Dubé, J. Claire 141–2, 142–3, 145, 182–83
Lillie, Mildred 50, 140
Lindh, J. Pernilla 116–17, 123
Lipshutz, Robert 71, 72, 75, 76, 77, 78
Lithwick, Dahlia 1–2
Loebl, Daphne 101

Lord Chancellor: reduction in power of role 94–5; role in judicial selection 88, 91–2, 94; "secret soundings" 27, 92, 98, 100, 112, 177 *see also* Irvine, Derry
Lorde, Audre 67
Lovenduski, Joni 67–8
Lucas, Jennifer 146

Mackay, Lord J. James Peter Hymers , Baron Mackay of Clashfern 95–6
Macken, J. Fidelma O'Kelly 63, 109, 114–15, 117, 120
Mackenzie Stuart, Lord Alexander 127
MacKinnon, Catherine 7, 13
Malta 124, 125
Mancini, G. Federico 111
Mansbridge, J. and Shames, S. L. 136–7
Mansbridge, Jane 89, 130–1, 132–3
Marshall, J. Thurgood 15, 38, 42, 168, 182
Martin, E. and Pyle, B. 32–3, 36
Martin, E. et al. *et al* 2002 36, 37, 38
Martin, Elaine: different voice arguments amongst female judiciary 5–6; disparate impact in judge selection 25–6; feminism as a variable in voting practices, study of 15, 29–30; as pioneer of scholarly investigation of female judges 23
Martin, Patricia Yancey 14, 28, 30, 162
Maryland nominating commission 27
Massachusetts Institute of Technology, and sex discrimination 138
McComb, J. Marshall 153–4
McDonald, J. Gabrielle Kirk 144
McKenna, Margaret: clashes with Bell 76–7; commitment to Carter's policy of racially and gender–diverse bench 71–2, 75, 77, 79, 80–1; dissatisfaction with nominating panels 76; pivotal role as feminist insider 20, 81, 82, 85; relationships with women's groups 72–3, 75, 78;
meaning-making 44, 45; *see also* emotions

media: coverage of gender composition of the judiciary (UK) 90–1, 101, 102; hostility towards female judges 142–3; looking for sex differences 3, 39, 61–2, 63, 159; role of 104–5; role in backlash 138; scrutiny of women judges 21, 46, 140, 152, 156, 158; stories about the judiciary (UK) 90; stories on the gender composition of the judiciary (UK) 91

Mellor, Julie 99

Menkel-Meadow, Carrie 35–6

Mertens de Wilmars, Josse 113

Michigan State Supreme Court 32

Miers, Harriet: conservatives block her appointment 37, 140–1, 178; nomination by Bush 85; withdrawal of her nomination 1, 20, 86, 149

Ministries for Women 67

Minnesota, system of choosing justices 53

Minnesota Democratic-Farmer-Labor Party (DFL) 52

Minnesota Supreme Court 44, 51, 52, 53, 55, 56, 62, 152, 157

Minnesota Women Lawyers (MWL) 53, 55, 56

Minnesota Women's Political Caucus 53, 56

Minow, Martha 13

Mitchell, John 70

mobilization, social: and emotions 44, 51, 56, 63, 183; lack of over gender and judiciary in the UK 88, 89–90, 97, 104; needed for gender diversity of judiciary 22, 49, 182; need strong public support 107

Mosk, J. Stanley 153, 158

Motley, Constance Baker 143–4

Ms. Magazine 60, 150

Murphy, J. Diana 37, 78

Murray, Pauli 164–5, 167

National Advisory Committee on Women 80

National Alliance of Women's Organizations 101

National Association of Women Judges (NAWJ) 5, 34, 69, 74, 80, 86

National Bar Association 82

National Organization for Women 68

National Organization for Women's Legal Defense and Education Fund 69, 74

national representation, judicial 108, 126–7, 133, 134

National Women's Political Caucus (NWPC) 69, 73

Nelson, Dorothy 153

Ness, Susan 73

The Netherlands 109, 118

Nevada v. Hibbs 35

Neuman, Linda Kinney 45–6

Nixon, Richard 50, 52, 70, 73, 75, 128, 140

nominating commissions; s*see* judicial nominating commissions

nondiscrimination 27, 116, 177–8, 179–181

nonessentialist arguments 4, 17, 18, 21

norms, adoption of new 47, 48

Obama, Barack: appointment of women to the judiciary 1, 22, 141, 161; commitment to policy of racially and gender-diverse bench 83, 181, 85–6; electoral campaign 13, 45, 61–2, 156

obscenity cases, impact of judges' gender on 30–1

O'Connor, J. Sandra Day: appointment of 46, 57, 68, 83, 109–10, 161, 178; belief that gender matters 170, 172, 173, 175; cohort (generational) effect 39, 41, 177; compared to Florence Allen 33–4; compared to Justice Ginsburg 15, 182; Cook's analysis of her stance on sex equality cases 3, 34–5, 38–9; debt to the NWPC 73; dismisses herself as employing distinctly feminine approach 5, 6, 17, 34–5; exclusion from large legal firms 25; replacement for 1, 22, 85, 149

O'Connor, K. and Segal, J. 35

Ó Dálaigh, J. Cearbhall 112
Omnibus Judgeship Act 74, 77, 79, 80,
    81–2
Ortega, Manuel Medina, MEP 119
Osamor, Martha 98–100
Overland, Sean G. 173

Palin, Sarah 2, 62, 159–60
Palmer, Barbara 35
parité movement 12–13, 15, 21, 163, 174
Parliament, number of women in 93
Peach Commission 96
People v. Tanner 154
Perpich, Rudolph-52, 53, 54–5, 56, 57,
    59, 62, 95
Perry, Barbara 126, 128, 129
Peters v. Kiff 168
Phillips, Anne 131–2, 133, 175
Pinochet, General Augustus, extradition
    case (UK) 94
Pitkin, Hanna Fenichel 126, 127, 131,
    132
policy implementation: crucial factors
    in 65, 75, 83, 86; diffusion 49–50;
    and political culture 47–8; role of
    litigation 97–8; symbolism of to
    certain groups 51–2; through
    insider–outsider collaboration 66,
    68–9, 74–5, 83, 85, 86, 184
policy windows 88, 107
political culture, state 47–50
politics: impact on judge selection 25–6;
    and judicial representativeness (ECJ)
    127–8, 129; relationship with the law
    (Europe) 111; and women candidates
    61–2
positive action 93, 116, 121, 132
Prashar, Baroness Usha 96
Prechal, J. Alexandra (Sacha) 109, 113,
    118, 132
presidents, records of judicial
    appointment 20, 37, 65, 68, 69, 70–1,
    84, 147, 178
protective legislation 14, 21
public defender offices, as important
    work area for female lawyers 41, 54,
    69–70, 79, 151, 155, 157

quantitative analysis 3–4, 22–3, 36,
    37–8, 42, 46, 185
Queen's Counsel 92–3, 95–7, 101, 119,
    182
Quintin, Odile 120, 123
quotas 12, 124, 163

race and racism 13, 14, 40, 143–4,
    164–9, 170, 171–3
Ragnemalm, J. Hans Olof 122–3
Ramsey County Women's Political
    Caucus 53
Reagan, Ronald: anti–feminist policies
    67; appointments as governor of
    California 154; appointment of
    O'Connor 25, 34, 57, 83; commits
    to first woman on Supreme Court
    50, 68, 74, 83; and geographical
    representation 178; lack of policy
    commitment to gender equality 52,
    83, 147; record of appointment of
    women to the judiciary 84
recusal, and women judges 143–4, 175,
    176
Reed, J. Bonnie 145
Rehnquist, J. William Hubbs 34, 35, 84,
    85, 168–9, 170, 172, 173, 178
Reid, Traciel 146
Reno, Janet 84
representation, theories of 108–110,
    126–133
representativeness (judicial): and
    independence 126; and non-merit
    factors for judicial selection 100, 103,
    120, 126–8, 129, 133, 139
Republican Party of Minnesota v. White 3
Republicans: support for Equal Rights
    Amendments and abortion
    liberalization 41, 138; voting patterns
    of 17, 31, 32, 34, 40, 42, 62, 84, 85,
    141, 146
Resnick, J. Alice Robie 147, 158
Reynoso, J. Cruz 153
Richards, J. Bertrand 100–1
Richardson, H.L. 154
Roberts, J. John 85, 141, 156, 178
Rochon, Thomas 89, 97, 104